CENTER FOR DEMOGRAPHIC STUDIES
REFERENCE LIBRARY

D1193008

DEMOGRAPHY LIBRARY
POPULATION STUDIES CTr.
UNIV OF PENNSYLVANIA
403 MCNEIL/6298

CENTER FOR DEMOGRAPHIC STUDIES
REFERENCE LIBRARY

social structure
and the family:
generational relations

DEMOGRAPHY LIBRARY
POPULATION STUDIES CTR.
UNIV OF PENNSYLVANIA
403 MCNEIL/6298

PRENTICE-HALL INTERNATIONAL, INC., *London*
PRENTICE-HALL OF AUSTRALIA, PTY., LTD., *Sydney*
PRENTICE-HALL OF CANADA, LTD., *Toronto*
PRENTICE-HALL OF INDIA (PRIVATE) LTD., *New Delhi*
PRENTICE-HALL OF JAPAN, INC., *Tokyo*

social structure
and the family:
generational relations

EDITED BY

ETHEL SHANAS
Department of Sociology and Committee on Human Development
University of Chicago

GORDON F. STREIB
Department of Sociology
Cornell University

A report of a Symposium sponsored by the
Program in Socio-Economic Studies of Aging, Duke University,
and the Special Projects Committee, The Psychological
and Social Science Section of the Gerontological Society.

PRENTICE-HALL, INC.
Englewood Cliffs, N.J.

PRENTICE-HALL SOCIOLOGY SERIES

Herbert Blumer, Editor

© 1965 by Prentice-Hall, Inc.
Englewood Cliffs, New Jersey

All rights reserved. No part of
this book may be reproduced, by
mimeograph or any other means, without
permission in writing from the publisher.

Library of Congress Catalog Card No.:
65-25258

Printed in the United States of America
C-81869

preface

The original drafts of the papers in the present volume were prepared for a Symposium on The Family, Intergenerational Relations and Social Structure held at Duke University, November 5-6, 1963, and sponsored by the Special Projects Committee of the Psychological and Social Science Section of the Gerontological Society and the Duke University Program in the Socio-Economic Aspects of Aging.

In 1961 Wilma Donahue, then chairman of the Section on Psychological and Social Sciences of the Gerontological Society, appointed a committee to identify special needs in the area of gerontology and to carry forward programs to meet these needs. The members of the original committee, representing the disciplines of economics, psychology, and sociology, were: Ethel Shanas, University of Chicago, chairman; Gordon F. Streib, Cornell University, vice-chairman; Carl Eisdorfer, Duke University; Lenore A. Epstein, Social Security Administration; Bernard Kutner, Albert L. Einstein College of Medicine; John C. McKinney, Duke University; Harold L. Orbach, University of Michigan; Irving Rosow, Western Reserve University; and Jacob Tuckman, Philadelphia Health Department. In the course of the life of the committee, Klaus F. Riegel, University of Michigan, Raymond G. Kuhlen, Syracuse University, and Joseph H. Britton of Pennsylvania State University were added to the membership.

The committee members agreed that there was need for a thoughtful consideration of the three-generation family in the United States and other Western societies. They felt that although a considerable body of information has been developed about older people and their roles within the social structure, much of what is said about the aged and many of the programs for older people are based not on facts but on social myths. This is particularly true in the area of family relationships.

The committee then decided to bring together scholars from anthropology, economics, law, psychiatry, sociology, social psychology, and social work to consider the three-generation family. To gain cross-cultural perspective, the committee invited scholars who could report on research in Denmark, Great Britain, and Africa. It was the deliberate intention of the organizers of the Symposium to invite persons of varying perspectives who were given broad assignments and complete freedom to develop their papers within the conceptual and theoretical context of their own disciplines.

The Symposium met at Duke University on November 5-6, 1963, at which time discussions were held of the papers which had been circulated in advance of the meeting. One result of the Symposium was that a number of authors chose to rewrite their papers in whole or part after the meeting. These final draft papers constitute the present volume. One of the features of the Symposium was the appointment of two critics, Dr. Kurt Back and Dr. Irving Rosow, who made oral criticisms of the papers and who then revised their observations and analyses for publication.

Financial support for the Symposium was given by the Program of Socio-Economic Studies in Aging of Duke University. The generous cooperation of Frank T. de Vyver, Director of this Program; R. Taylor Cole, Provost of Duke University; Alan Manchester, Dean of Trinity College, Duke University; and John C. McKinney, Chairman of the Department of Sociology and Anthropology at Duke University and a member of the Special Projects Committee, is gratefully acknowledged by the editors of this volume and their colleagues in the Special Projects Committee.

The help of Alan C. Kerckhoff with local Symposium arrangements at Durham is also greatly appreciated by the organizers.

A number of persons within the Gerontological Society have made a special contribution to this volume. They include Wilma Donahue, as chairman of the Section on Psychological and Social Sciences, Robert J. Havighurst and then, Ewald W. Busse M.D., as chairman of the Research Committee, and Robert W. Kleemeier, as Secretary of the Society and general consultant on procedure to the editors and organizers. These persons, along with the members of the Special Projects Committee, have sharpened the theoretical position which lies behind this book.

The editors should like to thank the contributors to the volume for their thoughtful papers and their patient and generous response to editorial queries.

They are indebted to Julia H. Martin who typed the final manuscript and assumed the responsibility for the format and correctness of the numerous footnotes. Finally, they are grateful to Herbert Blumer, Editor of the Prentice-Hall Sociology Series, and to Al Goodyear of Prentice-Hall, Inc., for their sustained support in the development of this publication.

ETHEL SHANAS
GORDON F. STREIB

contents

contributors
to this volume

KURT W. BACK is Professor of Sociology in the Department of Sociology and Anthropology at Duke University.

MARGARET BLENKNER is Director of Research, the Benjamin Rose Institute, Cleveland, Ohio.

ALVIN I. GOLDFARB, M.D. is Consultant on Special Services for the Aged of the New York State Department of Mental Hygiene and Associate Professor at the New York School of Psychiatry.

REUBEN HILL is Professor of Sociology and Director of the Minnesota Family Study Center at the University of Minnesota.

ALAN C. KERCKHOFF is Professor of Sociology in the Department of Sociology and Anthropology at Duke University.

JUANITA M. KREPS is Associate Professor of Economics in the Department of Economics and Business Administration at Duke University.

ROBERT A. LE VINE is Associate Professor of Anthropology in the Committee on Human Development at the University of Chicago.

EUGENE LITWAK is Associate Professor at the School of Social Work of the University of Michigan.

MAX RHEINSTEIN is Max Pam Professor of Comparative Law at the Law School of the University of Chicago.

MARGARET KEENEY ROSENHEIM is Associate Professor at the School of Social Service Administration of the University of Chicago.

IRVING ROSOW is Associate Professor of Sociology at Western Reserve University.

ETHEL SHANAS is Research Associate (Associate Professor) in the Department of Sociology and the Committee on Human Development at the University of Chicago; September, 1965, Professor of Sociology, University of Illinois, Chicago Circle.

JAN STEHOUWER is a Lecturer at the University of Aarhus in Denmark.

GORDON F. STREIB is Professor of Sociology and Chairman of the Department of Sociology at Cornell University.

MARVIN B. SUSSMAN is Professor of Sociology and Chairman of the Department of Sociology and Anthropology at Western Reserve University.

PETER TOWNSEND is Professor of Sociology at the University of Essex in England.

social structure
and the family:
generational relations

PART ONE   **introduction**

social structure
and the family:
generational relations

an introduction GORDON F. STREIB AND ETHEL SHANAS

One of the fascinating aspects of intellectual history is the way in which problems emerge and are transformed, and in turn, stimulate inquiries in new directions. The contemporary systematic study of the social aspects of aging was moved forward in the early 1950's by practical concerns—an increasing number of aged persons, the problem of their retirement, concern for their support, health, housing, and leisure. These considerations and others stimulated intellectuals in academia and persons responsible for policy and services in government agencies and in private organizations to examine the many ramifications of an aging population. A considerable body of knowledge about the social and psychological aspects of aging has been developed and much of it has been published.

Despite the growth in research and writing in social gerontology in the past decade, there are a number of important gaps in the field. One of these concerns the family, intergenerational relations, and the social structure.

The increase in life span has extended the duration of the family cycle. At the same time, changes have also occurred in the earlier part of this cycle. The age at marriage has been declining steadily, and first pregnancies are occurring at an earlier age. It follows from these two demographic facts, the increased life span and the earlier age of marriage, that persons are becoming grandparents earlier and remaining in the grandparent role for a longer time than formerly. These trends also suggest that Western societies in the future will have many more four-generation families than now exist.

The extended period which men spend in retirement raises the question of whether family contacts become a substitute for work interests. Do men become more concerned with their immediate family and their extended kin as their involvement with the world of work lessens? And, further, what sort of role reversals occur within the family as older men seek to fill their leisure with some of the tasks which formerly were the sole province of the older woman?

The implications of role reversal within the multigenerational family network have not been thoroughly explored or considered. The effects upon parents and middle-aged children of these children assuming the roles of provider, nurse, comforter, and decision-maker have hardly been touched upon in the literature.

Western industrial countries have been marked by the increasing intervention of government agencies into areas which were formerly supported and controlled by family and private agencies. In the United States, one of the major outcomes of this trend has been that most older people receive some part of their financial support from government sources. Thus, the pattern of dependency in this country has changed drastically from what it was one or two generations ago. The full impact of these programs of economic support as they relate to intergenerational relations has not been studied.

These shifts in social structure in the United States and other Western societies require a careful reexamination of the state of contemporary knowledge about older people and their families. Many of the current beliefs in this field are based on folklore, not evidence, and persist because scholars have failed to scrutinize the presuppositions on which they are constructed.

The tendency to neglect the later phases of the life cycle as these pertain to intergenerational relations stems in part from the over-emphasis in the social and psychological sciences on the early stages of the family. The social and emotional problems of older persons have received less attention. Sociologists of the family in particular have neglected this important area, perhaps because of their concern with courtship, dating, marriage, and child-rearing practices, and their emphasis on the nuclear family rather than intergenerational relations and the kin network.

The papers which follow represent the points of view of several different disciplines about the family, its intergenerational relations and social structure. The interdisciplinary orientation of the present volume is an expression of the belief of the editors and organizers that since little systematic attention has been given to intergenerational relations and social structure, an interdisciplinary approach would be the most fruitful way of approaching the subject for further development and conceptualization and would guarantee studies with a broader outlook. One of the purposes behind the work is to point out to readers — sociologists, economists, anthropologists, social workers, and others — that there are many intriguing and challenging problems concerning the family in later life which deserve further careful investigation. Some papers may have greater interest for a particular reader than others, but overall we view the work as the opening for further exploration of some new intellectual areas. Each contributor suggests either formally or by inference needed research on the multigenerational family within his own discipline. Further, perhaps even more important, each contributor to this volume suggests areas of research to those other disciplines concerned with the common problem.

The first two papers, those by Goldfarb and Blenkner, concentrate on the individual within the family structure. In "Psychodynamics and the Three-Generation Family," Goldfarb, a practicing analyst, develops the thesis that most individuals in contemporary Western culture are socialized for dependency not independence and that dependent relationships must be recognized as a "critical, common, and pervasive influence in family dynamics." Psychological dependency can be and is a cohesive social force in family and society, and it may flourish in just those interpersonal situations where it is overtly opposed.

Goldfarb states: "Information appears to be lacking about how interaction with grandparents affects the psychological development and personality attributes of family members." The Goldfarb paper should impress sociologists with the fact that population change, that is the addition of a generation to the family, has psychologic and psychiatric significance whether or not such an addition means a common household.

Margaret Blenkner evaluates current social-work theory and practice as these concern family relationships in later life. Blenkner points out that social-work theory is oriented toward the individual, and in so far as it deals with the family, toward the nuclear family of husband, wife, and children. She indicates that where the relationships between older parents and middle-aged children are dealt with in the social-work literature, the model used is role-reversal, the middle-aged child becoming "father to his father." Blenkner argues that the concept of "role-reversal" as used in social work and in much of the psychiatric literature is an incorrect one. Drawing on research evidence she states that when middle-aged children reach the "filial crisis" and resolve it successfully, the child assumes a new mature role, in which he views the parent as an adult in his own right with his own needs and his own virtues. As Blenkner puts it, the child reaches "filial maturity."

The Blenkner paper questions whether present social-work theory is really adequate to meet the needs of older persons and their middle-aged children. Her critique of contemporary theory implies that value judgements have blinded social workers to a true understanding of the roles of older parents and their children.

The papers by Sussman, Kerckhoff, and Hill report on empirical sociological studies of various aspects of intergenerational relations in the United States.

One of the prevailing stereotypes in the sociological study of the elderly is that the aged are rejected and cut off from their families. An accumulating body of facts exists to show that this is not the case. Drawing on extensive data, Sussman points out that we must reformulate theory concerning the isolated nuclear family, and view intergenerational relations in terms of kinship networks. From a large body of empirical studies, he demonstrates that kin networks are viable and widespread and that they must be taken into account if one is to understand the social structure of the contemporary United States. These kin networks are important both in the provision of material and nonmaterial mutual aid to their members and as a locus for social activities. As might be expected, empirical studies indicate the flow of aid tends largely to be from parents to adult children. The normative belief that young families should maintain financial autonomy seems to have been weakened and indeed almost to have disappeared in certain segments of the population.

Kerckhoff's empirical study examines from another perspective "the degree of nuclearity of our family structure." Using data obtained from interviews with older men and their wives, Kerckhoff distinguishes between normative and behavioral aspects of extended family relationships and indicates that these two dimensions are in a much more complex relationship than had been hypothesized.

"Decision Making and the Family Life Cycle" by Reuben Hill shows that the three generations, the grandparent, the parent, and the adult grandchild, respond differently to planning in several major problem areas. The grandchild generation is most active and the grandparent generation least active in all the areas of change studied: for example, in the areas of occupation, residential mobility, and financial decision. Hill's work suggests that one of the important ways to obtain understanding of intergenerational relations is to view the family in its cyclical phases. Contemporary sociology has tended to focus on only one phase of the family cycle, the phase of family formation. Attention given solely to the family life of old people may lead to similar errors of omission in the development of sociological theory.

Three papers, those by Stehouwer, Townsend, and LeVine, deal with intergenerational relations in societies other than the United States. Two of these papers deal with such relations in other industrialized societies, Denmark and Great Britain, and the third reports on intergenerational relations in African societies. Jan Stehouwer gives particular attention to the composition of the three-generation household in Denmark. He points out that contrary to popular belief three-generation households in Denmark are not kept together by occupational and economic dependence. Instead, such households are primarily formed when widowed parents who have health problems or physical handicaps move in with their children. The living arrangement preferred among older people in Denmark is to live apart from children, while at the same time having ready access to them. The Stehouwer paper also presents some interesting cross-national comparisons of household types and the relations between parents and children in Denmark, Britain, and the United States.

The Stehouwer study of old people in Denmark and his report of the comparative surveys of old people in Denmark, Britain, and the United States do not treat extensively with the psychological and emotional aspects of intergenerational relations. It is extremely valuable, therefore, to have, in Peter Townsend's paper, an analysis which reports some of these aspects of intergenerational life. The Townsend study is focussed on the factors which make for the institutionalization of the elderly in Britain. Although only a small percentage of older persons are institutionalized, the social and psychological processes involved throw light on the nature of intergenerational problems in the larger society. Of all forms of residence, old people least prefer the institution. It is therefore important to analyze, as Townsend does, those kinship lacks which result in institutionalization of the elderly. The paper clearly shows that intergenerational relations — and probably other subjects — can be fruitfully studied by directing one's focus not only upon problems which are common but also upon a problem area which occurs infrequently.

LeVine views the changes in intergenerational relations in Africa from the point of view of the anthropologist. Sociologists primarily interested in the dynamics of social stratification will find clues as to how kinship obligation may override different social and class strata in LeVine's discussion of the effect of Western culture on African kinship grouping and obligations. Kinship obligations, LeVine points out, do not change as rapidly as either patterns of residential dispersion resulting from employment or culture alienation resulting from Western education. The LeVine paper also points up the often neglected fact that tensions between generations may arise even in those societies which have well-defined kinship groupings.

The papers by Rosenheim, Rheinstein, and Kreps deal with intergenerational relations as these affect the structure of social welfare, the law, and the economy. In her consideration of contemporary social welfare activities, Rosenheim forthrightly expresses her position on a number of social policy issues which affect family life in the United States. She argues that the test of a successful welfare system is not only the standard of living which it makes possible, but also the freedom it confers on families to satisfy their own tastes and needs. Rosenheim's discussion of social welfare and its implication for family living serves to remind us that social welfare policies have empirical consequences.

Rheinstein in his paper "Motivation of Intergenerational Behavior by Norms of Law" emphasizes the relationship of the law and its social setting. Rheinstein deals with the way in which the law codifies the formal obligations of adult children and their parents. As long as a society is functioning without stress in a given area there is no need for law. The paucity in Western societies of legal strictures on the obligations of adult children and their parents is itself an indication of how these cultures have provided functional models for such relationships.

Juanita Kreps gives special attention to the economics of intergenerational relations. Kreps argues that the middle generation is now supporting both the old and the young through transfer payments. Individual family units are less and less responsible for the maintenance of their own dependents, both old people and children. Those persons in the labor force are supporting those outside the labor force. The Kreps paper raises the question of generational choice. Are those in the labor force willing to increase their level of support to both the young and the old to meet the increasing needs of these cohorts? Or, as the needs of the young and the old become greater, should there be a lessened level of support of one dependent group to better meet the needs of the other?

A theoretical analysis of the broad aspects of intergenerational relations in a democratic, industrialized society is given by Eugene Litwak. Litwak does this by focussing upon the way in which bureaucratic structures are related to families in terms of goal achievement. He develops a theory of shared functions, which can be applied to all areas of life; moreover, he illustrates the analytical power of the theory by a consideration of the sources and kind of aid a family receives from kinsmen and from formal organizations.

Kurt Back and Irving Rosow were asked to participate as critics in the original symposium. In their formal papers they give their reactions to the papers in this volume and their assessment of future needs in theory and research on the family, intergenerational relations, and social structure. Both critics are agreed that the papers demonstrate that the isolated nuclear family is not the "modal, functionally optimal type" in industrial society. They further agree that new theory and research is called for which recognizes the continuity of family structure under conditions of social change. There is clear need to develop new approaches and to adapt existing tools and models to study intergenerational relations.

Back suggests the way in which graph theory might be used to develop different degrees of network connections. Rosow proposes that input-output analysis be adapted to the study of intergenerational supports. He also proposes a coordinated study of public transfer payments and of a sample survey of families so that public transfer income may be related to other income at the family level.

The study of the family, social structure, and intergenerational relations is central to many problems in contemporary social science. In a rapidly changing world, the family becomes more important, not less important; kinship ties may assume different, but no less valuable, meanings to the individual. The present volume reflects what is known about these subjects and also indicates some of the gaps in our knowledge. An obvious need exists for further clarification of conceptual and theoretical issues, but important groundwork is presented here. While the topics under consideration have policy and planning implications, these have been dealt with only peripherally. This follows from our belief that while these implications are important, at this present point in time a research perspective in this general field seems more productive.

the individual
as the
focus of analysis

psychodynamics
and the
three-generation family   ALVIN I. GOLDFARB

DEMOGRAPHY LIBRARY
POPULATION STUDIES CTR.
UNIV OF PENNSYLVANIA
403 MCNE

Family relationships and the thoughts, feelings, and behavior of almost every adult have been directly or indirectly affected by the recent rapid increase in the number and proportion of aged persons in our society. Consequently, from the viewpoint of understanding and contributing to the stability of the family it seems likely, as suggested by Louisa P. Holt in 1952 that efforts:

> ... designed to increase the level of mental health among aged persons in our population might have as many beneficial effects in terms of the population generally as a program would that was designed specifically for its effect on children. There is reason to believe that parents' feelings toward their own parents powerfully affect their attitudes toward their children, and that this need not only be the result of their own parents' behavior long ago...[1]

[1]Community Services Committee, National Advisory Mental Health Council, National Institutes of Health, *Evaluation in Mental Health*, Public Health Service Publication No. 413 (Washington, D.C.: Government Printing Office, 1955), p. 15.

The new number of older persons in our population means that a great many families are now comprised of three or more generations. This, by increasing the complexity of personal interaction within the family, may present new problems of family relationships. The addition of a generation to a family may conceivably have a tendency to hold it together or to drive family members apart; moreover, such change may contribute to, or retard, the favorable development of the young and influence the degree or quality of socialization achieved. This population change is, therefore, not only of sociological and economic importance but also of psychologic and psychiatric significance.

Old age is now a life stage for which socialization should prepare the individual. Also, persons in our society need acculturation so that in each of their successive roles in life they can deal successfully with the aged persons and aged family members who will be a significant part of their environment. Nevertheless, there is no clarity about the role grandparents actually play; how school-age, young adult, middle-aged, or—as is now common—aged children respond to the interactional needs, demands, or supports of a grandparent generation. Current psychiatry generally regards the family as a two-generation nuclear unit consisting of the parents and young children. This tends to move grandparents out into the orbit of social environment.

Information appears to be lacking about how interaction with grandparents affects the psychological development and personality attributes of family members, what psychological constellations of thinking and feeling govern the behavior of grandparents in a family, and what thoughts and feelings are generated by the actual or feared separation from, or loss of contact with, children and grandchildren that may occur for a variety of reasons. Such information may increase our understanding of individual and societal development, and our ability to treat psychiatric problems of three-generational relationships. The course and social effect of problem situations that emerge with the development of three-, and even four-, generation interaction are not predictable from our present classification of available data. Books on psychodynamic theory or its application in practice, including works directly concerned with the structure, dynamics, or treatment of the family group, rarely mention the existence of grandparents, and almost never refer to them as influential or affected members of a family. At best—and this may be a reflection of the real situation— the family life of a young adult or of middle-aged children who have children of their own is generally discussed as though there were two co-existing but overlapping families, that of the person and his children and that of the person and his parents.

Psychodynamic theorists may have concentrated upon the nuclear family because, about sixty years ago when such formulations of human behavior began to crystallize, only three to four per cent of the population was chronologically old. There were then probably few living grandparents within clearly demarcated families as we now know them. The effect of aged persons upon family formation, family stability, and the rearing of grandchildren may have been minimal or may have escaped notice.

personal influence and psychodynamics

Although interaction of young and old — between the third and the first generations — has not been clearly defined in psychodynamic theory, the existence of strong interchanges of feelings between members of these age groups did not escape the notice of those who preceded or anticipated the emergence of psychoanalysis and psychodynamic concepts. Mesmerism is the historical antecedent of current psychodynamic theory, by way of hypnotism and psychoanalysis. The mesmerists explained influential personal interaction in terms of a postulated physical vital force often called magnetic.

Carl Sextus, a lay practitioner who wrote on hypnotism in 1893, provides us with a charming reification of influential psychological and emotional interaction between the young and the old. He recognized that only five to ten per cent of persons are not obviously susceptible to the influence of a hypnotist and believed that the hypnotic influence was literally a flowing of vital force from one to another. Many disorders could be attributed to a lack of "vital force" and were cured when "the vital force of the magnetiser is transmitted to the patient." As one proof of the existence and flow of vital force, he said:

> We know that it is healthy to live in an atmosphere filled with the restorative emanations given out by bodies young and full of vigor. We see in the third book of Kings that David lay with comely damsels to warm him and to give him a little strength. According to Galen and others, Greek doctors had long recognized in the treatment of sundry consumptions, the advantage of making the patients take nourishment from the breast of young healthy nurses; and experience had taught that "the effect is not the same when the milk is given after being caught in a vessel" ... There is not a housewife but knows that it is not good for a child to sleep with an aged person, though the latter enjoy perfect health.

Sextus continues:

> If we seek for ... a general instance of the influence of one human being on another as may seem like that mutual loss and gain and interchange of vital force, which is the principal wonder in mesmerism, we have only to look at the effects produced when young people sleep with old. Since the days of King David it had been known that the latter are strengthened at the expense of the former. Some painful instances of this have fallen under my own observation. Rev. Chancey Hare Townshend, A.M. relates a case in which the future well being of a person very dear to him was compromised. I was acquainted with an infirm old lady, who was so aware of the benefit that she derived from sleeping with young people, that with a horrid vampirism she always obliged her maids to share her bed, thus successively destroying the health of several attendants. Even among

animals it has been found that the young cannot be too closely associated with the old without suffering detriment. Young horses standing in a stable with old ones become less healthy.

"The celebrated German physiologist, Hufelang," he goes on to say, "has remarked on the longevity of school masters, and he attributes it to their living so constantly amidst the healthy emanations of young persons."[2]

One can easily understand how the young can have a supportive physical effect upon the old — can warm them and even nurse them, as pictured by Rubens and described by John Steinbeck — and that the old might transmit infection to, or weary the young. But there is an additional more "mysterious influence" of one person upon another which the mesmerists attempted to explain in terms of transfer of a vital force. This idea contributed to the development of our current psychodynamic concepts. In these early beliefs that the aged harm the young by draining them of a fluid or force, there is recognition that young persons and older persons may regard each other with mutual fear and hostility. The young may see the old as actually or potentially harmful: they can exert power vested in them by society, they can be restrictive, they can exact service, and they can destroy one's spirit, be burdensome, and injure one's health. Conversely, the old are envious of the young, are eager for their services, and may be angry in advance because they are aware that young persons react with resentment, refusal, or avoidance to the envy and the burdens thrust upon them.[3]

Our present-day psychodynamic descriptions of behavior, a great advance from the naive views of a vital force, also rest upon the assumption that one person can have influence upon another.

Current views and descriptions of psychodynamic mechanisms — the intrapsychic process by which thought, feeling, and, eventually, action are governed — rests upon the assumption that individuals are motivated, goal-seeking, tension-building and relieving, and hedonically controlled in their social and intrapersonal functioning. These descriptions are generally made in terms of psychic mechanisms or processes which facilitate or obstruct satisfaction of basic biologic and required needs, relief of tension, gratification, and adaptive adjustments. Psychodynamic concepts describe how these processes are organized, how internal equilibrium is maintained, and how social adjustments are made. These concepts are usually couched in terms of needs arising internally and contingent upon internal or external changes. These needs are satisfied by effector action, which is regulated and governed chiefly by learned, but also by innate, patterns of behavior, so as to effect, in personally and socially acceptable — also

[2]Carl Sextus, *Hypnotism*, 4th rev. ed. (Chicago: Carl Sextus, 1896), p. 112.
[3]Sextus leaves implicit and does not remark upon the fact that the young, while being "harmed" were taking from the old — receiving benefits — the schoolboys were taught, the domestics employed and paid, and the King's maiden elevated to a place of privilege through the great social power vested in him.

learned—ways, gratifying changes in the external environment or in the relief of tension.

Both overt and implicit actions of an individual appear to be very largely the result of parental influences which assist, elaborate, and help to pattern the person's evolution. The ability of the parents to influence the child appears to depend upon the child's need for the parent. This need, which makes it important for the child to be able to hold and use his parents, and the child's increasing awareness of his need for them provide the opportunity for parents to make suggestions which are likely to be followed. They are in a position to heighten the child's suggestibility and to make increasingly complex suggestions for immediate action and to make a great many suggestions for deferred—future—action. At first the child through direct contact with the mothering parent develops a capacity for feelingful—emotional—interchange, that is, ways of signalling need and pain and of communicating pleasure. A more detailed description of this interaction is given later in this chapter.

Current concepts of psychodynamics place great emphasis upon the genetically predetermined, internally arising needs which predicate a turning of the child to the parent for gratification, and the necessity for eduction of the child during the period of socialization away from the parent toward an "outsider" for gratifications, after suitable deferral of action. The turn of a child to a parent and attempts to hold the parent have been dealt with at length by various authors, beginning with Freud, as instinctive and inevitable, and as including an "Oedipal" stage. In this paper both the turn of the child to the parent and the development of "Oedipal" relationships is considered to be largely culturally conditioned and determined; the numerous biophysiologic mechanisms geared to aid adjustment, homeostasis, survival, and reproduction form the substrate, and the complex psychodynamic mechanisms and interactions may be considered to be culturally influenced elaborations of more basic behavioral constellations. This is elaborated upon when we consider the characteristics of the dependent relationship. Greater attention to cultural influence upon socializing techniques and to the effect of socializing influences upon the formation of basic, but modifiable, personality permits the recognition of personality characteristics, which in turn influence generational interaction. Their recognition, therefore, may be predictive of intergenerational dynamics and post-dictively "explanatory." An original description and classification is briefly presented in this paper.

socialization—type one and type two

The thesis of this paper is that socialization prepares an individual for the successive life roles that will be ascribed to him, or that he will achieve, and that this can be accomplished in two ways. The first is the one that is generally regarded in our Western culture as the aim of socialization: to provide the individual with skills, information, and psychological and emotional attributes which permit him efficiently and pleasurably to fulfill his roles, and what is more important, to instill a sense of purpose about doing so. He is acculturated so that he wants to do what he has to do.

The second method is to impel the individual toward acceptable social behavior by way of dependency ties and dependent relationships, which act as a social cohesive force and permit or force the more or less successful assumption of successive life roles even in the absence of skills, information, and rational social purpose: the individual may do what he has to do but does not do it because he wants to, but because he feels pressed or forced to do so.

The interaction of family members resulting from the first type of socialization will be largely cooperative, rational, efficient, and pleasurable; it will rest upon the individuals' internalization of cultural values and upon their successful identification with suitable models found in real life or in an idealized image of a suitable person. The second type of family interaction will be governed chiefly by dependent needs rather than by acknowledged or implicit cooperative behavior; relationships will be determined by culturally influenced, imperative individual needs rather than by any understanding and appreciation of the stated aims of socialization or subscription to such views.

If dependent relationships are recognized as a critical, common, and pervasive influence in family dynamics, we may have a means of understanding two- and three-generation interactions, which in their great variety and seeming extreme differences are otherwise difficult to group and classify. It may be especially helpful in understanding behavior of the grandparent generation, which painfully binds or burdens children or grandchildren, and the response of these second- and third-generation family members to the first generation. Furthermore, many relationships that pass for admirable adjustment and appear explicable in terms of love and respect may actually be seen to have their basis in dependent relationships. This bridges a gap between seemingly different psychodynamic patterns which have similar final common paths, and can help to explain how seemingly similar psychodynamic patterns may have different behavioral expressions. This is because of the differences basic to dependent and independent behavior which may otherwise appear to be identical. For example, a desire to marry and have children — to form a family of one's own — may appear to be derived from unhappiness in an unpleasant home life, or from the example of a happy home life as a child and adolescent. In both instances, this desire may be derived from dependent needs. A nondependent person may similarly marry and have children but as a self-fulfilling personality evolution based upon culturally defined goals; conversely, a pseudo-independent individual may yearn for successful marriage but be unable to achieve or maintain it because of dependent needs.

In this paper in an attempt to illuminate these matters the dependent relationship will be defined. The evolution of dependency in socialization and the contribution of this constellation to social stability and social structure will be briefly noted. Special reference will be made to dependency as a relational force in the three-generation family. Its chief characteristic—performing for or to please another as fundamental to the individual's sense of security—will be described and contrasted to the nondependent self-realization in which a capacity for cooperation or affectionate interchange with others is characteristic.

dependency and the dependent relationship in family members

Many aspects of both two- and three-generation family relationships that are of social and psychological significance can be conceptualized as centering upon, as being derived from, and as capable of being understood, in terms of a single psychodynamic constellation, dependency, and the process in which it exists, the dependent relationship. This constellation underlies and accounts for most of the events described in psychoanalytic literature as transference or transference phenomena; they are relationships in which the person depends upon another.

The scheme developed here is based upon clinical experience, and rests in large part upon observations of patient behavior with the physician. It can be argued that this is not a reflection of normal individual behavior nor of healthy or even average family interaction. This does not threaten the usefulness of the data for universal application, however, because it is implicit in the thesis that the capacity for dependent behavior develops in all individuals who survive infancy and early childhood, that it comprises a core of personal reaction around which more complex behavior is polarized and clustered, that it is transparently present in many and is easily discernible in others only at time of crises, and that it can be seen in most persons when behavior is examined from the point of view developed. We should emphasize that this is a unifying schematization of psychologic, psychiatric, and sociologic data for the purpose of clarifying human interaction and is not meant to be taken as the ultimate truth about human behavior.

Definition of Dependency   The term "dependency" denotes the behavior, both implicit and overt, of a person who believes himself to be weak or who is weak and in need of help, in relation to one who is, or he believes to be, strong, capable of helping him, and likely to do so if properly signalled, invoked, appealed to, or controlled. Dependent behavior, dependency, requires a target: the delegated powerful or "parental" figure. In the dependent relationship a person may be said to "parentify"[4] — that is to say he envisions the chosen other as a strong parent, and the process of delegation to the role may be termed "parentification."

This consists of an idealization, glamorization, or misinterpretation of the characteristics and motives of a selected individual, suitable to the needs of the parentifying or delegating "weak" person. Selection and delegation of "strong" persons to act as parentified figures — parental surrogate, helper, friend, confidante, or whatever term seems preferable or applicable — is more the rule for persons in our society than the exception. It can be recognized as a large component of what is called or regarded as "love" and is easily recognized in the "loving" heterosexual relationships portrayed in the Hollywood movie production, popular song, popular novel, and slick magazine story of our time. The preponderant number of persons socialized by our culture, and probably by all cultures, manifest dependent behavior overtly, either intermittently or continuously over their entire life span. The dependent relationship which gives rise to dependency as a psychodynamic constellation has its origin in infancy. This concept can be compared to the original description of transference.

Freud, in 1912, wrote of the development of the individual's capacity to love as the basis of transference. He seems to use the term "love" to designate the individual's desire, yearning, or need for gratification, pleasure, or relief from tension through the aid of another person:

> ... [E]very human being has acquired by the combined operation of inherent disposition and of external influences in childhood, a special individuality in the exercise of his capacity to love — that is, in the conditions that he sets up for loving, in the impulse he gratifies by it, and in the aims he sets out to achieve in it. This forms a *cliché* or stereotype in him, so to speak (or even several), which perpetually repeats and reproduces itself as life goes on, insofar as external circumstances and the nature of the accessible love-object permit, and is indeed itself to some extent modifiable by later impressions. . . . [O]f these feelings . . . only a . . . part is directed towards reality, and can be made use of by the conscious personality, of which it forms a part. The other part . . . has been held up in development, withheld from the conscious personality and from reality, and may either expend itself only in phantasy, or may remain completely buried in the unconscious so that the conscious personality is unaware of its existence. . . . [I]n anyone whose need for love is not being satisfactorily gratified in reality . . . [the previously unconscious feelings will inevitably be mobilized] by each new person coming upon the scene . . .[5]

From this it is clear that Freud verged upon describing what is here called the dependency relationship, parentification. This is probably better viewed as a search for aid or support. The individual

---

[4]This is the term suggested by Dr. Sandor Rado from whose views I have drawn liberally.

[5]Sigmund Freud, "The Dynamics of the Transference," *Collected Papers*, Volume II (New York: Basic Books, Inc., 1959), 312-313.

attempts to achieve an aim through a selected, delegated other person in ways which have their origin early in life, but are modified or reinforced by experience and which become insistent and repetitious in the absence of need fulfillment with the persistence of unrelieved tension. Such desires, yearnings, or needs for gratification by means of or with the help of another, he implies, can persist into later life. The search for aid in the face of feelings of tension, lack of pleasure, or the presence or discomfort, whether on the basis of primary needs or because of secondarily, culturally acquired needs, can be expected to occur at any age, and can be expected to be a search for actual assistance or for the promise or potentiality of help, which can be termed support.

Dependency as Search for Aid or Support   In this paper, for the purpose of understanding family interaction in terms of personality, a new scheme of personality classification is proposed and described; the scheme is based upon clinical observation of dependent and nondependent persons. "Dependency" is identified by the special attributes of the search for a parental surrogate as the goal of a search for aid.

The Search for Aid or Support can be schematized as follows:

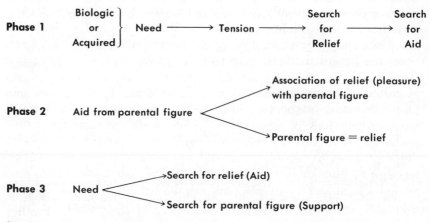

fig. 2-1   phases in the search for aid

In this way the developed individual learns to search for a parental surrogate as the means of obtaining relief from tension and gratification. This substitution of the person for the activity is borrowed when the search for relief by way of direct behavior is culturally discouraged and when the gratifying substitute through relationships with parental figures is encouraged. For example, the hungry child may be diverted from reaching out for the cookie so as not to spoil his appetite for supper, and to defer gratification by being drawn into substitute play or talk with the parent; similarly, adolescent sexual experimentation — a direct reaching out for self-gratification — may be discouraged by diversionary pursuits with parents or parent surrogates.

Most likely ways of searching for aid are learned first, and search for support is acquired as a secondary, conditioned development. For example, once hunger is discovered to be relieved by the mother, hunger may then provoke desire for the mother's aid; a next step in individual development is desire for the pleasure-providing mother's continued actual or potential presence as promising aid. This can be termed a security system in which the mother is the supportive element. If socialization results in personality development in which self-esteem, self-confidence, and purpose — sense of identity and motivation — rest upon real or illusory success in parentification, then a sense of helplessness and anxiety will eventuate in the search for support.

These psychodynamic mechanisms sparking the search for aid appear to be largely based upon the perpetuation of the child's original dependent relationship to the parent, reinforced and modified as he grows older. Some persons can evolve mechanisms for social interaction from the core of this original dependency, can modify them so greatly as they themselves develop, that they can achieve relationships on the basis of self-reliant independent types of interaction. Because these essentially different personality types — the dependent and the nondependent — seem to be the product of socialization processes and to be culturally determined rather than to be derived from an inherent, instinctual, inevitable constitution, what we call the psychodynamics of interpersonal relationships might perhaps better be called intrapersonal socio-dynamics. Although temperament must play a part, and, in special cases, a large part, in personality development, expressions of dependent or independent relationships can probably be traced to different family socializing experiences — different types of parental care and sibling interaction. The importance of nurture may well outweigh the greatest loading of nature. Socio-cultural and socio-economic conditions, in turn, undoubtedly influence the family climate through provision or deprivation of opportunity, incentive, and information.

Cultural influence can determine individual patterns of action by the effect of family dynamics and parental behavior upon attitudes toward self, what is feared, and how challenges or dangers are handled. In general, dependent socialization is to be expected if infants and children are reared where there is parental discord, relative disinterest in, or neglect of, the child, little supervision, inconsistency in parental attitude, behavior, or instruction, emphasis upon punishment rather than reward and on disapproval rather than approval as disciplinary measures, and where poor examples for emulation are provided, opportunities are scant, activity is restricted, and interested extended family or parental surrogates are absent or repellant.

Where there is only a short period of socialization, parents have little time to teach their children and often socialize their children most quickly by punishment and disapproval. Under harsh socio-economic conditions more persons are socialized as dependent. Under different conditions, where socialization is longer and "gentler," there is greater likelihood of developing nondependent persons.

However, even long periods of socialization that are inconsistent and punitive or socialization in affluent societies which relegate the young to the care of ignorant or neglecting nurses can favor the dependent type of socialization.

In short, dependent socialization, among others things, can be related to the development of individuals who feel helpless, frightened, and, therefore, in constant although unrecognized, need of a protective other person for at least partial alteration of disorganizing emergency emotion.

Socialization of the dependent type, "Type Two," appears to be simple, cheap, and rapid—that is to say family and social cohesion can be established under even primitive conditions, within relatively unstable families, and within a relatively short period of child-parent contact; in contrast, nondependent individuals require a prolonged dependency period for the evolution of a nondependent "Type One" personality which includes the acquisition of skills and techniques for personal relationships and, usually, of anxiety-free self-sufficiency.

The importance to us of these differences is that in our society the preponderance of the population appears to be developed as dependent; furthermore, of those who do develop as nondependent, a large number conduct themselves in conformity to the interpersonal value and the accepted mechanisms of social adaptation of the larger group of dependent persons. The reasons for this and the details of such persons' dependent functioning will not be developed here, but it may be helpful to present the subclassifications of dependent and nondependent functioning individuals to illustrate how dependent relationships come to be the common coin of personal interchange.

Personality, in terms of characteristic forms of dependent relationships or nondependent relationships, may be categorized or subclassified in the following groups, which are briefly described and discussed.

Types of Socialization   The first type of socialization, Type One, leads to the nondependent personality:

A. *Nondependent Personality Characteristics.*

1. Sense of purpose: depends upon internalized desire for self-realization combined with biologic urges toward survival and reproduction; self-assertion, necessary for survival, serves also for the improvement of the individual and social conditions.

2. Self-esteem: is enhanced and maintained by recognition of one's self as effective and capable of survival, of one's ability to

provide pleasure to the self, and of one's capacity for cooperative work and play with others; pride rests upon realistic appraisal of achievement.

3. Self-confidence: is established and augmented by recognition of one's ability and of one's achievements.

4. Pleasure: is obtained through the suitable recognition of tensions and needs, the identification of the means of achieving gratification within a socially and self-approved context, and the effective consummation of tension-relieving and gratifying behavior.

B. *Subtypes of Nondependent Personalities.*

1. Independent: rational, cooperative, and efficient functioning in social relationships; effectiveness not contingent upon overemotional reaction; affect—emotion—is attuned to individual goals and relevant to the situation.

2. Pseudo-dependent: rational social functioning modified by outward conformity to dependent behavior to avoid interpersonal complications. Because independence is disguised, subtype not easily recognized as independent.

3. Asocial, antisocial: openly exploitive behavior aimed directly at gratification of individual but not at social goals and without affectional ties. It can be argued that this should not be considered as a type of socialization; but it is included here not only for the purpose of comprehensive coverage, but because even asocial or antisocial behavior is, from the psychiatric standpoint, transactional and a product of socialization.

The second type of socialization, Type Two, leads to the dependent personality:

A. *Dependent Personality Characteristics.*

1. Sense of purpose: depends upon search for and holding— winning and controlling—others.

2. Self-esteem: through approval of others sought and won; and pride in self as one who can gain such approval.

3. Self-confidence: based on ability to identify, search for, and win others.

4. Pleasure: from service to, or effort toward accomplishment which pleases another. Pleasure in and from achievement is secondary to pleasure from its recognition by others.

B. *Subtypes of Dependent Personalities.*

1. Simple: open, transparent, obvious dependent relationships or strivings, often easily recognized and freely admitted by the dependent person as well as others.

2. Masked: highly elaborated disguised search, control, and exploitation of others; service is rationalized as a cultural value, a virtue, or good although its intent is to bind another; the individual

claims martyrdom at the hands of the delegated other; many mechanisms of "defense" as a means of converting ineffectual behavior into personally and socially useful activity; the individual attempts to repair the personality damage by making social virtue out of personal necessity, usually invoking reason but at the wrong time or in the wrong context. Thus—nothing ventured, nothing lost. Also, the rearing of many children under the guise of parental feeling but out of a need for reassuring, directive, devoted other person.

3. Pseudo-independent: brave and heroic, showy "masculinity," "femininity," or maternal behavior, usually with controlled anger on which self-assertion depends for break-through. Lip service to nondependent convictions, but for the purpose of another's regard; emulation rather than self-direction, or angry, defiant "go it alone" behavior because of disappointment in a parentified other—"surrogate" reaction.

These two types of socialization are not phases or stages in the evaluation of a personality. Each is a separate type, with its own characteristics as noted in the brief outline. Type Two is not an outgrowth of Type One in a predetermined instinctual developmental schema. Rather, according to this view of personality development, in the dependent relationship of infancy, childhood, and adolescence, individuals may be socialized toward the characteristics of either Type One, the nondependent personality, or Type Two, the dependent personality. The influence in one direction or another begins at birth. But these influences can be changed, even late in life, so that a shift of type is possible in either direction. However, complete shifts from dependence to nondependence are unlikely, from nondependence to dependence are even less likely. Some shifts within the major subtypes may be, in part, responsible for the emergence of pseudo-dependent and pseudo-independent types, but we must keep in mind that each of these "pseudo" subtypes is probably a clear-cut end product of individual socialization. One specific influence which appears capable of influencing a shift from one type of social functioning to another is *psychotherapy.* This process may offer the following for nondependent persons: for the independent who has "problems," information; for the pseudo-independent with social difficulties, help toward recognition of the more direct ways of achieving gratification and, by way of the pseudo-dependent supportive relationship with the therapist, perfection in functioning independently with more awareness of the pseudo-independent sociodynamics and more effective but less frequent use of them; for the asocial and antisocial nondependent, socialization toward affectionate relationships and cooperative attitudes toward nonharmful independence, or toward constructive pseudo-independence by way of a fostered pseudo-dependent patient-doctor relationship. Psychotherapy also aims to convert dependent persons to nondependent functioning. How frequently this can be achieved is questionable.

Certainly, simple dependents, by means of suggestion and instruction, can be greatly helped toward masked or pseudo-independent behavior. With considerable increase in social approval and increase in the approval or rewards from the others or other for whom they seek, pleasure may be increased and pain lessened.

Those dependent persons who fall into subtype two and three of Type Two, the "masked" and "pseudo-independent," probably comprise the major portion of our population. A fair share is also contributed by a subgroup of Type Ones, pseudo-dependents, who, although capable of functioning in an independent fashion, out of conformity or because of special situations which make it highly pertinent, function in a dependent manner.

The possibly puzzling behavior of a nondependent person as pseudo-dependent, may be understood as arising as follows: the nondependent in need, with another nondependent in need, will form a voluntary organization in which by way of cooperation the need is satisfied. But, when confronted by a "no-need" person, he may be required to act dependently, that is, behave pseudo-dependently if he is to obtain what he wishes. "No-needs" in relationship to other "no-needs" will be indifferent to each other, disinterestedly behaving in pseudo-dependent or independent ways; "needy" persons confronted by "counter-need" persons may at times relinquish independent types of functioning in favor of coercive dependent relationships, again as a form of pseudo-independence.

Thus, dependency functioning ranges from that of persons socialized as dependent and who have no other alternative, through seemingly independent functioning by dependent persons capable of simulation, to that of persons who are capable of nondependent relationships but who can also utilize dependent methods because of social pressures, with limitation of individual resources, or by choice. The social and psychiatric implications will not be discussed here. What is of importance is that by these definitions of personality the preponderance of persons, of necessity or by election, appear to function within the framework of dependent relationships.

In Figure 2-2 the products of socialization Type One and Type Two are grouped to show how, in the overlapping of overt behavioral manifestations, both types contribute to dependent relationships, which may be difficult to distinguish from each other without special study.

Persons in whom truly dependent behavior is a cohesive or disruptive force within the family should be distinguished from individuals in whom family formation or instability is related to their sociodynamic or independent type of functioning which conforms to social expectation. The distinction can be made between them by adequate attention to the characteristics noted above, and most surely by the use of "free associational" methods, which aid in the recognition of overdetermination of thought and action.

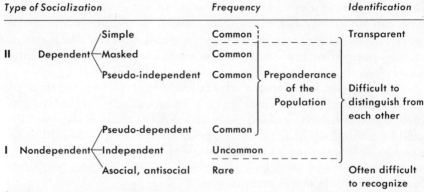

fig. 2-2   socialization and personality

Some additional characteristics differentiating the nondependent from the dependent personality, however, can be briefly described below to augment the description outlined above.

characteristics of the dependent relationship

Because the preponderance of the population appears to fall into one or another subgroup of dependent social behavior, the characteristics of the dependent relationship will be discussed in detail.

These characteristics must be considered in contrast to the features of nondependent relationships. The independent person, as observed previously, functions socially in a rational and cooperative manner and with relative effectiveness in achieving goals both alone and with the cooperation of others when required. He is capable of affection, trust, and patience, and can delay need gratifications for greater good at a later time according to the requirements of self and society.

The pseudo-dependent independent person is one who, in his rational social functioning, can recognize when conformity to socially valued dependent behavior is useful in avoiding friction and is harmless to himself and others. His is the dictum that when in Rome do as the Romans do. He may for example act in a sentimental way instead of solely with sentiment if this seems socially required, without self-depreciation or the loss of self-esteem which can otherwise be associated with sentimental attitudes.

The asocial group are independent persons, relatively rare, who have internalized little or no striving toward social functioning. They probably have lacked good or close care as infants. They are not always antisocial, but are rather unsocial or asocial. They are interested in other persons only as objects which can be used for the direct gratification of primary needs; they gain no gratification by way of the attitude of or relationship with the other person; they do not "parentify" or glamorize the person used as an object for goal achievement.

The person who is not socialized for self-reliance and cooperative family living but instead is dependent, has little primary desire to do what must be done to fulfill his successive roles and to realize his biosocial potential. His (or her) developing social orientation as a child will be more to play so as to be with someone else; he will tend to learn more to please another than for the pleasure of learning and being able to do; he will work for approval or admiration rather than because of interest in the work and pleasure from achievement; marriage will be to conform for social approval, to gain designated social position, and to acquire a supportive, helpful person; even reproduction and child-rearing will be more to please the mate, the parents, or the society, and in this way to make them more willing parental surrogates, rather than to achieve gratifying self-fulfillment. Social contributions are made for their effect in enhancing security, to obtain power or prestige so as to command and control rather than as an expanded expression of desire for individual and group survival and pleasure. We should note here that while other drives toward self-realizing behavior may be weak in the dependent person, the impulsion toward marriage and the courtship aspects of sexual behavior may be strong. In dating, courting, and marriage behavior, the varied patterns of "going steady," of courting, winning another, becoming disillusioned and running away, as in the "Don Juan" and "femme fatàle" patterns; of the frightened impotent male, the frigid or the "nymphomaniac" female; and of early marriage are all explicable in terms of a search for a supportive parental figure. The individual's search for friends and his striving for achievement, recognition, and success may also spring from his need and search for supportive others. The dependent person differs in all this from the person we evaluate as independent in that he does not seek to become and to be a self-pleasure-providing, self-reliant person, but instead he exerts himself to find a person who will give him a pleasurable sense of being valued and through whom he indirectly obtains gratification and tension relief. Even in sexual intimacy, participation is directed toward pleasing and winning the mate, or pleasure is gained because the other person can be held only if the relationship is enjoyed. This makes for the paradox of capacity for sexual pleasure and orgastic ability premaritally or when marriage is threatened, but such capacity is absent once marriage is attained or assured.

By contrast, the independent cultural product is an individual who seeks out socially acceptable life roles in personally and socially acceptable or tolerable ways; he obtains cooperation as necessary by way of constructive, efficient patterns of behavior. He has "internalized" the social values useful for self-realizing, cooperative behavior

and has learned to make quickly, often automatically, the responses
suitable to his ascribed or achieved role. The dependently socialized
person searches for aid and, even more obviously, for emotional support, for praise, and for external proofs of worth and ability. He ap-
preciates praise for effort as much as praise for achievement. At times
he is even more interested in effort than achievement, because actual
achievement, although praised and approved, might threaten his dependent status. There is thus in the dependent person a hidden fear of
success signalled by anxiety as it is approached and depression when
it is achieved. As one patient put it: "It threatens my insecurity."

Even reproduction becomes part of the search for aid. Not only is a
child conceived to please and hold an existing protective parent
figure, but also so that it may itself serve as a parent. Consequently, a
parent may inadvertantly "sexualize" the relationship with a child. A
mother may convey to her son that he is to fulfill for her what her
husband did not; that he is to be what her husband is not; that he will
really love, support, and care for her, as his father has not. The child is
made to feel he should, that he is expected to, compete with, rival, and
supplant his father. Daughters may be similarly imbued with the belief that it is their duty to supplant or replace the father in parental role
toward the mother, or to supplant the mother for the father. Many
variations of parentification of children can occur. Because, in our
Western society certain of these variations are so common, in some
subcultures specific variants appear to be universal. The resultant
internalized patterns and strivings, identification with and hostility to
the father or to the mother, together with yearning for and desire to
please one or another parent, may be mistaken for a biologically
predetermined aspect, or considered to be the whole of the dependency relationship. The very common middle-class pattern in our culture, in which a mother depreciates the father and motivates the son
toward identifying with an idealized image that she suggests, has led
to a belief in an instinctive Oedipal complex.

Fully as common now is parentification of a daughter by the
mother with indoctrination of the child that the male figure is demanding, violent, oppressive, and damaging. This results in a close tie to
the mother out of fear and need, in fear of men which accentuates the
need for the female parent, and to a search for a parent surrogate male
—out of dissatisfaction with the mother—in the guise of search for a
mate.

Because the behavior of a dependent person is contingent upon
another's personal supportive attributes, it can be recognized that the
dependent person has made out of what was once—in childhood—a
means to the end of achieving social and personal value, an end in
itself. When the dependent person has obtained a supportive person,
his psychodynamic situation may be a relatively stable one almost
indistinguishable from that of the effective self-reliant person. How-

ever, in the absence of a helpful supportive person, as when the parent-surrogate mate proves inadequate, the search for aid or support may be discernible as a compound that includes feelings of helplessness; anxiety; a rather transparent need for or desire for another person; ingratiating seductive behavior; anger towards persons sought after who, because they do not respond as desired, are regarded as rejecting, neglecting, or even harmful; self-justifying thought or behavior; self-punitive trends; and punishing attitudes or behavior toward the sought for, desired, but "neglecting" other. The life goal or purpose then emerges as a search for and as an attempt to gain and hold another who is selected and delegated to be the helpful one.

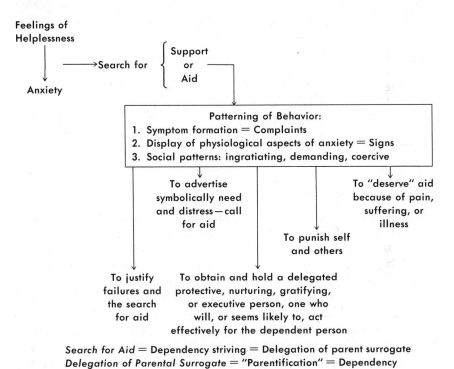

Feelings of Helplessness

Anxiety

→ **Search for** { **Support or Aid**

Patterning of Behavior:
1. Symptom formation = Complaints
2. Display of physiological aspects of anxiety = Signs
3. Social patterns: ingratiating, demanding, coercive

To advertise symbolically need and distress—call for aid

To "deserve" aid because of pain, suffering, or illness

To punish self and others

To justify failures and the search for aid

To obtain and hold a delegated protective, nurturing, gratifying, or executive person, one who will, or seems likely to, act effectively for the dependent person

Search for Aid = Dependency striving = Delegation of parent surrogate
Delegation of Parental Surrogate = "Parentification" = Dependency
Dependency = The exploitation of one believed to be strong by one who believes himself to be weak.

fig. 2-3   the search for aid

The patterns of search for aid as noted above can be recognized as occurring in certain common constellations which have a core of anger and often appear to be punitive and manipulative in their aims. Figure 2-4 illustrates their relationship to each other as a continuum of human response understandable in terms of dependent relationships.

How these patterns may be related to development and to intergenerational reaction is outlined in the next section.

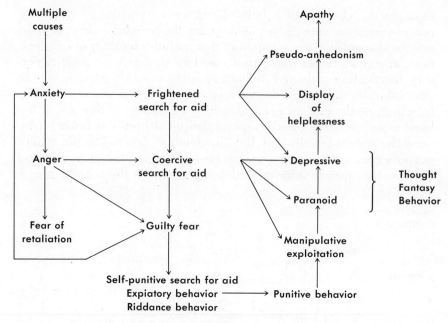

fig. 2-4   patterning of the search for aid

personality development

Infant-Parent   The human infant has a natural, primary dependence upon adults. To live, the infant must have extensive aids to
maintain its temperature, nutrition, and cleanliness, and to protect it
against harm. The inherent organization of the immature organism is
"set" to gravitate toward, signal for, and to accept the help it needs. It
seeks and tries to preserve the pleasant; it avoids and tends to reject
the unpleasant.

The helplessness and evidence of an infant in distress tends to
command adult provision of its needs. This adult orientation toward
the child is itself a product of early relationship and training in the
infancy of the parent; patterns of care for children are not instinctively
developed or spontaneously evolved. If good early care is absent,
patterns of parental care may fail to develop in the adult, or when
developed, may be adversely influenced by the individual's reaction
to the care he received in infancy and childhood. Within the matrix of
the early child-parent relationship there evolves, in a series of pleasurable or painful experiences with a strong protective other person,
an expectation for help and relief from tension and a conviction that
this relief can be demanded and received from another. This persists
in memory and in action as an emotional core around which ensuing
experiences are integrated.

While the gamut of hedonic mechanisms are geared for survival,
they are also subject to misdirection through faulty training or un-

fortunate circumstances. The type and quality of the care received, in conjunction with the inherited factors which are revealed in what we call temperament, appear to influence both the development of confident expectations of help and whether the relief of tension experienced with parental aid is entirely pleasurable or admixed with pain. The length of time tension is endured, and its intensity, may contribute to convictions that only painful feelings will solicit aid and/or comfort and that pleasure must be preceded by and paid for by pain.

The relatively well infant has a number of developmental tasks which may bring him into conflict with his mother. In his urge to stand, to crawl, to walk, to manipulate, and to taste, he must occasionally, if not often, be limited or restrained. Further, in the second year he becomes ready to and begins to learn bowel and bladder control. Parental haste, compulsive traits, or cultural bias may lead to child-parent conflict. As Rado describes, the child wants his way and the mother wants her way, leading to what he has called "the battle of the pot." In such a struggle the child, compelled by physiology, must eventually lose. He may take this as proof of his subservient, weak status, which is, therefore, accepted grudgingly and with many variations of rebellious, defiant, or other behavior aimed at bolstering self-esteem. Such struggle obviously can occur in behavioral areas. When victory on the part of the child is possible, such struggles may contribute to habitual modes of attempting to control and triumph over the delegated powerful parental figure. An important outcome of these struggles, which the parent may be drawn into or precipitate, is that the child learns to oppose self-gratification of his own needs because satisfaction is felt to be a frightening submission to another, or, conversely, that undiluted satisfaction is forbidden. The child comes to prefer control of another through painful self-denial to direct self-assertion, or to regard gratification as transgression. Furthermore, because his opposition and fear are in the context of a protective relationship, such struggle becomes the epitome of a secure situation. This may lead to polarization of behavior around struggle, domination, or submission rather than around a core of affectionate regard and reciprocally derived pleasure. The person becomes oriented toward "fight for fight's sake" and derives pleasure from struggling with parental surrogates because this is reminiscent of the secure, protected, sensually pleasurable infancy and early childhood in which struggles were the rule. Parental command, child refusal, parental insistence, withdrawal or struggle, punishment, tears, compliance, forgiveness, and then reward; or, disobedience, tears, pseudo-independent compliance, and then reward; or, tears, parental guilt, remorse, and reward may become painful sequences of behavior ending in pleasure.

The individual through these interactions with parent figures may develop a conviction that pain, suffering, discomfort, tension, or any "hunger" which provokes alertness and a search for relief must itself eventually force the appearance of gratifying parental help by means of having reached a peak of distress, or that pain suffered at the hand of a parent will eventually yield reward. Thus, in later life a desire for pleasure may give rise to a search for painful relationships with another as though this, rather than efforts on one's own behalf, will produce the desired result. Punitive complaining, open or disguised, which promises or elicits punitive retaliation, obvious or simply subjectively expressed as such, may be necessary for the capture of pleasure or as a price for its enjoyment.

This has been exemplified in popular songs, for example that one made relatively immortal by Fannie Brice: "He's my man, I love him so . . ." To the observer this may appear to be an enjoyment of or desire for pain or illness, or it may appear to be a method of commanding or punishing another through being in pain or ill, or being likely to become so. This behavior may actually be the only way the person knows to ask another for help, affection, or gratification. He behaves as though he must hurt so as to be helped, pay in advance to gain pleasure, suffer if he is to gain and enjoy what in a "sane society" he is actually welcome to take freely.

In adult's garb these patterns comprise some of the so-called "sado-masochistic" patterns. They are elaborated, modified, and reinforced in the post-infancy dependent relationship required for further socialization.

The Reinforcement or Modification of Infant-Parent Patterns The preschool child is not a completely helpless creature. On the contrary, he has considerable capacity for self-sufficiency and can survive with relatively little assistance in simple societies. In our own complex society, children remain hightly dependent and in need of considerable protection against the many hazards, partly because of their inquisitiveness, activity, and desire for independence.

The individual's values are largely contingent upon whether the culture in which he grows up is an essentially harsh or gentle one, that is to say, upon its protective, nurturant, and educational proclivities.

When parents encounter personal difficulties of socio-economic nature, they generally have difficulties in properly socializing their children. The result is a personality poorly socialized from the point of view of social welfare and cooperative behavior, often reinforced by socio-economically determined traditions of the child's peer group. Under these circumstances the development of a dependent type of behavior is socially favored.

Of profound importance to the preschool child are his parents' views about him. Maternal solicitude, a highly protective attitude, special attention to diet, and encouragement to rest, to avoid, or to take exercise engender ideas of fragility and vulnerability and favor incorporation of the mother's view in an exaggerated and self-restrictive way.

As the child moves into adolescence, to learn remains his chief task. However, he may also include work so that he can contribute to his own support or to that of his family. He enters a period of accelerated growth, both physical and sexual, with biological capacity for and drive toward reproduction. This, in our society, is generally controlled and prohibited, although with marked subcultural differences in attitude and modes of behavior. In the middle and upper classes, the adolescent remains largely dependent, and continues to learn by example and through formal training. He displays patterns of limited sexual activity, in which heterosexual relations are gingerly approached. There is emphasis on the aesthetic and more subtle aspects of heterosexual and other personal relations, which reciprocally influences other areas of activity. When contrasted to the lower-class adolescent whose dependence is not prolonged beyond the biological period, the middle- and upper-class adolescent appears more passive, intellectual, and less impulsive and rebellious, although oppositional behavior may be manifested verbally and in fantasy. Because of his passivity and the acceptance of special restraint and its internalization, he (or she) may be confused about his sexual role and fear he is homosexual when contrasting himself with adolescents fulfilling adult roles.

The adolescent in the lower socio-economic group places strong emphasis on independence, both financial and physical, and on "masculinity" if male or "femininity" if female. He wants a job, a car, and a girl, and usually gets all three early. She wants marriage. He is impulsive and tends to act by trial and error rather than to think through major or minor life problems. He has headaches and musculoskeletal symptoms. The adolescent girl may regard her menses as illness and disability. These patterns and symptoms may be used to manipulate surrogate parent figures who are longed for and being sought for as patterned by social presses, and early family formation may be the result.

Illness and impairment as a means of controlling others is common. Because of its utilization in coercive, angry, manipulative ways illness is simultaneously regarded as punishment and as a consequence of disobedience to the parents. The latter are often blamed, therefore, for misfortunes that occur. Illness is imputed to the parents, and what may be the result of one's own behavior is projected, as to cause, upon the parent surrogates. This characteristic becomes more important in middle age and old age when illness as an explanation of failure may be welcomed, and self-exoneration or self-justification is achieved by way of blaming, accusing, and destructively dealing with parent-surrogate mates, siblings, or children. Inversion of such projection often accentuates depressive patterns of middle life: the accused parent-figure is seen as accusing; the resulting vicious circularity of reasoning can be traced, as previously noted, to the pattern of search contingent upon socialization toward dependent relationships.

The following example of middle-class young adult relationship to mother, husband, and child illustrates some of these points.

case 1

Mrs. X., an only child of moderately well-to-do middle-class parents, was a popular and vivacious girl and was highly regarded by her teachers. She was not interested in going steady but was "rushed off her feet" and into marriage by a very eligible young man who became intensely devoted to her. She finished her college work simultaneously with his completion of graduate school, and they then went to live in his home, a city distant from her home and parents. She missed her parents greatly, made long visits with them, and was often reluctant to return to her husband. She felt generally listless, had multiple shifting somatic complaints, and disliked sexual intimacy. After several years they had a child to whom, as she saw it, the husband became very much attached, and for whose sake he seemed anxious to avoid marital discord. When the child was several years old, Mrs. X.'s father died. With her child, she left her husband "for a visit" to console her grief-stricken mother and to be, in turn, consoled by her. She found it extremely difficult to leave her mother and return to her husband, but on his insistence that she return home, she did so when her mother went along, first, to live with them, later, to live nearby. After about a year, on the advice of physicians seen by Mrs. X. because of her many complaints—at first extensively investigated medically, but finally regarded as psychiatric—the mother returned to her own home. Mrs. X. followed her on a visit after some months. Although bored and lonely with her mother, she felt very reluctant to return to her husband despite his pleas and the needs of the child for a stable home. Mrs. X.'s mother tended to examine her daughter's dilemma in detail with her—"never advising her, but always showing her both sides of the matter: that divorce was never certain to solve a personal problem, and that domestic problems are often as much the fault of the husband as of the wife." She admitted to the daughter, however, that she often felt that Mrs. X. may have made a poor choice of husband. Mrs. X. vacillated between thoughts of divorce and freedom, and fear of relative financial nonsupport and boredom at home with her mother; and between feelings—impressed on her by her husband—of duty and obligation to her own daughter, and of guilt about her mother's lonely widowed state and need for companionship.

Comment: The rivalry between mother-in-law and the daughter's husband for the physical presence of Mrs. X. appears to be clear. Implicit is a possible rivalry between Mrs. X.'s mother and Mrs. X.'s child. Mrs. X.'s indecision about whether to live with either her husband or her mother and the lack of expression of interest in living alone, now that she is thirty years old and feels she has made a poor marriage, is obvious. The accentuation of her problem, or her mother's, upon the death of her father, is also striking. We can assume that, here, there are at work individual psychodynamics which are disruptive of family cohesion and stability in view of the large distance between her mother's home and her own, but which are highly conducive to preserving geographic proximity and close relationship between herself, her family, and her mother and her mother's associates.

Mrs. X. is an illustration of the "dependent, simple type" of personality which serves family cohesion.

Behavioral Change with Aging   In the third and fourth decade of life, preoccupation with the image of oneself is common. There is a desire to improve one's self. Worries center about appearance, sexual morality, sexual performance, and one's relationship with others, the group, the nation, the universe. Later, in the fifth and sixth decades there is more concern about health, marital problems, economic security, and the political scene. Self-confidence appears to be highest for the female in the third and fourth decades, and maximum for the male in the sixth.

The middle-aged individual often has the burden of caring for his own children, himself, and his aged parents at a time when he begins to experience the first evidence of his own aging as indicated by fatigue or decrease in stamina and change in appearance. These may be times of change in status. Health, domestic life, economic situation, relationship to children and to parents, or individual self-esteem may be altered by changes in situation. For those who have been successful in defining their life goals, and in achieving or "guaranteeing" them, the middle years may be a time of prideful, pleasurable work and socialization. Reevaluation and revision of interests, friendships, occupation, family relationships, and personal views may lead to increased self-confidence and self-esteem, which in turn tends to lead to adaptability in the later years.

Middle age, however, may require revision of one's views of self or of previously cherished goals. There may be a forced change in the view of one's own status and a need to recognize without bitterness that there has been little realization of cherished goals. The need for revision of expectations causes many difficulties. Persons may become aware, for the first time, that they have failed to manipulate those around them in a manner that they hoped would be effective in enabling them to reach their goals. They become disillusioned about the efficacy of their way of life and their attempts toward achieving gratification by way of others. Previously masked behavior disorders now become more overt as persons exert more effort in their old ways or attempt to gain their ends by way of emphasis upon their failures. Consequently, for many, the middle years may be defined as a time of crises, disasters, catastrophes, impulsive changes in course, and of reaping and rueing. For those who succeed, they may be years of reevaluation, revision, and renewal of friendships, of interests, of confidence, and of self-esteem; for those who feel failure they are years of bitter recrimination and depression.

The following case illustrates some of these points.

case 2

Mr. O. is now 63 years old, and his wife is 50. His mother, who is now 93 years old, has lived in their home for 15 years, during which time their two children have grown to college age. His mother came to live with them on the death of her husband. The elder Mr. O. was a tyrannical, domineering, rigid, hot-tempered man who ruled the family absolutely and ruthlessly. The younger Mr. O., the middle child of three, knew he was least preferred by his mother and was completely subservient and devoted to his father after a defiant, unruly childhood. In the first year of his marriage, about 25 years ago, he was domineering, hypercritical of his wife, and continuously complaining about his business partner, one of his brothers. After the birth of his son, or at least when the child was old enough to talk, he began to dominate and criticize the boy, treating him so strictly and cruelly at times that his wife could not refrain from interfering. The boy grew fat and passively resistive of the father's prodding. Mr. O. regarded him as indolent and sabotaging. A first child, a girl born before the death of his father, was of less interest to Mr. O. Throughout their married life, Mrs. O. felt that he was "more married to his mother than to me." He was kind and respectful to his mother, and when she came to live with them, he kept the children quiet lest they disturb her in her physically separate quarters in the same house. Although throughout the period of his son's growing years his dominating abusiveness continued to be directed at the boy instead of to his wife, he nevertheless flew into furious rages at her about how she should talk to and control the son. He was sarcastic, mocked her, ridiculed her. She had great difficulty in tolerating his behavior but despite frequent impulses to leave him managed to stay on, taking care of the children and serving him in every way, as a good wife. One reason she persisted was because of his great generosity to her parents. During an obviously psychotic depression when he was 53, he became extremely considerate, sweet, and helpful; he seemed to cling to her, was compliant. She saw that his suffering was extreme and that his ingratiating submissive manner with the children frightened them, but she almost preferred that he remain ill because of the improvement in his attitude to her. Instead of rising at 5:00 A.M. to go work energetically all day and return exhausted and irritable at night, he kept reasonable hours, took time off, was interested in vacations. He accepted medical and psychiatric care, was docile, and was greatly concerned — often to tears — about the children, especially the son. He even consented to and arranged for psychiatric treatment of his troubled son. This was the first of several episodes in which what was usually Mr. Hyde became clearly Dr. Jekyll. His wife became interested in psychology, read and took courses, and became convinced that he was domineering because he felt weak and frightened, but had to put on a show that he was strong; the slightest suggestion from her that this was a possibility, however, threw him into a fury.

Comments: This man shows alternation in his behavior when he is well and when he is ill. When "well" he is abusive, domineering, and coercive, a tyrannical patriarch with his family, and he is ingratiating, clinging, and compliant with his mother just as he had been with respect to his tyrannical father. When he is "ill," he is clinging and ingratiating with his wife and son and shows masked hostility to his mother in his fright about her welfare.

The aim of this man's behavior has been to control others either by domination or by submission, whichever seemed to promise or guarantee protection contingent upon how he saw the strength of his selected, delegated parent surrogate. He may be considered an example of "masked" dependent, verging on the "pseudo-independent," type of socialization.

Old Age A person may be called aged when the processes of deterioration have reached the point of curtailing physical, psychological, intellectual, social, and economic activity.

As aging becomes manifest, persons who espouse "youthful views" about remaining vigorous and active, who resist believing that age must bring decline and disease, appear to have higher morale and to make a better adjustment, even though obviously ill and old, than those who have had conservative, pessimistic convictions of age as decline and deterioration. It appears that for many persons in our cultural setting a conviction of one's ability to master challenge and change, whether it be based upon the Type-II, dependent-personality conviction that one can find and hold another or upon the Type-I, independent-personality feelings of confidence and pride in one's self, is preservative of good interpersonal relations and contentment. In actuality, self-assertive persons with wide interests and many activities tend to remain alert and exhibit less evidence of mental defect than those with narrow and nonliterate pursuits. Thus, behavior in old age is to a considerable degree related to early education and to socioeconomic status. Possibly less literate and resourceful persons who can maintain their belief in their control over selected other persons can also remain relatively free of fear and its expressions. These persons, however, are more vulnerable to discomfort upon the loss of relatives and friends by death, illness, or removal.

The death of a friend or relative, especially of one who was younger, in some persons provokes extreme exacerbations of anxiety associated with feelings of both triumph and of guilt. The illness or death of an assisting supportive person, usually a spouse, may permit the emergence of previously masked intense dependency which then becomes burdensome to children or friends. The death of friends or relatives may appear to cause or increase the isolation of aged persons. The isolated person, actually one who was previously aided and supported by his family, emerges as a lonely, bored person who by way of a variety of complaints makes personal and social demands. His response to those around him may be first frightened and "searching," then angry; in each case it is inappropriate, and he may therefore be considered a nuisance, a danger, or endangered.

The case which follows gives an example of a dependent person in old age.

case 3

Mr. U., an 83 year old man, was noted to have failing memory and to be withdrawing rather large amounts of money from his none too ample resources without being able to account for how he used it. He had always been a boastful, pretentious person who prided himself on his business success, whereas his managerial status in his private concern had actually been arranged and maintained at first through the acumen of his wife and later by the help of his grown children and faithful employees. He had made a great show of effectiveness after his retirement. The advent of serious disabling illness in his wife made her not only unable to take care of his needs but also physically dependent upon him. The family was made aware that his home situation, his habits, and his failing memory presented a critical problem when they were called by the police to come to the station house for their father. When they arrived, he told them he had come to the police to help find their mother for whom he had searched everywhere all night. Worried, they asked him, "Have you called home while waiting for us?" "No," he replied, "I don't want to wake her up, she was asleep when I left."

Comment: The protective function the wife had for this man is obvious; less obvious until driven home by a chance remark, was the concretization of his search for his protective wife now that he is in the distressing situation of having lost her capable aid and of being pressed into her service. It is of interest that the grown children, with their own families of relatively grown children, stood by helplessly while this situation developed. The decline of the mother, which left her and her husband vulnerable and unprotected, was a problem about which the children felt concern, but they neither took action nor knew what action to take although they had been able to give material assistance to their father in the past. The search of this man, whose behavior also reflects brain damage, appears to be for the protective, motherly wife whose protection he never had to acknowledge in the past. His search is epitomized by the incident of appeal to the police. The once effective wife is now ineffective, gone, and he, both unprotected and burdened by her illness, leaves her to look for her. The ineffective replacement for the parent-substitute wife, the ill and depressed "new" Mrs. U., is left at home asleep and is not to be disturbed; she cannot be expected to be helpful in finding the woman for whom he seeks. There is an appeal for aid which takes him to the hopefully helpful police who force the children into action. He can be termed dependent, with a life pattern of pseudo-independent behavior; yet his behavior, based upon his need for the parent figure, is tending to bring and hold three generations together.

The following case illustrates how there may be a search for support in the guise of providing it, and how search for aid or support tends to interweave within a family and also to enlist the aid of outsiders.

case 4

Mrs. T. is 72 years old and childless, and has been a widow for two years. She is the oldest of three sisters. The youngest, a moderately mentally retarded spinster, lives with and keeps house for the widowed middle sister, Mrs. N., who works and regards herself as guardian of the youngest. Mrs. N. has a son and several grandchildren. Mrs. T. insists that she has regarded Mrs. N. as a "daughter" ever since their mother on her deathbed about 40 years ago told her to watch over her. Mrs. T. has many complaints about Mrs. N.'s disrespectful, unfeeling, unhelpful, and abandoning attitudes, actions, and statements; these have been redoubled since she lost her husband. During an illness of Mrs. N.'s, Mrs. T. repeatedly called all the physicians to assure herself that treatment was properly conducted; several times she tried to influence Mrs. N. to change to her own physician. She became indignant that Mrs. N. did not receive her advice graciously. As time went on and when Mrs. N.'s physician seemed to "brush her off," she accused Mrs. N. of the darkest ingratitude, of unsisterly and obnoxious behavior; she felt, on the other hand, that she herself had been patient, ever ready to help. Her late husband, she said, actually detested Mrs. N., but was nice to Mrs. N. because he recognized her needs and Mrs. T.'s responsibility.

Mrs. N. points out that Mrs. T. actually has always leaned heavily upon her for advice, reassurance, and companionship, and that she, Mrs. N., has been a lifelong confidante about Mrs. T.'s problems. Furthermore, Mrs. T. has become a constant visitor since her husband's death, in constant need of advice and reassurance. Mrs. N.'s son who, during this period had to be of assistance to his mother, became involved in multiple problems of his own with his wife and children, which then required his mother's assistance. When Mrs. N. turned her attention to him, Mrs. T. again became panic stricken and called doctors, friends, and relatives in disorganized and troublesome attempts to help Mrs. N. and to exhort them to prevail upon her sister to treat her more courteously and considerately.

Comment: Here we have an example of an older sister who appears to have delegated to a younger sister a parental role, disguising the relationship by insisting she has a maternal attitude and that she has taken over maternal responsibilities despite actions to the contrary and frank panic over an illness of the younger sister that threatened the loss of her dependent status. When Mrs. N. turned from her to help her own son and grandchildren, Mrs. T. become obviously frightened, demanding, and coercive in contrast to her previously condescending, controlling behavior. She may be considered as a "masked" dependent person who also can behave in a pseudo-independent fashion.

Failure to accept old age is not necessarily "ungraceful" aging, nor is it adequately explicable as "denial." Persons who do not develop feelings of helplessness, who maintain a conviction of strength and ability to cope with problems, are able to contend with the losses that constitute aging without becoming overwhelmed with anxiety. Many others become disillusioned about themselves, their prospects, and the world's beneficence. They become frightened and angry, and may display their feelings in one of a variety of patterns we call mental illness or invalidism.

The disillusionment that can occur with age is reflected by the fact that young adulthood or youth or childhood is so often retrospectively viewed as the happiest time of life by the old. Rarely is middle life or the later years so regarded. Feelings of contentment, vigor, desire, and interest decline in age and are replaced by feelings of uselessness and loneliness. The steadily mounting proportion of suicides, especially of men, in the fifth and later decades is one clear indication of mental distress and despair with aging.

Frightening, bewildering reminders of waning strength and impending dissolution may leave an aged person with feelings of defenselessness against his own decay, and he then faces life with feelings of fear and impending catastrophe. The preoccupation of old people with illness, operations, accidents, and violence are clues not only to resentments and rage, long-harbored or recently revived, but also to their own sense of vulnerability, their fear of damage, and their concern with the ultimate helpless state—death. Their preoccupations are like the nightmares which follow a catastrophic event. Much of the seemingly hypochondriacal complaining and agitated search for proper medical attention or for more salutary living conditions on the part of aged persons can be understood as their acting in terms of fears generated by feelings of helplessness in the face of awareness of mortality; they can be understood in the psychodynamic terms of search for support on the part of persons who have manifested the same behavior all their lives in other ways or as a search for aid patterned according to their knowledge and expectations on the part of relatively independent persons.

a psychodynamic construct of family interaction

The affirmed aim of socialization is to help individuals develop in a mutually cooperative society so that they may act independently or self-sufficiently to gain tension relief and gratification, and to make those adjustments suitable to the society in which they live. However, as a general aim of socialization, this aim may be what Lasswell would call a myth:

> The prerequisite of a stable order in the world is a universal body of symbols and practices sustaining an élite which propagates itself by peaceful methods and wields a monopoly of coercion which it is rarely necessary to apply to the uttermost. This means that the concensus on which order is based is necessarily nonrational; the world myth must be taken for granted by most of the population. The capacity of the generality of mankind to disembarrass themselves of the dominant legends of their early years is negligible, . . .[6]

The belief that the majority of persons is independent and self-reliant is probably unwarranted. The preponderance of our population appears to be socialized as dependent. This socialization is economical, it can be quick, and it affords a maximum of personal suggestibility and malleability. Such socialization is not a "plot," nor is it intentional on the part of "politicians." The suggestibility

[6]Harold D. Lasswell, "In Quest of a Myth: The Problem of World Unity," *A Study of Power*, Harold D. Lasswell, Charles E. Merriam, and T. V. Smith, eds. (New York: Free Press of Glencoe, Inc., 1950), p. 237.

and malleability of individuals together with their aggressiveness and irrationality is regarded rather as "human nature." There are many, however, who are delighted with social dependency and who happily try to, and do, make use of it.

Among those who make greatest use of individual suggestibility in our society are the members of the family themselves. Society vests authority in parental figures. This authority is added to actual strength and is utilized in a variety of ways, including the preservation of the family as an interactional unit.

One can conceive of a society in which the family supports and is supported by the individual so that he can perform effectively in other situations or social structures, which in turn support the family in a smooth and efficient interaction or transactional process. In such a social structure individuals would acquire goals and techniques, be motivated and have capacities for action, which would have them want to do what they have to do to maintain their family and social structure. Such a social structure would enable them successfully to assume and fulfill the successive patterns of action, the roles, required by their growth, development, aging, and changing position in the family and their society. This society could be static or changing. If changing, cultural influences upon the individual would encourage his desire to improve the culture and his abilities to do so at the proper time in acceptable ways, and there would be a concomitant wish and ability to alter society in accord with those technologic, intellectual, or value shifts that result from his efforts or those of others. These well-adjusted persons in a well-ordered society would be socialized toward self-socializing, efficient action and would find personal comfort or happiness in a highly gratifying society, in which families could be of any type—nuclear, extended, or network.

Socialization of the person would occur smoothly in this utopia because demands on the individual would not exceed his capacity as he develops. Challenges necessary for optimal functional growth or development would be optimally timed so as to be most effective. Under these circumstances of graded training in accord with biological readiness and requirements, the program of socialization begun within the family structure and aided by society would later continue in the community, aided by the family. In this way self-esteem, self-confidence, and ability would be developed in optimal amounts. Peer-group influences and teachers of all kinds would make their contributions to the family's socializing influence. Later the person himself, through his successful actions and the pleasures accompanying them, would reinforce and elaborate his already useful social actions. The gratifications to be gained by success as a personal carrier of culture as a parent, would then reinforce his well-socialized behavior while he transmits it. Marriage would serve as a social institution in which multiple gratification—sexual, intellectual, emotional, and pleasurable achievements—would occur in a relationship which enhances feelings of security. In marriage there would be a mutually acceptable division of labor and ready assistance for the relief of tensions; there would be assured opportunity for personal fulfillment as a companion and as part of a worthy social group.

In this society, family dynamics—the assumption of roles in accordance with changing age and ascribed or acquired change in status, duties, and privileges—would be relatively free of friction and discontent. Parental roles would interlock and complement each other, and children would find no difficulties in identifying themselves with effective persons of the same sex. In a family they would develop a secure sense of worth, self-confidence, and goals suitable to their temperament, intelligence, and opportunity, and they would receive family assistance toward the opportunities to realize their goals. Such socialization could conceivably result in a personality which permits the individual to adapt to his social environment affectionately, self-reliantly, cooperatively, and constructively.

However, in a complex society the learning period, the teaching provided, and the family condition and the social opportunities may not be adequate to assure development of such personality care and effective patterns of action. When a family is held together by social pressures, by individual needs for gratification, and by imperative needs for assistance rather than by a desire for mutual cooperation and pleasure, then the family will be vulnerable to dissolution. When the price of family assistance is high in terms of pain or distress, or when gratification is more easily obtainable elsewhere, then the family is vulnerable to dissolution. At this point, affectional ties of dependency may serve as a "second line" of social defense for family formation and for preservation of the family.

dependency as a cohesive force

Once the obligatory infantile and childhood dependency upon an individual who assumes a real parental role is over, dependent relationships are determined by what is learned in the relationship itself, but also by cultural factors which contribute to its modification and elaboration. The manifestation of dependency—who is delegated to a parental role, how this is done, and for what—may be complex and variable. Individuals can react to all around them, or, successively to selected persons, with dependency. Conversely, individuals in their turn may be themselves parentified, simultaneously or successively, by one or many other persons. While this pattern or constellation binds individuals, and therefore families, together, it can also promote disharmony and disruption because of its nature. It is an uncalled for and possibly unwelcome delegation of one person by another. On the other hand, it may sometimes appear to be a warm, friendly, inviting, admiring attitude which appeals to and seduces the delegated protector. At other times it may be directed at the selected person as a coercive ("love me or I'll kill myself"), painful attack.

The "ideal," "optimally socialized" (Type One) family is held together by affection, the automatization of good will. In the "ideal" family, parents are held together by affectionate bonds and reason; children in infancy are held to both parents by dependency, later (in childhood) by dependency and affection, later by affection and reason; children are held to each other by affection and affection plus reason; the parents are bound to the children by affection and reason.

The "nonideal" (Type Two) family is bound chiefly by dependency ties. However, there are many variations possible. Frequently family members are held together by social pressure; few members of the family have bonds to each other, and even these bonds are dependent relationships rather than voluntary and desired relationships, from the nondependent personality view. Thus, the parents may be held together and to their children only by social pressure, while their children are held to them by tenuous bonds of dependency.

Dependency may hold one parent to another, who in turn is bound by affection or who may have no bond other than reasoned tolerance of the arrangement. Mutual dependency is common. Parents may be dependent upon children who may have an affectionate bond or a reciprocal dependency relationship with them. Where parents or adult children in a family are bound to other adults by dependency, there is often a reciprocal dependent status which may appear to be an affectionate one.

Dependency may not be the only interpersonal tie, nor necessarily an exclusive one: it may coexist with reasoned cooperation, socially imposed collaboration, or fortuitous complementation. However, dependency, because it focuses the parental role, appears to be the most common and most important of the bonds that hold families together as a network of overlapping personal dependent relationships.

conclusion

This paper is not a comprehensive consideration of three-generation family relationships and individual psychodynamics. Instead, it is an attempt to describe personality characteristics which may lie behind, and possibly be useful as "explanations" of intergenerational friction, disharmony, or distress and paradoxically, of family cohesion and solidarity. For this purpose the concept of dependency striving, as an emotionally determined search for support or aid from others, is considered to form the core of personality, which can then evolve either as dependent or nondependent contingent upon childrearing practices. Nondependent persons are equipped for relatively rational cooperative behavior within the social context. Alternatively, dependency can serve to bind persons to each other either in crises or perennially as a way of life. No matter how much the expressions of behavior may resemble each other, the dependent individual behaves in a manner which has intrapsychic determinants that differ from those of nondependent persons.

From this point of view families are formed and held together because of social presses and needs for mutual aid and cooperative activity, but also because of affectional, that is to say, emotional ties. The affectional ties tend to be either affectionate, that is to say, empathic, tender, trusting, and pleasurable, in persons who are socialized as nondependent, or to be of a controlling type, by way of domination-submission behavioral characteristics, in which anger and fear predominate, in persons who are socialized as dependent. The preponderant number of families in our society appear to come into existence and to be held together on the basis of relatively nonaffectionate, that is to say, dominance-submission governed, dependent relationships.

These relationships which govern family interaction are determined by the socialization process which takes place within the family. Families with dependent relationships tend to perpetuate themselves in this manner, and families with nondependent relationships are prone to develop dependent personalities in their children under social or economic stress.

Individual indoctrination, or socialization, is a family function. Presumably the aim is to produce individuals capable of adjusting to social demands while gratifying personal innate and acquired needs, with consequent family formation, reproduction, and child-rearing as part of their contribution to the cultural pattern. This indoctrination is favored by the contactual relationships of mother and child which form a core of capacity for dependent relationship. These dependent relationships polarize added behavioral patterns, to which peers and parental surrogates contribute, first based upon mimicry, then upon the informal and formal learning which occurs within a dependency relationship with parents or parental figures. This relationship is one in which suggestibility is aroused, enhanced, and at least intermittently utilized so that suggestions can be accepted for immediate or deferred action, and the information, skills, and attitudes necessary for proper performance in successive life roles can be developed or acquired.

Internalization of parental attitudes and of the social values imparted through them, together with identification with an effective actual parent or an idealized parent image based upon existing models, but modified according to the developing yearnings and reason of the child, appear to be effective processes in the evolution of individuals with a high degree of self-esteem who are also capable of socially acceptable mastery of routine life problems, including family formation and child-rearing where socially practicable. "Nondependent socialization" produces an individual who is independent and self-sufficient, socially purposeful and cooperative.

The second type of socialization which occurs in the family is characterized by a tendency to form dependent relationships. Contributory to such socialization can be the burden of care for grandparents thrust upon parent figures, which interferes with their parental function with their children or sets examples for their children which result in a dependent personality.

Of paramount importance is the fact that dependency can be a cohesive force when socialization toward independence is not achieved or is considered socially undesirable. Socializing processes which cause impounding of self-assertion with respect to achieving relief from tension, the mastering of social problems — work, role fulfillment — and gratification develop dependent individuals.

The major thesis presented here is that dependency can be a cohesive, in fact it can be *the* cohesive, social force in the family and for society, although it may not necessarily be a desirable one. It can and does exist, in fact it seems to flourish, where it is most openly depreciated and overtly opposed. Such depreciation and opposition may be social modes of encouraging and fixing continuation of pseudo-independent — and thus dependent — behavior rather than actual obstacles to the development of dependent relationships.

A few key points about dependent relationships can be briefly stated:

1. The origin of dependency is in the child-parent relationship.

2. Its variants include pain-dependent-pleasure mechanisms.

3. It becomes sexualized and masquerades as passion, adult sexual interest, or affection.

4. It functions to guarantee such social institutions as marriage, despite its tendency to provide and to stem from marriages on the seamy side, by impelling individuals toward parent substitutes whom they tend to bind and hold.

5. It functions to guarantee child-rearing because it impels the person to child-bearing and caring for children to gratify needs to act like a parent. Such persons tend to seek and make parent substitutes of their children.

6. It tends to be a provider of pleasure, by way of the pleasures accruing to mastery, even where miscarried socialization or over-socialization has severely limited the individual's ability to provide and make use of pleasurable opportunities. It does this by way of the pleasures of control over others who can be fantasied as providers of pleasure, or from manipulation of them into doing so, rather than from the association itself.

7. It tends to provide purpose where individual capacity for self-realization in terms of productivity, the pleasurable achievement of status, and fulfillment of successive life roles has been impaired, destroyed, or failed to develop. It does so through the substitution of search for

and holding of the individual who is regarded as protective and a provider of pleasure. The means is substituted for the end.

8.   It provides for creativity by way of depressive reactions and yearning. Loss of self-esteem and loss of confidence in finding and holding the desired person yield to effort concentrated upon performance to win and please the other, with the incidental acquisition of skills and the expenditure of effort necessary for creative work.

9.   It provides opportunity for the repair of self-esteem in the face of failure. Inability to act is construed as humane and noncompetitive. Desirable goals are deprecated as of lesser value than the courtship and care of the idealized, desired, protective person or persons. Pride is taken in passivity, comforts are depreciated in favor of attitudes of abnegation. The means is again substituted for the end, a silk purse is made of a sow's ear, and pride is taken in one's deficiencies as faults are elevated to the place of virtues. The world is called dog-eat-dog, self-assertive persons are regarded as aggressive, success is depreciated as "phony," and in the face of those who can take care of themselves, and actually do so in a mutually cooperative manner, the individual may feel taken advantage of and perennially vulnerable. This may lead to anger and aggressivity.

10.   It provides, at times, opportunity for self-realization by way of aggressivity—anger—when the demands on the self in finding and holding the other become so onerous that defiance leads to performance for one's own self, spitefully, vengefully, or with a sense of victory over the other. Aggressivity is substituted for self-assertion and success may result.

The dependency ties which have been described are not the only possible ties in our society, but they appear to be more common than the rational, affectionate fulfillment of generational roles which occurs as the result of adequate internalization of social values and the identification with a suitable parent figure or an idealized image of a parent. Consequently, in terms of this conceptual scheme, three-generational family dynamics are usually characterized by the frequency with which dependent relationships assume importance as family integrative or disruptive forces. A grandparent generation tends to exert a governing or controlling action upon the dependent second generation who aim to gain its approval and favor as a means toward promise of aid for themselves or as an end in itself. In the absence of crisis a nuclear family group may react to this almost automatic dependent relationship as burdensome subservience. Individual members may, however, find great solace and support through appeal to, and contact with, the first generation; these familial ties appear to be culturally, not biologically determined.

Often, family closeness appears to be comprised of interlacing pain-filled personal relationships in which manipulative maneuvering is called, and mistaken for, affection, and in which guilt, a crushing sense of obligation, and a compulsive need for social compliance, joined with fear and inability to act with rational independence, combine to constitute a reciprocal bondage miscalled "love." These are persons whose family cohesion is based upon the socialization of the family members as dependent persons, whose pleasures are contingent upon their feeling that a parent surrogate is always available.

In such families, by occupying the middle generation, the first generation can force the environment to be harsh and depriving for the third generation, who, inadequately socialized, will in turn become highly demanding, dependent persons whose search for parental surrogates from youth to old age will contribute to family — and to social — disruption.

In conclusion, we should note that recognition that individuals can be socialized as dependent persons and can manifest their dependency in a variety of ways throughout their lives, contingent upon changing personal needs and situational demands, makes it unnecessary to conceptualize human behavior as "regressive." There is thus not really a "child-parent reversal" that takes place when an adult or an aged person looks to a child as to a parent. It is rather that a lifelong manifestation for a dependent person has emerged with greater clarity at this time than it has at others. Also, we need not postulate that individuals regress to previous modes of adaptation; manifestation of a dependent relationship is merely more transparent at some times than at others, often, because such relationships are less elaborately disguised or are displayed in socially less acceptable forms.

social work and family relationships in later life with some thoughts on filial maturity

MARGARET BLENKNER

Social work is not prepared, either theoretically or experimentally, to assist a growing group of persons in our society, namely, the middle-aged children of aging parents, those persons who today are facing the major task of attaining what might be termed "filial maturity."

Social-work theory and practice is oriented to the individual and to the nuclear family, composed of husband, wife, and young children. Its theories of intrapersonal and intrafamilial dynamics are almost entirely derived from psychoanalytic models, largely Freudian. In addition, of late, role theory,[1] crisis theory,[2] and transaction theory[3]

[1] See: Leonard S. Kogan, ed., *Social Science Theory and Social Work Research* (New York: National Association of Social Workers, 1960); Helen Harris Perlman, "The Role Concept and Social Casework: Some Explorations I: The 'Social' in Social Casework," *Sovial Service Review*, XXXV (December, 1961), 370-81; and "Identity Problems, Role, and Casework Treatment," *Social Service Review*, XXXVII (September, 1963), 307-18.

[2] See: Howard J. Parad and Gerald Caplan, "A Framework for Studying Families in Crisis," *Social Work*, V (July, 1960), 3-15; and Lydia Rapoport, "The State of Crisis: Some Theoretical Considerations," *Social Service Review*, XXVI (June, 1962), 211-17.

[3] See: Viola W. Weiss and Russell R. Monroe, "A Framework for Understanding Family Dynamics," *Social Casework*, XL (January and February, 1959), 3-9, 80-87; and Roy Grinker, Sr., *et. al.*, *Psychiatric Social Work: A Transactional Case Book* (New York: Basic Books, Inc., 1961).

have made their appearance on the social-work scene, but all are used within, and adumbrated by, the basic Freudian psychology—a psychology which views the apex of human development as that of "genital maturity" which, in the healthy personality, is attained in early adulthood and which, among other things, involves freeing oneself of the parental tie.

Social-work values are those of the democratic ethic, which places the individual and his right to self-actualization and self-determination in a central position, modified only by the competing rights of other individuals, *especially his child.*

The prototype of the family with which family social work primarily concerns itself is that of the *isolated* nuclear family, theorized by Parsons[4] to be the most functional type for modern industrial society as a replacement for the classical, but dysfunctional, extended family of earlier America.[5] Parsons' theory of the function of the family in the development and socialization of the child is congenial to social workers, and he is probably cited in current social work literature more often than any other sociologist because, although the theory is put up in Parsonian bottles, it is Freudian wine. Neither Parsonian nor Freudian theory, however, has any place for the middle-aged, or the aged parent except, in Freud's case, perhaps that of villain. This may be one of the reasons Parsons is struggling (so far with minimal results) to find a role for the old in America today.[6]

The concept of the isolated nuclear family as the modal and most functional family is coming under increasing attack in a recent wave of empiricism among sociologists, with Litwak's research seemingly the opening wedge.[7] This attack has now reached the point that, at the most recent meeting of the American Sociological Association, Sussman and Slater called for a reformulation of family theory, stating flatly that, "empirical evidence . . . makes it unnecessary to continue further descriptive work to establish the existence and functioning of the kin network in modern urban society."[8]

What then are some of the facts and ideas about the family and kinship system of modern America that social work should be aware of and ponder upon more than it has in recent years? How well does

[4]Talcott Parsons and Robert Bales, *Family, Socialization and Interaction Process* (New York: Free Press of Glencoe, Inc., 1955).

[5]Schorr, Litwak, and other American sociologists have questioned whether the classical extended family was ever a strictly American tradition, and feel rather that it was an immigrant one. See: Alvin Schorr, *Filial Responsibility in the Modern American Family*, U.S. Department of Health, Education, and Welfare (Washington, D.C.: Government Printing Office, 1960).

[6]Talcott Parsons, "The Aging in American Society," *Law and Contemporary Problems*, XXVII, No. 1 (1962), 22-35.

[7]Eugene Litwak, "Occupational Mobility and Extended Family Cohesion," and "Geographic Mobility and Extended Family Cohesion," *American Sociological Review*, XXV (February and June, 1960), 9-21, 385-94.

[8]Marvin B. Sussman and Sherwood B. Slater, "Re-Appraisal of Urban Kin Networks: Empirical Evidence," paper given at the 58th Annual Meeting of the American Sociological Association, Los Angeles, August, 1963 (mimeographed).

social work theory and practice fit these facts insofar as the middle-aged and aged are concerned?

The nuclear or conjugal family of today exists, not in isolation, but within a network of kin relationships extending horizontally among siblings and vertically among several generations, each of which is child or parent to another. Mutual aid flows mainly along the vertical, generational lines, followed by the horizontal sibling line, and, finally, by the more distant kin lines of aunts and uncles, nephews and nieces, and cousins.[9] Sussman and Burchinal describe the flow of economic aid among the adult members of the middle-class thus:[10]

> During the early years of the child's marriage the flow of aid is from parents to children. As children become middle-aged the stream may be reversed, children now help their aged parents. Middle-class, middle-aged children may be giving subsidies to young married children and aged parents at the same time. A frequent pattern of aid is to turn to the needs of aging and often ailing parents after children have been aided in beginning their marriage and careers. This pattern is more a function of high income of parents and the age of members of nuclear linked units than preference to help children over parents.[11]

Economic aid among kin in the middle class is more likely to take the form of cash subsidy than among the lower class, where the typical response to need of the aged and the young is that of shared living arrangements.[12]

Despite the still prevalent notion that the old are neglected or repudiated by their children, study after study has failed to produce evidence to support it, either here or abroad. Shanas,[13] Streib and Thompson,[14] as well as Townsend,[15] for example, all indicate that the older person prefers to maintain his independence as long as he can but that when he can no longer manage for himself, he expects his children to assume that responsibility; his children in turn expect to, and do, undertake it, particularly in terms of personal and protective services. For basic economic maintenance, both the old and their children look to governmental aid through a system of social security, but for other services children feel a strong obligation to assume the "tak-

---

[9]Marvin B. Sussman and Lee Burchinal, "Kin Family Network: Unheralded Structure in Current Conceptualizations of Family Functioning," *Marriage and Family Living*, XXIV (August, 1962), 231-40.

[10]Juanita M. Kreps, in a paper prepared for this same symposium, "The Economics of Intergenerational Relationships," describes the flow of nonvoluntary aid through taxation.

[11]Marvin B. Sussman and Lee Burchinal, "Parental Aid to Married Children: Implications for Family Functioning," *Marriage and Family Living*, XXIV (November, 1962), 320-32.

[12]Schorr, *Filial Responsibility in the Modern American Family, op. cit.*, pp. 8-14.

[13]Ethel Shanas, *The Health of Older People: A Social Survey* (Cambridge: Harvard University Press, 1962).

[14]Gordon F. Streib and Wayne Thompson, "The Older Person in a Family Context," *Handbook of Social Gerontology*, Clark Tibbitts, ed. (Chicago: University of Chicago Press, 1960), pp. 447-75.

[15]Peter Townsend, *The Family Life of Old People* (London: Routledge & Kegan Paul, Ltd., 1957).

ing care of" or "caretaker" function. This function is assumed voluntarily, without legal compulsion, as an affectional and ethical response
to parental need.[16] Included in this caretaker function are those idiosyncratic responses and services which do not lend themselves to stan-
dardization and uniformity and cannot be carried out through large-
scale bureaucratic organization in the way that the function of meeting
economic needs, for instance, can.[17]

Among the "expected and practiced roles," assumed by children
and other kin of old people, report Sussman and Burchinal, are the
giving of services involving "physical care, providing shelter, escorting, shopping, performing household tasks, sharing leisure time, etc."[18]
Since most older persons in the United States live near, if not with,
one or more of their children, these services are performed as needed
for the old parent or parent-couple living alone, as well as for those
sharing a household with kin.

Shanas[19] has vigorously attacked as a social myth, the "alienation
theory" which holds that "old people who live alone or apart from
their children are neglected by their children," and marshals convincing evidence to support her position, citing in addition to her own data
from the United States, the WHO report on *Mental Health Problems
of the Aging and the Aged* which summarizes reports of research from
various countries as follows:

> Wherever careful studies have been carried out in the industrialized
> countries the lasting devotion of children for their parents has been amply
> demonstrated. The great majority of old people are in regular contact with
> their children, relatives, or friends . . . Where distance permits, the gener-
> ations continue to shoulder their traditional obligations, of elders toward
> their children, and the children to the aged.[20]

In analyzing the sources of this myth of alienation, Shanas points
her finger at two groups: the aged themselves, especially *childless* old
people, and *professional* workers. "Childless old people, about one-
fifth of all old people in the United States," reports Shanas, "are the
most likely of all old people to believe that aged parents are neglected
by children." Professional workers, she speculates, see mainly the
aged who are without families or who have been alienated from their
families. "If these people did not already have problems, they would
be unknown to casework agencies, family service bureaus, public

[16]Schorr, *Filial Responsibility in the Modern American Family, op. cit.*, p. 33. Schorr
has covered so thoroughly the matter of legal compulsion of filial responsibility
that there is no need to expand on the matter. His monograph should be on the
shelves of every social worker, whether in or out of public welfare.

[17]See Litwak, "Occupational Mobility and Extended Family Cohesion," *op. cit.*, for
a discussion of bureaucratic versus family functions.

[18]Sussman and Burchinal, "Kin Family Network," *op. cit.*

[19]Ethel Shanas, "The Unmarried Old Person in the United States: Living Arrangements and Care in Illness, Myth and Fact," paper prepared for the International
Social Science Research Seminar in Gerontology, Markaryd, Sweden, August,
1963.

[20]World Health Organization, *Mental Health Problems of the Aging and the Aged*,
Technical Report Series, No. 171 (Geneva: World Health Organization, 1959).

housing authorities, home care services, etc." If they are alienated from their families, "such patterns ... usually do not appear for the first time in old age." The social myth of the alienation from their families of most old people, Shanas concludes, "is created and perpetuated by professional workers in the field of aging and by old people themselves."[21]

This is a strong indictment, but one could add to it. What Shanas may not be aware of is the unease, ambivalence, and plain ineptitude with which the average professional worker, in agencies not devoted specifically to serving the aging, meets the problem of alienation or, worse still, may compound or exacerbate it under the mistaken notion that his sole responsibility is to free the child from the parental tie, in line with his theory of personality development and nuclear family orientation. While it is often necessary to assist the child to complete his unfinished emancipation from the parent *in order that he may then be more free to help his parent,* this thinking is not readily apparent in much of what is done in family social work. The number of case records in which one reads of the worker "relieving his client's (the child's) guilt" or "alleviating separation-anxiety" is depressing, as is the number of times the worker is supported in this by the agency's psychiatric consultant. One is inclined to question whether caseworkers and psychiatrists know what the *normative* response of the adult, often middle-aged, child is to parental need, and to what extent they can grant absolution for failures in filial duty. Not all guilt is neurotic; real guilt serves a positive social and psychological function impelling a person toward change that can gratify him as well as those who otherwise may be hurt by his acts or failure to act.

One-fourth of the adults in the United States who are 45 years or over have at least one living parent, while four-fifths of the noninstitutionalized aged have living children.[22] We do not have the demographic data that matches up these adult parent-child pairs, however.[23] We do know, however, something of the characteristics of the child to whom the older parent turns, or would turn, for help in a crisis. This child is a *middle-aged woman,* either a daughter or other relative on whom the older person counts, and who expects to be counted on in times of illness or other stress.[24] If the situation requires, the older person moves into the child's home. Commenting on the comparative frequency with which aged parents move into son's *versus* daughter's homes, Nimkoff remarks:

> Apparently, if an aged parent has to be dependent, it is safer to be dependent on a daughter than on a son. Or, to state it differently, since the woman usually sets the tone of the home and has the major responsibility

---

[21]Shanas, "The Unmarried Old Person in the United States," *op. cit.*

[22]Shanas, *The Health of Older People, op. cit.*

[23]Some family life tables or parent-child life tables are badly needed. Perhaps the Census Bureau could remedy this lack if it could be convinced of its importance.

[24]Shanas, *The Health of Older People, op. cit.*

for the management of the home, it is more satisfactory to be dependent on a daughter than on a daughter-in-law.[25]

Not only does the woman perform the caretaking function for the old, it is also the woman who seeks help for them from nonfamily *I ssued* sources when she herself cannot give it. In a recent New York City study conducted in a voluntary family agency, the writers found a predominance of women among persons applying on behalf of an older person.[26] In a sample of 223 applications from or on behalf of a person 60 years or over, the application was made by the older person or his spouse in 39 per cent of the cases, by relatives other than spouse in 26 per cent, by nonrelated individuals in 16 per cent, and by social or health agency personnel in 15 per cent. Three-fourths of the applying relatives were women, usually daughters. Ranking behind nieces as a source of application came daughters-in-law. Sons ranked below daughters but equal to nieces and above nephews. Friends, usually women, were almost as frequent a source as children. The data indicate that a disproportionate number of never-married, divorced, and separated older persons seek help from the voluntary agency when compared to the general older population. As a consequence of the high proportion of never-married persons, the number of childless aged is higher than is true of the general population. Interestingly enough, this sample not only had fewer children but fewer siblings and other relatives. In other words, Shanas' contention that the older person who comes to the attention of the professional worker is less likely to have normal family resources to fall back on is supported by these data.

Some of the older persons sampled for the New York study were seeking help for *their parents,* or for a brother or sister, or in a few instances, a child or grandchild who could not manage for themselves and for whom the older applicant could no longer carry full responsibility owing to his own increasing needs.[27] This group causes one to raise serious question about "relative responsibility" clauses in welfare laws, or policies that do not take sufficient account of the problem of the middle-aged or older relative who is expected to carry financial responsibility for others. Their numbers are increasing and social policy must sooner or later take account of their predicament. In this New York study of older applicants for social agency help the problem categorized as "assisting another" was *positively* and significantly associated with financial problems, *negatively* associated with

[25]M. F. Nimkoff, "Changing Family Relationships of Older People in the United States During the Last Fifty Years," *Social and Psychological Aspects of Aging,* Clark Tibbitts and Wilma Donahue, eds. (New York: Columbia University Press, 1962), p. 409.

[26]Margaret Blenkner, Julius Jahn, and Edna Wasser, "Serving the Aging: An Experiment in Social Work and Public Health Nursing," prepublication draft, Community Service Society of New York, 1963 (mimeographed).

[27]Shanas found that about one in every ten persons to whom older persons said they would turn for help was 65 or older. See *Health of Older People, op. cit.,* p. 113.

problems involving the applicant's own housing and living arrangements, and not associated at all with any other problems. These facts tell a story: the older person who seeks help in assisting someone else does so primarily because of the financial strain he is under at a point where he must look to his own future. If he draws upon savings, he exposes himself to financial dependency later; if he carries the burden out of current income, he reduces the amount he can put aside for future emergencies; either way he is in a bind.

Except for economic need, however, the kinfolk of older people do not normally turn to social welfare programs for help for them; neither do they turn to institutional care except in extreme circumstances. The solution to the health and social needs of the oldster who can no longer entirely manage himself or his own affairs is, in the opinion of most Americans, that of having the older person move in with or close to a son or daughter. Less than one out of ten older people or their close kin think institutionalization is the proper answer.[28]

The thought of entering a home for the aged or a nursing home is extremely unpopular among the elderly. Among the older applicants interviewed in the previously mentioned New York study, only seven per cent selected "home for the aged" as their *preferred* dwelling place, despite the fact that many had applied for just that purpose, and none preferred living in a nursing or boarding home. Among a representative sample of *non*applicant New Yorkers 60 and over interviewed in the same study, only one per cent selected "home for the aged" and, like the applicants, none selected nursing or boarding home. Shanas found three per cent of her 65 years and over sample preferring such living arrangements. Her summarization of why older people feel the way they do about nursing homes and homes for the aged should be read and re-read by every social worker who counsels adult children regarding care of their aged parents. Below are some excerpts from it:

> Almost all older people view the move to a home for the aged or to a nursing home with fear and hostility. . . . All old people – without exception – believe that the move to an institution is the prelude to death. . . . [The old person] sees the move to an institution as a decisive change in living arrangements, the last change he will experience before he dies. . . . Finally, no matter what the extenuating circumstances, the older person who has children interprets the move to an institution as rejection by his children.[29]

Can one read this conclusion, founded on a nationwide and carefully chosen sample of some two thousand older Americans, and be glib about assuaging guilt or separation-anxiety?[30] True, sometimes the children and those trying to help have no alternative to placing the

[28]*Ibid.*, pp. 118-23.
[29]*Ibid.*, p. 102.
[30]One wonders in these cases just whose guilt or whose anxiety is being assuaged – the child's or the professional helper's?

parent in an institution, but why is there no alternative, why in America have two great humanitarian professions, medicine and social work, so abrogated their role of caring for the sick, the helpless, the confused that a highly profitable nursing home *industry* has grown up before their eyes to take over on a commercial basis a function that for all other age groups they jealously guard as their professional prerogative?

Why have we not developed the "home help" programs for the aged that European countries have? Why do we talk so often about homemaker or visiting housekeeper service for the aged and yet do so little about it that a USPHS survey made as recently as 1958 can report that for the whole United States, in one sample week, only 701 families with aged persons were actually receiving such service?[31]

Robins has attacked with considerable bitterness what he terms "the nursing solution to old age."[32] "The treatment [under social welfare auspices] of problems arising from tenuous parent-child relationships," he comments wryly, "has some of the characteristics of the disease." That the older people and their children who rejected the "nursing home solution" in the Shanas study may know better than the professional worker the full responsibility involved in such a decision is entirely possible. Evidence is beginning to pile up that placement or any abrupt transplantation of old people from familiar surroundings is hazardous and may indeed be a "prelude to death" for many of them.[33]

Robins also feels strongly that social welfare programs ignore the

---

[31]United States Public Health Service, *Homemaker Services in the United States, 1958 — A Nationwide Study,* United States Public Health Service Publication No. 644 (Washington, D.C.: Government Printing Office, 1959), p. 45.

[32]Arthur J. Robins, "Family Relations of the Aging in Three-Generation Households," *Social and Psychological Aspects of Aging,* Clark Tibbitts and Wilma Donahue, eds., *op. cit.,* pp. 464-74.

[33]One of the conclusions of the Blenkner, Jahn, Wasser study, "Serving the Aging," *op. cit.,* was that, "the negative association between applicant survival and amount and length of service, coupled with the positive association between amount and length of service and placement in protective settings, *leads one to hypothesize a negative association between removal of a client from his own home and his subsequent length of life.*

At least two studies of institutional populations moved from one institution to another indicate relocation of any sort may be hazardous. See: C. K. Aldrich and E. Mendkoff, "Relocation of the Aged and Disabled: A Mortality Study," *Journal of the American Geriatrics Society,* XI (March, 1963), 185-94; and N. Ferrari, "Institutionalization and Attitude Change in an Aged Population: A Field Study on Dissonance Theory," Doctoral dissertation, Western Reserve University, School of Applied Social Science, June, 1962.

In addition, Curt P. Richter, psychobiologist at Johns Hopkins, has reported some animal findings that may be relevant. See: "The Phenomenon of Unexplained Sudden Death in Animals and Man," *Physiological Bases of Psychiatry,* W. Horsley Gantt, ed., American Lecture Series (Springfield, Illinois: Charles C Thomas, Publisher, 1958), pp. 112-25.

The above reports should also give us some pause in our rush to remove old people from mental institutions, particularly those who have been there for years, or at the very least, to do some follow-up studies on death rates.

children who take on the task of providing a home for their aging parents. "We need to seek ways of maximizing the capacity of these families to be mutually supportive, and ways of minimizing intergenerational conflicts," he writes.[34] One might add that not only are children who assume such responsibilities ignored, but they are sometimes diverted from their filial obligations. One is reminded of Erikson's remark in *Young Man Luther* regarding his own profession, psychoanalysis: "We must grudgingly admit that even as we were trying to devise . . . a therapy for the few, we were led to promote an ethical disease among the many."[35]

The ethical aspects of attitudes toward the aged will not be put down by professional or scientific avoidance of the issue. "Old Age: A Moral Dilemma of an Affluent Society," Rosow titles one of his papers, and concludes eloquently:

> . . . the crucial people in the aging problem are not the old, but the younger age groups, for it is the rest of us who determine the status and position of the old person in the social order. What is at stake for the future is not only the alienation of the old from the young, but the alienation of the young from each other and of man from man. There is no way out of this dilemma, for young or old, without a basic re-ordering of our national aspirations and values of which the aging problem is but a token. Anything less than this will see us concentrating on superficial symptoms, especially tangible ones like housing the aged, and nibbling at the tattered edges of our problems without penetrating to their heart.[36]

Perhaps, if the social sciences and helping professions have any influence over society's values—and there is some reason to believe they do—it is time they stopped perpetuating alienation and started trying to remedy it. In this they may be behind the populace; if so it would not be the first time.

Turning to the individual, one of the more important phenomena of twentieth century America is the change occurring in the life cycle. Social workers are aware of the lengthened life span of the average person but not so aware of certain other changes or their implications. The span of the marriage cycle, for example, has lengthened 10 years since the turn of the century, owing both to earlier marriages and longer life expectancy. Parents are younger when their last child is born and younger when he marries. In 1959 the median age of the wife at birth of the last child was 26, of the husband 28. The median age of the parent at time of the last child's marriage was 47 for the wife, and 49 for the husband.[37] Whereas in 1890 the youngest child

[34]Robins, "Family Relationships of the Aging in Three-Generation Households," *op. cit.*, p. 473.

[35]Erik H. Erikson, *Young Man Luther,* Copyright © 1958, 1962 by Erik H. Erikson (New York: W. W. Norton & Company, Inc., 1958), p. 19.

[36]Irving Rosow, "Old Age: One Moral Dilemma of an Affluent Society," *The Gerontologist,* II (December, 1962), 182-91.

[37]Paul Glick, *et. al.*, "Family Formation and Family Composition: Trends and Prospects," paper read at Annual Meeting of the American Association for the Advancement of Science, Chicago: December, 1959.

married *after* the death of at least one of his parents, today he marries
some 15 or more years *before* this occurs.[38]

It is not only the chronological lengthening of life that is important, but the state of health and vigor in which those longer years are
spent. Men and women today are not physically or mentally old at 50,
although once this was true. (Earlier in the century Freud considered,
that ". . . near or above the fifties the elasticity of the mental processes,
on which treatment depends, is as a rule lacking—old people are no
longer educable.")[39] Most people today are not really old at 60; real
old age with serious accompanying infirmity comes to most in their
70's, while for some, serious limitation in their ability to manage independently does not come until their 80's. It is during this advanced
decade that many old people who have previously lived alone begin
to share a home with their children. Shanas reports that the proportion
of the unmarried elderly (widowed, divorced, and never-married) living alone stays at about the 50 per cent level until age 80, when there
is a sharp decline.[40] It must be remembered too, that many persons die
without ever having become old and infirm; the quick death from
cardiac failure or cerebral accident that strikes the still vigorous man,
or the aging, but still active, woman who succumbs to Asian flu are
examples in which the persons may never, until their short, final illness, have required care from anyone. Most older persons under 75
are quite capable of taking care of themselves and their affairs. They
neither want nor need to be "dependent," but they do want and need
someone they can *depend on* should illness or other crisis arise. There
is a vast difference in these two conceptions which is sometimes overlooked.

Another area where marked changes in the life cycle are occurring
is in the work life span, which has shortened for men, while increasing
for women so that the two sexes are moving toward each other: a fact
which will increasingly raise the economic status of the older woman
relative to men and in turn reduce the necessity for her to move into
her children's household for economic reasons alone. Proportionately
less than half as many men over 65 are working now as was true in
1900, while over four times as many women aged 45-54 are employed
now than was true at the turn of the century. Not only does the man
retire earlier than in the past, he begins to work later, remaining in
school and economically dependent on his parents. More and more
frequently he marries before he has started to work while his wife
enters the labor market to help support the family. The demands of the
technological revolution will increase, not diminish, the frequency
and social acceptability of this pattern. Nor, despite all the clamor, is

[38]Nimkoff, "Changing Family Relationships of Older People in the United States
During the Last Fifty Years," *op. cit.*

[39]Sigmund Freud, "On Psychotherapy," *Collected Papers,* I (New York: Basic
Books, Inc., 1st American edition, 1959), 258.

[40]Shanas, "The Unmarried Old Person in the United States," *op. cit.*

retirement likely to come later than it now does; quite the contrary, it is likely to come earlier. Organized labor is currently agitating for reduction of the age for Social Security benefits to 60 to meet the problem of decreasing job openings brought on by automation. There are signs on the horizon that the aging American may move into a new status, that of a leisure class who consume but do not produce because their product is not needed in an affluent society. As such, their role may come to be that of representing the ultimate reward of a productive youth and middle age. Social scientists and social workers might put their minds to this once in a while instead of forever casting about for "substitute roles" for the old to make them feel "useful."

The emotionally healthy and economically secure oldster is not likely to be much concerned about role or usefulness. As Cumming and Henry humorously remark regarding the ubiquitous survey question directed to the old—Do you feel useful to others?—"It has not been made clear why old people should be expected to feel this way." Amplifying this they comment:

> It is difficult to say why we assume that everyone desires to continue instrumental activity in a society where the performance of useful services is not inevitably tied up with being adequately cared for. Why is it not suggested instead that old people may want recognition for having been useful, for a history of successful instrumentality?[41]

The concepts of role-seeking and feelings of uselessness may well be a projection of the scientist whose pigeonholing drive is frustrated; *he* feels the old are useless because *he* cannot find a role for them. This does not necessarily mean that the oldster shares his needs or his feelings. Many old are content just to be and have been, if life is relatively pleasurable otherwise. Besides, the really old have a major task of their own, namely, to accustom themselves to the idea of death, which many do with a grace and thoughtfulness the young or middle aged cannot imagine.

How well equipped is social work to help the middle-aged child of aging parents? What does one find in the way of theory and practice? Therapeutics—the helping and healing process—should be goal directed within a forward-impelled conception of the client's or patient's life. This type of conception is sorely lacking for the latter half of life in the Freudian framework. Analogous to the fixation of personal development at the oral, anal, or phallic levels, psychiatry and those professions that take their theoretical cues from psychiatry have become "fixated" at the genital level in their *theoretical* development. Obviously something is wrong or lacking in a theory of personality that encompasses only one score of man's alloted three score years and ten—an allotment which, incidentally, American man has already passed. It is becoming increasingly sterile to view the latter two-thirds of life as mere repetition and reenactment of the first third. Psychiatric

[41]Elaine Cumming and William Henry, *Growing Old: The Process of Disengagement* (New York: Basic Books, Inc., 1961), p. 20.

and social-work theorists must begin conceiving of a stage *beyond genital maturity;* a stage that might be called *filial maturity,* a stage seen as part of the developmental sequence, representing the healthy transition from genital maturity to old age—which has its own sequence of stages already rather admirably conceived by Peck.[42]

Using developmental terminology, the *filial crisis* may be conceived to occur in most individuals in their forties or fifties, when the individual's parents can no longer be looked to as a rock of support in times of emotional trouble or economic stress but may themselves need their offspring's comfort and support. Successful accomplishment of the *filial task,* or performance of the filial role, promotes *filial maturity* which has its own gratification,[43] different from those of genital maturity, and leads into and prepares for successful accomplishment of the developmental tasks of old age—the last of which is to die.

The model of parent-child relationships and of individual development in later life to which one finds most frequent reference in psychiatric and social work literature is *role-reversal,* the child becoming "father to his father,"[44] or the therapist becoming parent figure to the old and senile patient.[45] In the writer's opinion, however, role-reversal is not a normal but a pathological development. Role-reversal may be a valuable concept in understanding the dynamics of the neurotic or immature but chronologically aging parent-child pair; it may serve the psychotherapist well in dealing with the senile or psychotic oldster; but, as a model of normal behavior, as an ideal image by which to measure or toward which to direct client or patient behavior, it is inappropriate and a dead-end. One may legitimately question whether the role-reversal concept is resorted to because it fits the facts, or because it fits the only theory the therapist has, for while it is true that the filial crisis marks childhood's end, the son or daughter does not thereby take on a parental role to his parent. He takes on the *filial* role, which involves being *depended on* and therefore being *dependable* insofar as his parent is concerned.

Healthy resolution of the filial crisis means leaving behind the rebellion and emancipation of adolescence and early adulthood and turning again to the parent, no longer as a child, but as a mature adult

[42]Robert Peck, "Psychological Developments in the Second Half of Life," *Psychological Aspects of Aging,* John E. Anderson, ed. (Washington, D.C.: American Psychological Association, 1956), pp. 42-53.

[43]Helen Perlman, writing in the *Social Service Review,* suggests a "turnabout in our perspectives—some consideration of the possibility that modifications or changes in personality may result from the exercise of ego functions that are inevitably involved in coping with role problems, and from feelings of gratification that may ensue." "Identity Problems, Role and Casework Treatment," XXXVII (September, 1963), 307-318.

[44]See: Arthur L. Rautman, "Role Reversal in Geriatrics," *Mental Hygiene,* XLVI (January, 1962), 116-20, for an excellent presentation of the role-reversal point of view.

[45]See: Allan Rechtschaffen, "Psychotherapy with Geriatric Patients: A Review of the Literature," *Journal of Gerontology,* XIV (January, 1959), 73-84, for a summarized presentation of the various approaches of psychotherapy.

with a new role and a different love, seeing him for the first time as an individual with his own rights, needs, limitations, and a life history that, to a large extent, made him the person he is long before his child existed.[46] This is what the parent wants of his children; this is what society expects; this is what many Americans accomplish, with varying degrees of success, in their late forties and fifties. It is one of the ways in which they prepare themselves for their own old age, through identification with the parent, as in childhood they similarly prepared for adulthood. As a stage in the developmental sequence, it has new and characteristic properties, "which cannot be wholly described in terms of earlier behavior or earlier influences but must be viewed in their own developmental context: the stage that is becoming."[47]

One of the major roles of the therapeutic professions can be that of helping the middle-aged client or patient accomplish this task to the best of his ability, for it will inevitably determine how successfully he meets the challenge of growing old. Social policy should support the middle aged in this task through social institutions designed to relieve excessive economic and social stresses and strains upon both parent and adult child, thereby freeing the child to carry out the affectional and idiosyncratic functions which bureaucracy can never adequately perform.

For the old person who has no children or other kin able to perform these latter functions, social work is the logical profession to step into the breach, but social work must prepare itself better than it has so far; it must insure that genuine alternatives are found to the "nursing home solution"; it must stop giving lip service to its slogan — keep the old in their own home — and make possible, *through rendering to old people in their homes,* the services, the comfort, the affectional concern, and the dependability that is expected of and given by adult children. There will always be some for whom group living in a highly protected setting is the preferred or necessary way of life, but both the old person and the caseworker trying to help must have some genuine *choice* in the matter, something they do not now have. The

---

[46]If the client has not achieved some measure of emancipation from the parent by the time the filial crisis arises, he will have considerable difficulty. It may then be quite appropriate for the professional helper to assist him in completing this task *so that he can proceed* to the filial stage. This is in accordance with Erikson's "epigenetic principle" whereby, "each item of the healthy personality is systematically related to all others, and they all depend on the proper development in the proper sequence of each item. . ." See: Erik H. Erikson, *Identity and the Life Cycle* (New York: International Universities Press, 1959), p. 53.

For illustrations of how helping the middle-aged child complete his emancipation may be used within the total goal of helping both parent and child, see: Marcella Farrar, "Mother-Daughter Conflicts Extended into Later Life," *Social Casework,* XXXVI (May, 1955), 202-207; and Margaret Ryder, "Casework with the Aged Parent and his Adult Children," *The Family,* XXVI (November, 1945), 243-50.

[47]Margaret Blenkner, "Developmental Considerations and the Older Client," *Relations of Development and Aging,* James Birren, ed. (Springfield, Illinois: Charles C Thomas, Publisher, 1964).

professional worker need not be afraid to assume the filial role. It is much more comfortable and gratifying than the one he has been trying to assume or than no role at all. It will help him, too, to move beyond genital maturity and thus integrate into himself the prospect of his own old age.[48]

Almost two out of five adult Americans alive today are in their forties and fifties—the age of the filial crisis. If family agencies and family-life educators would do a job of prevention, if they would forestall some of the problems of old age, this is the group with which to work. But first they must ask themselves, "Do we know how, do we have the theoretical tools and the professional values to give us direction in the preventive task?" The techniques exist, but they are not enough; theory and values will determine whether family workers meet the challenge.

[48]Rautman, "Role Reversal in Geriatrics," *op. cit.*, p. 120.

empirical studies
in the
united states

relationships of adult children with their parents in the united states

MARVIN B. SUSSMAN

A discussion of adult child-parent relationships without appropriate theoretical underpinnings would result in unlimited speculation and conjecture. This is not to say that this paper is completely devoid of speculation and conjecture. Science progresses toward truth by taking halting steps away from fiction.

The social scientist has learned from fellow compatriots in other disciplines that facts and events which appear to be disparate do have a logical and consistent order and meaning; that there are scientific laws which give a pattern and uniformity to facts, observations, and situations; and that the aim of the scientist is to discover these laws. The discovery of uniformities and patterns which give meaning to observations is furthered by the utilization of theory. Consequently, the first part of this paper will discuss a theoretical framework which gives meaning to existing parental relationships with adult children.

theoretical stance

The theoretical position assumed in this paper is that there exists in modern urban industrial societies, particularly in American society, an extended kin family system, highly integrated within a network of social relationships and mutual assistance, that operates along bilateral kin lines and vertically over several generations. The validity of this position is established by the accumulation of empirical evidence on the structure and functioning of urban kin networks based upon research undertaken during the last decade. In two review papers Sussman and Burchinal summarize the theoretical stance and supporting research.[1] In a more recent empirical study of a Cleveland metropolitan area sample, undertaken in 1961 and 1962, the evidence on the viability of an existing kinship structure carrying on extensive activities among kin is so convincing that we find it unnecessary to continue further descriptive work in order to establish the existence of the kin network in modern urban society. The far more important task at the present time is to determine the meaning and significance of kin network activities for the members of the system and to discover how the functions of the kin system affect the workings of other social systems in the society. Some of the data from this research will be presented later in this chapter.[2]

The establishment of the kin network as an existing and on-going social system obviously requires reformulation of current family theory. The new findings about family and kin are inconsistent with existing beliefs concerning the structure and function of the family as a social system. What is the current stance on family structure and function which is so inconsistent with new empirical findings concerned with the operations of the extended kin family system?

The historical thread linking the current popular notion of the independence and isolation of the nuclear family unit stretches back to the first quarter of the twentieth century when treatment of social phenomena in dualities and dichotomies became fashionable. Perhaps by coincidence, the statisticians of this same period were struggling with the four-fold contingency table and the appropriate tests to measure differences in observed and expected proportions. R. A. Fisher gave the world the "exact" test of chi-square.[3] (For sociologists I am uncertain whether this test is a bane or blessing. It may be equivalent to the aspirin which is used in medicine to treat most ill-

---

[1]Marvin B. Sussman and Lee Burchinal, "Kin Family Network: Unheralded Structure in Current Conceptualizations of Family Functioning," *Marriage and Family Living*, XXIV (August, 1962), 231-40; and "Parental Aid to Married Children: Implications for Family Functioning," *Marriage and Family Living*, XXIV (November, 1962), 320-32.

[2]Marvin B. Sussman and Sherwood B. Slater, "Re-Appraisal of Urban Kin Networks: Empirical Evidnce," paper given at American Sociological Association, Los Angeles, August, 1963.

[3]R. A. Fisher, *Statistical Methods for Research Workers* (London: Oliver and Boyd, 1925).

nesses.) Fisher encouraged his colleague, Yates, to produce the correction for continuity, a useful technique for establishing legitimate differences between observed and expected values when studying small samples.[4]

The link between the four-fold contingency table in statistics, which required dichotomization of data, and the "either-or," "yes or no" approach to the categorization of social phenomena may be a case of simultaneous discovery rather than one of interdisciplinary osmosis. Viewers of the social scene were witnessing the growth of large cities and the outcome of the industrial revolution. It was easy to discuss what was happening in terms of Gemeinschaft versus Gesellschaft, rural versus urban, kinship versus nuclear, low versus high social class, and the like. Even today we still converse in this vein: developed versus underdeveloped countries, haves versus have-nots, deviant versus nondeviant, and the like.

The work of the early theorists such as Weber, Durkheim, Simmel, Tönnies, Mannheim, and their later disciples stressed that the family in urban society was required to be an independent nuclear unit and, therefore, prone to be isolated, since social differentiation in urban societies requires of its members behavior appropriate to bureaucratic rather than familial norms. The assumption made by these theorists was that patterns of urban living were completely different from those found in rural society. City life required specialized social systems to take over the many functions once performed by members of the kin group. Moreover, the nuclear family consisting of husband and wife and offspring living independently from their kin was ideally suited to the demands of the economic system, a system which required a high degree of occupational and geographical mobility of its participants. Members of the nuclear family developed a set of mutual role expectations. Major obligations, interactions, and nurturance behavior now occurred primarily within the nuclear family unit. Relationships did exist between the nuclear family and other consanguineous relatives and relations by marriage of the kin group, but these relationships were insignificant for the maintenance of the individual conjugal family. According to the theoretical position outlined above, the new family structure, nuclear and isolated, was a social system adapted to meet the demands of a developing industrial society.

The theorists began to describe the changed functions of this new family system. By the time Ogburn wrote his classic paper on the changes in the functions of the American family,[5] there was common agreement that the basic functions performed by the nuclear family were procreation, status placement, biological and emotional main-

[4]F. Yates, "Contingency Tables Involving Small Numbers and the X^2 Test," *Journal of the Royal Statistical Society, Supplement I*, CCXVII (1934).

[5]William F. Ogburn, "The Family and its Functions," *Recent Social Trends*, Report of the President's Research Committee on Social Trends (New York: McGraw-Hill Book Company, 1934), pp. 661-708.

tenance, and socialization. These were presented in the context of the "isolated" nuclear family with little attention given to the activities of intergenerational and bilateral kin family networks in the areas of biological and emotional maintenance or socialization. Functions concerned with the economic, educational, protective, and consumptive activities of the family were said to have been taken over by the specialized institutions in the society.

The errors of these early theorists were of two types: errors of commission and errors of omission. The error of commission was to accept as *prima facie* evidence the breakdown of social structures and relationships or the development of deviant behavior as a permanent result of the transition from rural to urban society. For the family this view implied a similar breakdown of the kin structure resulting from its inability to cope with conditions on the urban scene. Durkheim's research on suicide suggested weaknesses in the new family structure and stressed the effects of isolation upon individuals.

During the initial period of change from one type of system to another, "social casualties" are likely to be high. The measurement of a casualty is usually couched in a rating of "normlessness," anomie, deviancy, and the like. The trials and tribulations of the immigrant in a new culture and of the migrant moving from one region to another, for example, from the rural South to cities of the North in the United States, have been amply illustrated in the published literature on racial and nationality group relations. "Marginality" is the concept used to describe the condition of individuals who are part of the dominant culture to a significant degree by having absorbed its aspirations but who are denied full participation. The marginal man is one who belongs to several reference groups which have conflicting values and identities.[6] As the Sherifs indicate, the marginal individual lacks a stable anchorage in his primary group and is pulled away by his identification with his reference group.[7] The Appalachian white migrant from West Virginia to such Northern cities as Chicago, Detroit, and Cleveland, soon after his arrival, is caught between the pushes and pulls of community expectations and new reference groups and the requirements for membership in back-home kin and friendship groups. The consequences of being unable to relate effectively to either group may be personal conflict; rebellion against self, group, and society; insecurity; and concomitant frustration.

The growth of marginality and the apparent breakdown of structures and functions during an initial period of transition within a society should not be confused with permanent change. Durkheim, however, did not indicate how the kin family after the initial onslaught upon its structure made the necessary adaptations for sustaining the

---

[6]Everett V. Stonequist, *The Marginal Man* (New York: Charles Scribner's Sons, 1937).

[7]Muzafer Sherif and Carolyn Sherif, *Groups in Harmony and Tension* (New York: Harper & Row, Publishers, 1953), pp. 172-73.

continuity of its component nuclear family units on through time.

It is probably unfair to attribute the beginning of the isolated nuclear family myth solely to Durkheim, or to Weber, Tönnies, Simmel, and Mannheim. Linton,[8] Wirth,[9] and Parsons,[10] writing in more recent times, have each taken the same position that the nuclear family unit consisting of husband, wife, and living offspring, independent from their kin-related families, is the ideal structure for meeting the demands of geographical and occupational mobility, such mobility being prerequisite to successful performance in modern industrial society. Success in the search for beginnings, however, does not disallow the existence of the current belief or effect changes in the current position. Reconceptualization of existing theoretical positions about the family will result only as a consequence of empirical evidence. Such data will be presented shortly. Nevertheless, apparently the error committed by both early social theorists and by later ones was the acceptance of the dichotomy fallacy.

Family sociologists followed the lead of the social theorists. Using the paradigm of the kin family of rural society versus the nuclear family of urban society, these sociologists found it sensible to categorize apparent changes in family functions and to give an explanation for these changes in terms of social conditions found in rural and urban societies. Moreover, the complexity of life in urban society made it exceedingly difficult to detect kinship structure and roles (this is still a difficult task), and few researchers had the skills or interest to establish the empirical bases for the new theoretical stance. Evidence based upon a single or a few cases, those that fitted the isolation mode, was used to substantiate the nuclear family theory. Specialized social systems had come into existence during the transition from a rural to an urban society. As these conditions persisted in the urban environment, *prima facie* evidence indicated that if the family unit was not shorn of its traditional functions, it at least shared the majority of them with these new social systems. The family was viewed as a weak and fragile unit prone to easy disruption and dissolution and almost completely dependent upon the other social systems of the society.

Without question, under the influence of increased urbanization, family structures became more nucleated, and nuclear units were to be found in separate residence apart from parents and consanguineal relatives. The nuclear unit within the kin system became dominant over any previous structural form. The new prominence of the nuclear

[8]Ralph Linton, "The Natural History of the Family," *The Family: Its Function and Destiny,* 2nd ed., Ruth N. Anshen, ed. (New York: Harper & Row, Publishers, 1959), pp. 45-46.

[9]Louis Wirth, "Urbanism as a Way of Life," *American Journal of Sociology,* XLIV (1938), 1-24.

[10]Talcott Parsons, "The Kinship System of the Contemporary United States," *American Anthropologist,* XLV (January, 1943), 22-38; "The Social Structure of the Family," in Anshen, *op. cit.,* pp. 263 ff.

unit as a family subsystem, however, did not mean that this unit abandoned the kin structure. Just as the error of commission was to accept the breakdown of social structures as a permanent result of the transition from a rural to an urban society, so the error of omission was to disregard social change. The social theorists ignored or were oblivious to the kinship studies being undertaken by their colleagues in anthropology.

One of Murdock's basic conclusions from his cross-cultural study of the social structures of approximately 250 societies was that kinship structures do not break down, dissolve, or even change radically as the result of culture contact with either more technologically advanced or equal societies.[11] Rather, such structures evolve and adjust over time, taking on activities and functions which for the most part are supportive of and adaptive to the changed conditions and emerging social systems. More recent work by anthropologists on the impact of Western society upon native political systems indicates that tribal systems do not change into bureaucratic ones. Instead, these native systems evolve and adapt and adjust to meet the changed conditions in and outside of the society. They sustain those elements of the structure which appear to be adaptable and functional under these changed conditions. Bennett and Despres have reviewed the role of kinship structure in the industrialization of a number of non-Western industrialized societies.[12] Unlike the common prescription which calls for activities according to bureaucratic norms, these economic systems function according to kin norms or adaptations of such kin norms.

Recent reports by historians question the assumed association of the emergence of the nuclear family unit with the beginning of industrialization and urbanization. These studies disclaim any basis for causality in the relationship between these two variables. Greenfield studied the process of industrialization in Western societies and concluded that the small nuclear family was not necessary or concomitant to this process.[13] Braun concluded from his study of Swiss towns during the early period of industrialization that rural families living in the fringe of the industrial area maintained stable kin ties and strengthened these ties further by earning supplementary income in nearby factories.[14] Row housing was eventually constructed close to factories and arranged to accommodate kin-related nuclear units.

Anthropological and historical studies supply only a portion of the argument against accepting the notion that the nuclear family

[11]George P. Murdock, *Social Structure* (New York: The Macmillan Company, 1960).

[12]John Bennett and Leo Despres, "Kinship and Instrumental Activities: A Theoretical Inquiry," *American Anthropologist*, LXII (April, 1960), 254-67; and Leo Despres, "A Function of Bilateral Kinship Patterns in a New England Industry," *Human Organization*, XVII (Summer, 1958), 15-22.

[13]Sidney M. Greenfield, "Industrialization and the Family in Sociological Theory," *American Journal of Sociology*, LXVII (November, 1961), 312-22.

[14]Rudolf Braun, *Industrialisierung und Volkslaben* (Erlenbach-Zürich: Rentsch, 1960).

emerged simultaneously with or as a consequence of the industrial revolution and that this family unit became a replacement for the kin family network. The more coercive empirical evidence for rejecting the fallacious dichotomy and for establishing the co-existence and blending of these two units into a coherent system of action in modern society emerges from field studies in England and in the United States on the family and the kinship network.

empirical evidence of kin network

Since 1950 there has been a plethora of studies undertaken in a variety of disciplines which support the notion that a viable kin network structure exists and that it has numerous functions supportive of the goals of other social systems. The major activities of the network are mutual aid (material and non-material) and social activities.

Sussman and Burchinal summarize these findings:[15]

1. Help patterns take many forms, including the exchange of services, gifts, advice and financial assistance. Financial aid patterns may be direct as in the case of the young married couples Burchinal interviewed; or indirect and subtle, such as the wide range of help patterns observed by Sussman,[16] Sharp and Axelrod.[17]

2. Such help patterns are probably more widespread in the middle and working class families and are more integral a feature of family relationships than has been appreciated by students of family behavior. Very few families included in available studies reported neither giving nor receiving aid from relatives . . .

3. The exchange of aid among families flows in several directions, from parents to children and vice versa, among siblings, and less frequently, from more distant relatives. However, financial assistance generally appears to flow from parents to children.

4. While there may be a difference in the absolute amount of financial aid received by families of middle and working class status, there are insignificant differences in the proportion of families in these two strata who report receiving, giving or exchanging economic assistance in some form.

[15]Marvin B. Sussman and Lee Burchinal, "Kin Family Network: Unheralded Structure in Current Conceptualizations of Family Functioning," *op. cit.*

[16]Marvin B. Sussman, "The Help Pattern in the Middle Class Family," *American Sociological Review*, XVIII (February, 1953), 22-28. For related analyses by the same author see, "Parental Participation in Mate Selection and Its Effect upon Family Continuity," *Social Forces*, XXXII (October, 1953), 76-81; "Family Continuity: Selective Factors Which Affect Relationships Between Families at Generational Levels," *Marriage and Family Living*, XVI (May, 1954), 112-20; "Activity Patterns of Post-Parental Couples and Their Relationship to Family Continuity," *Marriage and Family Living*, XXVII (November, 1955), 338-41; "The Isolated Nuclear Family: Fact or Fiction," *Social Problems*, VI (Spring, 1959), 333-40; and "Intergenerational Family Relationships and Social Role Changes in Middle Age," *Journal of Gerontology*, XV (1960), 71-75.

[17]Harry Sharp and Morris Axelrod, "Mutual Aid Among Relatives in an Urban Population," *Principles of Sociology*, Ronald Freedman and associates, eds. (New York: Holt, Rinehart & Winston, Inc., 1956), pp. 433-39.

5. Financial aid is received most commonly during the early years of married life. Parents are probably more likely to support financially "approved" than "disapproved" ones, such as elopements, interfaith and interracial marriages. Support can be disguised in the form of substantial sums of money or valuable gifts at Christmas, anniversaries or birthdays. High rates of parental support are probably associated with marriages of children while they are still in a dependency status; those among high school or college students are examples.

Social activities are principal functions of the kin family visitation, participation together in recreational activities, and ceremonial behavior significant to family unity. Major research findings are:

1. Disintegration of the extended family in urban areas because of lack of contact is unsupported and often the contrary situation is found. The difficulty in developing satisfactory primary relationships outside of the family in urban areas makes the extended family more important to the individual.[18]

2. Extended family get-togethers and joint recreational activities with kin dominate the leisure time pursuits of urban working-class members.[19]

3. Kinship visiting is a primary activity of urban dwelling and outranks visitation patterns found for friends, neighbors, or co-workers.[20]

4. Among urban middle classes there is an almost universal desire to have interaction with extended kin, but distance among independent nuclear related units is a limiting factor.[21]

5. The family network extends between generational ties of conjugal units. Some structures are identified as sibling bonds,[22] "occasional kin groups,"[23] family circles and cousin clubs.[24] These structures perform

[18]William H. Key, "Rural-Urban Differences and the Family," *Sociological Quarterly*, II (January, 1961), 49-56.

[19]F. Dotson, "Patterns of Voluntary Association Among Urban Working-Class Families," *American Sociological Review*, XVI (October, 1951), 687-93.

[20]Morris Axelrod, "Urban Structure and Social Participation," *American Sociological Review*, XXI (February, 1956), 13-18; Scott Greer, "Urbanism Reconsidered: A Comparative Study of Local Areas in a Metropolis," *American Sociological Review*, XXI (February, 1956), 19-25; Wendell Bell and M. D. Boat, "Urban Neighborhoods and Informal Social Relations," *American Journal of Sociology*, LXII (January, 1957), 391-98; Marvin B. Sussman and R. Clyde White, *Hough: A Study of Social Life and Change* (Cleveland: Western Reserve University Press, 1959); and Paul J. Reiss, "The Extended Kinship System of the Urban Middle Class," Ph.D. dissertation, Harvard University, 1959.

[21]E. Franklin Frazier, "The Impact of Urban Civilization upon Negro Family Life," *Cities and Society*, rev. ed., P. K. Hatt and A. S. Reiss, Jr., eds. (New York: Free Press of Glencoe, Inc., 1957), pp. 495-96.

[22]Elaine Cumming and David M. Schneider, "Sibling Solidarity: A Property of American Kinship," *American Anthropologist*, LXIII (June, 1961), 498-507.

[23]Millicent Ayoub, "American Child and His Relatives: Kindred in Southwest Ohio," project supported by the United States Public Health Service, 1961. Dr. Ayoub is continuing her studies under the subtitle, "The Nature of the Sibling Bond." She examines the solidarity or lack of it between siblings in four focal subsystems and at different stages of the life cycle. In her most recent work, "Family Revisions," she examines the implications of nonunilinear descent in American society.

[24]William E. Mitchell, "Descent Groups Among New York City Jews," *The Jewish Journal of Sociology*, III (1961), 121-128; "Lineality and Laterability in Urban

important recreational, ceremonial, mutual aid, and often economic functions.

Services performed regularly throughout the year or on occasions are additional functions of the family network. The findings from empirical studies are:

1. Shopping, escorting, care of children, advice-giving and counselling, cooperating with social agencies on counselling and welfare problems of family members, are types of day-to-day activities performed by members of the kin network.[25]

2. Services to old persons such as physical care, providing shelter, escorting, shopping, performing household tasks, sharing of leisure time, etc. are expected and practiced roles of children and other kin members. These acts of filial and kin responsibility are performed voluntarily without law or compulsion.[26]

3. Families or individual members on the move are serviced by units of the family network. Services range from supplying motel-type accommodations for vacationing kin passing through town, to scouting for homes and jobs for kin, and in providing supportive functions during the period of in-migration and transition from rural to the urban pattern of living.[27]

Jewish Ambilineages," read at the 60th Annual Meeting of the American Anthropological Association in Philadelphia, Pennsylvania, November 16, 1961; and William E. Mitchell and Hope J. Leichter, "Urban Ambilineages and Social Mobility," unpublished paper based on research from the project, "Studies in Family Interaction," sponsored jointly by the Jewish Family Service of New York City and the Russell Sage Foundation.

[25]Sussman, "The Help Pattern in the Middle Class Family," *op. cit.*, and Hope J. Leichter, "Kinship Values and Casework Intervention," *Casework Papers* (New York: Family Service Association of America, 1961). "Life Cycle Changes and Temporal Sequence in a Bilateral Kinship System," read at the American Sociological Association, Washington, D.C., 1958; "Normative Intervention in an Urban Bilateral Kinship System," paper read at the American Anthropological Association, 1959.

[26]John Kosa, Leo D. Rachiele, and Cyril O. Schommer, S.J., "Sharing the Home with Relatives," *Marriage and Family Living*, XXII (May, 1960), 129-31; Alvin L. Schorr, *Filial Responsibility in the Modern American Family*, Social Security Administration, U.S. Department of Health, Education, and Welfare (Washington, D.C.: Government Printing Office, 1960), pp. 11-18; Peter Townsend, *The Family Life of Old People: An Enquiry in East London* (London: Routledge & Kegan Paul, Ltd., 1957); Michael Young and Peter Willmott, *Family and Kinship in East London* (New York: Free Press of Glencoe, Inc., 1957); and Elizabeth J. Bott, *Family and Social Network* (London: Tavistock Publications, Ltd., 1957).

See Gordon F. Streib and Wayne E. Thompson, eds., *Adjustment in Retirement, Journal of Social Issues*, XIV, No. 3 (1958), whole number. Streib and Thompson have done the most creative thinking and analysis of data on these points. Streib's paper, "Family Patterns in Retirement," pp. 46-60 in this issue, is most pertinent. Ethel Shanas, "Older People and Their Families," paper given at the American Sociological Association, September, 1961. A more complete report is in *Family Relationships of Older People*, Health Information Foundation Research Series, 20 (New York: Health Information Foundation, 1961).

The best treatment of uses of leisure during the later years of life is found in Robert W. Kleemeier, ed., *Aging and Leisure* (New York: Oxford University Press, Inc., 1961). See particularly the chapters by Wilensky, Streib, and Thompson.

[27]Sussman and White, *Hough: A Study of Social Life and Change, op. cit;* C. Wright Mills, Clarence Senior, and Rose K. Goldsen, *The Puerto Rican Journey* (New York: Harper & Row, Publishers, 1950), pp. 51-55; James S. Brown, Harry K.

4. Services on occasions would include those performed at weddings or during periods of crisis, death, accident, disaster, and personal trouble of family members. A sense of moral obligation to give service or acknowledgement of one's kin appropriate to the occasion is found among kin members. The turning to kin when in trouble before using other agencies established for such purposes is the mode rather than the exception.[28]

5. General supportive behavior from members of the kin family network facilitates achievement and maintenance of family and community status.[29] Supportive behavior of kin appears to be instrumental in affecting fertility rates among component family members.[30]

A convergence of many of these findings occurs in the work of Eugene Litwak. In an extensive study of a middle-class population, Litwak tests two hypotheses on the functional properties of the isolated nuclear family for an industrial society: (a) occupational mobility is antithetical to extended family relations; (b) extended family relations are impossible as a result of geographical mobility. His findings, summarized briefly, are: 1) The extended kin family as a structure exists in modern urban society, at least among middle-class families; 2) extended family relations are possible in urban industrial society; 3) geographical propinquity is an unnecessary condition for these relationships; 4) occupational mobility is unhindered by the activities of the extended family — such activities as advice, financial assistance, temporary housing, and the like provide aid during such movement; and 5) the classical extended family of rural society or its

---

Schwarzweller, and Joseph J. Mangalam, "Kentucky Mountain Migration and the Stem Family: An American Variation on a Theme by LePlay," paper given at the American Sociological Association, September, 1961; Peter H. Rossi, *Why Families Move* (New York: Free Press of Glencoe, Inc., 1955), pp. 37-38; and Earl L. Koos, *Families in Trouble* (New York: King's Crown Press, 1946).

[28]Sussman, "Family Continuity: Selective Factors which Affect Relationships Between Families at Generational Levels," *op. cit.;* Seymour S. Bellin, *Family Kinship in Later Years* (New York: State Dept. of Mental Hygiene, Mental Health Research Unit Publication, 1960); Sharp and Axelrod, "Mutual Aid Among Relatives," *op. cit.;* and Enrico L. Quarantelli, "A Note on the Protective Function of the Family in Disasters," *Marriage and Family Living*, XXII (August, 1960), 263-64.

[29]Bernard Barber, "Family Status, Local-Community Status, and Social Stratification: Three Types of Social Ranking," *Pacific Sociological Review*, IV, No. 1 (Spring, 1961), 3-10. In this paper Barber challenges the current conceptualization of social class for designating an individual's position and power within a community. He differentiates social class position, family status, and local-community statuses into three types of social ranking. Each one has its own structure and functions; each allocates position, power, and prestige; and each has its own range of variation. The family kin network and support received from it determine family status.

[30]David Goldberg, "Some Recent Developments in Fertility Research," *Demographic and Economic Change in Developed Countries*, Reprint No. 7 (Princeton, N.J.: Princeton University Press, 1960). Recent fertility research has focused upon the relationship of family organization to differential fertility since variations in family planning and family size cannot be explained by differences in socio-economic status. One variable of family organization is the family kin network. Goldberg observes, "... and incidentally one which may ultimately prove fruitful in cross-cultural studies, is a consideration of the relative benevolence of the environment in defraying the economic and social costs of having children. Here it is hypothesized that the greater the amount of help available from one's community or kinship system the weaker the desire to prevent or postpone pregnancy." *Ibid.*, p. 9.

ethnic counterpart are unsuited for modern society, the isolated nuclear family is not the most functional type, the most functional being a modified extended kin family.[31]

Very few of the studies described above were undertaken specifically to investigate the validity of the position that there exists in modern urban society a functioning kin network. Samples used for the most part are inadequate in size and are not representative of a cross-section of a community's population.

In 1961 in Cleveland the validity of the kinship structure and function hypothesis was tested.[32] A stratified random sample of five hundred households was drawn, and an adult member of each household was interviewed. The stratification of the sample was based upon 221 census tracts located in the eastern section of the Cleveland metropolitan area. The five sample tracts were classified into five social classes: Negro working, Negro lower-middle, white lower, white middle, and white upper-middle.

The major hypothesis of the study was that there exists for urban nuclear family units an identifiable isolation-integration kin network continuum. Nuclear family units function along this continuum with most units found at the integration pole of the continuum. The specific hypothesis tested was that the nuclear family is not isolated from kin either functionally or through lack of propinquity.

For this project, *propinquity* was defined as the geographical distribution of the kin-related units. At the isolation pole of the propinquity continuum are located nuclear families without any reported kinsmen in the metropolitan area. At the integration pole are the units reporting all their known kin living in the metropolitan area. There are intermediate degrees of integration by propinquity between the antipodes of the continuum.

Function was measured by degree of communication and mutual aid between kin-related nuclear units. Frequency and extent of communication as measured by visits, telephone calls, and letter; and amount of mutual aid as assessed by type of financial help and services given and received are the two measures of the functional continuum. At one end of the functional continuum, the nuclear family neither communicates nor exchanges aid. At the other end, the functionally integrated unit has a pattern of extended communication and aid with kinsmen.

Two major conclusions from the Cleveland study are: (1) Nuclear family units function along an isolation-integration continuum. Almost 85 per cent are integrated in terms of propinquity, and no more than

[31]Eugene Litwak, "The Use of Extended Family Groups in the Achievement of Social Goals: Some Policy Implications," *Social Problems,* VII (Winter 1959-60), 177-87; "Occupational Mobility and Extended Family Cohesion," *American Sociological Review,* XXV (February, 1960), 9-21; "Geographical Mobility and Family Cohesion," *American Sociological Review,* XXVI (April, 1961), 258-71.
[32]Sussman and Slater, "Reappraisal of Urban Kin Networks: Empirical Evidence," *op. cit.*

25 per cent indicate isolation on any functional variable. (2) The majority of nuclear family units in this sample are members of an integrated kin network, both by propinquity and functionally, which cuts across lines of class, race, occupation, and education. The kin network is a pervasive social system blending with the *Gesellschaft* characteristics of modern urban society.

These conclusions from the Cleveland study establish the boundaries of a functioning kin network in a metropolitan area. The data, however, cannot be used to answer the historical question of whether the classical extended family found in rural society was replaced by a nuclear one, or whether the former evolved into the modified kin system described earlier in the chapter. The existence of the kin network in current urban society does support the contention that the early family theorists were in error. They confined their theorizing and research largely to the phenomena of immigrant movements to the United States and to in-migrant groups coming into the city to work, both events occurring during the period of urbanization in Western society associated with marked industrial expansion. The picture which emerged from their studies was one of anomie in family life, a consequence of the family's failure to make appropriate adjustments required of new migrants. The family life of the newcomer was disruptive, unstable, and anomic as described, but this condition was short lived. It existed only until the kin network could evolve a structure and effect functions compatible with the changed environmental conditions.

Unfortunately, the workplace of the factory was easy to describe as being cold and indifferent and thus as giving the individual a sense of aloneness and isolation. The belief was held that adjustment to the situation could be made much faster if the individual was unencumbered by kin ties and placed his greatest dependence upon small family units. A contrary position equally coherent and logical is that isolation, the coldness of the workplace, and the city as a steel and concrete bastion produced an even greater dependence of the individual upon kin. Sufficient empirical evidence exists to show that new in-migrants becoming established in the urban workplace use their kin as informants, job finders, innkeepers, and temporary providers.[33] It is within this context of extended kin family theory that the relationships of adult children and their parents are treated here.

the structural units of the extended nuclear kin family system

The basic unit of the kin system is the nuclear unit (subsystem) found usually in an independent household apart from kin. The kin system is composed of an x number of subsystems, and the possibili-

---

[33]William H. Key, "Rural-Urban Differences and the Family," *op. cit.;* and Sussman, "The Isolated Nuclear Family: Fact or Fiction," *op. cit.,* p. 340.

ties of various combinations in a multilineal descent system are unlimited. For this discussion we will limit the analysis of structure to four basic subsystem types. Murdock has delineated three basic types of units: the nuclear family of procreation, the nuclear family of orientation, and the affinal family.[34] Hill has suggested a fourth type, the family of gerontation.[35]

The nuclear family of procreation is one created by marriage and is composed of husband and wife and their offspring. The family of orientation is the one in which the individual is reared. It is composed of the individual's parents and siblings. Each spouse of the family of procreation belongs to a family of orientation. The gerontation nuclear family consists of these generationally linked nuclear units of parents, children, and grandparents. The affinal family consists of parents and siblings of the individual's spouse. An individual during his lifetime may be a member of all four of these subsystems. Upon marriage the individual creates the nuclear family of procreation. If his parents are living, he is a member of the family of orientation. He marries into the affinal family, and he is linked to the gerontation family as a grandson in kin obligations with his living grandparents.

The boundaries and links of these primary nuclear units are illustrated in Figure 4-1. The four nuclear units are independent of each

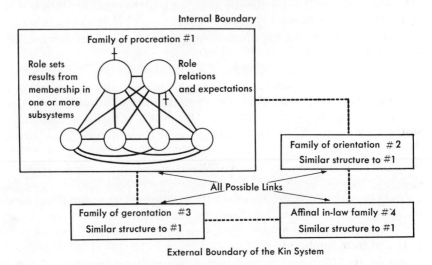

fig. 4-1   kin system of linked nuclear subsystems

other. They are linked to one another on the basis of affection, choice, and a widespread belief that relationships between these subsystems should occur in friendliness and without undue hardship or destruction of the independence and unity of each system.

[34]Murdock, *Social Structure, op. cit.*
[35]Reuben Hill has suggested this family form and uses it in work on decision making among generational families.

The boundary of each nuclear unit encompasses the internal affairs of the subsystem. These include role relationships and the associate processes concerned with the maintenance of the system. The internuclear unit linked boundary may envelop two or more nuclear subunits. Role relationships and expectations and joint activities within this boundary are governed by norms relative to the situation. All four nuclear units may form a kin system boundary within which the roles played vary according to situations, objectives, maintenance of the larger structure, and internal and external stresses produced by subsystems other than the family.

The family of gerontation subsystem is the appropriate one for the analysis of parents' relationships with adult children. It encompasses three generations and enables study of various relationships at different stages of the family life cycle.

the economic and social matrix of intergenerational family relationships

Since 1950 serious research has been undertaken on intergenerational family relationships. The foci of these studies have been upon mutual aid exchanged among families on different generational levels and upon existing social relationships among generational families. Work has begun on the meaning and significance of such continuous intergenerational relationships.

One series of studies focussed on the effects of early marriage upon the parents' willingness to subsidize these marriages. Most of these studies were with white, upper-middle class, Protestant and convenient college populations, and consequently most of the findings of these studies are limited in their general applicability for other populations in this society. The major conclusions of these studies are that while parents may threaten to withdraw support if their child marries "early," this rarely occurs. Surprisingly, college students have not completely accepted the subsidy norm and on the whole refuse lavish parental aid, but, on the other hand, they indicate a willingness to receive some subsidy during this early period of marriage.[36]

Another series of studies focussed on parental aid to young married children. Such aid was reported in an overwhelming majority of cases. During the early years of the marriage, the flow of financial aid was from the parent to the married child's family in a pattern of moderate help. Such aid took the form of financial assistance, loans or gifts of money for large expenditures, such as the purchase of a home, and some less direct assistance, as in gifts of furniture, household equip-

[36]J. L. Herman, "Should Parents Finance Youthful Marriages?" *Cosmopolitan,* CXLIX (1955), 82-85; Victor A. Christopherson, Joseph S. Vandiver, and Marie N. Kreuger, "The Married College Student," *Marriage and Family Living,* XXII (May, 1960), 122-28; and Lee G. Burchinal, "Comparisons of Factors Related to Adjustment in Pregnancy-Provoked and Non-Pregnancy Provoked Marriages," *Midwest Sociologist,* XXI (July, 1959), 92-96.

ment, and monies for such luxuries as inexpensive vacations and help around the home. Few of the respondents report giving continuous financial aid to children except in those instances where a trust fund had been established for a child, or an annuity became due, items which had usually been arranged many years prior to the marriage of the child. After an initial financial gift at marriage, financial gifts to children became limited to emergency help and to gifts at occasions for celebration such as birthdays and anniversaries of children and grandchildren. One major form of financial assistance was a "sizeable loan" to children at low or no interest.[37] Unfortunately, none of these studies of parental aid provides specific information on the amount of financial aid given to children.

Several recent investigations, however, are attempting to establish a cash nexus for such aid.[38] This step is required in order to establish the significance and implications of such aid for a variety of factors related to the functioning of generationally linked family systems. For example, there is no study reporting on the relationship to its total income of the amount of financial aid received by a particular family unit during a given period of time. Does the ratio of income earned to income received from family vary over time?

The problem of establishing the exact amount of financial aid given or received by a family or of stipulating a cash value for nonmaterial aid is difficult on several counts. Current folkways "limit" the asking of questions about financial aid. Respondents have difficulty in recalling the amount of financial aid received or given and the occasion for these contributions during a given period of time. Further, additional difficulties arise in placing a cash value on items which range from family heirlooms of sentimental value to those earmarked for the workshops of the Salvation Army or Goodwill Industries. At the present time, the lack of a quantifiable cash factor makes it difficult to analyze the economic condition of generationally linked families and the social significance of this economic linkage.[39]

The most conclusive finding in the mutual aid studies is that parents who are in their middle years at the time their children are beginning families of their own are at the giving end of the aid continuum. In one reported study, the flow of both financial aid and service activities is from parents to young respondents.

Data from this study are summarized in Table 4-1. As this table indicates, the respondent's family exchanged some form of help with

---

[37]Sussman, "The Help Pattern in the Middle Class Family," *op. cit.*, pp. 22-28.

[38]A. B. Clark and J. Warren, "Economic Contributions Made to Newly Married Couples by their Parents," *Memoir,* publication of New York State College of Home Economics, CCCLXXXII (1963), 3-23; and Sussman and Slater, "Reappraisal of Urban Kin Networks: Empirical Evidence," *op. cit.*

[39]Reuben Hill and his associates at the University of Minnesota are obtaining some information on economic exchanges. See Chapter VI, "Decision Making and the Family Life Cycle," below.

related kin in 93.3 per cent of all cases.[40] Two items of special interest are the giving and receiving of financial aid between respondents and their parental families. The young respondents gave assistance to their parents in 14.6 per cent of the cases, while 46.8 per cent of the respondents received financial aid from their parents.

table 4-1 direction of service network of respondent's family and related kin by major forms of help*

	direction of service network				
major forms of help and service	between respondent's family and related kin	from respondents to parents	from respondents to siblings	from parents to respondents	from siblings to respondents
	per cent	per cent	per cent	per cent	per cent
Any form of help	93.3	56.3	47.6	79.6	44.8
Help during illness	76.0	47.0	42.0	46.4	39.0
Financial aid	53.0	14.6	10.3	46.8	6.4
Care of children	46.8	4.0	29.5	20.5	10.8
Advice (personal and business)	31.0	2.0	3.0	26.5	4.5
Valuable gifts	22.0	3.4	2.3	17.6	3.4

*Totals do not add up to 100 per cent because many families received more than one form of help or service.
Source: Marvin B. Sussman, "The Isolated Nuclear Family: Fact or Fiction," *Social Problems,* VI (Spring, 1959), 338.

In a larger sample study of Detroit families, 70 per cent of the 730 wives interviewed indicated that their families both received some kind of help from relatives outside of their immediate household and gave help to such relatives, financial aid being twice as likely to come from parents as from siblings. In the Detroit data an inverse relationship was found between the age of the wife and receiving of financial aid. A larger percentage of wives in the younger age group compared to those in later periods of the family life cycle reported receiving financial assistance. Fifty-three per cent of the wives who were 29 years of age or younger, 36 per cent of the wives in the 30 to 34 year range, 18 per cent of the 45 to 49 range, and 20 per cent of the wives who were 60 or older reported receiving financial assistance. Most of the aid received by wives in the younger age groups came from parents.[41]

The pattern of aid from the parental family to the married child family is substantiated in two additional studies. In one study undertaken in Cleveland, a group of middle- and working-class family systems were matched by the number of nuclear-related families (parent and child) in their kin systems. A typical matched pair might be a middle-class and a working-class family, each composed of a middle-

[40]Sussman, "The Isolated Nuclear Family: Fact or Fiction," *op. cit.,* p. 338.
[41]Sharp and Axelrod, "Mutual Aid Among Relatives in an Urban Population," *op. cit.,* pp. 433-39.

aged parental-family couple who had three married children, each of whom was living in a separate household. The significance of difference between the social classes was determined by differences between these matched pairs and not by differences between the groups in the sample. The major findings of this study were that more middle-class than working-class parental and child families give and receive financial aid; there is no significant difference between classes in giving or receiving help during an illness of a family member; and, irrespective of class, the flow of financial aid, whatever the amount may be, is from parents to children.[42]

In a second larger study the findings are similar. The extent of financial aid differs by class and reflects the differences in life styles of the classes more than differences in willingness to participate in a mutual aid network. The flow of aid, while it may only trickle in the lower classes, is still in the direction of aid from parents to their married children during the young families' "launching period."[43]

The pattern and direction of financial aid calls into question the current belief that couples adhere to the norm of financial autonomy immediately after marriage. Among generationally linked nuclear families, the aid pattern is so persistent in its direction that the notion of the financial autonomy norm must be considered more of an ideal construct than an actual condition found extensively in society.

It is difficult to stipulate if the belief in the financial autonomy norm, so long held to be a cultural pattern in American society, is a by-product of the dichotomy fallacy described earlier. The belief in financial autonomy of young families probably is a cherished assumption in keeping with bureaucratic ideology and this is difficult to abandon in the face of mounting evidence. Calhoun reports that young married couples in colonial times were provided with some assistance to set up housekeeping.[44] Kin members, particularly parents, helped the young couple during the early rough days of marriage. Farming today is still largely an hereditary occupation, and the pattern of financial assistance of parent to child is verified repeatedly in studies of farm families.[45]

The method of giving financial aid has been simplified today because wealth is no longer invested solely in land but in certificates, titles, and coupons representing the wealth of industry, commerce, and business. The material increase in wealth and equity of families generally in American society during the past twenty years has

[42]Sussman, "Intergenerational Family Relationships and Social Role Changes in Middle Age," *op. cit.*, pp. 71-75.

[43]Sussman and Slater, "Reappraisal of Urban Kin Networks: Empirical Evidence," *op. cit.*

[44]Arthur W. Calhoun, *A Social History of the American Family*, Vol. II, reprinted paperback edition (New York: Barnes and Noble, 1960), 131-48.

[45]Roger W. Strohbehn and John F. Timmons, "Changing Paths to Farm Ownership," *Iowa Farm Science*, XIV (1960), 465-66.

provided middle-aged parents with the means for increased giving.

The current pattern of supporting young married children evolved out of a long history of such support and, during the last century, an increase in the length of time during which parents have assumed financial responsibility for their children. The current clarion call for young people to stay in high school and, if at all possible, to go to college (an effort to keep young people out of the labor market and to give them proper training) is an indicator of extended parental financial support for children. The educational hotbeds of the burgeoning suburbs and the growth of junior colleges during the last half-decade both attest to the increased financial responsibility being assumed by parents on all class levels. Today approximately 25 per cent of college undergraduates in the United States are married. While the employment of wives accounts for a good portion of the support of the young married man, it is obvious that he will accept money earned by persons other than himself without sustaining either permanent injury to his self-concept or to his feelings of obligation or commitment to the provider role. Whether the married male college student is more willing to accept the wages of his wife or a financial gift from his parents and how these relationships of receiving affect a number of dependent variables related to intra- and interfamily relationships are questions for research. Conditions today are such that parents expect to support their children for a long period of time until the children are properly launched into careers. Further, these parental expectations are largely shared by married children even though these expectations may not be overtly expressed.

Findings from attitude studies present a contrary view of the mutual aid pattern described above and support the position that the nuclear unit lives in a residence separate from other units and is financially independent and autonomous. Young couples, when asked about accepting aid from parental families, almost universally reject this as an acceptable source of income. Fifty-six per cent of the couples in one study disapproved of financial help from any source, although 90 per cent were actually receiving support from the federal government through the so-called G.I. Bill, which provided subsidies for veterans' educational costs.[46] It appears that the ideological stance of the young couple is to maintain an image of autonomy, and, perhaps, in a meaningful way, to avoid such aid if at all possible, but nevertheless not to reject such aid when it appears to assist in the achievement of economic stability and a level of living in consonance with the young couple's aspirations.

Middle-aged parents are equally adamant in stating their expectation that they will never receive support from their children. Many parents state, "We pray that we don't have to ask them for help." In all

[46]William F. Kenkel, "A Sociological Study of Married Student Veterans at the University of Maryland," Master's thesis, University of Maryland, 1950, pp. 56-75.

likelihood this is an overreaction, because one suspects that the pattern of actual giving to children is one subtle way of buying kinship insurance during the period of old age and senescence.

The evidence on financial aid from children to parents is confusing. In a study undertaken by Dinkel 20 years ago, largely with college samples, the conclusion was that young adult respondents were reluctant to support aged parents when there were other institutional sources of aid available.[47] Actual practices in supporting aged parents who are in economic straits vary considerably. Alvin Schorr points out that money contributions for parents is the only gift that can actually be compelled by law from children but that money aid is a relatively unimportant pattern.[48] From his review of research in the area, Schorr reports that assistance and services, something which cannot be compelled by law, are the dominant aid pattern. The recent finding by Shanas that married children are willing to assume responsibility for aged parents including financial aid, providing a home for them, and locating close to the residences of aged parents or vice-versa suggest a change in attitudes from the period of the 1940's (explored by Dinkel).[49] It is apparent that while the norm of post-marital financial independence persists for most individuals embarking upon marriage, it is being modified by social changes which are conducive to mutual aid patterns among generationally linked nuclear families. Such mutual aid contributes to the maintenance of the young family's standard of living and increasingly to the maintenance of aged parents during the latter's retirement.

In American society with each passing year the prospects for survival and living into old age increase. A three-generational family system of living grandparents, parents, and children is today very common. There is also a growing number of four-generation family systems.

Broad economic changes during the twentieth century present special financial problems to the parental generation, especially during their middle years, 40-55. Kreps in Chapter XII below indicates that with each passing year an increasing number of aged and young adults are being supported without contributing to the national productive output.[50] Automated processes in industry, government and private retirement programs, extended education for youth, and shortened working life along with other social phenomena have

[47]Robert M. Dinkel, "Parental-Child Conflict in Minnesota Families," *American Sociological Review*, VIII (August, 1943), pp. 412-19; and "Attitudes of Children Toward Supporting Aged Parents," *American Sociological Review*, IX (August, 1944), 370-79.

[48]Schorr, *Filial Responsibility in the Modern American Family, op. cit.*

[49]Shanas, *Family Relationships of Older People, op. cit.*; "Family Responsibility and the Health of Older People," *Journal of Gerontology*, XV (October, 1960), 408-11; and "Living Arrangements of Older People in the United States," *The Gerontologist*, I (March, 1961), 27-29.

[50]Juanita M. Kreps, "The Economics of Intergenerational Relationships," Chapter XII.

produced the conditions which now require the workforce (the mid-dle-aged generation for the most part) to support the other two genera-tions via taxes. Social Security payments and bond issues for expand-ing school facilities and operations are two types of taxes paid by the member of the middle-generational family regardless of whether he has children or retired parents. Kreps suggests further that the pattern of support in the United States is not within families but between generations. Moreover, the problem is less a matter of production than one of distribution and, therefore, a concern of policy and values rather than the usual readjustments of the economy.

In addition to the widespread growth of income maintenance programs for the nonworking adults financed through a governmental system of intergenerational transfer of funds by the middle genera-tional groups to the younger and older generations, there is still an interfamily exchange of support. In this interfamily exchange the mid-dle generation may have the burden of supporting and caring for aged parents as well as for their own young married and unmarried chil-dren. Adequate economic support for the aged during the 1960's is a particularly acute and basic problem for the middle generation. Many aged parents may not be insured under Old Age, Survivors, and Dis-ability Insurance (OASDI), or are not able to survive on OASDI income without other assistance. Many older people were unable to develop income-producing retirement programs during their working life. The prospects for the flow of aid in the 1960's are from the middle genera-tion to both the older and younger ones.

social relationships between parents and their adult children: asymmetry

In the discussion on mutual aid between kin family members, especially those between parents and their married children, no atten-tion was given to the symmetry of the aid pattern. It would be incor-rect to assume that aid from parents to children flows in a symmetrical pattern whereby sons and daughters each receive an equal amount of assistance. Data on amounts of aid given according to the sex, age, or ordinal position of the child are unavailable in reported studies. One study indicates, however, that male children are more likely to receive financial aid from parents, while daughters receive a larger proportion of services from parents.[51]

Most probably mutual aid patterns between parents and adult children are asymmetrical since intergenerational social relationships are of this order. Married daughters appear to have closer ties with their parents than married sons have with their parents. There is more frequent sharing of the household by married daughters and their parents and apparently a greater compatibility of mothers and daugh-ters than of mothers and daughters-in-law. Sweetser proposes a struc-tural hypothesis based upon cross-cultural research in which condi-

[51]Sussman, "The Help Pattern in the Middle Class Family," *op. cit.*

tions associated with potential tension and conflict between parents and child-in-law are established.[52] The structural hypothesis, developed from an initial cross-cultural study of 18 societies and subsequently verified on a sample of 111 societies, is that avoidance between parents and child-in-law will occur when the child-in-law is a stranger and a successor in the residential family grouping. The hypothesis has some applicability to the American family pattern because the daughter-in-law is most likely to be a "stranger" in her mother-in-law's house since most of the courting in American society takes place in the girl's home rather than in the home of her potential spouse. The daughter-in-law succeeds to the mother's important role, the care of her new husband, the mother's son. Since the daughter-in-law is successor to her mother-in-law, the two are less likely to share a household. But the mother-in-law does not find avoidance of her own daughter necessary because this daughter poses no threat of succession to the mother's position in the household.

These findings are in agreement with the statistical data supplied by Glick.[53] He finds that a higher percentage of the married females who are living with their spouse in the household of parents are daughters rather than daughters-in-law. Middle-aged and aged parents are more likely to call upon their daughters than their sons or daughters-in-law when they need assistance such as nursing care and other services.[54] Komarovsky has hypothesized that women, as a result of differential experience during adolescence, are much more attached to their parents than men. Daughters are more sheltered than sons and are required to be more constrained in their behavior away from home; thus their brothers have greater freedom to develop social relationships outside the family of procreation.[55] Stryker reports that young married wives are more dependent on their mothers than husbands are on theirs.[56] According to Komarovsky, when a spouse is very dependent upon his or her parents, difficulties with "in-laws" are more likely to arise than when the spouse is less dependent.

The findings of Komarovsky and Stryker support Sweetser's position that the married daughter is a stranger to her mother-in-law and at the same time is a successor to her in the male lineage. As a consequence, there is potential conflict and tension between mother-in-law and daughter-in-law. To this must be added the existence of a closer

[52]Dorrian Apple Sweetser, "Asymmetry in Intergenerational Family Relationships," *Social Forces*, XLI (May, 1963), 346-52.

[53]Paul C. Glick, *American Families* (New York: John Wiley and Sons, 1957), pp. 21-52.

[54]Shanas, *Family Relationships of Older People, op. cit.*; and Sussman, "The Help Pattern in the Middle Class Family," *op. cit.*

[55]Mirra Komarovsky, "Continuities in Family Research: A Case Study," *American Journal of Sociology*, LXII (July, 1956), 42-47.

[56]Sheldon Stryker, "The Adjustment of Married Offspring to their Parents," *American Sociological Review*, XX (April, 1955), 149-54.

association of the daughter than of the son with their respective parents. In primitive societies the problem of conflict and tension is handled by the custom of avoidance. In American society avoidance is often effected by geographical distance between nuclear related units even in the same metropolitan area.

Distance between residents of generationally linked nuclear units may be the necessary antidote for the potential conflict and tension inherent in the mother-in-law — daughter-in-law relationships. Under this arrangement, contact between family units is limited to selected occasions, thus permitting the nuclear family to function independently of other units yet related within the matrix of mutual aid and service provided by the extended kin network. The telephone, automobile, modern highways, and other means of high-speed transportation and communication are useful in linking the generational units for special activities and mutual benefit while allowing for independent functions of each component unit.

social relationship between parents and their adult children: crises and retirement

Crises The listing of "crises" with "retirement" does not imply a high correlation between these two conditions. Crisis has many definitions. A safe approach to a discussion of these is to think in terms of an answer to the question, "Where do you go when you got trouble?"[57] Or, a more verbal middle-class respondent might be asked which friends, relatives, or strangers (service agencies are sometimes conceived as such) he would rely upon for assistance when he faced a crisis situation. A disaster such as loss of one's home by fire or a chronic illness are types of acute and long-term crises usually requiring some form of assistance.

Disaster studies conducted during the past decade were reviewed by Quarantelli.[58] He reports that disaster victims seek out the extended kin family as a major source of help. The smaller the community, the more likely is the major source of assistance the kin group. The flow of aid from parents to children (established previously) makes it most likely that this is the pattern of aid during the long course of rehabilitation. Disaster infers heightened mutual assistance among kin along generational and bilateral lines in the immediate post-disaster period. The long-range rebuilding after a disaster will follow the particularistic pattern of each kin network with the economic condition of the kin units (as a consequence of the disaster)

[57]Earl Koos used a similar question to encourage working-class individuals to talk about themselves and their problems. *Families in Trouble, op. cit.*
[58]Enrico L. Quarantelli, "A Note on the Protective Function of the Family in Disasters," *op. cit.*, pp. 263-64.

being a dependent variable. Quarantelli's summary goes beyond the implications of parental aid to adult children. He adds another bit of evidence to the notion of the pervasiveness of the kinship network. He says:

> Disaster studies lend little support to the general proposition that the protective function has been basically relinquished and that the extended family is of little importance in mass societies. The kin group is the preferred, sought, and major source of short and long-run help in time of such crises. In this sense at least, the protective function is clearly still a major function of the extended family.[59]

Response to the illness of a member by others in the generationally linked kin network has been largely unstudied. Response to illness is indicated in several studies, but details on the nature and effort by kin members in "caring for their own" are largely a mystery. One study reported that middle-class mothers in their middle years responded almost unanimously to the request of their daughters for assistance during the latter's confinement. (These same mothers were less frequently asked for help by their daughters-in-law.) As to the time spent or activities performed in connection with this situation, however, one can only hazard a guess.[60]

In one study the response of the kin group to the long-term illness of one of its members was studied in relation to the larger study objective of determining the relationship and effect of sociologic, psychologic, and medical factors upon the course of achieved rehabilitation after discharge from a chronic illness and rehabilitation hospital.[61] Detailed analyses have been made of the responses of kin members to the ill member. Most of the ill patients (210 families in the study) are over 55 years of age, although there are a number of cases in the adolescent and early twenties group, for example, persons with spinal cord injuries and accident-victim amputees. Several findings emerge from this exploratory study which permit formulation of hypotheses for further testing.

Illness of an older member of the kin group results in almost instantaneous response from well members. As a rule, children of the ill member respond most vigorously, and one child assumes or is delegated the role of "responsible member." The illness does not appear to bring the nuclear units closer together or to destroy the already achieved integration. If the ill member has been in a highly integrated kin network and has experienced a high degree of intergenerational family continuity prior to his illness, he is most likely to be the recipient of large amounts of aid, service, and social attention during hospitalization and after his return to the community. The ill individual

---

[59]*Ibid.*, p. 264.

[60]Sussman, "The Help Pattern in the Middle Class Family," *op. cit.*

[61]Marvin B. Sussman and Morris W. Stroud, III, "Studies in Chronic Illness and the Family," Western Reserve University and Highland View Hospital, 1959-1964, mimeographed, pp. 1-25. A copy can be obtained by writing to Marvin B. Sussman.

who is isolated both in distance and function prior to hospitalization receives a minimum of assistance from kin. Although he may receive some response from kin at the beginning of his illness, he is essentially isolated after discharge from the hospital. The isolated older person is more likely than the kin-integrated individual to go into a nursing home after leaving the hospital. It appears that for this age group, chronic illness does not have an interfering effect upon the kinship pattern established prior to the onset of illness.

Chronic disability in the younger adult, on the other hand, has a very different effect upon the responses of kin members. The roles of the parents in the generationally linked network are most severely affected. In instances where adolescents are permanently injured, parents must take on new roles and expectations in order to handle the drastically altered interpersonal relationships within and outside of the family subsystem which result from the dependency of the child. Long-term dependency requires coping with the interventions of other social systems upon the family and the growing realization that the child is the central being in the family's interaction pattern. Family behavior is organized around the needs of the child, and other kin members such as grandparents are asked to perform supportive roles.

The married adult who becomes chronically ill and disabled presents even greater tasks for members of the family of gerontation. Often provider and mother roles are assumed by parents and grandparents. In this instance and in the instance of the adolescent child, the illness materially affects the structure and function of both the generationally linked nuclear units and the extended kin network. The behavior of the kin network when confronted by chronic illness and disability of kin members is now under further study.

Retirement Social relationships between aged parents and their children follow the pattern established in the middle years, that period after children have left their families of orientation to seek education, careers, marriage, or a combination of these.[62] During this "empty nest" stage, parents establish a basis for their retirement pattern which has reference to the continuity or discontinuity of intergenerational family relationships.

The conditions under which financial support links the aged to their middle-aged or younger children have already been described. Equally important during retirement is the need of aged parents for emotional support. Such support principally comes from continuous social relationships between the generations. It is difficult, however, to determine whether regular social activities intended to provide emotional support for aged parents are the consequence of a genuine sense of filial duty and obligation arising from the child's feeling of

[62]Gordon F. Streib, "Family Patterns in Retirement," *Journal of Social Issues,* XIV, No. 2 (1958), 46-60.

love and warmth for his parent,[63] or whether such activities are the consequence of long-ingrained rituals established in childhood.[64] Boyd, in a study on the emerging social roles of the four-generational family, presents evidence that genuine understanding and love characterize the emotional relationships which members of generation three (age range 20-40) express toward generation two (age range 40-70) and generation one (age range 60-90), and which members of generation two express toward generation one.[65] The social life of the small community, the site of Boyd's study, and the opportunity for sustained intergenerational relationships at various stages of the life cycle prior to old age may account for this finding. Brown's study of a Duke University population reports, however, that over two-thirds of the aged respondents visit with their children, while less than 20 per cent indicate close affectional ties with their children.[66]

Rosow is investigating the emotional relationships among the elderly because he finds such relationships to be a basic need for aged persons.[67] Rosow postulates a relationship between the older person's reliance upon family members for emotional support and the availability to him of opportunities for friendship. The more friends available to the aged person, the less he is dependent upon the family for emotional support. The greater the loss of roles by the aged person, the greater the dependence upon the family for emotional support.

This research should provide answers to the requirements, processes, and satisfactions of emotional needs of aged parents and their offspring. Another interesting question to which an answer may be forthcoming is whether the friendship group is a simulated and ritualistic nonconsanguine kin group performing functions similar to those of its consanguineal counterparts.

Bennett and Despres have described the Oynbun-Kokun and Hindu Jajman systems in Japan and the compadre system in the Philippines.[68] These two are organizational systems of nonkin which simulate blood-kinship ties and which serve various economic, social, ideological, and political objectives for their members. Despres believes that friendship groups in modern societies may be replicas of consanguineal kin structures, thus attesting to the pervasiveness of the kin network as a basic structural component of society.

[63]Schorr, *Filial Responsibility in the Modern American Family, op. cit.*

[64]James H. S. Bossard and Eleanor S. Boll, "Ritual in Family Living," *American Sociological Review*, XIV (August, 1949), 463-69.

[65]Rosamonde R. Boyd, "The Four-Generational Families of Upper, Middle, and Working Classes in Spartanburg, South Carolina," unpublished manuscript, pp. 1-26.

[66]Robert Brown, "Family Structure and Social Isolation of Older Persons," *Journal of Gerontology*, XV (1960), 170-74.

[67]Irving Rosow, "The Aged, Family and Friends," Project Statement, 1963, mimeographed, pp. 1-20.

[68]Bennett and Despres, "Kinship Structure and Instrumental Activities: A Theoretical Inquiry," *op. cit.*

parents, adult children, and economic activity

Mutual aid is an on-going activity between generationally linked kin members. Brief mention should be made, however, of economic and occupational activities of parents which on the surface at least appear to contradict the universality of action according to bureaucratic norms. Corporate structures today are said to operate with bureaucratic, universalistic, and impartial norms. Familialistic norms require loyalty and identification to the family and appropriate action in reference to these norms. In American business organizations which are family owned, there is conflict between these two sets of norms. The extent of the conflict is unknown since there are very few studies of this problem.[69] The task is to determine the extent of this conflict and the means employed to blend together into a common system of action apparently conflicting sets of paired norms.[70] Research on business and industrial organizations and the family is beginning in both England and the United States.[71]

The activities of parents in placing children in occupations or in situations favorable to successful occupational placement is another largely unexplored research area. The meaning and significance of such activities must be assessed for their compatibility with less particularistic norms which state that merit, ability, skill, and intelligence are the principal criteria in occupational placement. It may be that "who you know," such as influential parents, may be an equally important criterion for occupational selection and thus compatible with more universalistic norms.

Two illustrations describe this problem. In a large factory in the Cleveland metropolitan area which uses semiautomated assembly-line techniques, roughly 13 per cent of the men hired for summer work in the plant during 1963 were sons and other kindred of middle and high-ranked management.[72] The significance of this act is the fact that there is a plethora of unskilled workers available for these jobs in the Cleveland area. Wilson questioned 818 sergeants of a large metro-

---

[69]Despres, "A Function of Bilateral Kinship Patterns in a New England Industry," *op. cit.*

[70]Robert K. Merton, "The Ambivalence of Scientists," *Bulletin of Johns Hopkins Hospital*, CXII (1963), 77-97. Ambiguity and ambivalence resulting from norm inconsistencies is characteristic of all social systems. The difficult task is to blend inconsistent norms into a reasonably consistent pattern of action.

Marvin B. Sussman, "The Social Problems of the Sociologist," *Social Problems*, in press. The handling of norm inconsistencies in a work system is described.

[71]John Bennett has a study underway in St. Louis, Missouri, "Kinship in American Business Organization," reported at the Central States Anthropological Society, May, 1961.

Marvin B. Sussman is beginning a study on extended kin activities in business and individual organizations; and Cyril Sofer is considering a study in a related area concerned with ways executives and professionals resolve the conflict of loyalties between careers and families. *Personal Communication*, September, 1963.

[72]Anonymous: a graduate student in sociology at Western Reserve University completed this brief survey in October, 1963. He wishes to remain anonymous since he is employed by the company.

politan area police force in order to determine lines of ethnic and generational succession in the police officer's career.[73] The study population was divided into three groups by the nativity of their fathers: Irish, American, and European. Seventy per cent of the Irish compared to 55 per cent of the American and 34.2 per cent of the European had one or more relatives on the police force. Seventy-six per cent of the police relatives of the Irish were in the immediate family; 29.2 per cent had a father in the police force. Among the American group, 62.5 per cent of police relatives were in the immediate family; 24.9 per cent had fathers in the police force. Among the policemen of other European nativities with police relatives, 56.4 per cent of their police relatives were in the immediate family and 15.4 per cent had fathers who were policemen.

These two separate illustrations suggest patterns of family participation in occupational activities which are probably not uncommon in both corporate structures and in the professions. Further studies are required to determine the extent of such activities and their effects upon the functioning of economic and occupational systems.

The consumer patterns of family members on different generational levels are being studied by Hill and his associates.[74] These investigators are beginning with the individual's "want" for a particular hard goods item and then are reviewing the individual's evaluation of alternative courses of action, his planning, decision-making actions, and his satisfaction with decisions and action taken. Differences among three-generational families in their behavior as consumers as well as intergenerational influence upon consumer decisions are being studied.

Haller has raised several interesting questions regarding the significance of an emerging urban familism.[75] If individuals are intricately involved within a kin family network, will they be influenced by kin leaders and be less amenable to influence by outsiders such as the salesman of leisure-time products and other goods and services? Katz and Lazarsfeld have advanced the concept of the two-step flow of communication whereby opinion leaders in groups "expose" themselves to areas of knowledge which are of conern to the group (this is expected of them) and become "influentials" who are sought after by advice-seekers.[76] The decision-making process is virtually controlled

[73]James Q. Wilson, "Generational and Ethnic Differences Among Career Police Officers," paper given at the American Sociological Association, Los Angeles, 1963.

[74]Reuben Hill, "Judgment and Consumership in the Management of Family Resources," *Sociology and Social Research*, XLVII (July, 1963), 446-60; Joan Aldous and Reuben Hill, "Family Continuities Through Socialization Over Three Generations," paper given at the American Sociological Association, Los Angeles, 1963. See Hill, Chapter VI below.

[75]A. O. Haller, "The Urban Family," *American Journal of Sociology*, LXVI (May, 1961), 621-22.

[76]Elihu Katz and Paul F. Lazarsfeld, *Personal Influence* (New York: Free Press of Glencoe, Inc., 1955), pp. 309-34.

by these leaders. Hill's findings on consumer decision making may determine the applicability of this influence model and answer the more general questions raised by Haller and others concerning the effects of kin network activities upon the functioning of other social systems in the society.

parental aid model

Mutual aid and social relationships are the life blood activities of the kin network. An effort has been made to develop a theoretical model which can be used in the conceptualization of problems and the development of appropriate designs for the study of parental aid.[77]

The model (Figure 4-2) has been described in an earlier paper as follows:

Five general familial variables have been delineated as affecting the offering, acceptance or rejection of parental aid. These include the values of the family of orientation, the position of the family in the social structure, the economic level of the family, its family structure, and the pattern of relationships within the structure.

The types of parent-child economic support are classified into three major categories: goods, money, and services. Family emergencies or crises may result in multiple types of aids such as care of stricken family members and cash to pay for medical services. The major types of economic aid exchanges are enumerated but the list is not intended to be exhaustive.

The family system is influenced by other systems found within the society. Social systems such as the economic, the religious and the educational can either support or constrain parents in offering and children in accepting economic aid. Four societal factors support or constrain parental aid: the economic well being of people within the society; the demographic characteristics influencing the organization of the family, its structure shaped by organizational patterns of the larger society; and the family's value system which incorporated the dominant values of the society.

Twelve intervening variables may affect the giving and receiving of parental aid. These include the amount of aid given in a particular situation; expectations concerning aid and the basis for giving and receiving; the particular stage in the family cycle (requirements during the early years of childbearing are different from the later years when children are being sent to college); the occasion and technique used in giving aid without usurpation of provider roles; the expected return of parents; the residential location of the two sets of households; the social status of the family within the community and expectations concerning this status; the married child's image of the in-laws as helping or interfering persons; and

---

[77]Sussman and Burchinal, "Parental Aid to Married Children: Implications for Family Functioning," *op. cit.* Murray Straus constructed the original model which was modified by the authors. The model was first developed in a seminar, "Parental Aid to Married Children: Implication for Family Independence," Groves Conference on Marriage and Family, Columbus, Ohio, April, 1960.

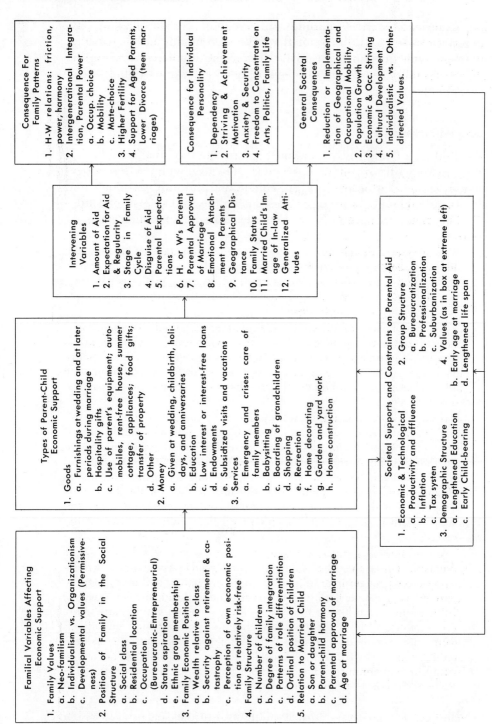

fig. 4-2. functional analysis of parental aid to married children.

Source: Adapted from Marvin B. Sussman and Lee Burchinal, "Parental Aid to Married Children: Implications for Family Functioning," *Marriage and Family Living,* XXIV (1962), 326.

generalized attitudes learned from interaction with in-laws, varied information sources and peer group experience.

Consequences of parental aid to married children are viewed in three areas, consequences for the family, consequences for the individual personality and consequences for the general society.

Aid may affect husband-wife marital relationships in strengthening or weakening marital relationships and in determining the allocation of power within the newly organized family. It may affect intergenerational relationships and strengthen parental authority in such areas as occupational choice, mobility of children and in mate selection. Aid may be related also to family size, the pattern of adjustment in old age and the rate of divorce particularly among younger married persons.

Parental aid given to children may affect the development of dependence, the motivation to achieve, increased personal anxiety, increased feelings of security and emancipation from mundane routines with freedom to concentrate on developments of skills and abilities and cultural interests. Opposite conditions may also prevail.

The general consequences for the society may be to reduce or further geographical or occupational mobility of families while maintaining a neolocal nuclear family system with a network of kin relationships. There are further consequences for population growth, economic and occupational striving of persons within the society, the cultural development of individuals, and current ideological systems.[78]

summary

The extended kin family network is the basic social system in American urban society within which parent-adult child relationships are identified, described, and analyzed. The network is a pervasive system and includes member nuclear units interlocked within a structure of social relationships and mutual aid.

The empirical evidence is conclusive on the existence of an extended kin family network in urban society. The evidence also refutes the notion that nuclear family units are isolated and dependent almost entirely for their maintenance and continuity upon the activities of other institutions and social systems. The activities of bilateral kin and intergenerational family linkages now require further study for their impact upon the behavior of nuclear family members and those of related social systems and institutions in the society.

The more general activities of the economic and social matrix among generationally linked nuclear units, particularly parents and their adult children, are described as being extensive. The flow of aid has been largely from parents to children with an increasing flow in the 1960's from middle-aged parents to grandparents; the financial autonomy norm has been weakened; parents play active roles in assuring successful economic stability and occupational placement of their children. Adult children have important social relationships with aged

---

[78]*Ibid.*, p. 327.

parents. The meaning and significance of these activities for component nuclear units and the functions of other social systems is largely unknown. Some suggestions are given. Research is beginning in a variety of settings which will provide clarification of the parental aid variable for its particular effect upon intergenerational family continuity, intrafamily activity, and functions of other social systems in the society.

A theoretical model is presented containing variables affecting patterns of support and implications of giving and receiving support. The model is intended to encourage the conceptualization of significant problems with appropriate research design relative to the study of parental aid.

nuclear and extended family relationships: a normative and behavioral analysis[1] ALAN C. KERCKHOFF

One of the issues widely discussed in sociological analyses of the contemporary American family is the degree of nucleation of our family structure. Most of these discussions take as their point of departure Talcott Parsons' treatment of this matter.[2] Given his concern with the systemic characteristics of social and cultural phenomena, a dominant theme in Parsons' works is the analysis of functional relationships among the various elements in our social system. He is particularly concerned with the relationship between family structure on the one hand and economic (or occupational) structure on the other. One central message is that a nucleated family structure is consistent with the industrial patterns we have developed.

This emphasis on nucleation has been questioned by a number of

[1]The research reported here was supported by a grant from the Ford Foundation to Duke University for "Socio-Economic Studies of Aging." The computations were carried out in the Duke University Computing Laboratory, which is supported in part by the National Science Foundation. The author is indebted to Adam Clarke Davis for his hours of careful work in processing these data and to Cyrus Johnson who first developed the normative typology used here.

[2]Although Parsons has discussed these issues in many of his writings, the first systematic statement of them, and one which still represents the central core of his analysis is: Talcott Parsons, "The Kinship System of the Contemporary United States," *American Anthropologist*, XLV (January, 1943), 22-38.

authors on the basis of both logical analysis and empirical data.[3] The burden of these writings has been that our family system is not *as* nucleated as Parsons' discussion would imply. Not only is there less geographic dispersion than would be expected from Parsons' analysis, but even in those families in which grown children move far away from their parents, a very viable relationship is often maintained between the generations.

One of the outcomes of this empirical-theoretical dialogue has been the differentiation among three-family types and an investigation of some of the correlates of each. Although there are different possible terms of identification of these three types, the author has chosen to use Litwak's terms, which are *extended, modified extended,* and *nuclear.* The first and third terms are, of course, the ones used earlier by Parsons and many others. The second, however, the modified extended, is a new concept which has evolved from the work of Parsons' critics.

Litwak has defined the modified extended family in relation to what he calls the "classical extended" and nuclear types. He says that the modified extended type:

> . . . differs from the "classical extended" family in that it does not demand geographical propinquity, occupational involvement, or nepotism, nor does it have an hierarchical authority structure. On the other hand, it differs from the isolated nuclear family structure in that it does provide significant continuing aid to the nuclear family.[4]

The differentiation of these three types of family systems forms the framework within which the present analysis is carried out.

The focus of the concern of the earlier discussions has been almost exclusively on the relationships between the conjugal unit and other relatives, especially the relationship between generations. The present paper is an attempt to examine another characteristic of the total system that may be expected to be related to the intergenerational pattern, namely, the structure of the conjugal relationship of the older couple. Before doing this, however, we must lay some additional theoretical groundwork.

The earlier Parsonian analysis of the nucleated family system in our society includes a discussion of the structure of both the intergenerational relationship and the conjugal pattern within each of the nucleated units. Given a systemic view of the total pattern of family life, we would expect that characteristics of the intergenerational relationship would be linked with characteristics of the conjugal relationship within each of the subunits of the system. According to Parsons' analysis of the nucleated system, which he sees as characteristic of our

---

[3]Marvin B. Sussman presents a review of this literature in his contribution to this volume, "Relationships of Adult Children with Their Parents in the United States," *supra,* Chapter IV.

[4]Eugene Litwak, "Occupational Mobility and Extended Family Cohesion," *American Sociological Review,* XXV (February, 1960), 10.

society, attenuation of intergenerational ties is associated with intensification of the conjugal tie.[5] Although most of his discussion has focussed on the conjugal relationship of the younger couple, a similar expectation with respect to the older couple seems in order. Viewing it as a whole, and contrasting it with other possible family systems, the nucleated system appears to be characterized by *both* minimal intergenerational ties and intense conjugal ties.

We may also hypothesize that a rather different type of conjugal relationship would be found in what Parsons has called an extended family system. Given salient outside points of reference (outside the conjugal unit, that is), we may reasonably expect that in an extended family system the conjugal relationship would be considerably less intense and functionally less important in the lives of the conjugal pair.

There is evidence that this is the case in fact even in some segments of Western society. Much of the evidence comes from a number of British studies which have noted that, especially in lower-class families, an important relationship is maintained between the mother and her married children (especially daughters).[6] In such a family system the father is much less important than his wife in the intergenerational link, *and* his relationship with his wife is not nearly as significant in the lives of either of the older spouses as would be expected in a nucleated family system.[7]

Thus, from earlier theoretical discussions, the findings of studies of intergenerational relations in this country, and the findings of total family networks in England, one may derive an hypothesis regarding the connection between the nature of the intergenerational link on the one hand and the nature of the conjugal tie on the other. The typology of intergenerational patterns referred to earlier—extended, modified extended, nuclear—may be used for that part of the hypothesis. We

[5]Parsons states, for instance, that: ". . . [in] comparison with other kinship systems, [the individual in our system is] drastically segregated from his family of orientation, both from his parents—and their forebears—and from his siblings. His first kinship loyalty is unequivocally to his spouse and then to their children if and when they are born. Moreover, his family of procreation, by virtue of a common household, income, and community status, becomes a solidary unit in the sense in which the segregation of the interests of individuals is relatively meaningless, whereas the segregation of these interests of ego from those of the family of orientation tends relatively to minimize solidarity with the latter." Parsons, "The Kinship System of the Contemporary United States," *op. cit.*, p. 30.

[6]This literature is also reviewed by Marvin B. Sussman in his contribution to this volume, "Relationships of Adult Children With Their Parents in the United States," Chapter IV.

[7]That this general relationship between intergenerational and conjugal patterns is not simply a class-linked phenomenon is indicated by Mogey's finding that a very different type of pattern may be found in lower-class families if the neighborhood context is altered through relocation. For our purposes, the significant aspect of Mogey's findings is that *both* the intergenerational and the conjugal pattern change in the new setting and they change in a way consistent with the present discussion. See John Mogey, *Family and Neighborhood* (London: Oxford University Press, 1956).

need terms, however, which help us focus on relevant dimensions of the conjugal relationship. For this purpose, the author has borrowed from Elizabeth Bott who differentiates between what she calls the "joint conjugal role-relationship" and the "segregated conjugal role-relationship." She defines these as follows:

> A joint conjugal role-relationship is one in which husband and wife carry out many activities together, with a minimum of task differentiation and separation of interests; in such cases husband and wife not only plan the affairs of the family together, but also exchange many household tasks and spend much of their leisure time together. A segregated conjugal role-relationship is one in which husband and wife have a clear differentiation of tasks and a considerable number of separate interests and activities; in such cases, husband and wife have a clearly defined division of labour into male tasks and female tasks; they expect to have different leisure pursuits; the husband has his friends outside the home and the wife has hers.[8]

This distinction seems particularly relevant to the present discussion, given the emphasis in many recent analyses of the American conjugal pattern on the "interpenetration of roles" or the "blurring of role distinctions." Evidently Bott's "joint conjugal role-relationship" is what one would expect in the nucleated family system as Parsons describes it.

Given these two sets of typologies, the general hypothesis which may be derived from the discussion thus far could be stated as follows:

A joint conjugal role-relationship will be found more often in association with a nuclear intergenerational relationship, and a segregated conjugal role-relationship will be found more often in association with an extended intergenerational relationship; the conjugal relationship of couples with a modified extended intergenerational relationship will be intermediate to those of the other two intergenerational types.[9]

Some of the earlier discussions of family relationships have focussed on norms or attitudes relevant to the family; others have focussed on behavioral data. When one speaks of "the structure of the American family," it is likely that he is referring to behavior, but this is not always the case. If we follow an institutional analysis (which is the usual Parsonian formulation), our concern is likely to be with normative data. It is at least equally legitimate, however, to investigate actual behavior patterns. Such a normative-behavioral distinction is, of course, a central one in much of sociological writing. Although the sociologist is largely concerned with the fact that normative

[8]Elizabeth Bott, "Urban Families: Conjugal Roles and Social Networks," *Human Relations*, VIII, No. 4 (1955), p. 346.
[9]Although the last part of this hypothesis is not clearly derivable from the earlier discussion, it is based on the assumption that the modified nuclear is an intermediate type between the other two. This is implicit in most recent discussions of this type, and the operational definition used in this study makes its middle position quite explicit.

definitions operate to control behavior, there is also explicit recognition that normative definitions and behavior are not always in accord.[10] Robin Williams, in his discussion of patterns of deviation from cultural prescriptions, for instance, differentiates between what he calls "normative structure" on the one hand and "patterns of conduct" on the other.[11] This type of differentiation is significant in the present discussion.

Research in the general area of inquiry within which the present paper is relevant has already demonstrated the following: (1) There is considerable variation in Western society in the normative definitions which are seen to apply to both conjugal and intergenerational relationships. (2) There is also considerable variation in the patterns of conduct followed in the various social units (families) to which these normative definitions apply. These demonstrated variations are what has led to the development of the typologies described above. However, if the kind of systemic formulations discussed earlier are applicable to units in our social system, one would expect that within these various units there would be a "strain toward consistency" between the two kinds of family relationship. In the most general sense, one would expect a strain toward consistency in three forms: (1) between the two patterns of conduct involved in [the normative orienta-] tion that given one type of normative orientation to the intergenera- relationships; (2) between the two patterns of conduct involved in these relationships; and (3) between the normative definitions and the behavioral patterns.

As it is stated, the general hypothesis offered here may then be interpreted in two different ways: (1) At the normative level of analysis, it acknowledges that family norms vary, and it makes the prediction that given one type of normative orientation to the intergenerational relationship in the family, one will also find a specifiable type of normative orientation to the conjugal relationship. (2) At the behavioral level, the hypothesis also assumes variation in patterns of conduct both between members of two generations and within the conjugal unit. It predicts that persons who are implicated in one kind of pattern of behavior with reference to their adult children will also be implicated in a specifiable pattern of behavior with reference to their spouses.

The fact that the same order of relationship is predicted at the behavioral and normative levels *implies* the assumption that behavior will be in accordance with normative definitions. As indicated, however, this relationship between norms and behavior is *always* a question to be answered by examination of the data rather than something that can be assumed at the outset. Thus, we must also examine

---

[10]That there is less than complete uniformity in the treatment of these matters is indicated by such controversies as that over whether the concept of "role" is normative or behavioral, whether it refers to what people *should* do or what they *do* do as occupants of social positions.

[11]Robin Williams, *American Society* (New York: Alfred A. Knopf, Inc., 1954), p. 537.

the relationship *between* the normative and behavioral data as well as the patterns *within* each set of data.

Finally, the form of the hypothesis also makes explicit the fact that we are using the individual family system as our unit of analysis rather than the society as a whole or large organized sub-units of the society (such as communities). Thus, any strain toward consistency that might be present is seen as either intrapsychic or interpersonal rather than interinstitutional or intergroup. As the later analysis according to occupational status implies, these data undoubtedly have relevance to larger units of analysis, but the conceptualization of the problem is not originally set at this broader level.

method

The general form in which the hypothesis is stated calls for data about three kinds of relationship: (1) the intergenerational relationship, (2) the conjugal relationship of the older couple, and (3) the conjugal relationship of couples in the younger generation.[12] The present study has data relevant to the first two of these relationships but not the third. The data were collected in extensive interviews with older white couples who were living together, and who were couples in which the man had either retired or was within five years of retirement. Husband and wife were interviewed simultaneously by two interviewers, normally in separated parts of the house. The lists of subjects were obtained from industrial, commercial, educational, and professional organizations all located in the Piedmont region of North Carolina. The subjects were chosen so as to maximize the occupational distribution of the husbands, and they are thus not to be considered as a representative sample of any particular population.[13]

Most, but not all, of these couples had children. In order to focus only on couples who had had an opportunity to develop both types of relationship relevant to our analysis, the analysis was restricted to

[12]Since younger couples may have intergenerational ties of a different type with the two parental couples, it would sometimes be difficult to say whether a younger couple have an extended, modified extended, or nuclear type of relationship with their parents. Of course, a parental couple may also have a different type of relationship with two of their married children, one being more or less "extended" than the other. In characterizing a system of relationships, therefore, one must limit oneself either to the *average* kind of relationship between the parents and their children (which is what has been done in the present study) or to a single parental couple-child relationship.

[13]It was necessary to choose between an area probability sample and a purposive sample in this study. The latter was chosen because our interest was in the pattern of relationships among a number of work- and family-related variables rather than in specifying the pattern of distribution of characteristics in any particular population. That is, in the present discussion we are concerned with the relationship between a type of intergenerational link on the one hand and a type of conjugal link on the other. No claim is made that the distribution of these types in our sample is representative of the distribution in any larger population.

those who had at least one child who was *either* married *or* at least twenty-five years of age. There was a total of 201 such couples.[14]

Intergenerational Family Type The earlier discussion of Litwak was particularly helpful in guiding the choice of operations in this area. The basic contribution of Litwak in this regard was the specification of the differences among what he calls the "classical extended," and "nuclear," and the "modified extended" types, as indicated in the quotation referred to earlier.

With reference to the criteria he enumerates, there was little evidence that parents in the present sample expected an authoritative relationship with their adult children, and there was little evidence of explicit occupational continuity between father and son (which was the author's interpretation of Litwak's phrase "occupational involvement"). There was no way of measuring "nepotism" in this study. Thus, the decision was made to focus on "geographical propinquity" and "continuing aid to the nuclear family" as the classificatory characteristics. The extended type was seen as having both propinquity and a high level of continuing aid, the modified extended as having a high level of continuing aid but not propinquity, and the nuclear type as having neither propinquity nor very much continuing aid.

At the normative level of analysis the criterion of propinquity was measured by agreement or disagreement with the following statement: "Married children should live close to their parents." The criterion of continuing aid was measured by a Likert scale (called Mutual Aid and Affection) made up of the following items:

1. Children should take care of their parents in whatever way necessary, when they are sick.

2. The older couple should take care of their children, in whatever way necessary, when they are sick.

3. The children should give their parents financial help.

4. The older couple should give their children financial help.

5. If children live nearby after they grow up, they should visit their parents at least once a week.

6. If children live nearby after they grow up, their parents should visit them at least once a week.

7. Children who live at a distance should write to their parents at least once a week.

8. Parents should write to their children who live at a distance at least once a week.

[14]The data to be presented involves, in most cases, measures based on multiple items. Difficulties of interviewing led to incomplete or inadequate responses from some of the individuals interviewed. There is a notable loss in sample size, therefore, in some of the analyses, since for a couple to be included, *all* items for *all* measures for *both* members of the couple must be available. Each table presents the frequencies used, so that the reader may take this loss into account in evaluating the results.

9. The children should feel responsible for their parents.
10. The older couple should feel responsible for their children.

Those subjects who agreed with seven or more of these items *and* who agreed that children should live close to their parents were classified as having extended family norms. Those who had equally high Mutual Aid and Affection scores but who did *not* agree with the propinquity item were classified as having modified extended norms. Those who agreed with six or less of the Mutual Aid and Affection items and who did not agree with the propinquity item were classified as having nuclear norms. There were two husbands and six wives who agreed with the propinquity item but who had low Mutual Aid and Affection scores. Since these did not fit into the typology, and since there were too few cases to warrant the creation of a new type, they were dropped from the analysis of the normative data. Table 5-1 presents the distribution of husbands and wives according to their position in our normative typology. Since their placement in this typology is based on the responses from the *individuals,* a husband and wife may very well end up in a different position. The significance of this fact for our analysis will be noted later.

table 5-1   distribution of husbands and wives
by normative typology

	extended	modified extended	nuclear
Husbands	62	92	45
Wives	40	116	39

An effort was made to construct a behavioral typology on the basis of items as similar as possible to those used in the normative typology. The criterion of propinquity was measured by an index of the average distance of a couple's children from the parental home. Each child's distance was classified according to a set of categories ranging from "in parent's home" to "more than 1,000 miles away," and the average of these categories was used as the family propinquity measure.[15] The criterion of continuing aid was met by an index made up of behavioral items similar to the normative items used in the Mutual Aid and Affection scale. It is called the Mutual Support index score and consists of the following items:

[15]The line between high- and low-propinquity families was drawn so that the average was fifty miles or less for high-propinquity families and more than fifty miles for low-propinquity families. There are difficulties with such a measure, of course, since it represents a large number of children in some cases and only one in others. The only alternatives that appeared to be available, however, were the degree of propinquity of the nearest or the most distant child. These were considered to be less useful measures both because approximately 80 per cent of the families had at least one child living within 15 miles, and because a given family might have both very near and very distant children. Although the solution adopted is hardly an ideal one, it seemed to be the best possible under the circumstances.

1. Have any of your children helped out when either of you were sick?

2. Have any of your children given advice on business or money matters?

3. Have you helped your children in any way when someone was sick in their family?

4. Have you given any of your children advice on business or money matters?

5. Have any of your children ever offered you financial assistance?

6. How willing would you say your children are to make sacrifices for you?

In each case, if there had not been a need for the particular type of assistance (such as in the illness of the parents), a score of 1 was given; if the need had been present and had been met, a score of 2 was given; if a need had been present and had not been met, a score of 0 was given.[16]

On the basis of these two measures, it was possible to divide the couples, first into those with low and high family-propinquity measures and, second, into those with high and low scores on the Mutual Support scale. The result, no matter what cut-off points were used on the two measures, was to create *four* rather than three empirical family types. In the final classification used, extended types were those with high propinquity scores (children lived relatively near by) and high Mutual Support index scores; modified extended types had low propinquity scores (children lived relatively far away) and high Mutual Support index scores; nuclear types had low propinquity and low Mutual Support scores. However, there was also a sizeable group which had high propinquity scores *and* low Mutual Support index scores. Since this group was of considerable size, it was retained for further analysis and was tentatively called the "individuated" type.[17]

Table 5-2 presents the number of cases in each of the four types. Since these are behavioral rather than normative types, there is only one type per couple rather than two.

---

[16]Here again, the problems of measurement are apparent. This system was considered superior, however, to the alternative of having a positive score only in those cases in which a need had been present and met. Responses from husbands and wives were very similar, so the husbands' responses were arbitrarily chosen for this analysis.

[17]The term is borrowed from Elizabeth Bott, although the use is somewhat different from hers. She defines the individuated family as one "separated off, differentiated out as a distinct, and to some extent autonomous, social group." "Urban Families: Conjugal Roles and Social Networks," *op. cit.*, p. 375. Such a definition could very well be seen as covering both the "nuclear" and the "individuated" types in the present study. The combination of geographical proximity and minimal mutual assistance, however, is seen as involving greater individuation than such minimal assistance combined with greater distance. This is so because there is increased opportunity for interaction when distances are reduced, and failure to provide assistance under those conditions amounts to active rejection of mutuality.

table 5-2   distribution of couples
by behavioral typology

Extended	59
Modified extended	38
Nuclear	50
Individuated	51

Conjugal Role Relationships Bott's differentiation between the joint and segregated conjugal role relationships involves a number of different characteristics. Not only were adequate data not available relevant to some of them, but any lack of correlation among them leads to the construction of a larger number of types than the sample size would justify. The operational definitions used for these types, therefore, were in terms of the single characteristic of a "division of labor." This characteristic was chosen because of its importance in earlier discussions of the American nuclear family system. A Likert scale of normative items, called Task Sharing, was used which consisted of the following items:

1. Yard work is the man's job, and his wife should not be expected to help with it.

2. Unless it is absolutely necessary for the family support, a wife should not work.

3. Housework is for women. A man should not do housework.

4. A man should simply "stay out of the way" as far as housework is concerned.

5. Certain family tasks are "women's work" and other tasks are "men's work," and it is best to keep them separate.

6. Although fathers are concerned with their children's welfare, the raising of children is really the mother's job.

7. When the children need to be punished or scolded, the father should do it.

8. When it comes to money matters, what the man says should be the rule.

9. A woman's place is in the home, not on a job.

These items were scored so that a high score indicated an acceptance of task sharing by husbands and wives, and a low score indicated a preference for task segregation and specialization.

An exact behavioral counterpart to this scale was not possible, but an index that was seen as very close to it was constructed. It consisted of responses to items which asked "Who does" the following tasks in the family:

1. Washes and dries the dishes.

2. Pays the monthly bills.

3. Sweeps and scrubs the floors.

4. Does the grocery shopping.

5. Makes the beds on weekends.

6. Dusts the furniture.
7. Does minor household repairs.
8. Hangs out the clothes to dry.
9. Sets the table.

For each item the possible responses were: wife always; wife usually; usually done together; sometimes one, sometimes the other; husband usually; husband always. A score of 0 was given if the wife always does it, a score of 5 was given if the husband always does it, with the intermediate responses being scored accordingly. The final index was an average of the scores on the individual items.[18] Since a high score indicates a high degree of household task performance by the husband, this index is called Husband's Participation.[19] It is considered here as an index of the degree to which the husband had assumed responsibility for some of the tasks traditionally carried out by wives, and it is thus also an index of the degree to which the separation of "men's work" and "women's work" is maintained in the conjugal unit. The two measures of the conjugal relationship, therefore, are measures of normative acceptance of task sharing and the actual degree of husband's participation in tasks that are traditionally carried out by wives.

Since the measures of the conjugal relationship were single scales, and those relevant to the intergenerational relationship were typologies, the approach in data analysis was to examine the variation of the conjugal measures among the intergenerational types. This was done independently for the normative and the behavioral measures, thus providing two different tests of the hypothesis.[20] It is also possible, of course, to examine the relationship between the behavioral and the normative measures, and such analysis will be referred to later in the discussion.

findings

Turning first to a test of the general hypothesis with normative data, we may compute the mean Task Sharing scores for husbands and wives who are normatively classified into the three intergenerational

[18]This averaging was necessary because occasionally a task was done by neither husband nor wife but by a maid, a child, or someone else. This information was collected from both husband and wife. Since their responses were generally quite similar, the husband's responses were arbitrarily chosen for this analysis.

[19]An alternative method of scoring these items was to give a high score for a response indicating a sharing of a task and a low score for a response indicating one person always does it. The results of this alternative method, however, were the same as for the one used here because of the fact that these are generally women's tasks and the husband's participation in any of them involved a sharing of the usual wifely role. This is borne out by the fact that none of the men scored very high on this index, and the average score was below 2.0 out of a possible 5.0.

[20]Actually, since the normative data were collected from husbands and wives independently, there are two tests of the hypothesis at the normative and one at the behavioral level of analysis.

types. The expectation, on the basis of the general hypothesis, is that
persons who normatively subscribe to an extended family pattern
should have lower Task Sharing scores than those who subscribe to a
modified extended pattern, and the latter will also be lower than those
who subscribe to a nuclear pattern. Table 5-3 presents the mean Task
Sharing scores for husbands and wives according to their normative
intergenerational type. The order, in both cases, is as predicted in the
hypothesis. There does, therefore, seem to be evidence of a connection between our older couples' normative definition of their relationship with each other and their normative definition of their relationship with their children.

table 5-3   mean task sharing scores of husbands
and wives by normative type

	extended	modified extended	nuclear
Husbands	14.83	17.67	18.66
N =	58	89	42
Wives	17.88	17.96	22.73
N =	37	114	38

The differences reported in Table 5-3 are not very great, however,
especially the difference between the mean wives' scores of the extended and modified types. The fact that these were scores derived
from answers given by *individuals* rather than the couple led to the
further consideration of these data in the light of *couple* responses.
The basic notion in this further analysis was that the relationship
hypothesized, if it were a valid one, should appear more clearly in
couples in which there was normative consensus with respect to intergenerational type. In such consensus couples, the intrapsychic strain
toward consistency is reinforced by interpersonal forces, but the opposite is true in nonconsensus couples. Rather than the three original
types, such an analysis calls for an examination of the mean Task
Sharing responses given by couples falling into nine types defined in
terms of the husband's intergenerational type *and* the wife's intergenerational type. Thus we have an extended-extended type, an
extended-modified extended type, an extended-nuclear type, and so
on, given the nine combinations of husbands' and wives' intergenerational types. Within each of these groups, the mean Task Sharing
score can again be computed. The refined hypothesis being examined
is that the original relationship predicted should be more clearly
present in the three pure types (the extended-extended, the modified-
modified, and the nuclear-nuclear types).

The results of this analysis are presented in Tables 5-4 and 5-5 for
husbands and wives respectively. The cells in which we are mainly
interested are those along the upper left to lower right diagonal. As

expected, the ordering of means in these cells is from low to high, and the difference between cells is greater than in the original analysis. This provides even more impressive support for the hypothesis phrased in normative terms, especially since these data represent two independent tests of the hypothesis.

There is also an additional pattern in these two tables, especially in Table 5-4, one which was not predicted but which is in keeping with the general logic which led to this further analysis of the norma-

table 5-4 mean task sharing scores of husbands by normative type of husband and wife

husband's normative type	wife's normative type		
	extended	modified extended	nuclear
Extended	12.06	15.91	16.40
N =	17	36	5
Modified Extended	16.07	17.64	19.19
N =	14	59	16
Nuclear	15.33	18.89	21.53
N =	6	19	17

tive data. Not only are the means along the critical diagonal in the predicted order, the great majority of the other means in the two tables follow a very consistent pattern. Husbands who fit the extended

table 5-5 mean task sharing scores of wives by normative type of husband and wife

husband's normative type	wife's normative type		
	extended	modified extended	nuclear
Extended	16.50	17.75	19.20
N =	17	36	5
Modified Extended	19.43	18.16	21.63
N =	14	59	16
Nuclear	18.17	17.74	24.81
N =	6	19	17

type and are paired with wives of the extended type have the lowest mean score of *any* combined type and the nuclear-nuclear cell has the highest mean score of *any* in the table. The same is true for Table 5-5. Not only this, but extended-type husbands have increasingly higher mean scores when they are paired with modified-type wives or nuclear-type wives. The same is true in general for all types of wives and husbands. That is, the general trend is to have higher mean scores as we move down the rows from left to right in the columns of Tables 5-4 and 5-5. There are only three out of eighteen cells that deviate from this order. There is, thus, rather impressive evidence not only of a normative conjugal-intergenerational link in these tables, but there is also evidence of a degree of normative influence on this dimension within the conjugal unit itself. Evidently the normative strain toward consistency operates at both the intrapsychic level and the interpersonal level.

The data based on behavioral definitions of the relevant variables produced very different results. The four-way typology of extended, modified extended, nuclear, and individuated was used to classify couples, and the mean Husband's Participation score was then computed for each of these groups of couples. Table 5-6 reports the results of this analysis. Ignoring the individuated type for the moment, the general hypothesis calls for the lowest mean Husband's Participation score to be in the extended-type cell and the highest to be in the nuclear-type cell. In fact, the reverse is true. Although the differences are rather small, we find more participation of husbands in household

table 5-6   mean husband's participation scores by behavioral type

extended	modified extended	nuclear	individuated
2.08	2.00	1.89	1.84
N = 59	38	50	51

tasks in those families having an extended structure and less in those having a nuclear structure. Actually, the lowest participation rate is found in our fourth type, the individuated.

With regard to the original general hypothesis, therefore, not only do the behavioral data not support the hypothesis, they even follow a slightly opposite pattern to that hypothesized. We thus seem to have very inconsistent results depending on whether we pursue the logic of our hypothesis at the normative or the behavioral level of analysis. The evidence at the normative level is clearly in accord with the hypothesis. Persons (husbands or wives) who espouse extended intergenerational norms also prefer a segregation of tasks between husband and wife, and those who espouse nuclear intergenerational norms also reject such task segregation. On the other hand, there seems to be basically no association between the "actual" (behavioral) relationship with one's adult children and the relationship with one's spouse. Couples who maintain a relationship of propinquity and mutual support (an extended relationship) with their children are just as likely to share household tasks as those who maintain a nuclear relationship with their children.

discussion

The strikingly different results from the two types of analysis require a close look at the relationships between the normative and behavioral levels. This can be done by cross-tabulating each normative measure with its matching behavioral measure. When this is done, the results are what would be expected from the findings reported above. Although there is a positive relationship in all cases, the number of deviant cases is very high. If we divide the Task Sharing scores at the median into high and low and do the same for Husband's Participation scores, only 57 per cent of the wives who prescribe to either high or low Task Sharing have husbands whose participation is of the same general level. The relationship is even weaker between the husbands' Task Sharing scores and their participation, only 55 per cent espousing norms generally in keeping with their own behavior. A similar finding results when we relate the normative and behavioral measures for propinquity and intergenerational relations. In fact, if we use our intergenerational typologies in the cross-tabulation, only 32 per cent of the husbands' and 25 per cent of the wives' normative types agree perfectly with their intergenerational behavior types.

It would be difficult to argue that the measures used here are such as to warrant an expectation of a perfect relationship between the measures at the normative and behavioral levels. However, this degree of deviation between the two strongly suggests that a clarification of these findings will require more than a critique of the operational definitions used.

An attempt at a partial clarification has been made within the limits of the present study. This attempt is based on the assumption that the measures used in this study are generally valid and that there must, therefore, be considerable deviation between the norms the respondents espoused and the patterns of behavior in which they engaged. The analysis thus focuses on two basic issues. First, we will note that it is possible to differentiate more than one type of deviation from these normative definitions. Second, based on the assumption that behavioral deviations from norms are likely to be caused by some kind of structural constraint in the overall situation in which the actor finds himself, the data will be examined to see if actors differentially situated in our society behave differently in relation to the norms they espouse.

All of the normative measures used in this study are based on statements to the effect that a person "should" do some particular thing. If one agrees with such a statement, he is in effect calling for a specific kind of behavior (often under specified circumstances) from someone (himself or another). This means that if this behavior is not forthcoming, there is a clear deviation from his normative definition. On the other hand, if one disagrees with such a statement, he is very probably not saying that a person should *not* behave in the specified

manner. He is rather probably indicating that it is not *necessary* for a
person to do so. For instance, if I agree with the statement: "Children
should give their parents financial help," and if I have children, I am
clearly implying that I think my children should give me financial
help. If they do not give me such help, they are violating my normative definition of our relationship. On the other hand, if I disagree
with that statement, it does not necessarily imply that I am normatively opposed to their giving me financial help; it more likely indicates that I do not think it is their obligation to do so. If they do not
give me financial help, of course, their failure to do so does not violate
my norms. But what if they *do* give me financial help? Is this a violation of my norms? Without making a complete analysis of the semantic
and philosophical implications of this question, it seems safe to state
that if we do call this a deviation from our normative definitions, it is of
a very different order than the first type noted above.

   We thus seem to have two rather different kinds of possible deviations from the normative definitions used in this study. The first kind,
which involves a failure on the part of the actor to perform an act
called for by the norm, will be referred to as a "counter-norm" deviation. The second kind, which involves the performance of an act
which is not called for by the norm, will be referred to as a "non-
norm" deviation.

   When we turn to the second matter, that of finding indications of
structural constraints which might help us understand the deviations
from normative definitions, the considerable dispersion of our subjects along a socio-economic continuum is useful. Although it is hardly
a wholly adequate index, the current or preretirement occupational
position of the husband is a useful indicator of variations in general
life style of our subjects. We know, for instance, that men and women
in the higher occupational groups are more likely to maintain organizational and other kinds of ties outside the family than are those in
lower occupational groups. They are thus more likely to have diverse
interests and activities than persons in other occupational groups. We
also may expect that in general the children of higher occupation
couples will be more mobile geographically than are those of other
couples and will not be as accessible for daily contact. In general, we
might expect that the "life space" of older persons in the higher occupation group is wider than that of other oldsters and generally involves more opportunities for extrafamilial activities. In that sense,
then, the social milieu in which the lower occupation oldster lives is
generally more "constraining" than that of other older persons. It also
seems reasonable to assume that those in lower occupations would be
both more likely to have need of assistance and have fewer resources
to provide it, or at least fewer financial resources.

   With this kind of logic in mind, then, the subjects of this study
were divided into three general groups according to the current or

preretirement occupation of the husband.[21] An examination was then made of the normative and behavioral patterns within each of these three groups. A report of the full details of this analysis would consume an unwarranted amount of space, but a general description of the patterns within the groups is in order. To simplify this description, a sketch of the top and bottom occupational groups will be presented, since in almost all characteristics the middle group was found to be between the other two.

Husbands and wives in the upper occupational group score relatively high on Task Sharing, but the husbands do not participate in household tasks any more than do those in other occupational groups. Thus, many cases occur in which both husband and wife reject the norm of task segregation (which is the form of the items in this scale), but the husband does not participate in household tasks to any great degree. The tendency is for the normative definitions of intergenerational relationships to fit the nuclear classification most frequently with relatively few in the extended type. The same is generally true at the behavioral level, this group having the highest proportion of cases in which the normative and behavioral intergenerational types are the same. However, the proportion scoring high on the Mutual Aid behavioral scale is not very different from those in the other occupational groups. Thus, although there *is* less propinquity of children in this group than in the others, there is not any great difference in mutual aid. Since their norms do not call for mutual aid, they have, relatively speaking, an excess of aid beyond that normatively prescribed. In fact, with regard to both division of labor and mutual aid, there is a higher non-norm/counter-norm ratio in this group than in any other. That is, when behavior does deviate from norms, it is less likely to involve a direct conflict between norm and behavior.

There is relatively low acceptance of Task Sharing by both husbands and wives in the lower occupation group, but, in spite of this, husbands are about equally likely to participate in household tasks as are husbands in the other two groups. Thus, the men often participate in the face of counter-norms. At both the normative and behavioral levels, there is a preponderance of the extended types and relatively few nuclear types. However, the Mutual Support behavioral scores are not notably different from those in the other groups. This group

[21]The three occupational subgroups used were: Upper (professional and higher management), Middle (white collar and skilled), Lower (semiskilled, service, and unskilled). Since most unskilled labor is carried out by Negroes in the industries covered in the study, the Lower group is composed almost entirely of semiskilled and service workers. Also, the Upper group is heavily weighted in the direction of professionals, about half of our sample in that category being doctors, lawyers, or college professors.

A similar analysis using retired-working as a control was also carried out. Although the retirees did participate more than the preretirees, the pattern of relationships between participation and behavioral family type was approximately the same. There were no notable differences.

has the lowest proportion of cases in which the normative and behavioral intergenerational types are identical. This is in part because this group also has the highest proportion of cases in the individuated behavioral type. Thus, although propinquity norms are generally adhered to, there is considerable deviation between norms of mutual aid and the actual behavior, and this deviation is again of the type involving counter-norm behavior.

We find, therefore, that there are two rather different patterns of norms, as well as different norm-behavior relationships in these occupational groups. Except for propinquity, however, there is little difference among them on the behavioral measure. Although deviations from norms occur in all three groups in rather sizeable proportions, there is a higher proportion of non-norm deviations in the upper occupational group and a higher proportion of counter-norm deviations in the lower group.

The interpretation of these findings suggested by the earlier discussion is in terms of situational constraints or breadth of life space. According to this interpretation, within the conjugal unit lower occupation husbands are viewed as having few alternatives to family participation in spite of their (and their wives') normative rejection of task sharing. With respect to intergenerational relations, one might turn to economic factors as an explanation and point to the probability that children of the lower occupation parents are not able to help them, nor are the parents financially able to help their children. It may very well be that such factors are quite relevant to the findings presented here.

Another kind of interpretation of these findings comes to mind, however, an interpretation which involves a dynamic very relevant to the body of literature on the changing structure of the American family system. This interpretation takes into account the probability of structural shifts through time and examines their probable effect on the kinds of data reported here.

If the general pattern of change in our society is as Parsons and others have indicated, it is toward the nuclear normative pattern. In terms of the operations used here, this is in the direction of fewer expectations with regard to propinquity and mutual aid and greater acceptance of task sharing. If, as the data presented here seem to indicate, this general pattern of change is most rapid in the higher occupational group of oldsters and least notable in the lower occupational group, certain expectations follow. We would expect, for instance, that those oldsters in upper occupational groups have reached a point on this continuum of shifting normative definitions nearer to that which is modal for younger members of our society (a point near the "nuclear" end of the continuum). We might expect, therefore, that such oldsters would espouse norms nearer to those espoused by their children than would be true of older members of lower occupational groups. That is, we would expect a greater normative gap between lower occupation oldsters (who would be expected to be nearer the "extended" end of the continuum) and their children (who would be expected to be nearer the "nuclear" end) than between upper occupation oldsters and their children. If this is true, and if an individual's behavior is likely at least to approximate the norms he espouses, the children of lower occupation oldsters would tend to behave in a way that directly contradicts the older persons' norms (counter-norm behavior). Similarly, the conjugal norms of such children would also be expected to deviate from those of their parents. On the other hand, we would expect the upper occupation group of oldsters to have children whose norms with regard to both conjugal and intergenerational relationships would be much more in accord with their own. These norms do not *require* intergenerational mutual aid, but they do not rule it out either. Thus, any children's behavior that deviates from the norms espoused by their parents in such cases is most likely to be non-norm behavior.

Although it goes well beyond the content of this very limited study, it may be worth suggesting that a more intensive analysis of such factors in the entire norm-behavior intergenerational system might lead to some clarification of the issues raised by the controversy over whether we are moving in a direction of a nuclear or a modified-extended family system. It seems reasonable to expect that a rather different picture of the system of relationships among the various family members would emerge, depending on whether we examine normative or behavioral indexes of these relationships. For instance, our modal pattern may be becoming a nuclear one at the normative level but a modified-extended one at the behavioral level. This would mean that increasingly deviations from norms would be in the non-norm direction rather than the counter-norm direction.

The evidence collected thus far clearly indicates that there is an impressive amount of intrafamilial mutual support in the form of friendly contact, services, and financial aid, even when the generations are separated by considerable distances. On the other hand, there is equally impressive evidence that most people, old and young alike, support the norm of nuclear family independence. This evidence is usually in the form of answers to attitude questions, and indicates that independence is the desired state, *if conditions permit.* Such findings seem to fit the kind of argument developed above. The norm appears to be one of maximizing independence by not *requiring* (for self or other) intergenerational assistance. It does not, on the other hand, rule out a willingness to assist (or accept assistance) if assistance is required.

Within this general pattern, however, we must also recognize the strong probability of there being considerable variation in norms, in patterns of behavior, and in the norm-behavior relationship. In order to investigate such patterns of relationship adequately, we must use the two-generational family network (at least) as our unit of analysis, rather than using samples of old people, or a probability sample of a neighborhood, or even couples of a single generation, as was done in this study. Most data on family relationships have been collected from persons in only one of the relevant statuses or at best from persons in the several statuses who are not necessarily connected to each other. As the limited data of this study indicate, the kind of intrapsychic relationship between two sets of norms may be, at least in part, a function of the interpersonal relationship within a significant sub-unit of the larger family. We would expect similar associations at both the intrapsychic and interpersonal levels when comprehensive data are available relevant to all significant members of the family.

summary

Through the use of data collected in interviews with husbands and wives having adult children, the adequacy of the following hypothesis has been examined:

A joint conjugal role-relationship will be found more often in association with a nuclear intergenerational relationship, and a segregated conjugal role relationship will be found more often in association with an extended intergenerational relationship; the conjugal relationship of couples with a modified-extended intergenerational relationship will be intermediate to those of the other two intergenerational types.

Both normative and behavioral data were used in this analysis. The hypothesis was supported by the normative but not by the behavioral data. An analysis of the relationships between these two types of data indicates that there is considerable deviation between normative definitions and actual behavior in the families studied. Some of the deviation is in direct opposition to normative definitions (counter-norm behavior), and some behavior is deviant in the sense that the normative definitions do not require it, but they do not oppose it (non-norm behavior). When the data are examined according to the occupational level of the husband, it is clear that there are differences in the normative-behavioral patterns of the three occupational groupings used. Among other things, there is more counter-norm behavior in the lower occupation group than in the other two. These differences are interpreted in terms of assumptions about the probable characteristics of the entire two-generational structure. It is suggested that analyses of total two-generation structures at both the normative and behavioral levels may shed further light on the controversy over what "is" the modal family pattern in our society.

decision making
and the
family life cycle

REUBEN HILL

The focus of this chapter concerns the decisions pertinent to the family in later life, the timing of these decisions, and the division of power within the family for making decisions. In fulfilling this assignment we draw upon the insights suggested by an emerging conceptual framework, the family development approach to family study, and we utilize some intergenerational research findings from the Minnesota Consumership Study of three generations which reflects this approach. We begin with a description of the conceptual framework and follow with some of the assertions it suggests about decision making at different points in the life cycle, concluding with a set of empirical findings comparing three generations of the same family lines in their decision making over a twelve-month period.

the conceptual framework of family development

The developmental approach is the youngest of seven conceptual frameworks used in family study identified by Hill and associates[1]

[1]Reuben Hill, Alvin M. Katz, and Richard Simpson, "An Inventory of Marriage and Family Research," *Marriage and Family Living*, XIX (February, 1957), 89-92.

through their Inventory of Research in Marriage and Family Behavior from the content analysis of several hundred pieces of research on marriage and the family published in America during the past thirty years. The analysis included search for the key concepts used, the foci peculiar to the approach, and the definitions of the family implied (if not explicitly given) by those using the approach. A recent article describes in some detail five of these frameworks, their properties, and the assumptions on which they have been built.[2] With the exception of the developmental, a basic shortcoming of all the frameworks analyzed to date has been their failure to cope systematically with the social time dimension. Where process concepts dealing with the dynamics of change were utilized, they failed to specify time in units appropriate to families and therefore had limited value in assembling generalizations about family change.

Properties of the Family Developmental Approach   The family development approach emphasizes the time dimension neglected by the other conceptual frameworks dealing with the family, but its focus is on the family as a small group, the nuclear family occupying a common household. The time units employed encompass the family life span expressed in stages of development but subdivided into years of marriage.

The approach is eclectic in its incorporation of the compatible sections of several other approaches to the study of the family. From rural sociology the family development theorists have borrowed the concept of stages of the family life cycle which they have greatly elaborated, giving the phasing of the life cycle a theoretical rationale. From child psychology and human development have come the concepts of developmental needs and tasks. From the sociologists engaged in work on the sociology of the professions we have borrowed the concepts of career, viewing the family as a convergence of inter-contingent careers of the positions of husband and wife, later of parents and children. From the structure-function and interactional schools has been borrowed the trio of concepts, position, role, and norms, particularly as these involve age and sex roles and changing family size. The many concepts associated with the family as a system of interacting personalities find their place in the modifications of the concept of role seen in role-playing, role-taking, reciprocity of roles, and role differentiation. These several concepts have been assembled together in a frame of reference that furnishes an opportunity for accretion of generalizations about the internal development of families from their formation in the engagement and wedding to their dissolution in divorce or death. The scope and organization of this framework may be described as follows:

[2]Reuben Hill and Donald A. Hansen, "The Identification of Conceptual Frameworks Utilized in Family Study," *Marriage and Family Living*, XXII (November, 1960), 299-311.

The family development approach views the family as a small group system, intricately organized internally into paired positions of husband-father, wife-mother, son-brother, and daughter-sister. Norms prescribing the appropriate role behavior for each of these positions specify how reciprocal relations are to be maintained, as well as how role behavior may change with changing ages of the occupants of these positions. This intimate small group has a predictable natural history, designated by stages beginning with the simple husband-wife pair and becoming more and more complex as members are added and new positions created, with the number of interpersonal relations reaching a peak with the birth of the last child, stabilizing for a brief period, to become less and less complex subsequently with the launching of adult children into jobs and marriage as the group contracts in size once again to the dyadic interactions of the husband-wife pair. As the age composition of the family changes, so do the age-role expectations for occupants of the positions in the family, and so does the quality of interaction among family members.

Viewed social psychologically and developmentally, the family is an arena of interacting personalities, each striving to obtain the satisfaction of his desires. Parents often defer the satisfaction of their own immediate needs, however, in building complementary roles between themselves and their children. At some stages of development, parents and children are good company; at other stages, their diverse developmental strivings may be strikingly incompatible.[3]

An immediate by-product of this conceptual framework has been its sensitizing effect upon researchers utilizing the family as the unit of study. Any research which seeks to generalize about families without taking into account the variation caused by the stages of family development represented in the sample will leave much variance unaccounted for, just as studies which ignore social class differences leave much unexplained. Buying patterns, saving patterns, and mobility patterns can be expected to vary greatly over the family life span, as will many other family behaviors as yet unassessed by family life-cycle categories.

Using the family developmental approach to behavior to analyze decision making in the family urges us to ask certain questions and to anticipate certain regularities. First of all, the approach divides the family cycle into stages of growth and development which have been demarcated by application of role theory to the changing positions in a family as it moves forward in time. The role content of the several positions in the family constitutes the *role complex* of the family at a given point in time. A stage of development would change, according to the framework, each time a fundamental change in the age role content in the positions making up the family occurs, or in other words each time the family's role complex changes.

[3]Reuben Hill, "Patterns of Decision Making and the Accumulation of Family Assets," *Household Decision Making*, Nelson Foote, ed. (New York: New York University Press, 1961), p. 63.

The theoretically most sophisticated schemes for differentiating stages of the family life span today utilize three sets of data as indicators of change in role complex:

A first criterion used for dividing up the life span is the observable "number of positions in the family," which permits inferring stages of "expansion," of "stability," and of "contraction" to be blocked off. Changes in stages of development (because fundamental changes in role complex occur) would be required by the birth of the first child, launching of first child into marriage, and launching of last child.

A second criterion involves the age composition of the family, which reflects indirectly the *family's complex of age role expectations in reciprocity* at any one time in the history of the family. This criterion requires that a stage be changed each time the role complex changes in any degree. If we were engaged in undertaking case studies of individual families, this procedure would be most interesting to follow, but in seeking to differentiate stages of development for large numbers of families it would be highly impractical to designate a new stage each time the complex of age role expectations changed, since there would be almost as many different combinations of stages (family careers) as there are families in the study. Duvall, reflecting the judgments of the various committees working on the problem since 1948, chose a simpler solution to the problem in her text.[4] She suggests that it is sufficient to change stages of development each time the oldest child shifts from one significant age category to another. Of all the children, to be sure, the oldest child's development is the most significant for the shift in role content in the parents' positions, since his experiences present new and different problems which as yet the family has not encountered and bring about the most modification of role content in all other positions in the family. The significant age categories in which changes would be expected to occur in our society include: infant, preschool child, school child, adolescent, young adult, middle-aged adult, and aged adult.

A third criterion involves the change in the age role content in the husband-father position which occurs with his retirement from active employment. For the mother who has not been gainfully employed, her retirement from active mothering occurs with the launching of her last child into marriage and is captured in the shift in the family's role complex from the launching center to the post-parental stage.

Employing these three sets of readily available data of numbers of positions in the family, age composition of the family, and employment status of the father, several stages of the family life span can be differentiated, each representing a distinctive role complex, as follows: Stage I Establishment (newly married, childless); II New Parents (infant-3 years); III Preschool Family (child 3-6 years and possi-

[4]Evelyn M. Duvall, *Family Development* (Philadelphia: J. B. Lippincott Co., 1962).

bly younger siblings); IV School-Age Family (oldest child 6-12 years, possibly younger siblings); V Family with Adolescent (oldest 13-19, possibly younger siblings); VI Family with Young Adult (oldest 20, until first child leaves home); VII Family as Launching Center (from departure of first to last child); VIII Post-parental Family, The Middle Years (after children have left home until father retires); IX Aging Family (after retirement of father).

Some Generalizations Which Flow From the Framework. The view of the stages of the family life cycle as distinctive role complexes opens up the way for anticipating the content of family interaction for each of these stages. If we begin by looking at the focus of this conference on the aging family, we can readily see that the aged generation will be disproportionately found in Stage IX, with some representatives still in Stage VIII. The numerical composition of the family for both of these stages, in contrast with those which preceded them, is simple and stable — two positions with only one interpersonal relationship to maintain, a companionate dyad. This can be quite a contraction for large families. For the family of ten persons in which the author grew up, for example, there was a contraction from forty-five interpersonal relationships, which constituted the number the author's parents coped with before launching their eight children into jobs and marriage, to one in the post-parental period. The parental role content of the two positions which are left in the family in the post-parental stage (Stage VIII), as opposed to the spousal role content, is in the process of continuous redefinition, and by the time the couple enters Stage IX, almost fourteen years later, the nurturant, guiding, and socializing content will have largely disappeared in favor of a more symmetrical set of norms of mutual aid and reciprocity in exchanges between the generations.

The stages of family development are suggestive also of contrasts in needs, in volume of plans, and in willingness to take risks in the form of purchases and other commitments which affect the direction of decisions in the family. At the beginning of the family's life span, in Stages I-IV, the family tends to be future oriented, living with rapidly expanding needs for shelter spaces, for facilities, durable goods, and means of transportation. Needs press heavily on resources as the ratio of dependents to earners mounts, and we would accordingly expect that the volume of plans and decisions to make residential moves, to remodel, to purchase goods, to change jobs, and to purchase protective insurances to be very high. We would also expect concomitantly that the willingness to accept help from kin and peers as well as the utilization of credit from commercial sources would also be greater than at any other period in the life span.

In Stages V-VI, the stages of rearing school-age and adolescent children, we would expect the family to be more oriented to the here and now, to have achieved some equilibrium of interaction, but to be still heavily pressed with high needs for housing and added facilities.

In Stage VII, the stage of launching children into jobs and marriage, the family undergoes maximum contraction in size and experiences an irregular but slow decline in pressure of needs on resources. In many families the wife-mother has returned to the labor force, providing a double income to equalize the costs of higher education and of marrying off the children. The uncertainties and ambiguities of in-law roles and of grandparental roles are introduced into the positions of the family heads during this period. There are also complications of establishing mutually agreeable helping patterns for the newly married children through gift giving, exchanges, and loans.

In Stage VIII the family enters a stage of recovery financially, often with two earners, with disposable income for the first time since Stage I. The disposable income may be invested for retirement, but may also be turned to upgrading the level of living of the post-parental couple and helping both married offspring and their own aged parents. For some mothers it is a period of retirement from the protective roles that have been central to the career of wife and mother, so that they experience many of the adjustments to loss of functions which the breadwinner experiences at retirement. Mothers who have entered the labor force, on the other hand, experience the adjustments of loss of functions when retiring from their jobs years later. We would expect for the family as a whole that this would be a period of continued high volume of economic activity and, therefore, of decision making.

In Stage IX, with both spouses retired, we expect a net change in the direction of giving, restrictions on the helping of married offspring who are now economically established, and a reversal of roles with the aged receiving more help than they give. There will be sharply restricted economic activity over the years which remain. In this stage particularly we would expect the family to be more oriented to the past, making accordingly fewer attempts to structure the future.

From the standpoint of decision making, then, the framework has suggested a number of regularities which are relevant while leaving room for the discovery of many others. It has suggested that the sheer volume of economic activity will rise rapidly at the beginning of the life span of the family, level off, and then decline. Indeed, that is probably the excuse to call the family life span a life cycle, since so many behaviors are of this order: residential mobility, occupational mobility, complexities of family interaction owing to changing plurality patterns, and so on. Long-term as against short-run type planning will be expected to appear more in the early than in the middle and late stages of family development because of the different time orientations of the generations.

The framework does not tell us anything about the relative success the families will have in preplanning their economic activities at various points in the life span, nor whether families will be more or less rational in their decision making at the beginning, in the middle, or at the end of the life span. The framework tells us little indeed about expected changes in power allocation or the allocation of duties in the family over the life span, although some empirical studies using the framework have advanced some findings on these issues.[5] These are among the discoveries we can anticipate in studying families empirically by stages of development.

empirical findings

To answer the questions raised in this paper we should ideally have available longitudinal data on decision making over the entire life span of a cohort of couples who entered marriage in the same year. No such data have ever been collected in the history of family research, in part because of the cost and continuity of research organization required. The few data that we do have were collected in synthetic longitudinal studies of various types drawn from cross-sectional samples. A sample of couples of different durations of marriage is interviewed and the resulting responses aggregated as if they were drawn from a marital cohort moving over time. The study of decision making by Blood and Wolfe is of this type.[6] They demonstrate that the husband's power in the family structure increases from the honeymoon period, Stage I, where there are no children, to Stage II-III with young children, and declines slowly through the various subsequent stages of family development into the post-parental period, Stage VIII, after which it drops sharply as the husband retires in Stage IX. In recent years this same device of aggregating cross-sectional samples to construct the life cycle of families has been widely carried out in making generalizations about consumer behavior: the timing of home ownership, automobile ownership, the acquisition of television sets, automatic dryers, and so on.[7] The hazards of generalizing from such synthetic longitudinal studies have been covered in some detail elsewhere in which the author discusses the relative advantages and disadvantages of five methodological short cuts that have been devised to circumvent the costs and travail of longitudinal research with families.[8]

In this paper we turn to the least unsatisfactory set of data availa-

---

[5]See especially the summary of this area of research by James M. Rollins, "Two Empirical Tests of a Parsonian Theory of Family Authority Patterns," *The Family Life Coordinator*, XII (January-April, 1963), 13, and Tables III and V, 20.

[6]Robert O. Blood, Jr. and Donald M. Wolfe, *Husbands and Wives* (New York: Free Press of Glencoe, Inc., 1960), pp. 41-44.

[7]See, for example, the several chapters on the issue in *Consumer Behavior*, Vol. II, *The Life Cycle and Consumer Behavior*, Lincoln H. Clark, ed. (New York: New York University Press, 1955), 28-58, 61-66.

[8]Reuben Hill, "Methodological Issues in Family Development Research," *Family Process* (in press).

ble about decision making over the life cycle. We are drawing from data obtained from an intergenerational sample and are treating the data obtained from the youngest of three generations as representative of the early stages of the cycle, the data from the parent generation as representative of the middle stages, and the responses from the grandparent generation as depicting the last stages of development. By placing findings of the other two generations in juxtaposition with those from the grandparent generation, we can gain some idea of the distinguishing characteristics of decision making among older couples. The findings we cite are valuable in their own right but should be used cautiously when generalizing about changes in decision making over the life cycle. It would be more defensible to refer to our findings as changes in decision making over three generations.

The data which we shall use for an empirical description of decision making have been collected as part of the Minnesota Consumership Study. The areas of planning and decision making covered included eight recurring problems requiring long-range planning and fairly elaborate decision making: residential location, redecoration, remodeling, acquisition of durable goods and of automobiles, changes in the family's financial portfolio in savings, investments, insurance, provisions for retirement, and changes of occupation (change of job by husband, entering or leaving labor force by wife). Methods of data collection have included four semistructured interviews with wives, one joint interview with both spouses, tests and questionnaires filled out by both spouses, and direct observation of stress situations by interviewers.

The choice of intact families drawn from three generations of the same family line assures us relative homogeneity of family culture. Moreover, it provides us with three contrast groups to highlight the differences in decision making over the life span. A description of the families selected will make this even clearer.

selection of families

An intergenerational sample of intact families linked through three generations living within fifty miles of Minneapolis-St. Paul was obtained from area probability samples of the metropolitan area. Three hundred and twelve nuclear families, composed of 100 grandparent families, 105 parent families, and 107 young married families, survived four waves of interviews covering a year's observations. These families are ecologically dispersed within the metropolitan area and its hinterland; they are well distributed by social class and economic levels, but are somewhat more stable residentially than comparable families without three-generation linkages. The three generations have the following characteristics:

1. Age: Grandparents 60-80; parents 40-60; married children 20-30.

2. Ethnic make-up: Grandparents, 1/4 Scandinavian, 1/2 other Northern European, balance Southern European; parents and children, similar.

3. Religious affiliation: 1/3 Catholic, 2/3 Protestant (Lutheran dominant), some Jewish. High continuity of religious affiliation from generation to generation.

4. Income: Grandparents, $1,000 to $6,000; 1/2 under $2,000
    Parents, $1,000 to $20,000; 1/2 under $5,000
    Married children, $2,000 to $10,000; 1/2 under $4,000.

5. Children in residence: Grandparents, no children at home; parents, 2/3 with children still at home; married children, 1/10 no children yet, 2/3 with children all below school age, 1/5 with children of school age under 12 years of age.

From the descriptive statements about the generations given above, we can see that the three generations do present contrast groups which may be viewed developmentally as well as intergenerationally. The married child generation is concentrated in Stages II-IV, Families with Infants, Preschool, and School-Age Children; the parent generation has, of course, already launched at least one child so is found heavily represented in Stage VII, The Family as Launching Center (71 per cent), and Stage VIII, The Post-parental Family (24 per cent); the grandparent generation is found entirely in the very last stage of retirement, Stage IX, with two-thirds of its couples in the 71-80-year age bracket. Because of the system of drawing this sample by generations, we have very few families in Stage V, Families with Adolescents, and Stage VI, Families with Young Adults. For the purposes of this paper the contrasts of life in the different sectors of the life cycle are sharper, however, than if we had drawn a more representative sample. Having three generations of the same family line assures us that the differences noted over the life span are more likely to be developmental differences than class or educational differences.

With this background let us turn to the performance of the three generations over a twelve-month period in 1958 to highlight the similarities and differences found among the three generations. We begin with a comparative picture of the financial and housing constraints operative on the three generations, as well as the types of problems perceived as requiring help over the twelve-month period. Second, we shall examine the location of power in decision making and degree of differentiation of sex roles by generation. Third, our research design permits us to examine within several areas of activity the volume of plans enunciated and actions taken, the planning horizons, the proportion of plans fulfilled, the degree of rationality in decision making, and the degree of satisfaction expressed with the actions taken. Our empirical overview will conclude with some of the correlates of planning, rationality, and satisfaction in the grandparent generation.

situational constraints affecting decision making

We must remember that each of the three generations has had a different history before entering the twelve-month period of observation. The grandparent generation is educationally, occupationally, and financially handicapped compared with the younger generations. Educationally grandfathers averaged 6 years of schooling, fathers 9 years, and grandsons 12.6 years. Occupationally the grandfathers began lowest on the scale and have made the slowest movement upward. There has been an acceleration of occupational upgrading generation by generation when each is compared year by year since marriage. In each successive generation, more of the wives have worked during the first several years of marriage and more have returned to work after their children grew up. In all economic matters we can say that the married child generation is destined to outstrip the previous generations based on the achievements of each generation during the first ten years of marriage. In home ownership the married child generation has already exceeded the grandparent generation (80 per cent homeowners) and is where the parent generation was only after twenty years of marriage. In acquisition of durable goods the married child generation has overtaken the grandparent generation and is at a point in its inventory where the parent generation was after thirty-five years of marriage—the same can be said for bathroom and bedroom spaces in the home and other amenities. This has not been done at the expense of protective insurances or retirement provisions, for the married child generation is well along in the acquisition of a portfolio of insurances and investments. Over 50 per cent have retirement provisions over and beyond Social Security and 95 per cent have life insurance. This married child generation starts its marriage with 82 per cent covered, which is higher than their grandparents ever reached, and is as high as their parents achieved after thirty years of marriage.

As predicted from our family development theory, the pressure of members on resources is greatest in the early stages of the life cycle. As the study began, the married children had the most children resident in the home (two) and had the fewest rooms per family (4.6). Grandparents had no children and had the next highest number of rooms (4.9). The parent generation had the most rooms (5.6) with two thirds of the families having a child still at home. In quality of housing,however, grandparents had the lowest ratal values, and more of them lived in the lowest grade neighborhoods, two thirds in Class C and Class D areas compared with 50 per cent among the parent generation.

We earlier indicated substantial differences in average income and in the range of income among the three generations, with grandparents averaging below-subsistence incomes (one-half under $2,000). We asked families for their subjective definition of the adequacy of their current income in terms of its sufficiency to buy necessities and luxuries. Table 6-1 tabulates the responses of the three

table 6-1   percentage distribution of responses
on adequacy of family income by generation

responses	grandparents per cent	parents per cent	married children per cent
Total	100.0	100.0	100.0
Do without many needed things	28.0	4.7	1.2
Have the things we need, but none of the extras	23.5	5.9	4.8
Have the things we need, and a few of the extras	30.5	61.0	76.0
Have the things we need, and any extras we want	3.5	14.2	16.8
Have the things we need and any extras we want, and still have money left over to save or invest	14.5	14.2	1.2
Number of families	85	85	83

generations in percentage form and suggests that the grandparent generation feels the financial squeeze more than the other two generations. Half of them are barely meeting the necessities, but 14.5 per cent are on easy street.[9] Three-fourths of the married child group checked the median expression, "We have the things we need and a few of the extras." Only one couple in this generation, however, feels really "flush." The parents are not only factually better off (in income, housing, and durable goods), but they feel more comfortable, distributing their answers towards the luxury end of the scale.

Degree of Interdependence for Mutual Aid   We have indicated earlier in this chapter that family development theory anticipates some reversals in dependency-interdependency relations among the generations by stage of development. In the last of the four interviews respondents in each generation were asked to give an accounting of help given and received during the year from all sources including immediate and extended kin, peers, church, social agencies, private specialists, and commercial sources in the problem areas of illness, child care, household management, emotional gratification, and economic assistance.

When examined by vulnerability to problems requiring help, the parent generation was lowest in vulnerability (44.7 per cent receiving no help of a stressor problem-area nature); the grandparent generation was next lowest (32.9 per cent receiving no help due to crises). The

[9]The responses of the grandparent generation are somewhat comparable to the findings for Grand Rapids, Michigan, where a survey of people sixty and over reported about the adequacy of their income to meet their needs as follows: 15 per cent couldn't make ends meet, 66 per cent had just enough to get along on, and 15 per cent had more than was needed. At the affluent end of the scale, it will be seen both populations have about 15 per cent who have more than they need. At the depressed end, the Minneapolis sample has a higher proportion in poverty. See Richard M. Williams, "Changing Status, Roles, and Relationships," *Handbook of Social Gerontology*, Clark Tibbitts, ed. (Chicago: University of Chicago Press, 1961), pp. 283-84.

married child generation with its infant-age dependents was most vulnerable (only 21 per cent receiving no help of a crisis nature during the year).[10]

The three generations reported an involvement in a vast nexus of transfers of one sort or another during the year, over five thousand, of which 3,781 were quite clearly help exchanges. Table 6-2 has been prepared to demonstrate the social networks within which help is exchanged. First of all, we note that help exchanges within the vertical kin (giving and receiving help, other generations) exceeds all other categories in the social networks for each of the generations. This is especially true for the grandparents for whom 65 per cent of the instances of help received was familial (from children, the parent generation, or grandchildren) compared with 53 per cent for the parent generation and 44 per cent for the married grandchildren. The child generation operates in a wider flung network of exchanges with a less concentrated pattern especially of giving within the vertical kin line (only 28 per cent) and giving proportionately more than the other

table 6-2   comparison of help instances given to help instances received by generation and by various sources over a year's period*

generation	source or recipient	per cent of help instances: given	per cent of help instances: received	total instances of help
	Total	100	100	
	Other generations	47	65	521
Grandparent	Peers	15	16	148
	Horizontal and vertical kin once removed	9	8	80
	All other agencies	29	10	206
		N = 574	381	955
	Total	100	100	
	Other generations	44	53	637
Parent	Peers	17	21	246
	Horizontal and vertical kin once removed	14	20	212
	All other agencies	25	6	252
		N = 890	457	1347
	Total	100	100	
	Other generations	28	44	516
Married children	Peers	22	20	316
	Horizontal and vertical kin once removed	25	27	380
	All other agencies	25	9	267
		N = 844	635	1479
	Total instances of help	2308	1473	3781

*Per cents may not total 100 due to rounding.

[10]We are indebted to Robert Macdonald for the analysis and interpretation of these data on intergenerational exchanges. His doctoral thesis has been built from the data collected in the fourth wave of interviews of this research. See Robert Macdonald, "Intergenerational Family Helping Patterns," Ph.D. thesis, University of Minnesota, 1964.

generations to horizontal and vertical kin once removed (siblings, cousins, aunts, uncles, nieces, and nephews), 25 per cent compared to 14 per cent for the parent generation and only 9 per cent for the grandparents. To all other sources (religious organizations, health and welfare agencies, and other specialists), the grandparents give proportionately the most (29 per cent) followed by the other two generations at 25 per cent each. Age mates are least likely to be recipients of help for the parent and child generation, whereas for the aged generation the horizontal and vertical kin once removed are least seen as targets for help.

In general we note that help instances given exceed those received for all generations and for virtually all categories of the social network. The level of giving is highest for the parent generation and lowest for the grandparents. The child generation leads in volume of receiving as might be expected, given its heavy needs.

table 6-3   comparison of help received and help given by generation for chief problem areas*

	economic		emotional gratification		household management		child care		illness	
	gave	received	gave	received	gave	received	gave	received	gave	received
	per cent	per cent	per cent	per cent	per cent	per cent	per cent	per cent	per cent	per cent
Total	100	100	100	100	100	100	100	100	100	100
Grandparents	26	34	23	42	21	52	16	0	32	61
Parents	41	17	47	37	47	23	50	23	21	21
Married children	34	49	31	21	33	25	34	78	47	18

*Per cents may not total 100 due to rounding.

In Table 6-3 we have looked much more intensively at the 1,674 exchanges which occurred exclusively among the three generations by type of help provided or received. The parent generation, within this narrower network, is again the most active in giving help and the married child generation the most frequent recipient of help. The grandparent generation both gave and received least of the three generations in help items of all kinds. The parent generation is the sociometric star of the interchanges, giving more to the married children and to the grandparents than either gives to the other. The parent generation also receives in exchange more from the grandparents and from the married children than either grandparents or grandchildren receive in their interchanges. By area of need grandparents required more help in the problem of illness (61 per cent), household management (52 per cent), and emotional gratification (42 per cent), whereas the married child generation received help especially in the problem areas of child care (78 per cent) and of economic assistance (49 per cent).

Perhaps the most interesting findings in Table 6-3 are those which compare percentages receiving and giving help in five categories by generation. The parent generation quite clearly gives more help than it receives in all five areas of exchange. The grandparents, in sharp contrast, receive substantially more help than they give in all areas except child care where they have, obviously, no need of help. The married child generation gives more than it receives in three areas — emotional gratification, household management, and illness. This generation, on the other hand, receives more than it gives in the economic-assistance and child-care areas. We get from this table a most interesting picture of changes in symbiosis over the generations. In the beginning of the life span the married child generation is apparently quite willing to receive various kinds of help and perceives itself more or less in equilibrium in its giving and receiving. It appears to benefit more from exchanges that are reciprocal than does the grandparent generation. The grandparents perceive themselves as both meager givers and high receivers, almost in a *dependency status,* whereas the parent generation, in contrast, is high in giving and modest in receiving, a *patron-type status.* Only the married child generation appears high both in giving and receiving, a *status* of *high reciprocity* and *interdependence* within its social network.

With this further evidence of the differences among the generations in the patterns of needs and interdependency, which point up the parent generation as the more affluent, the more supportive, and the more sustaining, and the younger and older generations in greater need, let us turn briefly to the differences in family structure in the division of power in decision making and in the allocation of family tasks.

marital power structure and decision making

Two expressions of family role structure are currently viewed as relevant for identifying the locus of power in a family: who makes the decisions, and who performs specified services within the family. The first is the marital authority pattern and the second the division of labor pattern.

We obtained two appraisals of the locus of power in decision making. In one we asked the spouses to indicate who usually makes the final decision with respect to six problems: what house or apartment to take, how much life insurance and what types, whether the wife shall work gainfully, whether the husband changes his job, whether a doctor is called when a family member is ill, and where to spend vacations. The responses were scored in such a way that husband-centeredness, wife-centeredness, and equalitarian patterns can be identified in decision making.[11] Interviewers, in a joint interview with

[11]For the system of scoring see the discussion in Blood and Wolfe, *Husbands and Wives, op. cit.,* p. 21.

both spouses, were also asked to record data which would permit classifying the families with respect to authority patterns. They recorded who did most of the talking, who exercised most influence, and who seemed to have the last word in a series of problems posed to families. The results are shown in Table 6-4.

table 6-4   percentage distribution of families on authority patterns in husband-wife relations by generation

authority pattern	self-reported			observer reported		
	married child	parent	grand-parent	married child	parent	grand-parent
Total	100	100	100	100	100	100
Husband-centered	15	12	22	40	24	34
Equalitarian	80	82	69	42	47	28
Wife-centered	5	6	9	18	29	38
Number of families	107	100	94	96	90	74

The findings by Blood and Wolfe cited earlier suggest that the husband is more active in decision making when the children are very young, because he is involved also much more in performing home-centered child-care duties which he gradually drifts out of as the children mature and his occupational demands become greater.[12] This would account for the decrease in husband dominance over most of the family cycle and the upturn in the post-parental period, but would not account for the sharp drop in husband power in retirement. Our findings from the interviewer's reports do show both a decline in husband dominance from the early stages represented by the married child generation and an increase in wife dominance into the last stage of the cycle. Equalitarianism appears especially modest in the grandparent generation compared with the earlier stages of development. We should note that the observers' reports identified much less equalitarianism and substantially more wife-centeredness in all three generations than the self-reports. It would be particularly hazardous to generalize self-reported patterns for the different stages of the life cycle, since the ideologies about marital power have been changing so radically over the period represented by the respondents that we may be getting differences in beliefs about what "ought to be" rather than a valid description about what are the patterns of authority in the family.

Role Allocation Patterns   Historically, there has been a clear-cut division of tasks and responsibilities by gender within the family. The husband has traditionally been the breadwinner and keeper of the family purse, has worked in the yard, and has done the repair jobs around the house, and the wife has been the housekeeper, cook, and nurse. With many wives now gainfully employed, husbands in contemporary families have been involved in crossing the sex line to

[12]*Ibid.*, pp. 41-44.

undertake housekeeping tasks formerly done only by women, and wives have shared yard work and finances, thus creating a fluidity of role allocation and considerably more sharing of tasks together.

Examination of Table 6-5 suggests that specialization (jobs done exclusively by one spouse alone) increases over the life span, with the married child generation least specialized and the grandparent generation highest in complete segregation of the spouses in the performance of tasks. Flexibility is most characteristic of the youngest generation.

Role conventionality (division of labor with men doing only men's work and women doing only women's work), by contrast, is less frequently practiced by the three generations, with much crossing of sex lines and even reversals of traditional roles. Nevertheless, there is greater conventionality as we move over the life span from the married child generation to the grandparent generation, with the number of conventional couples more than double those in the earlier stages of the cycle. Not to be outdone, however, the grandparent generation is also heavily represented in the couples that are most unconventional, with both husband and wife crossing the sex line and/or completely reversing the conventional roles by reversing the division of labor. These so-called role reversals may possibly occur during periods in which one spouse or the other is sick and cannot perform their usual roles. With both spouses retired, there is also more time and opportunity to try out opposite gender roles.

table 6-5   percentage distribution of families by generation on role specialization and role conventionality

	married child	parent	grandparent
Role Specialization			
Total	100	100	100
High specialization, both spouses always do certain household tasks	57	65	78
Medium specialization, spouses usually but not always do the same specified tasks	37	29	14
Low specialization, great shifting about in who does tasks	6	6	8
Role Conventionality			
Total	100	100	100
Both conventional in doing sex-typed tasks, and/or wife conventional with husband only crossing the line	17	21	42
Husband conventional, wife crossing line, and/or both crossing line	70	62	32
Combinations of unconventionality: both crossing line and systematic role reversals	13	17	26
Number of Families	107	100	98

decision-making patterns by generation

Let us turn now to the observations recorded in the economic activities of the three generations during the twelve months of the study. They may be conceptualized as falling into the four phases of a consumption cycle beginning with the identification of unmet needs in the form of plans (Phase 1), an intervening process of decision making in choosing the best course of action (Phase 2), followed by an action of purchase or residence move or job change (Phase 3), ending with an evaluation of the adequacy of the action as satisfying or dissatisfying (Phase 4).

Respondents were asked on the first, second, and third interviews of the panel whether the family was seriously considering moving, acquiring an automobile or any of twenty-four different durable goods, making a job change, doing any remodeling or redecorating, or making any major changes in their financial portfolio of insurances, investments, or savings. If the answer was affirmative, the respondent was then asked if he had a definite time in mind for the action. This gave the planning horizon: within three months, four to six months, seven to nine months, ten to twelve months, more than twelve months, or no definite time. Responses in the category "within three months" were classified "immediate plans," within the categories four to twelve months "longer plans," in contrast to those in the category "no definite time," which were classified as "indefinite plans."

Plans were voiced during the year of the study about as frequently as action occurred during the same year. However, not all planners acted, nor did all actors plan. During the second, third, and fourth interviews, respondents were asked what actions they had taken during the period intervening since the previous interview. If plans and actions differed, either as to content or timing, an explanation was sought for the discrepancy.

Volume of Plans and Actions   Table 6-6 provides a summary tabulation of the number of plans and actions by areas of activity and by generation. Differences in total volume of plans made by the three generations are striking and follow precisely the order hypothesized earlier from family development theory. The child generation expressed 677 plans of all kinds during the year of the study, the parents 482 plans, and the grandparents 229 plans. This greater propensity of the child generation to verbalize wants as purchase plans is highest in durable goods, where it is twice as great as in the parent generation and seven times the volume of such plans in the grandparent generation. Intergenerational differences in volume of plans were least in the financial and remodeling-redecorating areas, but even here the children consistently led, the grandparents consistently lagged. In three areas—automobile, financial, and remodeling-redecorating—the parents resembled their married children in volume of plans. In three they did not—these were plans for durable acquisitions and for resi-

table 6-6   numbers of plans and actions
by areas of activity and by generation

areas of activity	grandparents		parents		children		total	
	plans	actions	plans	actions	plans	actions	plans	actions
Durables acquisitions								
Number	29	53	101	118	206	148	336	319
Average per family	.29	.53	.97	1.12	1.92	1.38	1.1	1.0
Automobile acquisitions								
Number	8	3	37	40	44	45	89	88
Average per family	.08	.03	.35	.38	.41	.42	.30	.30
Residential moves								
Number	23	9	27	8	76	37	126	54
Average per family	.23	.09	.26	.08	.71	.35	.40	.20
Occupational changes								
Number	6	10	6	26	30	55	42	91
Average per family	.06	.10	.06	.25	.28	.51	.10	.30
Financial changes								
Number	74	51	135	108	139	145	348	304
Average per family	.74	.51	1.28	1.03	1.30	1.35	1.1	1.0
Remodeling-redecorating								
Number	89	54	176	100	182	113	447	267
Average per family	.89	.54	1.68	.95	1.70	1.05	1.4	0.9
Total								
Number	229	180	482	400	677	543	1388	1123
Average per family	2.3	1.8	4.6	3.8	6.4	5.0	4.4	3.6
N =	100		105		107		312	

dential and occupational change. In the two latter areas, they are virtually as stable and settled as the grandparents.

From family development theory we have anticipated that the
content of plans will vary over the life span — more acquiring, moving,
and job changes in the beginning of the cycle; more attempts to make
present quarters over in the older generation. Examining the grandparent generation's announcement of plans more closely for content,
we note that changes contemplated were highest in reworking the
housing arrangements by remodeling or redecorating or by changing
residence completely. Closely approximating these changes were
changes in the financial portfolio. The grandparents anticipated more
changes than occurred as did the other two generations, but in the area
of durable goods acquisitions the grandparents actually acquired more
items than they planned to. This looks like impulsive behavior, but as
we shall see later in joining individual plans with the fulfilling of
plans, many of the grandparents' acquisitions came as unanticipated
gifts.

Despite the fact that actions may outnumber plans in specific generations and specific areas, it is apparent that the child generation not
only makes more plans but also takes action more frequently than the
two older generations in every area recorded. The grandparent generation is mildly active in only three areas — durables, financial, and
remodeling-redecorating — and even here does not come close to the
level maintained by the two younger generations.

Types of Plans Made   In Table 6-7 the numbers of plans of various types for each generation occurring during the planning intervals have been aggregated. Certain small but consistent differences are apparent. The child generation is more likely to assign a definite point in time to intended actions, including purchases. The proportion of all its plans that are definite is 61 per cent for the youngest generation and somewhat less for the other two generations, as is also shown in this table.

table 6-7   types of plans made, by generation,
six areas of activity, aggregated

	total		grandparents		parents		children	
	number	per cent	number	per cent	number	per cent	number	per cent
All plans	1388	100	229	100	482	100	677	100
Definite plans	816	58	126	55	276	57	414	61
Immediate plans	452	32	78	34	160	33	214	32
Longer-run plans	364	26	48	21	116	24	200	29
Indefinite plans	572	42	103	45	206	43	263	39
Ratios								
Definite plans: Indefinite plans	1.45		1.21		1.35		1.55	
Immediate plans: Longer-run plans	1.24		1.62		1.44		1.07	
N =	312		100		105		107	

The ratio of definite plans to indefinite plans places the child generation at the top, the parent generation in the middle, and the grandparent generation at the bottom in relative commitment to undertake actions in the future. The ratio of immediate plans to longer-run plans, on the other hand, qualifies this impression, since among definite planners the grandparent generation has the shortest horizon and the parents next. As we hypothesized earlier from family development theory, plans of the child generation are more frequently of a longer horizon, suggesting that they are more confident of their capacity to realize these plans even if they are less sure of how long it will take. As families age, both confidence and time perspective may diminish, while knowledge and realism about what is feasible increase.

Plan Fulfillment   The payoff in analyzing the characteristics of plans is to discover which types of plans carry over most consistently into actions and how the generations compare in their relative success in this regard. Table 6-8 demonstrates clearly the higher predictiveness of definite plans over indefinite plans in all three generations. Definite plans are twice as likely to carry over into action as indefinite plans in each of the three generations. Among definite plans, those which are immediate, having horizons of three months or less, are about three times more likely to be fulfilled than longer-run plans.

table 6-8   plan fulfillment ratios by types of plans and by generation

planning completion ratios	total	grandparents	parents	children
Definite plans fulfilled: Definite plans	.39	.48	.37	.39
Immediate plans fulfilled: Immediate plans	.58	.67	.53	.57
Longer-run plans fulfilled: Longer-run plans	.22	.22	.21	.22
Indefinite plans fulfilled: Indefinite plans	.19	.26	.17	.18
Total plans fulfilled: total plans	.31	.37	.29	.31

By generation, it is apparent that the grandparent generation, which made the fewest plans and took the fewest actions, fulfilled the highest proportion of its plans; the parent generation, which showed a moderate number of both plans and actions, fulfilled the lowest proportion of plans. The distribution of types of plans made by the grandparents probably accounts in part for its greater success in following through on its enunciated plans. The grandparent generation makes its best record with immediate plans, of which two-thirds are carried out.

The two younger generations are more like each other in their performance than either is like the grandparents. The parents' poor fulfillment record may reflect a different style of planning, supported by their significantly greater discretionary income, compared with the other two generations. The parent generation has fewer needs and can take actions without prior planning because of its greater income, so it appears more frequently as acting without advance planning. The child generation has a high level of needs; these needs are salient enough to be verbalized frequently into plans, which are then carried into action. The grandparent generation has fewer pressing needs, but its income is so low that it must be more circumspect in planning.

An explanation of the greater rate of fulfillment of the grandparents' plans may lie in their distribution among types of plans and among areas of activity. Turning back to Table 6-5, we see that this generation has few plans for acquiring automobiles or durable goods, where the fulfillment rates appear to be lower than in other areas of activity, and concentrates more in remodeling-redecorating and in residential changes, where fulfillment rates are generally higher. Examination of the fulfillment rates of the plans of the grandparent generation in these latter areas of activity shows them indeed to run several per cent higher than those of the other two generations, particularly where the plans are definite rather than indefinite. Thus the grandparent generation's record in plan fulfillment is partly accounted for by its propensity for a lower volume of planning and actions, partly by the types of plans which it enunciates, and partly by the areas of economic activity in which it has been most active.

Rationality in Decision Making Intervening between the enunciation of a plan and the follow-through of the action taken is a choice-making process, namely, the process of choosing and deciding on the appropriate actions to be taken in implementing the plan expressed. We have attempted to scale this process on the dimension of rationality by specifying the indicators of rationality in decision making and arraying them in a score which ranges from zero to eight. For every action taken during the year the family was asked to show what had been done before taking action to assure the best outcome possible. The several steps taken were arrayed by the frequency with which they were taken, from those which were taken by most families through to those taken by only a few. For example, let us illustrate the steps which indicated rationality. Most actions were taken on the information members within the immediate family circle were able to provide. Fewer families actually went to the next step of seeking alternatives, fewer yet had a set family policy, while the last item to scale, or the item the fewest families answered positively, was the seeking of information from experts outside the immediate family. From this array it appears that the family first utilizes its immediate members as sources of information, evaluates the costs, and finally projects the outcomes of the alternatives they propose. Only as a last step does the family leave the home to seek alternatives.

Table 6-9 presents the distribution of scale types among the three generations based upon the extent to which the actions taken by them were preceded by activities of high rationality or low rationality in arriving at a decision. The grandparent generation is lowest on rationality, with an average score of 4.61. The child generation is especially high in rationality, with an average score of 5.88 compared to 5.17 for the parent generation. The married child generation is particularly likely to seek information outside the immediate family

table 6-9   distribution of rationality scale
type scores by generation*

scale scores	children		parents		grandparents	
	number	per cent	number	per cent	number	per cent
	367	100	258	100	98	100
8	112	31	42	16	19	19
7	65	18	46	18	10	10
6	60	16	50	19	13	13
5	33	9	28	11	8	8
4	25	7	29	11	15	15
3	28	8	26	10	8	8
2	19	5	19	7	7	7
1	11	3	9	4	5	5
0	14	4	9	4	13	13
Reproducibility:	90%		88.9%		87.4%	
		Chi Square = 16.36		P = 0.01		

*Per cents may not total 100 due to rounding.

(Scale Type 8) before undertaking a residence move or making a durable goods purchase, for example. Thirty-one per cent of all its actions were first preceded by using all eight methods of obtaining information and evaluating solutions. Parents and grandparents were less active in this respect, since only 16 per cent and 19 per cent of their respective actions carried them to all sources of information. As far as utilizing only the information the family could provide, the grandparent generation ended its evidence seeking with its immediate family on 70 per cent of its actions, the parents on two-thirds, and the children on one-half of their actions. We may speculate that the reason the child generation is the more active in seeking outside information is that it is in the process of formulating its consumption patterns while the parents and grandparents have an accumulation of agreements and of past experience upon which to draw. We will discuss in more detail the correlates of rationality in decision making shortly, but it is of interest to speculate whether families begin the life cycle more rational in weighing the satisfactions and costs of projected actions, only to become more impulsive as the marriage matures. One way of specifying this phenomenon would be to see if, within the generations, rationality decreases with years married.

Within the parent generation, those parents married longest (31-40 years) have the lowest rationality score, but those in the middle category, 26-30 years married, have the highest. Among the grandparents, the older spouses are the most rational, planning more circumspectly. Among the married children the relationship is equivocal, with the older group (5-15 years married) being both high and low in their performance while the very young marrieds, largely childless, have middle rationality scores. Within the married child generation, age at marriage is closely associated with rationality in decision making. Those above average age at marriage (more rational in timing the marriage) are also highest in rationality scores over the year's observation. We must conclude that the finding of an inverse relationship between rationality in decision making and generation is not a function of years married, nor ages of spouses, but may be a function of some other factors such as educational training and style of planning, which run contrary to generational phenomena.

Satisfaction with Outcome of the Decision   In considering decision making over the life span, we should consider the way families evaluate the outcome of decision making. We have constructed satisfaction with outcome scores from the answers to two questions: If you could start over again, would you make the same decision? If you could return the item purchased, push a button and be back in your old residence, and so forth, would you do it? In general all three generations were affirmative about most of the decisions and most of the actions taken. When all three generations are merged, 72 per cent of the families were classified in the category "high satisfaction with outcome." This includes only families that claimed they would do nothing to alter the decisions made nor to repudiate the actions taken over the twelve months of the study. Taken separately, the parent generation is most affirming (77 per cent high satisfaction), the grandparent next (75 per cent), and the child generation least (66 per cent).

We recognize that such high frequency of unqualified affirmation may carry heavy components of self-justification for many of the actions evaluated. Our indicator may be telling us more about the distribution of the propensity to rationalize past actions than it does about the actual gratifications experienced in the consumption process.

Within generations, age of spouses appears related to expressions of satisfaction. The youngest age group among the married child generation (20-25 years of age) is critical in significantly large numbers (38 per cent dissatisfaction), while within the grandparent generation the eighty-year-olders are significantly more satisfied than expected by chance (85 per cent satisfaction).

This brings to a close the description of decision-making patterns by generation over the life span. Because of the high interest of the participants in this symposium in the aged, we will now attempt to describe the family properties associated with both high and low performance in the different phases of the consumption process from need identification in the form of plans, through rationality in decision making, to degree of satisfaction with outcome.

correlates of consumership in the grandparent generation

The grandparent generation has experienced the various phases of the consumption process differently from the younger generations. Having fewer needs they have made fewer plans, fewer decisions, fewer actions, and have experienced fewer frustrations with the untoward consequences of actions, hence have expressed high satisfaction with the fewer actions taken.

Low Versus High Needs   Only in the grandparent generation do we have any families who went through the year without either plans or actions. These families share a common pattern. The syndrome is one of extremely aged couples married longer than their peers, living alone without dependents, with higher lifetime income and higher current income than average. The spouses have lower than average education and are both retired. The family organization is characterized by restrictiveness, disengagement from outside contacts, no social participation and wife not working gainfully, conventional division of sex roles, and a wife-dominant authority system. The marital climate is good with high marital agreement and high marital integration.

High volume of plans is characteristic of a minority of the grandparent generation, but this minority shows higher education of spouses, more equalitarian power relations between spouses, and more dissatisfaction with marriage. In the older generation it is the couples who are dissatisfied with marriage who are high in unmet needs and who report these as plans.

Low Versus High Rationality in Decision Making   The grandparent generation was the lowest of the three generations in conforming to the patterns of rationality in decision making. Among the grandparents those who are lowest in rationality are younger than average, have higher education, are more flexible in sex role allocation with some role crossing, and show low marital communication. In this respect they parallel the syndrome of the families with a high volume of plans. It is surprising to find the lowest rationality among the couples where both spouses had high education and the highest rationality where both spouses were poorly educated, because this situation is reversed in the married child generation. In the grandparent generation education may have enabled the couples to formulate policies and rules short-circuiting the many components of decision making that give high scores on our scale for rationality.

High rationality among grandparents is found among the less well educated but higher levels occupationally, among the couples of high marital communication but relatively low marital integration and agreement. Again, we see an association between disenchantment with the marriage and more careful consumership.

High Versus Low Satisfaction with Outcome   Associated with high satisfaction are properties which differ in many respects from those associated with low needs and low rationality, which constitute the other modal behaviors of the grandparent generation. From the standpoint of the stage of the life span, high satisfaction is associated with older husbands, older marriages, and higher lifetime income — essentially the same syndrome found among the families of low volume of plans. In terms of social competences, however, high satisfaction is associated with high education, with continued employment of the husband, and with location in the upper classes, which differs almost at every point from the properties of families of low volume of plans and low rationality.

In the language of family organization, high satisfaction does resemble the low-needs families, since the pattern is one of restrictiveness in family organization: authoritarian decision making, conventionality of sex roles, no social participation, and wife not gainfully employed.

Turning to marital climate, high satisfaction presents a new syndrome; namely, low marital agreement accompanied by high communication, which is quite different from the pattern associated with low rationality.

Low satisfaction with one's decisions, in sharp contrast, is found associated with social participation and gainful employment of the wife and with unconventionality in sex-role allocation (role-reversals).

summary and conclusions

We have looked at the phenomenon of decision making over the life cycle in this chapter, utilizing the conceptual framework of family development as our lenses, to give focus and specificity to our observations. The framework has enabled us to anticipate more of a propensity to plan in the earlier stages of family development compared with the middle and later stages, because of greater needs; likewise we anticipated longer horizons because in the earlier stages the couples are more likely to be future oriented. The framework also permitted us to anticipate greater stability and simplicity of interaction in decision making and greater disengagement from commitments and from one's social network of helping agents in the latter stages of the cycle.

These expectations were examined in an unusual intergenerational sample. It consisted of 312 intact families linked through three generations living within the metropolitan area of the Twin Cities of Minneapolis-St. Paul. The sample was composed of 100 grandparent families (aged 60-80), 105 parent families (aged 40-60), and 107 married children (aged 20-30). The data were obtained by a series of panel interviews scheduled over a twelve-month period covering the decisions undertaken in seven recurring problem areas requiring long-range planning and fairly elaborate decision making: residential location, remodeling, redecorating, acquisition of automobile and durable goods, changes in financial investments and insurances, and job changes.

The performance of the three generations over the year's period tells us much about the types of problems which provoke decisions, the type of decisions and the way they are made, as well as the consequences of decisions.

The three generations began the year's period under quite different situational constraints. The married child generation was under high pressure of needs on resources, the parent generation was in a state of relative affluence with a margin of disposable income, and the grandparent generation was close to the borderline of poverty.

Over the year's period the history of help exchanges demonstrated the greater vulnerability of the married child generation to problems requiring assistance, particularly in the realms of child care and economic assistance. The grandparent generation was especially in need of assistance in the problem areas of illness, household management, and emotional gratification. The parent generation was highest in receiving no help but did receive much attention in the area of emotional gratification. In several thousand different help exchanges the generations fared quite differently. The parent generation acted more as *patron*, giving to both grandparents and married children and receiving markedly less than it gave. The grandparent generation, in contrast, received more than it gave in virtually all problem areas, demonstrating a *dependency status*. The married child generation was more nearly in balance in its giving and receiving, demonstrating high reciprocity in its exchanges.

The location of power in decision making showed an increase within our sample in wife-centeredness and a decrease in husband-centeredness and equalitarianism as we move from the married child generation into the parent generation and on to the grandparent generation in the last stage of the life cycle.

A few generalizations may be made about the extent of planning, the degree of rationality in decisions made, and of satisfaction with outcomes as the three generations are contrasted:

1. The married child generation does the most planning in every area of activity studied; the grandparent generation does the least.

2. The child generation is the most active of the three generations and the grandparent generation is the least active in every area of activity studied.

3. More plans are made than actions undertaken by each generation except in the area of occupational change, where actions substantially outnumber plans.

4. The child generation is the most likely to be definite in setting a date for taking action and to have a longer horizon in planning; the grandparent generation is the most often indefinite, but, if definite, most likely to enunciate plans of short horizon.

5. Definite plans are carried into action more frequently, and among definite plans, the short-run are more likely to be fulfilled than the longer-run plans in all generations.

6. The grandparent generation, which made the fewest plans and took the fewest actions, fulfilled the highest proportion of its plans; the parent generation, which showed a moderate number of both plans and actions, fulfilled the lowest proportion of plans.

7. The majority of the changes completed by all three generations were not planned in advance.

8. The components of rational decision making are more faithfully met in the married child generation than in the other two generations; the grandparent generation is lowest of the three. The child generation is most likely to search for information outside the immediate family, to weigh satisfactions among alternatives, and to take into account long-term as well as short-term consequences before taking action than are the more seasoned generations.

9. In evaluating the outcome of decisions and actions, the parent generation is most likely to be completely satisfied, the grandparent generation next, and the married child generation least.

It would indeed be hazardous to attempt any sweeping propositions about decision making over the life span from the many miniature generalizations brought together in this paper. We have shown that the three generations representing different phases of the life cycle have been distinctive in responding to the stimuli of recurring problems requiring thoughtful planning. The married child generation, near the beginning of its family cycle, and the grandparent generation, approaching the end of its life span, have been farthest apart in their decision-making behavior over the year of observation. The parent generation more typically has fallen in between these two extremes, as might be expected from its position in the life cycle. Indeed we see some support in our observations of the three generations for the theory of disengagement, progressive reduction of life spaces, and retreat from arenas of activity enunciated by Cumming and her associates.[13] Further research using longitudinal methods should be undertaken to further test this provocative theory.

[13]Elaine Cumming, Lois R. Dean, D.S. Newell, and Isabel McCaffrey, "Disengagement—A Tentative Theory of Aging," *Sociometry*, XXIII (March, 1960), 23-35.

relation between generations and the three-generation household in denmark

PART FOUR cross-societal
studies

relations between generations and the three-generation household in denmark[1]

JAN STEHOUWER

Until about the beginning of this century it was still common and sometimes even preferred that one of the adult children remain with his parents, even after marriage. This has changed. Urban growth, industrialization, and mechanization of agriculture have contributed to the individualization of the nuclear family and have made generations less dependent on each other in both urban and rural areas. There is considerable evidence that elderly people now want to live near their adult chilren, but not with them.[2]

Considering this development, one is inclined to wonder what has happened to the household of three generations as well as to relations between generations not living under the same roof. This paper deals with these questions in relation to the situation in Denmark. The paper is divided into three parts.

In the first part, the living arrangements of elderly people in Denmark, their proximity to children, and their contact with children are

[1]This research has been financed by a grant from the United States National Institutes of Health, MH 05509 and the Public Health Service, Chronic Disease Division, CH 0052-03.

[2]Gordon F. Streib, "Family Patterns in Retirement," *Journal of Social Issues*, XIV, No. 2 (1958), 46-60; Leopold Rosenmayr and Eva Köckeis, "Propositions for a Sociological Theory of Ageing and the Family," *International Social Science Journal*, XV, No. 3 (1963), 410-426.

described briefly. It has often been assumed that the aged in modern industrial societies are isolated from their children, especially in urban areas. The first part of this paper will deal with this question. Further, the situation of the aged in Denmark will be compared with equivalent data from sample surveys in Great Britain and the United States.

The second part of this paper will deal with factors which contribute to the establishment and maintenance of three-generation households and to the occurrence of such households in Denmark. Compared with non-Scandinavian European countries, Denmark has remarkably few people who live in three-generation households.

This observation leads to the third part of this paper, which deals with the relations between generations in Denmark. The fact that Denmark has a long-established tradition of social pension systems, health insurance, and housing policy for the aged makes the study of relations between generations an attractive object for cross-national comparisons.

The data of this paper derive from two sources. The first source is the study of the social well-being of the aged in Denmark, which is a part of a cross-national study in social gerontology, carried out in Britain, the United States, and Denmark.[3] The second source is the screening interview on household composition and health conditions, carried out by the Danish National Institute for Social Research in 1961, which was used as the sampling basis for three national sample surveys in Denmark. The data about the number and the composition of three-generation households in Denmark are a by-product of this sample survey.[4]

the living arrangements of elderly people:
the proximity of children
and the frequency of contact

Urbanization and industrialization in Denmark started relatively late compared with other Western European countries. Denmark has a population of about 4.5 million people, one-third of whom live in the

---

[3]This study is financed by grants from the United States National Institute of Mental Health and the United States Public Health Service, Community Health Services, Bureau of State Services, in all three countries. The general aim of this study is to secure comparable data about health, physical capacity, the employment status, the family relations, and the economic status of elderly people in these countries. In each country roughly 2,500 persons aged 65 and over were interviewed during April-July, 1962. The national teams used the same sampling methods, questionnaires which included mainly comparable cross-national questions, similar definitions of variables, and similar interviewer instructions. The responsible investigators are Denmark, Henning Friis and Jan Stehouwer; Great Britain, Peter Townsend; the United States, Ethel Shanas. See Henning Friis, "Cross-National Research on Old Age," *International Social Science Journal*, XV, No. 3 (1963), 451-55.

[4]A 0.7 per cent stratified area probability sample of about 10,000 households.

metropolitan area of Copenhagen. Another third live in the provincial towns, which range from less than 2,000 to almost 180,000 inhabitants. Approximately half of those in provincial towns live in communities with less than 30,000 inhabitants. The rest of the population live in the rural areas of the country.

Approximately 6 per cent of the people aged 65 and over live in institutions.[5] Among older people who live in private households it is more common to live apart from children than together with them. Those elderly who live with children live with unmarried children. Very few elderly people in Denmark live with married children.

Differences within Denmark   As one might expect, we find the largest proportion of married elderly people living with children in the rural parts of the country. Our results show that in Denmark in rural areas nearly one-fifth of the elderly people live together with children. This, however, does not mean that these households function as traditional farm families of more than two generations living and working together. This type of household has nearly disappeared in Denmark.

The elderly living in the provincial towns differ from the elderly in Copenhagen as well as from those in the extreme rural areas in living arrangements as well as in relations to their children.[6] In the provincial towns we find the largest proportion of elderly married people who live only with their spouse and the largest proportion who have their nearest child at a distance of more than 60 transport minutes, and the number of those who have not seen a child within the last month is about twice as high as that reported for Copenhagen or the extreme rural areas.

Among the unmarried aged we find almost the same pattern. Again the proportion of those who live alone is highest in the provincial towns. About twice as many in the provincial towns as in the Copenhagen area have their nearest child at a transport distance of more than 60 minutes. Contrary to the situation of married people, we find no significant differences in the frequency of contact with children for those who are single whether they live in Copenhagen, the provincial towns, or the rural areas.

Table 7-1 indicates that the probability that all children move away from the areas where their parents live is highest in the provincial towns, somewhat lower in the rural areas, and lowest in Copenhagen.

Our data reveal that one has to be careful with the hypothesis that urbanization leads to spatial separation between generations and towards isolation of the aged. The inclination for parents and children to see one another may still be greatest in the rural areas, but the possi-

[5]There are only estimates about the number of elderly people in nonprivate households. Census data are not yet available.
[6]Extreme rural areas are areas with less than 10 per cent of the population living in the built-up area of the community.

table 7-1 the living arrangements of people aged 62 and over, their proximity to nearest child, and contact with children in areas of denmark*

marital status and living arrangements	copenhagen per cent	provincial towns per cent	rural areas per cent	extreme rural per cent	whole country per cent
Married					
Total	100.0	100.0	100.0	100.0	100.0
Living with:					
Spouse only	77.9	84.0	75.3	60.8	77.8
Unmarried children	17.3	12.3	17.6	19.6	16.5
Married children	0.3	0.4	2.8	8.4	1.4
Others	4.5	3.3	4.3	11.2	4.3
N =	353	559	324	396	1632
Unmarried					
Total	100.0	100.0	100.0	100.0	100.0
Living alone	61.8	73.7	43.9	47.0	60.8
Living with:					
Unmarried children	19.2	14.5	30.3	22.6	19.6
Married children	5.5	3.9	12.1	19.5	8.4
Others	13.5	7.9	13.7	10.9	11.2
N =	297	330	132	164	923
Married (not living with children)					
Nearest child more than hour away	6.4	25.0	17.4	19.0	18.1
Child not seen in last month	4.0	8.3	8.5	4.3	6.5
N =	296	492	260	300	1348
Unmarried (not living with children)					
Nearest child more than hour away	8.6	17.9	16.7	12.0	14.5
Child not seen in last month	10.3	8.4	12.8	10.1	9.8
N =	233	274	78	99	648

*Includes only persons with living children.

Source: Jan Stehouwer, "Urban-Rural Differences in Contact between the Aged and their Children in Denmark," paper prepared for the International Social Science Research Seminar in Gerontology, Markaryd, Sweden, 1963.

bilities of contact are greatest in Copenhagen—because the parents will more frequently find a child within the limited and densely populated area of Copenhagen than within any other area of the same size.

The Living Arrangements of People with Living Children, in Denmark, Great Britain, and the United States Nearly three out of four elderly persons aged 65 or over in Denmark, Britain, and the United States have at least one living child. The proportions without children are: Great Britain, 23.6 per cent, United States, 24.4 per cent, and Denmark, 24.5 per cent. Compared with Britain and the United States, however, we find that Denmark has the lowest proportion of elderly people—single or married—who live together with their children. As Table 7-2 shows, we find in Denmark only 8.7 per cent of the aged who are unmarried living together with married children compared to 18.6 per cent in the United States and 24.2 per cent in Britain. In Denmark we find no difference in the proportion of elderly people living together with the family of the married daughter or married son. In Britain, the majority of the elderly, single as well as married, who live with married children live together with the family of a married

table 7-2   the living arrangements of people aged 65
and over who have living children

marital status and living arrangements	britain per cent	united states per cent	denmark per cent
Married			
Total	100.0	100.0	100.0
Living with:*			
Spouse only	63.8	77.9	79.8
Married daughter	4.7	1.0	0.4
Married son	0.8	1.1	1.2
Unmarried child	25.9	14.6	14.9
Sibling	1.5	1.3	0.3
Grandchild	1.5	2.3	0.7
Other relative	0.6	0.8	0.3
Nonrelative only	1.2	1.0	2.4
N =	1022	1169	1183
Divorced, widowed, or single			
Total	100.0	100.0†	100.0
Living alone	38.7	46.5	61.1
Living with:*			
Married daughter	19.7	14.5	4.5
Married son	7.4	4.1	4.1
Unmarried child	26.8	24.1	18.4
Sibling	2.6	2.5	1.0
Grandchild	0.7	2.2	1.4
Other relative	0.9	1.4	0.8
Nonrelative only	3.2	4.6	8.7
N =	889	843	828

*Listing in priority order.
†Per cents do not add to total because of rounding.

daughter.[7] In the United States typically single persons living with married children, live together with a daughter's family.

The Proximity of Children and the Frequency of Contact Between Aged Parents and Their Children   Although relatively few people in Denmark live together with their children, most old people live within a short distance from at least one child. Table 7-3 shows that about one out of eight elderly people in Denmark and Britain have their nearest child at a distance of more than 60 transport minutes. In the United States the proportion is one to six. Our data support results from other surveys, which show that parents and children generally settle in the vicinity of each other.[8] In this respect, we find striking similarities among the three countries. Looking at the proportion of children living at a long distance from their parents, we must remember that the three countries vary greatly in size, which makes the relatively small number of elderly people with their nearest child within more than 60 transport minutes in the United States even more surprising compared with the corresponding proportions found in Denmark and Great Britain.

[7]Peter Townsend, "The Family of Three Generations," paper presented at the International Social Science Research Seminar in Gerontology, Markaryd, Sweden, August, 1963.

[8]Leopold Rosenmayr and Eva Köckeis, "A Method to Assess Living Arrangements and Housing Problems of the Aged," paper presented at the International Social Science Research Seminar in Gerontology, Markaryd, Sweden, August, 1963.

table 7-3   the proximity of the nearest child to people aged 65 and over in great britain, the united states, and denmark*

	people with living children		
proximity of the nearest child	britain per cent	united states per cent	denmark per cent
Total	100.0†	100.0	100.0
Same household	41.9	27.6	20.1
10 minute's journey or less	23.5	33.1	32.0
11-30 minute's journey	15.9	15.7	23.0
31 minute's—1 hour	7.6	7.2	12.4
Over 1 hour but less than one day	9.1	11.2	11.2
1-day journey or more	1.9	5.2	1.3
N =	1911	2012	2009

*Unclassifiable 0, 0, and 4 respectively.
†Per cents do not add to total because of rounding.
Source: Adapted from Peter Townsend, "The Family of Three Generations," paper prepared for the International Social Science Research Seminar in Gerontology, Markaryd, Sweden, August 1963.

The majority of elderly people with living children are in daily or weekly contact with at least one of them. The proportion of people who have not seen a child within the last week is one in six in the United States and even smaller in Denmark and Britain. In Denmark this means that although very few elderly people live together with their children, the majority of them have daily or weekly contact with at least one child. Table 7-4 shows that about two-thirds of the elderly in each country have seen at least one of their children today or yesterday. Among the British about 40 per cent of those with children live with a child, in Denmark only about 20 per cent. The data in Table 7-4 indicate that "not living together in Denmark" is highly compensated for by daily contact.

Summarizing our major results as to the living arrangements of the aged in Denmark, the proximity of children, and the frequency of contact with children, and the comparison with Great Britain and the United States, we can conclude that in spite of the fact that Denmark

table 7-4   when people aged 65 and over last saw one of their children*

	people with living children		
last time child seen	britain per cent	united states per cent	denmark per cent
Total	100.0	100.0	100.0
Today or yesterday	69.3	65.0	62.3
Within previous seven days	17.3	18.7	21.8
Within previous month	7.4	6.8	9.8
Within previous year	4.2	7.0	4.8
More than a year ago	1.8	2.5	1.3
N =	1906	1996	2001

*Unclassifiable: 6, 16, and 12 for Britain, the United States, and Denmark respectively.

has a very high proportion of aged who live apart from their children, we find no differences in the proximity of the nearest child and the frequencies of contact with children between Denmark and the two other countries involved in this cross-national survey.

These results raise two questions: first, what has happened to the household of three generations in Denmark and, secondly, what are the relations between generations when elderly people do not live together with their children. In the next two sections we will try to throw some light on these problems.

the three-generation household

Why do so few elderly people in Denmark live in households consisting of three successive generations? Why in general do we find so few elderly people in Denmark who live with their children? The higher degree of institutionalization of elderly people in Denmark, compared for example with the United States, 6 per cent compared to 4 per cent, may have caused some of the difference — but evidently not the whole. The next pages shall first deal with factors which contribute to the establishment of three-generational living, secondly we shall summarize some recent evidence about the occurrence of three-generation households in Western European countries, and finally we shall describe the structure of the three-generation households which are still found in Denmark.

The Establishment of Three-Generation-Households   Various reasons exist for the establishment of temporary or permanent three-generation households. In general, two main causes for such households can be distinguished: (1) dependence originating because the family functions as a joint enterprise involving two or more generations working together, and (2) need for help and care, offered either by first or second generation.

Economic dependence has traditionally been considered as one of the main reasons which have led to the establishment of three-generation households. Le Play's "La Famille Souche" in which one of the sons inherits the farm or business owned by his father, and continues to keep it for the family, is a good example of this kind of economic and functional dependence which leads to three-generational living, especially among farmers and small entrepreneurs.[9] In rural areas of Western Europe this type of farm family has been rather common and mainly patrilocal in structure.[10]

The need for help and care can be the reason for three-generational living in various circumstances. In some instances, the first or older generation offers help. Some such households are estab-

---

[9]Frédéric Le Play, *L'Organisation de la famille*, 3rd ed. (Tours: A. Mame et fils, 1884).

[10]J. P. Kruijt, "Het gezin sedert de middeleeuwen," *Sociologisch Bulletin*, 4 e Jaargang, No. 3 (1950) p. 81.

lished, more or less on a temporary basis, for example, when an adult child marries, and the young couple must wait to get a dwelling for themselves. In these cases, a housing shortage may be a factor which contributes to the establishment of temporary three-generation households. A recent study of the housing conditions of newly married couples in Copenhagen, for example, has shown that 23 per cent of all couples start married life living with either his or her parents, and in a great number of cases the first child is born in this household.[11] Young and Willmot reported the same sort of households in East London.[12]

Another typical example of help offered by the first generation is seen when an unmarried daughter (or married, but temporarily separated from her husband) continues or returns to live with her own family. This has been a common pattern especially in times of war.[13]

Evacuation and acute shortage of houses caused by the destruction of war have also been common reasons for temporary and even permanent establishment of three-generation households, either in the family of the first or second generation.[14]

Finally, declining health among elderly people and the reduction of their capacity to take care of themselves are common reasons for the establishment of three-generation households in many countries. Instead of moving into an institution, the aged parents move to live with their children.

Discussing the structure of the three-generation household in Germany, Baumert makes the distinction between the new and the old type of three-generational living.[15] In the old traditional type of three-generation household, at least one of the children remains with the parents and in many cases continues to work on the farm or in the business which has been owned by the family for generations. In this type of household economic and occupational dependence together with family traditions is the main reason for three-generational living. In the new type, according to Baumert, the members of the second generation move away from the parental home, establish their own families, and later invite the parent(s) to live with them in cases of the former's widowhood, declining health, or physical incapacity.

[11]K. Auken, *Familien lever* (Copenhagen: Gad, 1962), pp. 59 ff.

[12]Michael Young and Peter Willmott, *Family and Kinship in East London,* Pelican, A 595 (Harmondsworth, Middlesex: Penguin Book Company, 1962), p. 31.

[13]William M. Smith, Jr., Joseph H. Britton, and Jean O. Britton, *Relationships Within Three-Generation Households,* College of Home Economics Research Publication No. 155 (University Park: The Pennsylvania State University, 1958), p. 16. See also K. Ishwaran, *Family Life in the Netherlands* (The Hague: Van Keulen, 1959), Chapter on: "The Impact of the War on the Family," pp. 92 ff.

[14]Enrico Quarantelli, "A Note on the Protective Function of the Family in Disasters," *Marriage and Family Living,* XXII (August, 1960), 263-64. See also Marvin B. Sussman's review of the literature on this topic in his contribution in Chapter IV of this volume.

[15]Gerhard Baumert, "Changes in the Family and the Position of Older Persons in Germany," *Social and Psychological Aspects of Aging,* Clark Tibbitts and Wilma Donahue, eds. (New York: Columbia University Press, 1962), pp. 416 ff.

Having no data for retrospective comparisons, it is doubtful whether we are able to speak about old and new types of three-generation households. It is indisputable that the number of three-generation households was larger about a century ago than it is now. It is also correct that the so-called "old type" or Le Play's "La Famille Souche" has been a frequent household type in the rural areas of Western Europe. This does not allow us to assume, however, that the other type of household, in which the first generation moves into the household of the second, is particularly new. Perhaps, this latter type is more urban than rural in origin. The lack of public care for the aged, the absence of medical care, and the very unattractive institutions for the aged a hundred or even only fifty years ago must have been conditions which frequently contributed to the establishment of the three-generation household in urban areas. The three-generation household in which the children take care of their parent(s) who have moved into their household is not a new one. It may well be the remainder of an old, and perhaps traditionally urban type.

The Three-Generation Household in Western Europe   Does the three-generation household still exist in Western Europe, and where do we find it? This is the next question which should be answered before we turn to a more detailed analysis of three-generational living in Denmark. There is evidence that the three-generation household is still a common arrangement among the population of poor agricultural and economically backward regions within a number of Western European countries, such as Italy,[16] the Netherlands,[17] and even Germany.[18]

The number of three-generation households in Europe is smallest in urban areas. In rural areas their frequency seems to vary with the regional traditions and the prosperity of agriculture.

Rural sociologists in the Netherlands have ascertained that relatively many three-generation households still exist along the German frontier. The extended family system in Holland is confined to the sandy areas in the east and the middle of the country—which, up to the beginning of this century, as a result of geographical as well as social factors, have been extremely isolated. The farm family in these areas until recently has been a production as well as a consumption unit. Being small, the farms need no hired labor. Each member of the

[16]Aurelia Florea, *L'Anziano in Famiglia* (Roma: Comitato Italiano Per Gli Anziani, 1962) and some unpublished tabulations from a sample survey in rural parts of North and South Italy.

[17]E. W. Hofstee and G. A. Kooy, "Traditional Households and Neighborhood Groups, Survivals of the Genealogical-Territorial Societal Pattern in Eastern Parts of the Netherlands," *Transactions of the World Sociological Congress*, Vol. IV, Part II (Amsterdam: International Sociological Association, 1954), 76 ff.

[18]Baumert, "Changes in the Family and the Position of Older Persons in Germany," *op. cit.*

family and even sometimes members of the extended kin group are to some degree engaged in the farm work.[19]

In Baumert's study of Darmstadt in 1950 (see Table 7-5) 42 per cent of the full-time farm families had an extended family system of three or more generations living together. In contrast, only 5 per cent of the families in the city he studied lived in a three-generation household.

In Vienna, Rosenmayr and Köckeis found that almost 4 per cent of all households consist of three generations living together.[20] In one of six of these households the members of both adult generations were still married. In all other cases, either the grandparent or the parent (or even both) were widowed. From this, Rosenmayr and Köckeis conclude that "joint households thus seem hardly ever to be maintained throughout adult life in urban industrial society but rather re-established when other relationships break off."[21]

table 7-5   number of generations living together in urban and rural families in a west german city and its hinterland, percentage distribution

number of generations	urban families (N = 387)	rural families			
		total (N = 434)	nonfarm	part-time farm	full-time farm
One	36	25	27	35	7
Two	59	62	64	49	51
Three	5	12	9	15	37
Four		1		1	5

Source: Gerhard Baumert, "Changes in the Family and the Position of Older Persons in Germany," *Social and Psychological Aspects of Aging,* Clark Tibbitts and Wilma Donahue, eds. (New York: Columbia University Press, 1962), p. 420.

The Three-Generation Household in Denmark   Two of every hundred households in Denmark include three or more generations. Although the majority of the three-generation households in Denmark include aged persons, in a substantial proportion the first or grandparent generation is still at the stage where the youngest children are about to get married and leave the household. Both in absolute and relative terms we find most of these in the country and only a few in the Copenhagen metropolitan area and in the provincial towns.

[19]Hofstee and Kooy, "Traditional Households and Neighborhood Group," *op. cit.* See also: K. Ishwaran, *Family Life in the Netherlands, op. cit.,* p. 40: "The extended family is confined to those areas which the Netherlanders themselves describe as 'old,' 'primitive,' 'outdated' and 'undeveloped.'"

[20]Rosenmayr and Köckeis, "A Method to Assess Living Arrangements and Housing Problems of the Aged," *op. cit.,* p. 5.

[21]*Ibid.* A similar conclusion is reported by Robins in an American study. Robins found that in Columbia, Missouri the combined household was formed on an average of ten years after the children's marriage. Arthur J. Robins, "Family Relations in Three-Generation Households," *Social and Psychological Aspects of Aging,* Clark Tibbitts and Wilma Donahue, eds. (New York: Columbia University Press, 1962), p. 470.

When we look at the population aged 65 and over who have children, we find that 5.1 per cent live in three-generation households. In the United States the proportion is 8.1 per cent and in Great Britain 13.4 per cent.

Why is the number of three-generation households so limited in Denmark? There are two main conditions in Denmark which may have prevented three-generational living and diminished the number of households of this kind. First, for the country as a whole, the long tradition of care and the housing policy for the aged have diminished dependency among generations. This tradition may have contributed to the fact that there has been far less pressure in Denmark, than, for example, in the Netherlands and the United States to make adult children take care of their aged parents.[22] Recent trends in the housing policy for the aged show that everything possible is done to keep old people independent in their own dwellings. Institutionalization is a final solution only in cases where the elderly person is not able to take care of himself. Second, the housing conditions of Denmark serve to prevent three generations from living together. Three-generational living is dependent on large housing units, and this condition exists in Denmark only to a very limited extent, especially in urban areas. In Denmark, as well as in the other Scandinavian countries, the average dwelling has only two or three rooms.

Furthermore, in rural areas, the structure of agriculture and the high degree of mechanization of farm work have limited the need of unpaid family workers (except for the wife of the small-holder). Rural areas with a long tradition of three-generation households, such as can be found in the Netherlands, do not exist in Denmark. Finally, we must take into account that Denmark has had no major part in either the First World War or the Second. The country has not had the problem of war-widows, nor the acute housing shortage caused by war destruction which is still apparent in much of Western Europe.

The Composition of Three-Generation Households in Denmark   The most common arrangement in three-generation households in Denmark is that of widowed parents living with their married children and grandchildren.

In only one of six cases do three-generation households consist of two married couples of successive generations. Households consisting of a married couple and single children and grandchildren also occur in the same proportion.

Nearly 70 per cent of the households in which the parent(s) live in the household of one of their children are found in rural areas of the country. About 50 per cent of the households with a member of the

---

[22]See for example Ethel Shanas, *The Health of Older People: A Social Survey* (Cambridge, Mass.: Harvard University Press, 1962), Chapter VI, "Older People and Their Families," pp. 107-41; and J. Diederich, *Levensomstandighedenvan bejaarden in kleinere en middelgrote gemeenten van Nederland* (Amsterdam: Nationale Raad voor Maatschappelijk Wek's Gravenhage, Netherlands, 1958).

table 7-6   the composition of three-generation households in denmark

head of household	per cent
Total	100.0
1st generation	
Married couple, married child(ren), possibly other child(ren), grandchild(ren) and possibly others	10.5
Married couple, unmarried child(ren), and grandchild(ren) and possibly others	14.8
Unmarried head, married child(ren), and grandchild(ren) and possibly others	8.6
Unmarried head, unmarried child(ren), and grandchild(ren) and possibly others	11.7
2nd generation	
Married parents, married child(ren), and grandchild(ren) and possibly others	6.2
Married parents, unmarried child(ren), and grandchild(ren) and possibly others	1.9
Unmarried parent, married child(ren), and grandchild(ren) and possibly others	44.4
Unmarried parent, unmarried child(ren), and grandchild(ren) and possibly others	1.9
N =	162
Total number of households in sample	8634

first generation as head are also found in the rural areas of the country. Neither these households, nor the ones where the parents have moved into the household of one of the children, however, represent a typical rural tradition in three-generational living. The very small numbers of different types of three-generation households indicate in themselves that we are unable to speak of tradition in this respect.

The observation that there are households in urban areas in which two younger generations stay in the household of the first generation can be explained by current housing conditions. The proportion of elderly people who occupy large dwellings is larger than the proportion of young families with space for three-generational living.

table 7-7   distribution of three-generation households, urban and rural denmark

area	all three-generation households per cent	generation of head		frequency in total sample per cent	distribution of total sample per cent
		first per cent	second per cent		
Total	100.0	100.0	100.0	1.9	100.0
Copenhagen area	19.1	20.3	18.2	1.2	29.9
Provincial towns and suburbs	21.6	32.4	12.5	1.2	35.1
Rural districts	59.3	47.3	69.3	3.1	35.0
N =	162	74	88		8636

There is considerable evidence that the three-generation household, as it has survived in Denmark, is a subsidiary system rather than a system kept together by occupational and economic dependence. Very few households consist of two married couples. The majority consist of a single parent, usually widowed, living with children. Of these parents, the majority are women. Data about health and physical capacity of all family members of the household show that 55.4 per cent of all three-generation households in Denmark, compared to 15.4 per cent of all households, have at least one member with health troubles or physical handicaps.

Our results correspond very closely to observations made by Rosenmayr and Köckeis. They summarize their findings from a micro-census in Vienna and two federal states in Austria by saying "that intergenerational households are nearly always retained or reestablished only if and when one of their members (either of the older or of the younger generation) would otherwise have to live quite alone, or at least not in a family household."[23]

table 7-8   illness, health troubles, and physical handicaps among members of three-generation households in denmark*

members with complaints	number of households per cent
Total	100.0
None	44.6
Head of household only	13.6
Spouse of head only	11.7
Both head and spouse	5.6
Other member, related to head	12.3
Head and other related member	6.8
Spouse of head and other related member	1.8
Head and spouse of head and other member	1.8
No information	1.8
N =	162

*Households with member(s) who are ill, have complaints about health, or have a physical handicap. Refers to long-term, not temporary illness.

relations between generations in separate households

Since we find that Denmark has very few three-generation households, one is inclined to ask: How about relations between generations in Denmark in general? Is the vanishing three-generation household a sign of a weakening of relations between the elderly and their children?

In the beginning of this paper, we have shown that, in spite of certain marked differences in the living arrangements of the elderly in Denmark, compared with Great Britain and and the United States, we find remarkable similarities between the elderly population of the three countries as far as the frequency of contact with their children and the proximity of their children is concerned.

Living together in a common household imposes a functional as well as an emotional dependence on all household members apart from the dependence which exists because of family and kinship ties. To what extent is the fact that generations live apart from each other in Denmark a symbol of functional independence between generations, although a pattern of regular contact is maintained? In the last part of this paper we will deal with some aspects of relations between generations which may give some answers to this question.

[23]Rosenmayr and Köckeis, "A Method to Assess Living Arrangements and Housing Problems of the Aged," *op. cit.*

Patterns of Mutual Help and Assistance in Denmark   Help given to children is one of the indicators of the extent to which the aged parent is involved in the daily life of the adult children. In Denmark as a whole, 27.7 per cent of the people aged 65 and over reported that they are able to help their children with various things, such as repairs, housekeeping, and taking care of the grandchildren. The proportion of elderly people who say that they help their children is largest in the rural areas, nearly as large in Copenhagen, and lowest in the provincial towns.

table 7-9   are you able to do anything for your children?

answers of persons aged 65 and over with living children	copenhagen area per cent	provincial towns per cent	rural areas per cent	whole country per cent
Total	100.0	100.0	100.0	100.0
Yes	28.1	22.6	31.9	27.7
No	70.7	76.7	67.3	71.5
No information	1.2	0.7	0.8	0.8
	N = 516	707	789	2012

When people become ill, they become dependent on help. All elderly people in the national sample survey were asked whether they had been in bed because of illness during the last 12 months. Those who had been ill were asked some further questions about who helped them with various things, such as preparing meals, housekeeping, shopping, and care. Those who had not been ill were asked questions about who would help them in case of illness. The answers given by those persons with living children tell us something about the extent to which children in fact do help the elderly and to what extent the elderly expect help from them.

About four out of five elderly married people expect their spouses to prepare their meals during illness, and about the same proportion in fact received help from their spouses in this situation. Less than one of ten married elderly people expect their children to help them with meals, but the proportion of those who actually get help from their children with the preparing of meals is slightly larger.

Three out of five single people who live with a child expect one of their children to take care of meals, and something less than this proportion get this help. Among those who are single and live alone, only two of five expect and get help from children with meals. Unmarried elderly people who live alone are in the worst situation when ill. About 10 per cent of those who had not been ill during the last 12 months answered that there would be no one to help them with meals during illness. Among those who had been ill, we found about 20 per cent who had no help with meal preparation during their illness.

Finally, it is interesting to see that relatively more elderly people expect to receive help from local social agencies, such as community home helpers, than people who actually get help from these authori-

table 7-10 expectations of help with meal preparation during illness compared with the help given*

| persons aged 65 and over with living children | ill during last 12 months who helped with your meals? | | | | not ill during last 12 months who would help with your meals, if you became ill? | | | |
| | unmarried | | married | | unmarried | | married | |
priority code	alone per cent	with others per cent	spouse only per cent	spouse and others per cent	alone per cent	with others per cent	spouse only per cent	spouse and others per cent
Total	100.0	100.0	100.0	100.0	100.0	100.0	100.0	100.0
No one	20.6	3.6	2.5	1.5	9.3	2.0	0.6	1.2
Spouse only	...	...	65.0	61.7	...	...	71.6	63.2
Spouse and others	...	...	12.8	10.3	...	...	9.6	18.7
Child in household	4.8	58.9	0.6	16.2	3.0	51.2	0.6	7.6
Child outside household	35.8	7.1	7.2	...	36.8	9.2	5.3	1.7
Relative in household	...	11.6	...	...	0.9	16.6	...	0.6
Relative outside household	13.3	5.4	0.9	4.5	15.6	3.4	1.3	0.6
Social services	15.2	4.5	3.8	...	29.0	14.6	8.7	5.8
Others	10.3	8.9	6.9	5.8	3.6	3.0	1.3	0.6
No information	...	...	0.3	...	1.8	...	1.0	...
N =	165	112	320	68	334	205	619	171

*Total sample interviewed except 17 persons who are bedfast and 5 who did not respond to the question whether they had been ill during the last 12 months.

ties. For the elderly population as a whole, we find that about one of eight expect that they will receive help during illness from local social agencies, but about one out of eighteen gets this kind of service. Table 7-10 shows the difference between the number of people who expect help and those who get help from social services for all categories.

Relations Between Generations in Denmark, Compared with Great Britain and the United States As already mentioned, we find that in Denmark about one of four elderly people report that they were able to help their children. In Great Britain as well as the United States we find that the proportion of elderly people who help their children, and thus take an active part in the life of their children and grandchildren, is much higher. In Great Britain nearly half, and in the United States more than half of the elderly population aged 65 or over, reported that they helped their children.

table 7-11 the living arrangements, the proximity of the nearest child, the contact with children, and patterns of mutual help of people aged 65 and over with living children, in denmark, great britain, and the united states

living arrangements and relationships with children	denmark per cent	britain per cent	united states per cent
Proximity of Children:			
Children in the same household	20.1	41.9	27.6
Nearest child at more than one hour's transport distance	12.5	11.0	16.4
Contact with Children:			
Have seen at least one child today or yesterday	62.3	69.3	65.0
Have stayed overnight with child within last 12 months	20.0	29.5	42.9
Have had children staying overnight within last 12 months	20.1	26.2	46.0
Help to Children:			
Those able to do anything for children	27.7	46.9	52.5
Those able to do anything for grandchildren*	13.3	32.8	49.6
Help from Children:			
Received a regular money allowance within last 12 months	2.5	4.1	4.2
Received occasional money gifts within last 12 months	6.2	20.3	34.9
N =	2012	1911	2012

*Percentage computed only for those who have grandchildren. Denmark N = 1845, Britain N = 1719, and United States N = 1873.

The same pattern is observed concerning help to grandchildren. Only 13.3 per cent of the Danish respondents reported that they helped their grandchildren, while the percentages in Britain and the United States are 46.9 per cent and 52.5 per cent respectively.

To stay overnight with children or to have the children staying during holidays and other occasions is relatively uncommon in Denmark, where about one out of five parents has stayed with his child(ren) or has had a child(ren) staying with him in the previous year. In the United States little less than half of all older people with children have stayed with children or have had children staying over-night with them. These differences are even more striking when we take into account that there are relatively fewer elderly people in Denmark who live with their children than in the United States.

We must, however, take into consideration, that there may be several conditions which may make staying overnight more common in the United States than in Denmark. First of all, housing conditions in the United States permit overnight visitors to a larger extent than is true in Denmark. Secondly, we must remember that Denmark is a small country, whereas the geographical conditions in the United States make it probable that at least one of the children lives at a long distance from the parents, which makes overnight stays desirable dur-ing visits.

A regular money allowance from children is rather uncommon in all three countries. The proportion of elderly people who have re-ceived a regular allowance during the past 12 months is smallest in Denmark and highest in the United States. Receiving occasional money gifts from children is a regular phenomenon in Britain and the United States, but rare in Denmark. In Denmark, one of every seven-teen old people reported that they had received money gifts from their children during the last 12 months. In Britain, one of five, and in the United States, one of three had received occasional money gifts.

In comparing economic support given by children to their elderly parents in Denmark, Britain, and the United States we have to take into account that the Danish taxation system, in contrast to that of the other two countries, does not permit the deduction of economic sup-port to relatives in the annual income declaration. We should also mention that as far back as to the first codified rules on help to the poor, the sick, and the aged (1799), the Danish Social Security Acts never have had a rule that public relief of the aged (and other groups) is given on the condition that the children are unable to support their parents.

Summarizing the few comparable observations about relations be-tween generations in the three countries, which are available at this stage of our cross-national research, it seems that elderly people in Denmark are in regular contact with their children and live close to them. Unlike Great Britain and the United States, however, contact seems to be limited to visiting and is not the result of functional de-pendence. Compared with Britain and the United States, the elderly in Denmark seem to take a less active part in the lives of their chil-dren. Neither do they seem to be as dependent on help from their children as are the aged in England and the United States.

In evaluating these preliminary results from our cross-national survey one has to make certain reservations. First of all, we must be aware of the fact that some of the differences in the help patterns among generations in the three countries can be explained by structural differences in the populations concerned. The fact that we find a very large number of people in Britain saying that they are able to help their children can be a function of the extremely large proportion of elderly people in Britain living with their children. In this respect the Danish and American populations are more alike—which makes the differences in help patterns between these two countries more striking. Other structural differences between the three national samples will also have to be taken into account, such as proportions of married and unmarried elderly people, and the average number of children.[24]

We have already mentioned that Denmark has a long tradition of care for the aged—and especially a long-established pension system. Health insurance societies were formed in the middle of the nineteenth century and furnished the basis upon which the present nationwide system in Denmark is established.

The movement towards keeping the aged out of institutions—and if possible, in their own homes or in special apartment houses with a low rent—has been supported by a system of municipal home care. In this respect, the aged in Denmark are able to be more independent of their children, as far as housekeeping, nursing, and other sorts of help are concerned.

Apart from these factors, however, there are other circumstances which should prevent a complete detachment of generations. More than 30 per cent of the married women in Denmark are in the labor force, and in the large towns the proportion is even higher. Nevertheless, it seems that the grandmother in Denmark has taken the place of the mother only to a very limited extent in regard to taking care of children. The environment of the small town and the rural areas which is typical of the country ought to be ideal for the development of intensive relations between generations. This does not seem to be the case in Denmark where we find nearly equal and low proportions of elderly people in Copenhagen and rural areas who say that they help their children. Denmark seems to be an example of a country in which generations live in close contact with each other but with a relatively low degree of functional dependence.

Obviously the differences in mutual help patterns reported here only tell us something about the degree of functional interdependence of aged parents and their children and nothing about the emotional quality of intergenerational relations in these three countries.

But, in spite of these reservations, one cannot help but ask about the causes of such pronounced differences in patterns of mutual help between Denmark on one side, and Britain and the United States on the other.

---

[24]We have to take into account that the observations in intergenerational relations in the three countries are based on sample surveys with the aged in private households only. Differences in the degree of institutionalization of the aged in the three countries, however, is not great enough to be the cause of the observed difference.

summary and conclusions

The lengthening of the average lifetime of man in modern Western societies has increased the possibility of having family members or relatives in two or three generations apart from one's own. In spite of this development the household consisting of members from three successive generations seems to be a disappearing structure in most parts of Western Europe as well as in the United States. The increasing proportion of elderly people in the populations of almost every country with a high degree of industrialization and urbanization makes the study of intergenerational relationships a topic of general interest for theorists as well as social practitioners.

In this paper we have dealt with three aspects of intergenerational relations in Denmark. In the first part we have described living arrangements of elderly people in Denmark, their contact with children, and the proximity of children.

Observations within the country show that:

1. Urbanization has not led to spatial separation of elderly parents and their children. As expected, we find the largest proportion of elderly people who live together with adult children in the rural areas of the country. Nevertheless, relatively more elderly people in the small provincial towns than in the metropolitan area of Copenhagen live apart from their children.

2. Urbanization has not contributed to a reduction of regular visiting between the aged and their children. The largest proportion of elderly people who have not had contact with at least one child within the last month is found in the provincial towns. The lowest proportion is found in the Copenhagen area and not in rural areas as one might expect.

Cross-national observations in this research area reveal that:

3. The proportion of people aged 65 and over with living children who share a household with their children is largest in Britain and lowest in Denmark.

4. Elderly people in all three countries tend to live in the vicinity of their children.

5. Most elderly people in all three countries are in regular contact with at least one of their children.

The second part of this paper has dealt with the household of three generations in Denmark.

In Western Europe as well as the United States the three-generation household still exists, but it is a disappearing structure, especially in highly industrialized regions, where we find only very small proportions of the population living together in households of three or more generations. Denmark, in particular, is an example of a country with a very small proportion of three-generation households, in spite of the fact that about 25 per cent of the population lives in rural areas. This situation, which may seem to contradict some beliefs about the association between rural life and three-generation households, has to be evaluated against the background of a long tradition of social policy for the aged and a typical Scandinavian tradition of small housing, factors which limit the need and the possibilities of three-generational living.

Observations based on a national household sample show that:

6. The majority of three-generation households in Denmark are found in the rural areas of the country, whereas the remainder are equally divided between Copenhagen and the provincial towns.

7. There are nearly equal proportions of households in which the first and second generations are reported to be the head of the household.

8. One-third of all three-generation households consist of a married couple in the first generation. Only one of six households consists of two married couples of successive generations. In two out of three households we find a single member, either among the first or the second generation.

9. In more than half of all three-generation households, at least one member has health complaints or a physical incapacity.

10. Married elderly people who share a household more often live with the family of their married son than with the family of a married daughter. These households are found only in rural areas.

11. Widows more often live with married daughters than with married sons.

The traditional extended family system, consisting of three or more generations closely related to each other in an occupational and economic interdependent unit, is a type which is nearly nonexistent in Denmark. Among the disappearing three-generation households in Denmark, that which remains functions as a subsidiary system in which either first- or second-generation members are dependent on care and help from other family members. This is a type of household which has a less traditional reputation but which nevertheless must have existed for centuries, perhaps especially in urban areas.

In the last part of this paper we deal with relations between generations not living together in Denmark, Great Britain, and the United States.

Our main observation is that, in spite of similarities in regard to the proximity of the children and contact with children, there are striking differences between Denmark and the other two countries. In regard to an older parent's staying overnight with children, children's staying overnight with parents, and patterns of mutual help and assistance, we find that:

12. More than twice as great a proportion of elderly people in the United States as in Denmark stay with children overnight or have children staying with them.

13. In Denmark about one of four elderly people reports that he is

able to help his children. In Britain and the United States, about one of two was able to help his children.

14. Correspondingly, we find that relatively few Danish grandparents were able to help their grandchildren with various things.

15. Regular financial support from children is a rare phenomenon in all three countries. Occasional money gifts from children occur more frequently than regular financial support. The proportion of elderly people who receive occasional financial support from their children is lowest in Denmark and highest in the United States.

Our cross-national observations show that Denmark is an example of a country in which the generations live in close contact with each other but with a very low degree of mutual functional dependence. In spite of the fact that the same proportion of elderly people in Denmark, Britain, and the United States are in regular contact with their children and live near them, we find in Denmark very low proportions of elderly people who are able to help their children or who are supported by their children.

These observations have to be evaluated against the background of two conditions. First, we must remember that Denmark, being a country with a relatively moderate degree of urbanization, many small towns, and large rural areas, must be in many respects the ideal environment for the development and maintenance of strong intergenerational relations. This is confirmed by the large proportions of elderly people who are in nearly daily contact with children, and who live in the neighbourhood of their children. Second, we must take into account that Denmark has a long tradition for social security and care for the aged. This tradition may have reduced functional dependence among generations, but it does not seem to have influenced the frequency of contact between generations. Compared with the United States and Britain, Denmark seems to be a country where expectations about help between generations are reduced to a minimum, without influencing the degree of voluntary contact.

the effects of family structure on the likelihood of admission to an institution in old age: the application of a general theory[1]

PETER TOWNSEND

Before the early 1950's practically no intensive or far-ranging empirical studies of family relationships in Western society had been carried out. Since that time a number of surveys — at first local but afterwards even regional and national — have finally established the fact that in urban as well as rural areas, and in upper as well as lower occupational status groups, close associations between a number of relatives belonging to the wider family of three or four generations, even when not living together under the same roof, are normal.

The implications for social science are not yet fully appreciated. The author suspects that the study of many intricate social problems of divorce, poverty, criminal recidivism, class antagonisms, and adjustment in adolescence or retirement will gain fresh stimulus and directions. The author also suspects that family or kinship theory of an entirely new genre will be developed partly as a consequence and will henceforth play a much larger role in the development of sociological thought.

[1] The author is grateful to his colleagues on the residential Homes survey: Robert Pinker, Brian Rees, Mrs. June O'Brien, and his wife, Ruth; and also to those who gave greatest assistance on the more recent survey of all types of institutions: Miss Sheila Benson, Mrs. Caroline Woodroffe, and Miss Jan Walker.

This paper gives one application of what is, as yet, crude theory. The theory is that an individual's behaviour in nonfamilial as well as familial society is affected by the composition, the structure, and the organization of the nuclear (or immediate) and extended families to which he belongs. The specific form of this general hypothesis is that the likelihood of admission to an institution in old age, particularly a residential institution, is partly contingent on family composition, structure, and organization, and not only on incapacity, homelessness, and lack of socio-economic resources. The paper is, therefore, concerned with the reasons for the admission of old people to residential Homes and other institutions. It is based mainly on data collected in a survey carried out during 1958-1960 in England and Wales. During this survey a random sample of 173 public and private institutions and Homes were visited (of a total of over 3,000 in the country) by a small team of research officers. Statistical information about 8,517 residents (of whom 7,689 were of pensionable age) was obtained, and questionnaires were completed for 530 residents of pensionable age (489 of whom were interviewed) who had been admitted to these 173 establishments in the previous four months. Similar questionnaires were completed for a further 136 residents who had been admitted in this period but who had since died, been transferred to hospitals, or gone home.[2]

There were no previous inquiries into institutional care, drawing upon systematic interviewing techniques, on which we could build. Some mentally and physically handicapped persons were able to answer only some of our questions or could not answer any. Rather than weaken our conclusions by leaving them out of the analysis, we sought every means possible of getting information about them. We wrote out questions for those who were stone deaf, talked to mentally handicapped persons in private, and were occasionally delighted to get responses which had not been anticipated by the staff. Through a process of checking by personal observation and with staff, matrons, and case records, we were able to complete or nearly complete all the questionnaires.

In 1963 a wider survey was carried out. This involved a random sample of all persons aged 65 and over living in geriatric and psychiatric hospitals, nursing Homes, and residential Homes throughout Britain, and one of the chief aims was to discover in what ways the institutional differed from the general elderly population in family structure and social circumstances. The inquiry was designed to supplement the British part of a cross-national survey of persons aged 65 and over, who were living in private households, which was carried

[2]Peter Townsend, *The Last Refuge: A Survey of Residential Institutions and Homes for the Aged in England and Wales* (London: Routledge & Kegan Paul, Ltd., 1962). The research was financed by the Nuffield Foundation.

out in the United States, Denmark, and Britain in 1962.[3] Altogether 126 hospitals and other institutions were visited, and approximately one in every 200 patients and residents of this age in the country were interviewed. Statistical information for another one in every 200 was collected.[4] These data were being processed at the time of writing, late 1963.

hypotheses and definitions

The general context of structural theory should be indicated briefly before the survey data are described. There are a number of common types of kinship groups, but perhaps the two most common in Western industrialized societies are the immediate or nuclear family consisting of one or both parents and their unmarried children living in one household. Any two of its members stand in one of the following eight relationships to each other: wife/husband; mother/unmarried son, mother/unmarried daughter, father/unmarried son, and father/unmarried daughter; unmarried brother/unmarried brother, unmarried brother/unmarried sister, and unmarried sister/unmarried sister. The *extended family* may be defined as consisting of a group of relatives, usually larger in number than the immediate or nuclear family, in which at least two of its members stand in a relationship other than any of those of the immediate family, who live in one, two, or more households, and, if more than one, usually in a single locality, who share common domestic, social, and economic activities throughout each week. It generally consists of three (or four) generations of relatives — grandparents (and greatgrandparents), one or more of the married children (together with children-in-law), and grandchildren — although it may comprise the immediate or nuclear families of two married siblings, say, when making up more than one household.

These different groups or clusters of individuals serve particular psychological and social functions. Otherwise they would not exist. That is why the biological ties between the members are reinforced. But we should remember that each cluster is drawn from a larger aggregate of kin, which has a definite structure; that is, it is made up of different individual elements in a particular relationship. This is the

---

[3]See, for example, Henning Friis, "Cross-National Research on Old Age," *International Social Science Journal*, XV, No. 3 (1963), 451-55; and Ethel Shanas, "Some Observations on Cross-National Surveys of Aging," *The Gerontologist*, III (March, 1963), 7-9. The British research was supported by grants MH-05511-02 and CH-00053-02 respectively from the National Institute of Mental Health and the Community Health Services Division, Bureau of State Services, of the United States Public Health Service.

[4]For an account of research method see Peter Townsend and Caroline Woodroffe, "Sampling the Populations of Hospitals, Nursing Homes and Residential Institutions," unpublished paper presented to an International Social Science Research Seminar in Gerontology, Markaryd, Sweden, August 5-9, 1963.

"kinship network," and although its possible extensions are infinite, it may be restricted, for all practical purposes, to that aggregate of surviving kin known to an individual or to the other members of the immediate and extended families to which he belongs. Besides the eight primary relationships which could exist within the immediate family, there are the relationships which already exist, at the time of marriage, on the husband's side and on the wife's side. Other links are developed as the children themselves marry and rear the next generation.[5] Individual relatives may group themselves differently for different purposes.

Great diversity exists in the structure of each kinship network and also among the component immediate and extended families. Few attempts have yet been made to examine such variations systematically within a society. The relationship between two individuals in a family group will be affected, for example, by their sex, their marital status, their difference in age, the generation to which they belong, whether they have a biological or an affinal relationship, and what that relationship is.[6] When we consider not two individuals but a largish family group, these individual characteristics might be combined in many different ways.

Human beings belong to households and families rather as neutrons and electrons belong to atoms and molecules. The effect of an adult marrying or a child being born is like adding an extra neutron to an existing molecular structure or introducing a new particle into a human cell. Perhaps after an initial period of random or "exploratory" reaction, the component units will settle down into a new pattern of relationships and behaviour. They divide, and coalesce.[7] Put crudely, the composition or structure of the whole will determine (1) the behaviour of the whole, (2) the relation between any two particular units, and (3) the "character" of any individual unit. More exactly:

1. The collective behaviour of any corporate group of kin will vary according to (a) the composition of the group, and (b) the network of kin into which the group is knitted;

2. The quality and intensity of the relationship between any two members of an immediate or extended family or a kinship network will vary according to the structure of that family or network;

3. The character or personality of an individual will vary according to

[5]For an analysis of the different structural possibilities see George Peter Murdock, *Social Structure* (New York: The Macmillan Company, 1960), particularly Chapter 6.

[6]See Murdock's discussion of the principles employed by human societies in the linguistic classification and differentiation of kinsmen, *ibid.*, pp. 101-106.

[7]Firth, for example, notes the difficulty of separating "one set of kinship ties from that of others in the same system; they are like a set of forces in delicately poised equilibrium; if one is disturbed, others must respond in adjustment also." Raymond Firth, *We The Tikopia* (London: George Allen & Unwin, 1936), p. 218. See also George C. Homans, *The Human Group* (London: Routledge & Kegan Paul, Ltd., 1951), particularly Chapter 10.

the structure of the immediate and extended families in which he is
reared and to which, as an adult, he belongs.

These may be treated as provisional hypotheses. For example, we
are saying that in the "immediate" family of parents and young children the form and character of the relationship between man and wife,
and each parent and each child, as well as their individual personalities, will tend to differ according to the number and sex of their dependent children. Thus, husbands and wives would behave
differently towards each other in the families of different structure
illustrated in Figure 8-1, as would fathers and sons, mothers and sons,
and brothers and sisters.

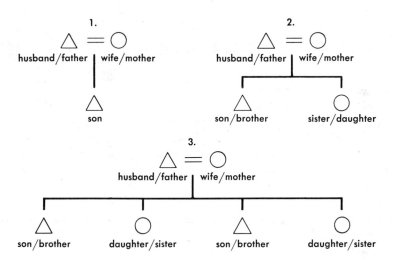

fig. 8-1   three simple forms of the immediate family of parents and dependent children

But to pursue these variations solely within the context of the
immediate family is not enough. The husbands and fathers are themselves sons and brothers, and their relationships with their wives and
children cannot be understood except in the context of the structure of
the extended family (in our clear but limited sense) and at least the
adjoining sectors of the kinship network. Thus, one study showed that
husbands help their wives less often and share fewer pursuits with
them when daughters or other female relatives live at home or nearby;
and that unmarried or otherwise childless people have closer relationships with brothers and sisters (and particularly close relationships
when both siblings remain unmarried) than people with children.[8]
Again, people have a significantly closer relationship with children-
in-law when they possess no children of like sex. Indeed, the relationship seems to be particularly close when the child-in-law's parents are
dead or living at a distance. To some extent, daughters-in-law substi-

[8]Peter Townsend, *The Family Life of Old People* (Harmondsworth, Middlesex:
Penguin Books, 1963), pp. 66, 86-88, 120-23.

tute for daughters, and sons-in-law for sons.[9] The effects of changes in structure are shown illustratively in Figure 8-2.

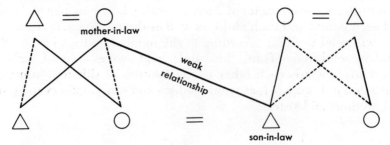

1. More usual relationship

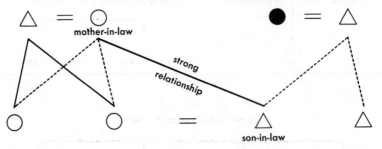

2. Mother-in-law with no son; son-in-law whose mother is dead

fig. 8-2   effects of difference in family structure on relationship between mother-in-law and son

These examples do no more than suggest how it may be possible to obtain some insight into personality and family relationships through the testing of certain hypotheses involving kinship structure. For the present we shall have to rely on rather simple correlations. There is too little empirical evidence about the actual relationship between different pairs of relatives and about variations in kinship structure to allow sophisticated validation or theory.

the elderly living in residential homes in england and wales

Old people seeking residential care form a very small minority of the elderly population. In England and Wales in 1959 approximately 17 per 1,000 persons aged 65 and over lived in Homes run by local councils, voluntary organizations, and private individuals under the provisions of Part III of the National Assistance Act of 1948 (and about another 24-25 per 1,000 were patients in hospitals and nursing Homes). About two-thirds of them lived in local council Homes and the others in voluntary and private Homes. Half of those in the council

[9]*Ibid.*, pp. 100-102.

Homes were in old poor-law institutions, and the other half in converted and newly built Homes opened since the war.

A survey carried out at this time showed that by contrast with the general population of 65 and over, the older people living in Homes are, first, much older. The proportion rises steeply with advancing age, reaching 50 per 1,000 for both sexes in the early eighties. Second, there are proportionately as many women as men aged 65 and over among them, although there tend to be more men than women of each particular marital status. Third, there are relatively several times more unmarried and widowed than married persons among them. One striking fact is that between 140 and 150 of unmarried persons aged 85 and over live in residential Homes.[10] Table 8-1 gives estimates based on information about some 7,500 old people living in a sample of 173 establishments in 1958-59.

table 8-1   number per thousand old people of a given age, sex, and marital status in england and wales who were living in residential homes in 1958-1959*

sex and age	all persons	marital status		
		unmarried	married	widowed and divorced
Men				
65-69	5	42	1	12
70-74	12	81	1	22
75-79	23	104	4	35
80-84	48	154	11	63
85+	63	137	16	74
All ages	17	82	3	37
Women				
65-69	3	13	1	3
70-74	9	27	2	8
75-79	19	48	3	17
80-84	41	88	8	38
85+	79	152	40	66
All ages	17	42	2	19

*Estimated from information about 7,689 persons of pensionable age in a sample of 173 institutions and Homes.

Source: The table is based on population figures for 30 June 1958, published by the Registrar General, though the distribution by marital status of the three oldest age-groups had to be estimated from information given in *The Report by the Government Actuary on the Second Quinquennial Review of National Insurance* (London: Her Majesty's Stationery Office, 1960). The information about elderly residents was collected during visits to the Homes in the sample between October 1958 and September 1959.

The residential population includes not only a disproportionately large number of unmarried persons but also of married persons without children. Twenty-eight per cent of men and 35 per cent of women of pensionable age in the sample who were married, widowed, or

[10]In 1951, 85 of every 1,000 bachelors, and 59 of every 1,000 spinsters, who were aged 75 and over, were in National Health Service hospitals in England and Wales. No information is available for those aged 85 and over. It therefore seems likely that about a quarter of unmarried persons of 85 years of age and over live in institutions of various kinds. Brian Abel-Smith and Richard M. Titmuss, *The Cost of the National Health Service* (London: Cambridge University Press, 1956), p. 140.

divorced had no surviving child, compared with an estimated 15 to 16 per cent of both sexes in the elderly population. Altogether we found that nearly 60 per cent of the residential population were childless, compared with 24 per cent of the elderly population.[11] Indeed as many as 14 per cent of the residents had no known relative.

the lack of close relatives

When we consider the fuller information from our sample of new residents as distinct from the information from our sample of all residents we find confirmation of the same trends. Proportionately more of the persons admitted to Homes are drawn from the older age groups. Forty per cent of the men and 45 per cent of the women in the sample were aged 80 or over compared with 14 per cent and 12 per cent respectively among the general population of pensionable age.

The new residents also differ strikingly from the general population in marital status. The proportion of unmarried persons admitted is much larger than the proportion of widowed and divorced persons, and many times larger than the proportion of married persons. Far more men than women of a particular marital status are also admitted. We estimated that in the year of our survey approximately 25 in every 1,000 bachelors aged 65 and over, compared with 15 in every 1,000 spinsters of that age, entered a Home. For widowers and widows the figures were 19 and 9 respectively, and for married men and married women 2 and 1 respectively. Despite this sharp difference between the sexes it is nonetheless true that (1) more women than men, in absolute numbers, are admitted, and (2) the relative proportions of men and women admitted are almost the same — there being just a slight excess of men. The reason is that there are far more women than men in the elderly population (61 per cent of those aged 65 and over), and there are also relatively more widows than widowers. Table 8-2 shows the results in more detail.

Such results are merely the surface indications of underlying social phenomena. The new residents differ in other ways from the general population. A disproportionately large number of those who are married, or widowed, are childless. This is shown in Table 8-3.[12] Nearly three-quarters of the childless persons in the sample had never had children, the others had lost their children.

We may consider further the two main groups. Those with no surviving children formed 51 per cent of the sample. Nearly three-fifths of them had at least one surviving brother or sister and described

[11]Estimates for the elderly population are based on provisional data from the survey in 1962 of persons aged 65 and over living in private households in Britain.

[12]In visiting a sample of residential institutions we gained information about all those admitted within the previous four months, including those who had since died or left. It proved impossible to obtain complete information about the latter, numbering 136. The account in the rest of this paper refers only to the 530 persons who still resided in the institutions on the day of our visits.

table 8-2 number per thousand old people of a given age, sex,
and marital status in england and wales who had
entered residential homes in 1958-1959*

		marital status		
sex and age	all persons	unmarried	married	widowed and divorced
Men				
65-69	3	17	1	11
70-74	5	20	2	10
75-79	11	30	3	21
80-84	23	50	11	30
85+	26	33	13	31
All ages	8	25	2	19
Women				
65-69	1	5	1	1
70-74	5	11	1	7
75-79	9	17	1	11
80-84	16	33	6	13
85+	26	39	28	23
All ages	7	15	1	9

*On the basis of a sample of 666 admissions to old people's Homes.

table 8-3 the possession of surviving children by new residents
and by the elderly population*

surviving children	new residents		population of pensionable age	
	men per cent	women per cent	men per cent	women per cent
Total	100	100	100	100
None (unmarried)	26	33	8	15
None (once married)	18	23	13	13
At least one	56	44	79	72
N =	204	323	2,072,000	4,543,000

*Sample of 530 new residents of old people's Homes; total population of pensionable age. One man and two women among new residents were unclassifiable.

Source: The percentages of men and women of pensionable age who are unmarried are taken from population figures for 1958. The figures for once married but childless persons are tentative estimates based on two sources: the *Registrar General's Statistical Review*, 1958 (infertility rates of deceased women), and D. V. Glass and E. Grebenik, *The Trend and Pattern of Fertility in Great Britain, A Report on the Family Census of 1946* (London: Her Majesty's Stationery Office, 1954).

where they lived; others had nieces, nephews, and cousins, but a tenth were unable to name with confidence the whereabouts of any surviving relative.

The new residents with surviving children (including step- and adopted children) numbered less than 49 per cent. Compared with the general population a disproportionately large number of them had one child (29 per cent) or two only (30 per cent).[13] Rather more of them had sons than daughters (79 per cent compared with 73 per cent), whereas

[13] Of those aged 75 and over with children who were interviewed in the British survey of 1962, 25 per cent had one child and 23 per cent two children. Scrutiny of fertility data obtained in successive Censuses broadly confirms these figures.

in the general population the opposite holds (76 per cent compared with 78 per cent), as Table 8-4 shows. Indeed, the table almost certainly understates the true difference in family structure between the two populations, because the new residents consist mainly of persons aged 75 and over who belong to a generation which had larger numbers of children than the one immediately succeeding it.[14] It is also important to note that only 43 per cent of the men and 31 per cent of the women in the sample had a surviving daughter.

table 8-4   family structure of new residents and the elderly population*

number and sex of children	new residents of homes per cent	old people living in their own homes per cent
Total	100.0†	100.0
One son only	15,6	11.7
One daughter only	13.7	13.7
Two or more sons, no daughter	10.9	9.9
Two or more daughters, no son	7.0	10.4
Children of both sexes	52.7	54.3
N=	256	3,092

*Sample of 530 new residents of old people's Homes; sample of 4,067 persons aged 65 and over in private households in Britain. There were also 271 (and three unclassifiable) and 973 (and two unclassifiable) who had no children.
†Per cents do not equal total because of rounding.

Of the new residents having children 8 per cent had step- or adopted children only and a further 3 per cent step- and putative children. These proportions may be higher than in the elderly population as a whole. Nearly a fifth of persons with children had no grandchildren, and altogether only 46 per cent of the men and 39 per cent of the women in the sample were grandparents.

These facts about family structure and status are clearly important in explaining social insecurity. Many of those we interviewed were well aware of their isolation. A widow said: "I never thought I'd come to this. It makes a difference not having a daughter or a son." Another widow wept when she spoke about her family background: "We buried our Charlie and our Bill (nephews). My favourite nephew came to live in Scarborough and he helped me and then he died. He clung to me like a mother. I used to tell my husband when we didn't get any children, '*You* won't feel it when you get older but *I* will.'"

This was as though one were looking at the commonest relationships of society through the wrong end of a telescope, through the eyes of people who had not experienced them. Bachelors and widowers affirmed the importance of wives, and childless persons of children. Men and women alike seemed to recognize that the ability to go on living in a normal community was weakened in old age if there

---

[14]The data from the 1962 survey which would allow us to standardize for age are not available at the time of writing.

were no relatives of succeeding generations to replace the loss, by death and illness, of relatives of the same or of preceding generations. Such relatives also provide links with the rest of society. An old person's acquaintances and friends can be his daughter's neighbors, his son's workmates, his grandchild's school-friends. Family relationships extend into and merge with the whole community. It is usually more difficult to maintain other social relationships when family relationships do not exist.

the elderly living in all types of institutions in britain

The wider survey completed in 1963 bears out much of the account given above. In institutions of all kinds there are relatively more women than men in each age group above 65, but the difference becomes marked only for those 75 years of age and over. As Table 8-5 shows, about twice as many unmarried as widowed elderly persons are in institutions, and many fewer married than either widowed or unmarried persons are in institutions. The individual breakdowns of the table for each type of institution are, of course, subject to substantial sampling errors, but these breakdowns do suggest variations in population patterns. The proportion of persons in psychiatric hospitals does not rise so sharply with age as in other institutions, and the relative excess of unmarried persons in them is even greater than elsewhere. For example, 4.4 per cent of unmarried men and 2.6 per cent of unmarried women of 65 and over are psychiatric inpatients, compared with 0.7 per cent and 0.9 per cent respectively of the the widowed.

table 8-5　number per thousand old people of a given age, sex, and marital status in britain who were living in institutions in 1963*

sex and age	all persons	unmarried	married	widowed and divorced
Men				
65-69	1.3	7.2	0.6	2.5
70-74	2.1	12.2	0.8	3.3
75-79	3.6	15.0	1.4	4.4
80-84	6.0	13.5	3.0	7.4
85+	11.9	19.0	4.7	14.5
All ages	2.9	11.5	1.0	5.5
Women				
65-69	1.4	4.8	0.6	1.2
70-74	2.3	5.6	1.0	2.4
75-79	4.5	8.8	1.7	4.5
80-84	8.9	17.4	3.6	8.1
85+	15.3	26.1	11.2	13.5
All ages	4.0	8.6	1.2	4.5

*Based on a sample of 2,205. The estimates are provisional only. They do not cover some 25,000 elderly patients in general and teaching hospitals (in a total institutional elderly population estimated to number 266,000). Population figures by marital status and age for 1963 were not yet available at the time of writing and estimates for 1962 have been used. Twenty-nine persons in the sample were unclassifiable.

Table 8-6 shows in summary form the marked differences in marital status between the elderly institutional and the total elderly population, but also brings out some of the differences between the populations of each main type of institution. Even in nonpsychiatric hospitals (which here include private nursing Homes as well as geriatric hospitals), there is a disproportionate excess of unmarried persons.

table 8-6   the marital status of the elderly institutional
and the total elderly population in britain, 1963*

marital status	all institutions per cent	residential homes per cent	psychiatric hospitals per cent	non- psychiatric hospitals per cent	total britain per cent
Men					
Total	100.0	100.0	100.0	100.0	100.0
Unmarried	31.8	30.2	47.4	19.4	7.9
Married	24.2	13.8	32.4	34.9	69.2
Widowed and divorced	44.0	56.0	20.2	45.7	22.9
N=	666	318	173	175	2,333,000
Women					
Total	100.0	100.0	100.0	100.0	100.0
Unmarried	33.5	35.7	38.3	26.4	15.6
Married	9.7	5.3	16.5	9.9	33.6
Widowed and divorced	56.8	59.0	45.2	63.7	50.8
N =	1,500	642	392	466	3,736,000

*Sample of 2,205 persons aged 65 and over; total population of 65 and over. Unclassifiable, 39 in the sample.

A disproportionately large number of persons in institutions who are married or divorced are childless: amounting to 27 per cent in this sample, compared with 15 per cent in the elderly population as a whole. If the unmarried without children are included, the childless comprised 49.5 per cent of the men and 49.9 per cent of the women in all types of institutions, as Table 8-7 shows.

table 8-7   the possession of surviving children by the elderly
institutional and the elderly noninstitutional population*

surviving children	all institutions		private households	
	men per cent	women per cent	men per cent	women per cent
Total	100.0†	100.0	100.0	100.0
None (unmarried)	33.0	32.5	4.4	13.9
None (once married)	16.5	16.5	14.9	13.2
At least one	19.3	20.6	20.7	18.3
More than one	31.3	30.4	60.0	54.6
N =	643	1469	1629	2436

*Institutional sample of 2,205; private household sample of 4,067. Unclassifiable, 93 in the institutional sample (many of whom were known to be married or widowed but whether they had children was not known). Two in the private household sample were unclassifiable.
†Per cents do not equal total because of rounding.

Over one-third of those in institutions with children have only one, compared with a quarter of the elderly noninstitutional population. Relatively fewer of them have daughters, too, amounting to 72 per cent in this sample compared with 78 per cent of the elderly noninstitutional population. Table 8-8 shows some of the differences in family structure.

table 8-8   family structure of the elderly institutional and noninstitutional population*

number and sex of children	all institutions per cent	private households per cent
Total	100.0	100.0
One son	18.1	11.7
One daughter	18.1	13.7
Two or more sons, no daughter	10.0	9.9
Two or more daughters, no son	6.7	10.4
Children of both sexes	47.1	54.3
N =	508	3092

*Institutional sample of 1,102; private household sample of 4,067. Information about family was obtained only from half the institutional sample of 2,205. The unmarried are also excluded in this table. Unclassifiable, 32 and 2 respectively.

Even as regards other relatives the institutional population is not rich. Over 40 per cent of those in the sample had no brothers or sisters, compared with 22 per cent in the private household population. Of those with children fewer had grandchildren (82 per cent compared with 87 per cent), though, because of their advanced age more of them had great-grandchildren. Altogether, 7 per cent had no known relative.

Compared with the unmarried and otherwise childless, those who possess children are more often incapacitated, as Table 8-9 shows. In fact, the table implies that many old people with children continue to live at home to an advanced stage of infirmity before seeking admission to an institution.

table 8-9   incapacity of the elderly institutional population, according to possession of children*

Personal incapacity	no children per cent	one child only per cent	more than one child per cent
Total	100.0	100.0	100.0
None or slight	28.3	25.1	21.0
Moderate	24.2	13.4	22.2
Severe	27.3	32.6	27.1
Bedfast	20.2	28.9	29.7
N =	550	187	347

*Institutional sample of 1102. A measure of personal incapacity was based on answers to questions involving mobility, and capacity to wash, bathe, dress, and cut toenails. Unclassifiable, 18.

the loss of supporting relatives

Detailed illustrations of family circumstances were obtained in the first inquiry of residential Homes. In many personal accounts the sudden loss of a supporting relative was plainly critical. A wife died or went into a hospital. A son was killed in an accident. A daughter emigrated to Canada with her husband and family. A widowed sister became more infirm and moved to live with her married children. A niece was no longer able to live with her aunt because she took a residential nursing appointment. The death or the sudden illness of close relatives were the most common events precipitating admission. Table 8-10 shows how many old people had recently lost a close relative, and it may understate the actual numbers.

By losing a close relative, an individual experiences "desolation" and not necessarily "isolation." Only when there are no other relatives to replace or compensate for the loss does he experience the latter. This is what characterized the situation of many people in the sample. They had few, or no, substitute sources of help and affection. An infirm woman lived ten miles from two sisters aged 85 and 86 and a niece who was a semi-invalid, and depended almost entirely upon her husband until his sudden death four months earlier. Another had gone into the hospital after the successive deaths of her husband and only son: "I've only a niece, and I've never seen much of her. It isn't like your own son or daughter. She couldn't look after me now."

Widowers were particularly insecure. In old age a man often seems to depend more on his wife than she on him. When he loses her, he often talks touchingly of his desolation: "You lose your wife. You lose your home. You lose your health. It's only natural to feel down sometimes. Your don't know what it is in the night with nobody with you. When a man loses his wife, he's like a bird with only one wing. It's more than half of you gone." Over 25 per cent of the widowers in the sample had lost their wives within the three years previous

table 8-10   recent loss of a close relative*

loss of close relative within previous 3 years	per cent of old persons
Total	100
By death before admission	19
By hospitalization or emigration before admission	8
By death or otherwise after admission	4
No evidence of loss	69
N =	530

*Sample of 530 new residents of old people's Homes. "Close relative" defined as a spouse, child, or any other relative (for example, brother, sister, niece) with whom the old person was living or on whom had been placed considerable material and emotional dependence.

to their admission, and a further 23 per cent within six years, compared with 15 per cent and 13 per cent respectively of widows. Again the comparative paucity of substitute sources of help was noticeable.

Sometimes old persons entered an institution more in anticipation of the loss of a relative rather than as a direct consequence. One woman's son, a serviceman, was to be posted abroad and she left her home a month before his departure. Other people took the same step before the death of a close relative or in the knowledge of their impending hospitalization. Sometimes they were not themselves very infirm and regarded the prospective loss of a relative as a warning which they must heed. An ex-schoolteacher, for example, said that she would have no relatives once her sister, who was suffering from cancer, died. "Unless I was to die suddenly I knew that sooner or later I should come to physical dependence of some sort. I knew that I would be unable to call on any help." Studied anticipation of this kind was rare, however.

The loss of a relative often led to a series of changes in old persons' living arrangements rather than immediate admission to an institution. They felt obliged or were persuaded to give up their homes and sell their furniture. They tried living with one person and then with another. Family resources were sometimes limited, or close relationships with a new household could not be established, and spells of ill-health added to the difficulties. People who even after an initial misfortune had a fierce sense of independence and of self-reliance seemed gradually to weaken and become insecure after several unsettling changes of residence. To lose a close relative and one's home at an advanced age and then to move, or be moved, to another home, hospital, nursing Home, or old people's Home creates bewilderment, resignation, and near despair. Old people rarely choose to make a new life for themselves. Their security consists in attachment to home, locality, former relationships, even personal possessions. To be denied some or all of these is to be denied access to life itself. Or so many people appeared to feel. The fact that such changes had occurred at all seemed in itself to be a contributory cause of admission.

We were unable to keep an exhaustive check on the social changes experienced by many new residents. Sometimes the facts were difficult to explore and, particularly when a person had come direct from a hospital, the admitting authority had no record whatever of previous social history. Such ignorance on the part of officials and staff who have to cope with frail and bewildered old people itself explains why the latter often gave an impression of lacking social identity. A quarter of the sample had lived in at least three different private households, hospitals, or other institutions during the three years previous to their admission. Many of the changes had occurred as a result of administrative decisions taken by a public authority. Some people had lived in as many as seven, eight, or nine different places.

Changes such as these help to explain why it was often difficult to determine with confidence the chief event precipitating admission.

Mrs. Llandaff, a widow of 75, is an alert and intelligent woman but is blind as well as being physically incapacitated. "I had my own home. My son lived next door, and he had four boys and two girls. He sold his taxi business and went up to the Beacons to farm, and I went with him. That was after the war. Then he took a fish and chip shop in Swansea. He died five years ago without a will, and my daughter-in-law got his money. I stayed with her for two years, and then my niece offered me a room. I was with her for over a year, and then she had a nervous breakdown. That's why I went to these Homes. I was 3 weeks in one in Gloucestershire, but I was unhappy, and then I was advised to go back to the one in Wales. I do exactly what they tell me. I was there two years, and then I went to a hospital for nine months. The almoner said I should come here."

This example indicates the complicated history of many new residents. Some had lived for a few months with a succession of relatives; others had transferred from one hospital, nursing Home, or old people's Home to another. A number resorted to a number of different lodging houses, hostels, huts, caravans, and disused sheds which scarcely deserve the name of "home." These misfortunes were not confined to working-class people. The widow of a tailor, for example, had sold her house and had lived in turn with her three children, well-to-do people living in various parts of Surrey and Sussex, and then in three separate guest-houses in the brief space of three years before entering an institution.

separation from family and community

To the lack or the sudden loss of close relatives we can add geographical separation from family and community as a cause of isolation in old age. If old people live alone, it is supposed, then they are isolated. Field studies have, however, shown that relatives may live in separate households and still maintain very close associations, seeing each other often in the day and performing reciprocal services. Much evidence suggests that old people often prefer this arrangement to living with their children. And although modern means of transport make it feasible for relatives to keep in touch when they live miles apart, in practice arrangements between relatives work out best when they live within easy walking distance of one another.

For this reason considerable importance was attached in this survey to finding out the nearness of relatives to an old person before he entered an institution, as well as to finding out whether there were relatives in the same household. Among the 530 persons in the sample there were 256 with at least one surviving child; when last living in a private household, or in a lodging house or hotel, 39 per cent had not lived within a mile of any of their children (another 42 per cent having been in the same household, and the remaining 19 per cent in the same neighborhood). In the elderly population as a whole the comparable figure is estimated to be about 30 per cent at the most.[15]

The tendency for a higher proportion of the institutionalized old people to be geographically separated from relatives appears also to be shared by those who do not possess children. There were 157 persons in the sample who did not have children but who had at least one surviving brother or sister; 62 per cent had not lived with a brother or sister or within a mile of one. There were also 110 persons who possessed neither brothers and sisters nor children; 70 per cent of them had not lived with or near any other relative. Altogether, 5 per cent of the sample had no relatives, and a further 36 per cent, while possessing at least one relative, had not lived within a mile of them prior to their admission to an institution. A careful check revealed that few of these people lived even within five miles of a relative.[16]

The general impression was very different from that gained in surveys of the outside community. In interviewing old people living at home one frequently gets in a marvellous tangle tracing a complicated network of family relationships. There are sons and daughters, grandchildren and greatgrandchildren, brothers and sisters each with their offspring, and sometimes there are many households related one with the other in the same locality. If one household falls out of favor, another takes its place. In this survey such instances were comparatively rare. Even the occasional person who talked, say, of having "a field full of relatives" in the same town was more often referring to first and second cousins than to close relatives. Again and again we met persons previously living with or near just one relative (sometimes just an aged brother or sister) who represented all that was left of the family in the entire district. Altogether nearly 70 per cent of the sample had not been related, when they were living at home, to anyone living in another household within a mile radius. This figure is made up of 32 per cent who had in fact lived with relatives or other persons and as many as 38 per cent who had lived alone or in lodging houses, hostels, and the like. The picture of social isolation presented by these statistics is very marked.

[15]The survey of persons aged 65 and over in Britain in 1962 showed that 35 per cent of those with children were *not living within ten minute's journey of at least one of their children*. While it is difficult to compare the results from applying the two criteria, a pilot study has shown that some of these actually lived within a mile. In another survey of six different areas of Britain, only 25 per cent of the old people lived more than 15 minute's walk from any of their children. Dorothy Cole Wedderburn, with John Utting, *The Economic Circumstances of Old People* (Welwyn, Herts: The Codicote Press, 1962).

[16]So far as it was possible to judge, isolation from relatives did not vary strikingly according to the social class of old people. But in the interviews, old people of low occupational status frequently remarked on a child who was a doctor, a business executive, a civil servant, a matron, a school headmistress, and so on, and who had not lived near them or seen them often. It seemed that differences in class between the generations may be one important cause of separation from family, and hence of liability to admission to an institution in old age. Unfortunately our data did not allow a rigorous check.

Our data imply that fewer old people with relatives at hand find it necessary to enter institutions. If this is true, then we should also expect those among them who do find it necessary to be more infirm. In other words we might infer that those with relatives at hand are able to go on living at home to a more advanced stage of infirmity than would otherwise be possible. If confirmed, this inference has many implications for social policy. Table 8-11 perhaps supplies one of the most important results to emerge so far from our statistical analysis.

Persons who had been living alone were significantly less infirm than persons living with their children or with others. And among the former, persons with no relative living nearby tended to be less infirm than the rest.[17] These differences applied to both men and women, and did not appear to be accounted for by any other possible explanation, such as the loss of a home, bad housing, or the differing incidence of marital status, social class, or income.

table 8-11   incapacity of persons admitted from different types of private household*

		prior living arrangements			
		living alone			
incapacity for self-care	all living arrangements per cent	no relative within a mile per cent	relative(s) within a mile per cent	living with children per cent	living with other relatives per cent
Total	100	100†	100	100	100
Very slight	31	39	30	24	29
Slight	28	33	25	26	23
Moderate	22	17	30	26	21
Severe	19	10	15	24	27
N =	281	87	47	70	77

*Sample of 530 new residents of old people's Homes. Persons admitted from hospitals and other institutions excluded. Incapacity for self-care based on a special rating covering 16 items. Unclassifiable, 2.
*Per cents may not total 100 due to rounding.

the consequences of isolation

It is, of course, difficult to establish the facts about isolation from family. There are almost infinite variations in its structure, and it is hard sometimes to know whom to count as a member. Should we refuse, for example, to count an old person as isolated from his family if a first cousin lives in the next street? Defining the family is not the only difficulty. There are more subtle complications. An only daughter

[17]Incapacity was measured at some point between one day and four months after admission (averaging 8 weeks), and it may be argued that it would be wrong to correlate this with previous social conditions. This is a fair criticism, and it is true that we found evidence of some individuals improving or deteriorating in health in the early weeks after entering institutions. But so short a period of time had elapsed that the capacities of the majority seemed broadly to correspond with their capacities at admission. It seems reasonable, therefore, to attempt the correlation, even if it is not as sharp as is desirable.

may live in the next street, but she may be bedfast with cancer and, therefore, have few contacts with her parents. Alternatively she may live twenty miles away, but, because she is comparatively well off, can telephone daily and come over frequently in her car, sometimes taking her mother home with her for weekends. The definitions adopted for the purpose of measurement are necessarily imprecise.

Despite these difficulties the data we have described help to indicate why so many of the persons interviewed in this survey were isolated at a time when they had come to need help of one kind or another. Left largely to their own resources, they were compelled to give up many previous activities. Their health suffered for want of proper meals, and their homes became shabby. By the time some crisis forced an outsider to intervene, they needed more than stop-gap measures of support. The following two examples include much that is common to many histories.

> Mrs. Henry is a widow of 90. "My husband died eight years ago. He had his own painting and decorating business. I was living alone in a large house, and I let rooms. When I got rid of the tenants, I didn't want any more. I've only one sister and she's 85. She recommended me to come in a Home. When I first came to Bristol, she lived near me, but her husband had to move because of his firm — so when my husband died I had no one. I couldn't manage any more. My place went to rack and ruin. God was good to me. I was sitting by the fire and I fell down. I called upon God to help me get away from the fender. I wriggled my way across the room and opened the door. Then it took me just the same and threw me down. I called out 'come and help me please.' My neighbor came and then the doctor. I'd wanted a bungalow, but I thought it over and told the president of the Darby and Joan that I'd changed my mind. I haven't the money now. I came here a few weeks afterwards." There was no evidence of any help being given by statutory or voluntary domiciliary services.

> Mr. Carruthers, a former photographer of 68, is fairly active but complains of melancholia. Certainly he talks morosely. "I was living on fish and chips and pasties. My nerves were so bad I couldn't make decisions. I came in because I was beginning to feel so poorly." He is a bachelor and has only one sister, who is in a mental hospital. His only other relative, a "step-cousin," lived a mile away but "is in bad health and I haven't seen much of her in recent years. I didn't see much of anyone and got in a dirty state." The case record indicated that though he might have been helped to remain at home for longer, he had been found in such neglected conditions, first by a chance visitor and then by his doctor, that it was "impossible to instal the services of a home help" and "the case must be treated as a dire emergency."

Neighbors were sometimes extraordinarily helpful, in going to the shops, cooking meals, and making fires, but often they did not expect, nor were they expected, to undertake continuous services. As one woman living in a rural cottage aptly put it: "I couldn't be on my own all the winter. I had to depend on my neighbors."

Some isolated people had relatives living at a distance. We tried to find out why they had not gone to live with one of them. Of all the old people formerly living alone, 20 per cent had no relatives to go to, or had lost touch with them, 18 per cent said the accommodation was insufficient to take another person, and 22 per cent said the relative most likely to help them was ill or infirm. Most of the rest said either that they were unwilling to impose on any relative or expected difficulties to arise, but it is interesting to note that these were chiefly persons who lived at a considerable distance and had not had close associations with relatives in the recent past. The great majority lacked alternative social resources.

There is little doubt that an answer has still to be found through social policy to the problem of isolation in old age. We encountered numerous instances of persons living in tragic circumstances. The following extract from one case record was not at all unusual: "Destitute. Verminous. Admitted from home to the General Hospital in indescribable state with broken arm of several weeks standing. Home closed by sanitary authorities." Instances resulting in death are frequently reported in the press.

difficulties of living with the family

But what accounts for the admission of those who are not isolated, particularly those formerly living with other people? In the entire sample of new residents interviewed, 46 per cent had lived with others, usually relatives, before entering a Home (including those who had first gone to a hospital). We should remember that fewer of them than of those living alone had entered a Home and also that more of them had reached an advanced state of infirmity. About a third of them had lived with their married children and a tenth with unmarried or widowed children, but about a half had been living only with persons of about the same age as themselves—husbands or wives, siblings, other relatives such as cousins, sisters-in-law, and friends.

The old people had no possiblity of moving to an independent or alternative home of their own for a number of reasons, including shortage of money and lack of the right kind of housing. We sought to establish whether there were other relatives with whom they might be able to make a home. Although we would not claim to have been able to explore this question properly, the evidence we gained is of some interest. Thirty-five per cent had no other relative to whom they could turn; 25 per cent said that the relative to whom they would first be drawn could not accommodate them because of housing difficulties; and a further 21 per cent said they could not be accommodated because of illness or infirmity in the household. About a tenth said personal relationships would be difficult, and an equal proportion said that they refused to impose on these relatives. The majority clearly had little alternative but to live where they were.

What were their household problems, which may have partly explained their admission to a Home? There were first those who had

experienced acute difficulties of accommodation (excluding those living in housing with unsatisfactory amenities), and numbering 29 per
cent. They were significantly less infirm than the rest, a fact which
reinforced the importance we attached to accommodation problems in
explaining the admission of people to Homes. Many of them were
obliged to leave their homes because another member of the household was going into the hospital or was moving elsewhere or there was
a clear threat of the family being evicted. There were also a number of
people living in overcrowded conditions who took matters into their
own hands. One said, "I slept in the sitting room with my two grandchildren, and as they were growing up, my daughter and I thought it
was best for me to leave. There was only one bedroom. I didn't have to
go."

Second, there were those living with relatives who were themselves ill, infirm, or of advanced age. They numbered 36 per cent. One
widower lived with an unmarried son who was blind. The 58-year-old
daughter of another man of 81 was mostly confined to bed because of a
heart complaint and shortly after he entered an institution, was taken
to a hospital. A widow said that both her daughter and son-in-law were
ill: "She is going into the hospital for an operation, and he is a very
sick man with ulcers. My other daughter is in Canada and as I was
getting older, I didn't want to be a trouble to anyone." Sometimes the
illness or infirmity of a relative was the most obvious reason for an old
person's inability to go on living in the household. Often it was only
one of several reasons, which included overcrowding, financial
difficulties, and friction with a son-in-law or daughter-in-law.

It is difficult to classify the circumstances of the remaining 35 per
cent or so. Some were infirm and alone in the day while a son or
daughter was at work. Others relied on the services of a daughter-in-
law, say, who also had a part-time job as well as young children to
attend to. A number had a variety of problems, such as the woman
formerly living with a widowed sister-in-law who attended to a bedfast mother of 80 living next door. And the man whose daughter-in-law
was about to have a baby and who said that after seven years she felt
she could "cope with the old man no longer." Many old people themselves referred to the nervousness and strain placed upon a relative
because of their illness or infirmity. It was interesting to note how
often they drew attention to the continuity of strain. "My son and his
wife hadn't had a holiday for six years."

There were, of course, many references to friction with some other
member of the household, usually an in-law. In analyzing both the
case records and what old people had to say about the reasons for their
admission, we kept careful note of any evidence of poor relationships
with any other member of the household. Twenty-seven per cent of
those formerly living with others had experienced difficulties of this
kind (including those who had provoked them). Interestingly enough
these had rarely arisen when old people were living with brothers or

sisters, unmarried or widowed children, or a distant blood relative. Only one or two talked of a husband's hostility or intolerance, and though a few men complained about the attitudes of their wives, they were exceptional. One spoke of a third marriage which was a failure; another of a "housekeeper" with whom he had lived for 15 years, and a third of a wife 25 years his junior.

The problem appeared to have been greatest when a daughter-in-law or son-in-law had been living in the home. Personal frictions of one kind or another were reported in nearly a half of such households, occurring more often when there were sons and daughters-in-law than when there were daughters and sons-in-law (50 per cent compared with 35 per cent). This finding applied equally to old men and old women, whether or not they had spent a period in a hospital first. The person who told us that "a wife's mother comes before a husband's mother" seemed to be broadly correct.

Mrs. Mooney, a widow of 82 renowned for her belligerent language, formerly lived with her married daughter and family. "My daughter's husband said to me, 'You're nowt but an old nag,' and I goes up to him and I says, 'If I'm an old nag, it's thee has made me one, with coming to look after thy wife and looking after thy children. You were fain to run to me when thy wife were ready to be confined. Put that in your pipe and smoke it.' He said, 'It's time you went,' and I gave him such a one across his chops, and I says 'Take that.' I thought there'd be nowt left of me if I stopped with that lot. My daughter said she'd found a nice place for me." Mrs. Mooney is very infirm, is anaemic and incontinent, and can scarcely walk. She had been living in a small house not only with her married daughter and son-in-law but with an unmarried daughter and five grandchildren. The case file reports that her daughter was ill with a "nervous complaint."

Often the daughter-in-law or son-in-law was singled out as the main source of trouble. "He couldn't stand me and asked me to leave. He used to put his fist in my face." "She wouldn't speak to me and threw the meals at me. She led me a terrible life." But sometimes a son or a daughter was blamed instead or as well. Indeed a few children appeared to possess little affection for their parents and to feel under no obligation to give them much assistance.

Mr. Farmer is an infirm widower of 78. He is an ex-regimental sergeant major who had had rather fleeting relations with his wife and children in over 20 years of army service. His only son wrote this letter to the welfare department: "He is so completely unreasonable and uncooperative that one is prevented from doing anything for him. I would not have him in my home until the day comes when I'm prepared to have my family life smashed to pieces. . . . If he doesn't get individual personal attention, if everyone's routine is not geared to his, he becomes aggressive. You may think I'm a little callous . . . but the fact is that having searched my memory of my relationship with my father, I cannot find any single experience, not even as a boy, which could raise a spark of warmth or appreciation. Having him in my home while it would undoubtedly solve his problems would create 5 others — one for each member of my family."

But one catches here a note of something more than the mere want of affection and of a sense of duty that is normally displayed in the relationship between children and parents — the man's loss of contact with his family for many years. In one instance after another we became aware not only of the influence of housing problems and of abnormal pressures of physical defect or infirmity on the personal relationships between members of a household but also of the influence exerted by abnormal family history or structure.

Among the new residents with surviving children, over a quarter had unusual family relationships; there were those who had deserted their families ten, twenty, and thirty years previously and now had few or no contacts with them; those whose *children* had themselves deserted wives or husbands; those who had made a "common law" marriage after the death of their wives or husbands, sometimes regarded by the children as an offense to the memory of a parent; those with step-children ("When I took the mother, I had to take the children. Now she's dead, I don't look for them, and they don't look for me."); and those who, for various reasons, including imprisonment and prostitution, had lived apart from their families for many years before returning to them in old age. Without knowing more about the family relationships of the general population, it is difficult to determine the significance of such vicissitudes, but they are not likely to be as common.

Some antipathies, therefore, had their roots not only in problems of housing and disability but also in abnormalities of family history or structure. But how extreme had personal animosities proved to be, and how far had children shown themselves to be unwilling to care for their aged parents?

In attempting to put this matter into perspective two important facts should be remembered. First, there was much more evidence of genuine affection and of loyalty between parent and child than the reverse, even among the rather exceptional families encountered in this survey. People talked again and again of the love and solicitude shown by children, and we came across many examples of the financial and personal sacrifices made by a child. The following letter was received by a local authority welfare department (and the old man concerned was subsequently admitted to an institution).

Dear Sir,

I wonder if you could help me on this matter. You see I have my father living with me, he is going on 93; he is not ill, and of course he doesn't get up, only to go to the back. You see I wanted a holiday, just a week. I am sorely in need of this break. I feel if I don't get one I shall be ill. . . . It wants someone here all the time. I was wondering if you know of a widow or elderly couple who would live here for a week and would be trustworthy and reliable. I don't want him sent away anywhere. I have had him 28 years and have not got anywhere farther than the bottom of the road. I would be grateful for any suggestions.

I am, yours truly . . .

Second, while old people wanted to be in close touch with their families, they did not want to impose too much upon them. "I had home trouble. My daughter and son-in-law didn't get on well, and I'd been there some years. He asked me to leave. The children are growing up and there's not much room. I wouldn't go back to stay but I'd like to be near and see them often." "My daughter looked after me for 13 years and I'm blind. No one could want for better. But young couples are best left on their own. It's wrong to interfere. It's all right for a time, but they've their own lives to lead and I'd sooner be independent."

Of course, some people may not have revealed their real feelings about their relationships with children. Moreover, except in the course of some preliminary work, we were unable to learn the children's side of the story. Rather more intensive inquiry would be needed to obtain a properly balanced interpretation. But our interviews suggested that the crisis that had developed in some households was rarely attributable to the indifference or hostility of children.

Fundamentally, it was attributable to the forced expression, because of a lack of social resources to deal with problems of housing and disability, of tensions which smoulder beneath the surface in almost any household in which there are in-laws. The ties of blood can only with difficulty be reconciled with those of marriage and usually only by segregation in role and in space. A married person may happily accept the temporary transference of a partner's devotion or affection in times of family adversity, particularly if it can be expressed away from home. But in the home a variety of circumstances can bring them quickly to a breaking point. A wife may have parents living nearby as well as her own children to attend to; she may have come to accept the presence of her husband's mother in the home, even when the old woman is infirm. But once the mother becomes really frail and can no longer do much in the house or has one or two falls, the somewhat tenuous relationship that has been built up snaps. Memories of former discord are raked to the surface. The wife feels that her first obligations are to her husband, her children, and her own parents; her husband loves his mother and does not want to lose her. He goes on putting off the evil day, hoping for a solution until, more often than not, his wife presents him with an ultimatum. "You must choose between me and your mother." He seeks outside help in solving the problem, and the old person decides, "They don't want me."

These are the dramatic, apparently final, statements which catch our attention. Yet no one who attempts any thorough investigation of the circumstances of any individual can find it easy to apportion blame. There are all kinds of extenuating circumstances, frequently difficult to unravel, which may bring a household to the breaking point. A son may be physically ill, or have spent periods in and out of a mental hospital, or a daughter may have the strain of dividing her attentions between children, paid employment, and an infirm parent. Or there may be peculiarities in the family relationships themselves. As we have seen, an old man may have been out of touch with his family for twenty years because of service in the army, and it is not easy to renew intimate relationships. A woman may have left her husband and family to live with another man, and we can hardly expect them to feel so warmly towards her in her old age, even if they give her a home. We cannot ignore facts such as these even if it is difficult to evaluate their significance. What stands out throughout our analysis is the absence of practicable alternatives, of supporting relatives, friends, and social services.

intergenerational tensions and extended family structures in africa[1]

ROBERT A. LE VINE

A Western observer of extended family organization in non-Western societies is likely to be impressed initially with its socially beneficial aspects. By contrast with how little a Western individual may rely on his family and kinship relations, the mutual dependence among kinsmen in many non-Western societies is indeed impressive. The extended family can be seen as providing care for the aged, the infirm, and the unemployed (thus obviating the need for public assistance to such persons); facilitating the redistribution of wealth from the economically privileged to their less fortunate kinsmen; and making each individual feel secure in the knowledge that he will not face the adversities of life alone. The author believes it is true not only that extended family relations have these beneficial functions in many societies of Africa and Asia, but also that their role is frequently indispensable at the level of economic and institutional development presently obtained in those areas.

[1]The writing of this paper was assisted by a Research Career Development Award granted by the National Institutes of Health and was carried out while the author was a Fellow of the Foundations' Fund for Research in Psychiatry.

A growing body of anthropological evidence and anecdotal material indicates that, whatever the gains to society from extended family organization, it is often accompanied by manifestations of fear and hostility within its cohesive groupings. We hear of the frequency of suicide among the desperate young married women of traditional China seeking to escape from their tyrannical mothers-in-law. From North India it is reported that young wives develop hysterical seizures when marital obligations force their return to residence with their husbands' families. Assassins are hired to help settle internal family quarrels in Egyptian villages. Fraternal tensions within domestic groups are extremely widespread from China to West Africa, and in Africa the prevalence of polygyny results in divisive quarrels between the paternally connected sons of different mothers. Accusations of witchcraft and sorcery—a common medium for the expression of hostility—tend to be concentrated among kinsmen in East African societies. Parricide is a marked phenomenon in at least one Uganda tribe. The antagonisms between father and son in societies with patrilineal inheritance and descent, and between mother's brother and sister's son in those of matrilineal inheritance and descent, have been repeatedly documented in African studies. The burden of such disparate fragments of data is that the very structures which entail kinship obligations beyond the nuclear family engender antagonisms which may ultimately be registered in homicide, suicide, litigation, and other forms of interpersonal conflict.

Concerning the societies of sub-Saharan Africa, the author proposes to discuss three questions which have relevance to this symposium on intergenerational relations: (1) What aspects of extended family structure generate intergenerational tensions? (2) What institutionalized mechanisms exist to "manage" these tensions, that is, to minimize their socially disruptive effects? (3) How have intergenerational relations been affected by or reacted to economic and educational changes stemming from Western contact?

typical tensions in african extended family structures

To understand intergenerational tensions in Africa, one must bear in mind the organizational context within which such tensions arise in African extended family structures. By the latter we refer to domestic groups in which adults of two or more generations reside in close proximity and to groupings such as a minimal lineage which is based on a principle of descent and which may or may not coincide with a domestic residential group. In virtually every agricultural society of Africa there can be found some multigenerational primary group, based on kinship or a combination of kinship and residence, which represents the primary sphere of mutual dependence and common interest of its members. (In some societies an individual is a member of several such groups, with the important societal consequences that Fortes, Gluckman, and others have been at such pains to point out.) Regardless of whether this primary group is residentially concentrated, it is a multifunctional unit, usually involving joint property-holding, subsistence activities, judicial action, and ritual. These important functions, most frequently vested in extrafamilial institutions in industrial societies, require a high degree of formal organization within the African extended family structures.

The formal organization of the extended family unit involves clearly defined positions of leadership, which are invested with the power to make authoritative decisions concerning the functions of the group, that is, decisions concerning property, the allocation of economic resources, labor, the settlement of disputes, the application of sanctions to offenders, and religious activities. The occupant of a leadership position, often elderly, may have considerable common power within the group and a highly visible and respected position as its representative vis-à-vis other groups. Thus social prestige combined with the intrinsic rewards of the exercise of authority serve to make the assumption of a leadership position attractive to eligible members of an extended family group. If there is no rigid rule of succession such as primogeniture, considerations of ability, loyalty, or wealth then play a part in the selection of a successor to the leader, and the position may become the object of competition among group members. The competition may begin long before the position is vacant, and factions may form around each of the pretenders. If, on the other hand, there is a rigid rule of succession to leadership, overt competition may be eliminated, but tensions nevertheless can arise, primarily because the term of office is not definite. In many African societies the leader of an extended family group remains in office until his death. He may suspect his successor of wishing to hasten his death, and this may be more or less true. Thus the knowledge that the advancement of one is dependent upon the demise of the other causes the relations between the leader and his prospective successor to be strained, despite the high degree of respect paid to the aged.

We should not assume that these potentialities for tension over succession to leadership positions are made manifest in all or even the majority of African family situations. These tensions are widely recognized, however, and are likely to be found most conspicuously in those extended family units whose leadership positions carry with them political authority outside the family or considerable wealth.

A major task of extended family units is the allocation and transfer of those economic resources in which the group as a whole has at least residual rights and which may be jointly exploited or shared on some commonly accepted basis. The importance of this function to each individual member can hardly be overemphasized, for his livelihood and life chances are often derived entirely from his access to family property. In these agricultural societies men often spend their entire lives cultivating land and/or herding livestock which they received by virtue of their descent group membership and which will be transferred by that group upon their deaths.

In addition to inherited property, descent group membership often confers rights of usufruct for commonly held pastures, sources of water, and other economic resources. Furthermore, a man is often dependent on his kin group to raise the livestock, cash, or other goods necessary to pay his brideprice, and in the polygynous societies of Africa this is not simply a one-time occurrence in his lifetime. Unless there are extremely rigid rules for the inheritance of property upon death, its transfer before death (in case of brideprice), the sharing of income from the sale or exploitation of group property, and the sharing of usufruct rights — opportunities for competition and conflict within the descent group are likely to abound. The decision-makers of the group, in performing their allocative functions, are constantly confronted with the possibility that one member will claim to have been deprived of his rightful share and another member will attempt to gain more than his rightful share.

Where an elder may name his own heir or favor some heirs over others in the distribution of property, there is the expectable competition for his favor. Even where the rules of inheritance are rigid, inequalities within the group lead to resentments, and cases come up which are not adequately covered by the body of unwritten rules. These potentialities for conflict over economic resources exist within small-scale domestic groups as well as within corporate property-holding descent groups, although the exact nature of the conflicts vary according to the role of each unit in the allocative system.

In identifying points of tension in these extended family structures, we have been describing them almost as one would describe any formal organization in which there are positions of leadership and in which desired resources are shared, allocated, and transferred among the members. We have done this to emphasize the features which these kinship groupings have in common with any organization in which the transfer of power and property as the membership changes over time provides occasions for competition and conflict. However, as kinship groups, African extended family structures have other features which are not found in nonfamilial occupational and associational groups. One distinctive feature is that membership and experience in the organization begins at birth. Inevitably, at least some of one's fellow members are persons one has known from earliest childhood. This affords opportunities to base group solidarity on early affective ties, which may be very close, but it also means that the resentments and rivalries engendered in the early years may affect performance in adult relationships within the group. The emotional intensity of such long-standing hostilities may be greater than that characterizing the competition of strangers. While suppressed in everyday behavior, these grudges formed in childhood may flare into the open when a crisis occurs, pitting brother against brother, son against father, or nephew against uncle.

Another feature of these kinship groups not found in other formal organizations is the importance of sexuality and close affective bonds based on sexual unions. The struggle for power and property is complicated by matters relating to fertility, sexual possessiveness and jealousy, and incest taboos. Some of these matters are governed by rules which members may be tempted to violate; others (like fertility or sexual potency) may be matters of chance as far as group regulation goes, but which create inequalities and humiliations within the group which lead to resentments and jealousy.

We need not elaborate further on how a family group is different from a nonfamilial group. The point of this discussion is that the African extended family structures carry out economic and quasi-political functions in an atmosphere which is charged with emotions derived from childhood experience and sexual concerns. The tensions to be observed in such groups, then, result not only from conflicts over power and property, but from the fact that economic cooperation and authority relations are carried on between adults who have had intimate childhood contact and who are in some way concerned with each other's sexual behavior.

With this general organizational context in mind, we can proceed to the dyadic relationships in which intrafamilial tensions typically appear, and thus gain an impression of the sources of intergenerational tension. Since the points of tension vary with the type of kinship system and structural unit, we shall concentrate the discussion on one structural type, the patrilocal, polygynous extended family, which is propably most widespread in sub-Saharan Africa. By the "patrilocal, polygynous extended family" we refer to a domestic grouping typically comprised of at least one man of the senior generation with his several wives, his married sons and their wives and unmarried children, and other persons related by blood to one of the senior men. These others may be an aged parent of a senior man or a divorced or widowed sister. Such a family unit is basically a localized patrilineage plus the wives and unmarried daughters of the lineage members. In most areas each married woman and each adult male has a hut (or in some urban groups, a room) of her or his own. Groups of uterine brothers tend to form cohesive subgroups as they grow to maturity.

Two words of warning must be offered concerning the generality of the picture of this structural type being presented here. First of all, even in societies where it is most frequent, many persons will be found living in different family arrangements. This is not simply because of factors which make reality deviate from the ideal, but because the type as presented here actually represents only one phase in the developmental cycle of domestic groups in such societies.[2] These cycles also vary from one group to another, but frequently there is a formative phase in which the second generation has not yet been married and a later phase of dissolution in which the older generation has died off and the adult brothers have not yet set up their separate domestic groups. Secondly, patrilocal, polygynous extended families vary widely from one African society to another on so many characteristics — size, solidarity, internal ranking patterns, relation to wider kin groupings — that the type must be considered an abstraction of a few elements from a diverse set of instances.

The following dyadic relationships represent the most typical points of strain in patrilocal, polygynous extended families as found in sub-Saharan Africa.

Father — Son   Here the tension often centers about the father's fear that the son, particularly the eldest, will wish to hasten his death in order to gain independence from the old man or replace him as head of the family. In societies where the father is expected to transfer goods to his son for brideprice payment, conflict may arise over the father's delaying the transfer and/or the son's appropriating the goods in advance of formal permission from the father. The sexual rights of father and son also present problems: where the father exercises authoritarian domination over his sons, the danger exists that he will commit adultery with their wives, and this danger is recognized in many African groups. On the other hand, when the father is a senescent polygynist, wealthy enough to acquire numerous young wives but not virile enough to keep them sexually satisfied, the danger exists that the sons will commit adultery with his younger wives. In some groups — where the sons inherit these wives upon the father's death — this may be overlooked when the father is very old, but in others it is a real source of conflict. Illustrative material on father-son conflict is presented below.

Co-wife   The polygynous situation is fraught with potentialities for conflict. If the husband bestows more attention or material benefits on one wife or the other or if he favors one's child over another, resentment may turn into open hostility. Even if the husband acts equitably, the sterility of a woman who has a fecund co-wife, or the failure in school of a child when the co-wife's child proves brilliant, can lead to conflict. The more the co-wife relationship involves uncertainty as to the present or future distribution of advantages among the wives and their children, the more likely that hostility will result. The hostility reaches a peak where the wives' own efforts play a part in determining how much their sons will inherit from the father. Factors which diminish conflict between co-wives are hierarchical status relations (either through the appointment of one chief wife who dominates or through

[2]See P. H. Gulliver and R. F. Gray, eds., *The Family Estate in Africa* (London: Routledge & Kegan Paul, Ltd., 1964).

a rank ordering of all), a large age differential, and the residential separation of the wives. The hostility among co-wives is frequently expressed as accusations of witchcraft and sorcery.[3]

Brother—Brother   In polygynous families it is most common for half-brothers to feel competitive and somewhat hostile to one another, while uterine brothers form a cohesive and mutually loyal group. This represents the continuation of co-wife hostility in the second generation of the family, but it may also reflect the contemporary situation in which the young men find themselves. If their mothers have been mutually hostile for a long time, their respective sons are likely to have taken over the feelings of hostility of their mothers, toward whom they feel protective and loyal. However, in some societies, uterine brothers are classed together as a single unit for purposes of inheritance, so that they have a mutual interest in fighting for a larger share for their subgroup. The sons in patrilocal, polygynous families are responsible for the care of their own mother in the latter's old age, and the recognition of this, together with the intense loyalty which sons in these families develop toward their mother, often makes them resentful of any ill treatment which she might receive from their father as she grows older. As an example of such ill treatment, the father may take young wives and seek to favor them over the older. Among the Gusii of Kenya, the author observed a situation in which a man with three wives had so antagonized his sons by the oldest wife by favoritism shown toward the youngest wife that when he sought to modernize his farm, involving moving the hut of the oldest wife but not depriving her of any economic benefits, these sons assaulted him.

More frequently, however, the sons display their loyalty to their mother in hostility to their half-brothers over the allocation of resources. Actually, uterine brothers may also enter into conflict with one another over property, especially where the family was monogamous, where no living heirs remain from the co-wives, or where the division of resources between uterine segments has already taken place and is no longer at issue. The generational equivalence of siblings makes brothers in a patrilineal inheritance system natural competitors for property and power, and if they are not strictly ranked, conflict may result.

Mother-in-law—Daughter-in-law   In the patrilocal family, the woman comes as a relative stranger to reside with her husband's family; in many African groups, she comes from people who are regarded as enemies by her husband's kinsmen. This situation occasions a certain measure of mutual suspicion at the outset of the marriage as well as considerable fear on the part of the bride. She usually is in closest contact with her mother-in-law, who inducts her into the

[3]See Robert A. LeVine, "Witchcraft and Co-Wife Proximity in Southwestern Kenya," *Ethnology,* I (January, 1962), 39-45.

women's life in the family and directs her work in the home, fields, and markets. If a woman does not get along well in her husband's family and wants to break off the marriage, she is likely to claim that her mother-in-law does not treat her well and that the old woman practices witchcraft. In some cases the accusation of witchcraft appears to be fabricated by the bride in order to arouse the sympathy of her own kinsmen so that they will support her efforts to get out of the marriage, but there can be no doubt that other young women are genuinely afraid of their mothers-in-law and suspect them of evil doings.

We should note, however, that the tension between a woman and her mother-in-law is primarily a phenomenon of the first year or so of marriage. If it is intense, the marriage will be broken off; otherwise, the wife is likely to be accustomed to and to become friendly with her husband's mother. The situation in African societies is quite different from that in areas like North India where the mother-in-law's extreme domination is a strain on her son's wives for many years. In the latter situation all the women are confined in the house and its adjacent courtyards, attending exclusively to domestic tasks under the supervision of the mother-in-law. In most African groups, a wife not only has her own hut but also becomes quickly autonomous in her economic activity, cultivating fields allotted to her or trading on her own in the market. She may serve her mother-in-law and relieve the older woman of many oncrous tasks, but the wife's separate house, independent occupation, and freedom to travel on her own prevent her from being excessively dominated. Thus the resentment and desperation common among the younger wives in the extended families of India and others parts of Asia are rare in African societies. The author does not consider the mother-in-law — daughter-in-law relationship a point of great strain in African extended families.

From this review of tensions in dyadic relationships within the patrilocal, polygynous extended family, it is apparent that the major point of *intergenerational* strain is the father-son relationship. The sources of this strain are as follows: (1) Both father and son recognize that the latter will replace the former upon his death in at least some of his roles (that is, as family head, possessor of economic resources, sexual partner to the wives), and further that the adult son is capable of doing so immediately. This raises the possibility that as the father becomes senile, his sons will presume upon their inheritance, in contradiction to the patriarchal norms of the extended family, and contrary to the deepest wishes of the father. (2) The authoritarian father may be tempted to deprive his adult sons of the prerogatives they have as husbands and fathers in their own right, especially by having sexual relations with their wives. (3) Uterine brothers in a polygynous family form a faction with their mother and may rise to her defense against the father when they believe the latter is maltreating her. As this last point makes clear, any severe conflict within an extended family of this type is likely to be translated into father-son conflict because jural authority in the family is concentrated primarily in the father and secondarily in his sons and eventual heirs.

illustrative cases of intergenerational tension

The two ethnographic cases which follow are examples of inter-generational tension which is overt and relatively unregulated. In both cases the anthropologist reporting the facts has identified an alleged structural source of tension to explain the manifestation of hostility across generations in a family group.

In an analysis of homicide (99 cases) and suicide (68 cases) among the Gisu of Uganda, La Fontaine found evidence to indicate that inter-generational homicide among men was more common than intragenerational killing, and that the age group most heavily represented among the male killers—roughly 25-35—was the same as that most heavily represented among the male suicides.[4]

The ethnographer's analysis of the homicide situation is as follows:

> ... [W]here the exact relationship is known, there are eleven fathers and father's brothers killed to only five brothers. In two cases in which the father's brother was killed, the father was dead and the victim of the murder stood *in loco parentis* to the murderer. Three of the brothers are elder brothers and hence in a position of some authority vis-à-vis the murderers. As in most patrilineal societies, a man is subject to the authority of his senior male agnates [patrilineal kinsmen] who also control property, land, and cattle, which is the means by which status is acquired in this society. Identity of interest, mutual loyalty and cooperation between agnates are continually stressed, and the fact that these very mutual interests may feed personal rivalries and jealousies for which there exists no outlet, means that the actual relationship is very different from the ideal. Conflict results in a greater strain on the junior party because legal and jural rights secure the position of the senior, whereas ideals of what is just are the only safeguards of the junior man's claims. Thus a "good" father in Gisu society provides his son with land and the cattle with which to obtain a wife, but the son cannot sue his father if he fails in this duty. He can extort what he considers his due only by resorting to means which are socially disapproved.[5]
>
> ... [H]omicide is primarily committed by young men ...
> The peak period appears to be between 25 and 30. The ethnographic facts show that this is a difficult period for Gisu men. By this time they have achieved adulthood, by undergoing the rites of circumcision. There being no further gradation of men into formal age sets, a young circumcised man has the same formal status, in the society as a whole, as his seniors. After circumcision, a man is entitled to the privileges of an adult male and the

[4]Jean La Fontaine, "Homicide and Suicide among the Gisu," *African Homicide and Suicide,* Paul Bohannon, ed. (Princeton: Princeton University Press, 1960), pp. 94-129. Copyright Princeton University Press.
[5]*Ibid.,* pp. 107-108.

chief of these is the headship of his own family. In order to set up his own family, a man must have his own land and cattle, and it is his father's duty to provide him with them. However, the possession of large herds and much land mean high status in the community. An old man who is still vigorous is reluctant to relinquish to his son what he has acquired. To this rivalry is added another element which makes for conflict: although a man does achieve a change in ascribed status by passing through the *rite de passage* of circumcision, the structure of authority within the social group does not change. He is still subordinate to the authority of his seniors. But the inequality in terms of formal status that formerly supported this inequality of power no longer exists. Not only has the formal position changed but the newly-circumcised man begins to demand actual equality. Conflict between a man and his father is increased.[6]

La Fontaine adduces approximately the same factors to account for the high suicide rate of young men who are between the age of circumcision (at 16-20) and age 40. For a man in this age group, the disparity between his theoretical status as an independent adult equal to his father and his actual lack of access to the material advantages which would give him *de facto* independence is seen as frustrating and as resulting in suicide, as other legitimate outlets for aggression have been blocked. The ethnographer implies that some men are not equal to the struggle with their elders required to establish themselves socially, and that they are more likely to give up during this post-circumcision period than at any other time.

The second case involves a pair of *matrilineal* societies in the Nuba hills of the Sudan. As described in a well-known study by Nadel, the Korongo and Mesakin have many cultural similarities, including the pattern of the child of six or seven years of age moving from his father's house to that of his mother's brother, whose property (primarily cattle) he will eventually inherit.[7] The life of men from adolescence onwards revolves about a formal division into age classes, each of which is characterized by the right to engage in particular sporting contests — light wrestling, strenuous wrestling, and spearfighting — which serve as exhibitions of masculinity. The stage of strenuous wrestling marks the peak of physical vigor, while spearfighting is regarded as appropriate to the physical decline believed to be brought about by sexual relations, after which men must give up these exhibitions of masculinity altogether. When a boy who has reached puberty engages in his first sporting contest, his mother's brother ceremoniously bestows upon him an important gift — an animal from the uncle's herd — which Nadel refers to as the "anticipated inheritance," since the vernacular word for inheritance is applied to it.

Concerning divergences between the two groups, Nadel tells us that the Korongo "have no witchcraft beliefs at all" (which is probably

[6]*Ibid.*, pp. 108-109.
[7]Siegfried F. Nadel, "Witchcraft in Four African Societies: An Essay in Comparison," *American Anthropologist*, LIV (January, 1952), 18-29.

an exaggeration), while the Mesakin are obsessed by fears of witch-craft:

> Mesakin witchcraft is believed to operate only between maternal kin, especially between a mother's brother and a sister's son, the older relative assailing the younger. Mesakin witchcraft further operates only if there is a reason ... and the latter is almost invariably a quarrel over the "antici-pated inheritance"...[8]

Although the mother's brother in Korongo never refuses to give this special gift (though he may postpone it), his Mesakin counterpart always refuses to give it at first, and it often has to be taken by force, as it cannot legitimately be postponed. "Quarrels over it between the youth and his mother's brother are the rule; and if by any chance the former falls ill, dies, or suffers some other misfortune, the older man is invariably suspected of having employed witchcraft."[9]

To explain this difference in intergenerational conflict between the two groups, Nadel looks to divergences in their organization of social age. The Korongo have a total of six age grades, four of which involve the above mentioned physical contests, from which men withdraw gradually around the age of thirty, after having tapered off their participation and their visits to the young men's cattle camps. The sixth age grade begins around fifty with actual physical decline. In Mesakin, there are only three age grades of males: prepubertal, that of youths before parenthood (approximately 13-25), and that of men from parenthood until death. All of the athletic contests are concen-trated in the 13-25 age grade, and a man must abruptly withdraw from them as well as from life in the cattle camps when he leaves this age grade. Nadel regards the uncle's gift to his sister's son as a re-minder to the older man of his own withdrawal from the life of sport, in both societies. Among the Korongo, however, withdrawal comes later, social aging is in any event gradual, and the presentation of the gift can be postponed. The Korongo uncle is thereby cushioned against the implications which the anticipated inheritance has for the decline of his own masculinity. The Mesakin uncle, however, who is not prepared for his withdrawal and consignment to old man status, must go through it earlier and more abruptly, and he may not postpone the presentation of the gift to his newly active nephew. His resent-ment concerning his transition to the status of someone whose mascu-line vigor is being dissipated by sexual activity is vented upon his nephew—who replaces him in the life of the cattle camps—in the form of an illegitimate refusal to give the anticipated inheritance. The maternal uncle is openly jealous of his nephew, and his ungracious behavior makes him a likely target for accusations of witchcraft.

Both of these ethnographic cases of intergenerational tension involve an older man reluctant to give up status-conferring advantages

[8]*Ibid.*, p. 23.
[9]*Ibid.*

to his legitimate heir at a time when it is socially required that he do so. In the Gisu case, traditional regulations favor the older man, and it is the younger who resorts to illegitimate aggression. In Mesakin, however, society is on the side of the younger man claiming his due, and it is the elder whose resentment at being pushed out of active life leads him to be hostile in an unacceptable manner. This fear by a man of symbolic replacement by his sister's son in a matrilineal society is so similar to the fear of fathers vis-à-vis their sons in patrilineal societies that it can be taken as evidence that intergenerational conflicts in African kinship systems tend to follow lines of inheritance and succession.

The best published example of overt recognition of intergenerational tension in a patrilineal society is the report by Fortes on the Tallensi of northern Ghana.[10] The most pertinent passages follow:

> [A son] does eventually take the place of his father in the life of the community and could be suspected of wanting to hurry on the day when this will happen. His desire for independence is liable ... to run counter to his father's plans and demands. Every advance in his social and economic development might be interpreted as an added threat to his father's dominance. He will not be his own master until he has no father.... Tallensi themselves make no bones about the matter. "Your oldest son is your rival," ... the men say bluntly.... "Look at my oldest son," an elder once said to me. "He would not care if I should die tomorrow. Then he would inherit all my possessions...."
>
> This candor in fathers is not matched by their sons, who never admit the rivalry.... This is as one might expect, for it is the fathers who feel the threat to their dominance; and they feel it the more strongly as they grow older and their powers decline....[11]
>
> Tallensi explain the rivalry between father and son by means of the mystical concept of the *Yin* or personal Destiny. There is, they say, an inborn antagonism between the *Yin* of a father and the *Yin* of his eldest son. While the son is still young his *Yin* is weak, but as he grows older his *Yin* grows more powerful and wants to make him master of his own affairs. The son's *Yin* wants to destroy the father's *Yin;* but the father's *Yin* desires the father to live and be well and remain master of the house. ... Therefore it will try to destroy the son's *Yin*, and if it is the stronger *Yin* it will cause misfortune and perhaps death to the son.[12]

The idea that a father might anticipate the rivalry of his son and want to kill him is not limited to the Tallensi in West Africa. For example, Melville and Frances Herskovits report that Dahomean folklore contains many tales of men who killed their sons to prevent being overthrown by them.[13]

[10]Meyer Fortes, *The Web of Kinship among the Tallensi* (London: Oxford University Press, 1949).
[11]*Ibid.*, p. 225.
[12]*Ibid.*, pp. 226-27.
[13]Melville and Frances Herskovits, "Sibling Rivalry, the Oedipus Complex, and Myth," *Journal of American Folklore*, LXXI (January, 1958), 1-15.

the control of intergenerational tension

In one of his B.B.C. lectures on conflict in Africa, Max Gluckman noted:

> ... [T]here is this constant general difference between African domestic relations and our own — in Africa there is a whole series of rules to regularize relations within the family. And it is striking that while on the one hand the members of the family are brought together by these rules, on the other hand they are forced apart and estranged from one another.[14]

The thesis of this section is that customary patterns of estrangement — ranging from formality of interaction to outright avoidance — operate in some African societies to prevent intergenerational tensions of the type described above from disrupting the functioning of extended family groups. In other words, these patterns are cultural reactions to the tensions, that is, institutionalized attempts to avert conflict by minimizing emotional intensity in those dyadic relationships which are fraught with tension and in which open hostility would prove disruptive to group functioning. This hypothesis contrasts with, though it does not necessarily contradict that of Gluckman, who asserts that patterns of intrafamilial estrangement have as their primary function the integration of the individual in the extrafamilial social order and the consequent strengthening of total-society cohesion.

Some illustrations are needed to indicate the strength and elaboration of intergenerational avoidance patterns in African societies. Probably the most striking example is a custom which is found in a variety of forms among many groups involving millions of people in the Western Sudan, which is on the southern margins of the Sahara Desert in West Africa. This is the custom of avoidance of the first child, which has been described by Fortes for the Tallensi, by Skinner for the Mossi of the Voltaic Republic (north of Ghana),[15] and by Smith for the Hausa of Northern Nigeria.[16] The avoidance takes a different form in different tribes.

The Hausa taboo on social intercourse between a first-born and his parents is so strong initially that first-born children shortly after weaning are often sent to be raised by relatives, and only as adults can they have even the most restrained contact with their parents, taking care not to look them in the face. Tallensi first-born, on the other hand, are raised by their own parents but observe special taboos from the age of seven onwards, concerning eating with their father and touching his property, and these taboos are intensified for the first-born son as he becomes older. Soon after the time of his marriage, a first-born

---

[14]Max Gluckman, *Custom and Conflict in Africa* (New York: Free Press of Glencoe, Inc., 1955), p. 55.

[15]Elliott Skinner, "Intergenerational Conflict among the Mossi: Father and Son," *Journal of Conflict Resolution*, V (March, 1961), pp. 55-60.

[16]M. G. Smith, "Introduction," *Baba of Karo*, M. F. Smith, ed. (New York: Philosophical Library, 1955).

son and his father must not meet face to face in the gateway of their common homestead. Eventually, when he has children reaching adolescence, the Tallensi first-born son separates himself from his father by cutting a private gateway for himself in the family homestead.

Skinner's discussion of Mossi father-son avoidance illustrates the relation of this pattern to intergenerational tension. Although the first son is most likely to be a father's heir and successor, he is raised by his maternal relatives.

> A first son does not return to his father's compound until he is past puberty, but does visit him from time to time. These visits are quite formal and from very early time the first son is taught to be circumspect with his father. He learns to efface himself before his father and not to seek attention from him even though he sees younger siblings playing with him. When the boy does return home he is made to live with other young men of the extended family either within the compound or in special young men's quarters outside the compound....[17]

> Mossi fathers are so sensitive about being eventually replaced by their sons that they often resent the boys' growth and development. The first son is the target of this fear and hostility because he is the one who will benefit most from the father's death. However, if the first son happens to die, then the son who is next in line becomes the subject of his father's uneasiness. Mossi men have been known to upbraid their sons for growing beards, the significance of which is seen in the fact that men do grow beards as a sign of mourning on the death of their father.... As a rule, Mossi fathers tend to avoid any situation in which their eldest sons may be compared with them. For example, a man and his grown son do not walk together for fear of the embarassment which would be created if a stranger, not recognizing the age differential between them, greeted the son before he greeted the father.[18]

After his father's death, the eldest son must go through a very elaborate series of ceremonies aimed at demonstrating to the father's spirit that he did not usurp his father's property or have sexual relations with his father's wives during the old man's lifetime; these ceremonies are prerequisite to his actual inheritance. Skinner interprets the prohibitions, avoidances, and ritual proofs of good will imposed on the eldest son as safeguarding the continuity of the patrilineal family group from the potentially disruptive tension inherent in Mossi father-son relations. Similarly, Fortes (in an earlier analysis) interprets the Tallensi first-born taboos primarily in terms of avoiding the danger that a son will usurp his father's status in regard to procreation, property, and ritual relation to the ancestor spirits.[19] Although the existence of such taboos in other relationships indicates they may have other functions as well, they tend to be most intense between

[17]Elliott Skinner, "Intergenerational Conflict among the Mossi: Father and Son," *op. cit.*, p. 56.

[18]*Ibid.*, p. 57.

[19]Fortes, *The Web of Kinship among the Tallensi, op. cit.*, pp. 225-27.

father and son, and it is there that their role in the management of intergenerational tension to preserve family functioning and continuity is most evident.

On the other side of Africa, in the Kenya highlands north and east of Lake Victoria, are a number of related peoples who also have intergenerational taboos, although of a different type. Among the Gusii, these prohibitions exist between a person and every kinsman of his parents' generation, although they are most intense for men in regard to their own fathers.[20] The relevant persons of the parents' generation are referred to by a name which indicates that one experiences sexual shame in their presence, and indeed Gusii define the relationships in terms of the avoidance of sexual discussion or bodily contact of any kind. A man may not shake hands with these parental kinsmen, although he does with persons of his own generation, and he may not sleep in the same house with them, bathe with them, or be seen naked by them, or witness the mating of animals jointly with them. He must also be generally deferential to them and not contradict them. The taboo on sexual talk is so strong that a man may not inform his own father that his wife is pregnant; it must be done through intermediaries. These taboos, like those in the Western Sudan, put the burden of responsibility on the younger man, and in addition give the father a powerful weapon for humbling his son through extreme embarassment or worse: a father's curse involves the old man exposing and manipulating his genitals before his mortified son. However, the avoidance pattern does work both ways: a father may not enter his married son's house even though it is part of the homestead of which he is the head. Gusii fathers adhere to this so strictly that they will not enter a son's house to take out some chairs when guests arrive, even when there are no other chairs and there is no one else at home to fetch them. Father's brothers are allowed to enter one room in their nephew's house but must enter through an inconvenient opening from the cattle pen rather than through the main door.

These customs, which may appear to an outsider like bizarre ritual inconveniences, are taken by the Gusii themselves to be at the core of their morality, and though the Gusii are not very articulate about their significance, clearly these customs symbolically represent a mutual restraint which not only prevents the sons from sexual usurpation but also excludes the elders from the most private lives of their subordinate kinsmen. Unlike many other African peoples, Gusii are not allowed to inherit their father's widows, so that they attempt to eliminate any possibility for the occurrence of sexual jealousy between father and son. The writer's own interpretation of this is that the strict sexual morality of the Gusii would tend to make sexual jealousy a more disruptive area of father-son conflict than it would be in less

[20]See Robert A. LeVine and Barbara B. LeVine, "Nyansongo: A Gusii Community in Kenya," *Six Cultures: Studies of Child Rearing*, Beatrice B. Whiting, ed. (New York: John Wiley & Sons, Inc., 1963), pp. 115-202.

restrictive societies, and thus intergenerational avoidance is more elaborated in this area. In African groups such as the Tallensi where
prerogatives of ritual access to the ancestors are more important than
they are for the Gusii, intergenerational avoidance is concomitantly
more elaborately focussed about participation in ritual.

Thus African extended family structures appear to generate not
only characteristic intergenerational tensions but also characteristic
institutions for managing these tensions and avoiding disruption of
group functioning. As the author has asserted elsewhere,[21] the co-wife
hostility characteristic in certain types of African polygynous families
is diminished in some societies by increasing the distance between
the residences of the co-wives, thus reducing their opportunities for
contact. Intergenerational avoidance also reduces opportunities for
contact—and hence friction—between potentially hostile persons, but
it also tends to stereotype and inhibit their interaction by setting up
explicit rules which if adhered to will allow their necessary cooperation while by-passing their areas of potential conflict. Even where
avoidances do not reach the peak of explicitness described herein,
there is much formality of intergenerational interaction in African extended families. This formality is another way of increasing social and
emotional distance between persons whose hostility would be disruptive to operation of the family group in the many areas of life which are
not usually familial functions in Western societies.

We should note, nonetheless, that avoidance and its approximation in formality were not the only ways of managing intergenerational
tension in traditional Africa. An extremely important way—which
amounts to avoidance but is not *prescribed*—is the emigration of those
youths who had most difficulties in getting along with their elders in
the domestic group. Until recently, much of Africa was in a frontier
condition, with abundant land open to anyone who would cultivate it.
Even in societies that might be described as patrilocal, many sons did
move out to new land, and this movement provided a safety valve for
tensions in the family. In fact, some of the worst cases of unregulated
father-son tension described in the ethnographic literature—that of
the Gisu as described above and the Nyakyusa of southern Tangan-
yika as described by Gulliver[22]—have occurred in areas where land
scarcity has rapidly become a serious problem in recent years. In
those areas—particularly the Nyakyusa—sons could fend for themselves and did not have to depend on their fathers. In consequence,
father-son relations, particularly concerning property, did not have to
be as strictly regulated as in other African societies. Land scarcity has
made sons highly dependent on their fathers (and father's brothers) for
allocation of land, and this has aroused conflicts for which the family

[21]Robert A. LeVine, "Witchcraft and Co-Wife Proximity in Southwestern Kenya,"
    op. cit.
[22]P. H. Gulliver, "Land Shortage, Social Change, and Social Conflict in East Africa,"
    Journal of Conflict Resolution, V (March, 1961), 16-26.

structure was unprepared institutionally. Thus it appears that emigration as a mechanism for the control of intergenerational tension is highly vulnerable to contraction in land areas available for new settlement.

adaptation to new conditions

The impact of changes introduced by Western contact on the relations between generations in African families merits more extensive analysis than can be given here. However, one modern consequence of the pattern of intergenerational relations described above must be mentioned. The estrangement involved in formality and/or avoidance between fathers and sons conditions an individual to view intimacy and obligation as quite separate modes of behavior, inhering in different relationships. A son grows up recognizing many obligations to his father but is distinctly not intimate with him, and to a lesser extent this emphasis on obligation as opposed to intimacy holds for many relationships in African extended families. Thus when the individual leaves home, becomes educated in Western schools, and enters the modern occupational system, his remoteness from his natal family, though diminishing his opportunities for intimacy with them even further, does little to diminish his obligation. In fact, as a relatively privileged member of an extended kinship group, he finds himself saddled with obligations to many members of the groups with whom he was not previously acquainted let alone intimate. The claims they press upon him must nevertheless be honored in some degree, and the individual tends to yield to these claims because he was trained to recognize obligation independent of intimacy, a point which many Westerners fail to understand.

Thus the residential dispersion of individuals for reasons of employment, and their alienation from their cultural origins through Western education, occur more rapidly than the dissolution of extended kinship obligations. In the transitional situation characteristic of the most rapidly developing parts of equatorial Africa, this results in a redistribution of income from the well-paid educated elite to their poorer kinsmen, and thus militates against the development of a rigidly organized class system. Furthermore, the emphasis on obligation rather than intimacy mitigates intergenerational conflict over differing cultural standards. The uneducated, rural parent whose successful Westernized son recognizes his duty to give financial aid to family members and to exert influence on their behalf, makes relatively little protest over the son's radically different way of life. In this sense, the educated elite may be said to buy their way out of cultural conflict with the older generation. If they fulfill their heavy kinship obligations, the educated are able to make a more drastic cultural transition with less intergenerational friction than we are used to seeing in our rapidly changing Western societies.

PART FIVE

social welfare,
the law,
the economy

social welfare
and its implications
for family living   MARGARET KEENEY ROSENHEIM

The particular subject to be considered in this paper is the development of social welfare in the United States as it has affected the family living arrangements of the poor. Anyone who undertakes to examine this matter is conscious of spading material which has already been turned over by students in a number of disciplines and professions. Those who are professionally concerned with the structure and function of the family, for example, have remarked on the impact of economic status and of poverty in particular on family life. Students of social welfare, with primary interest in the scope, financing, and operation of income maintenance and service programs, have assessed these programs in terms of their meaning to economically deprived individuals. Relatively less attention, however, has been devoted to considering the impact of existing social welfare provisions on patterns of family life, nor has it been customary to evaluate the soundness of welfare policy, at a given point in time, in terms of its significance for family relationships. As we trace the rise of social welfare programs in this country, it is the author's aim to identify points where these programs impinge on freedom of family choice and to propose that the effect of programs on the range of available choices is a highly relevant criterion by which to gauge their appropriateness as instruments of contemporary economic and social policy.

Clearly, detailed and systematic treatment of social welfare from this point of view necessarily must proceed from an exhaustive search into a huge stockpile of relevant documents. This paper, while based on what is meant to be a solid set of facts, is far from being so ambitious an undertaking. Rather, it is principally an attempt to marshal some impressions with the hope of stimulating further inquiry and discussion.[1]

Whether we recognize the fact or not, "it is the task of each generation to define (or redefine) its concept of poverty."[2] A corollary to this proposition is that each generation decide whether its population suffers from an appreciable burden of poverty and, if so, what to do about it. Insofar as the palliatives adopted are designed to satisfy basic maintenance needs, the eligibility requirements or conditions of use attached to these poverty-alleviating devices may significantly affect the personal choices open to family members and the patterns of living which the family has created. For a full appreciation of the role of the family in our modern society, and particularly its role in reference to dependent aged persons, it is, therefore, desirable to identify the basic stance which a political community takes toward those who are in need.

Recent popular notice of the issue of poverty in the United States represents a belated awakening of policymakers to the unpleasant facts of life — to human deprivation, in the first instance, and to a picture of large-scale unemployment distributed in certain regions and concentrated in vulnerable groups. The keen awareness of low-income status which reports and articles now manifest is undoubtedly tied in with our recognition that the problems of dependency show no signs of abatement. Indeed, given current trends in population and employment, these problems will probably become more acute. All prognostications point to a future in which producers in the economy will be supporting a larger group of nonproducers than heretofore — more children under 18 and adults over 64 in relation to the 18-64 age group. Not only will the size of this potentially dependent group grow, by all accounts, but its impact on the economy will be augmented by

[1]The substantial set of footnotes which follow amply attests to my indebtedness for ideas and materials to many sources. In addition, however, the writer gratefully acknowledges her heavy reliance on a number of colleagues and on the participants at the Duke Symposium. In particular, I owe to Eugene Litwak insight into an important aspect of relatives' support laws. Withal, I willingly assume full responsibility for the contents of the paper.
[2]Richard M. Titmuss, "The Welfare State: Images and Realities," *Social Service Review*, XXXVII (March, 1963), 8.

such factors as longer periods of schooling for youth and a smaller proportion of employed persons among the aged. Add to these predictions certain unpleasant features of today's labor market—the relative decrease in expansion of job opportunities as compared to population growth, for example—and we face a picture of continuing, growing income-maintenance need, which presents momentous challenges to a social welfare system. It presents, furthermore, a lively danger that the public will conclude that the system itself produces dependency and should, therefore, bear sole responsibility for eliminating it.

It is commonplace to say that the inauguration of the Social Security System nearly thirty years ago has brought about the most remarkable changes in the expectations of millions of Americans and has greatly altered their personal situations when and if confronted with old age, disability, childhood dependency, or certain other economically incapacitating conditions. These are changes which have been reviewed many times by commentators the world over. Yet repetition should not obscure the fact that since 1935 the status of the needy in the United States has been dramatically improved. It may be stating the obvious to maintain that persons in want are better off today than in an earlier era. Such a statement may also give false comfort and support to critics who argue that these groups are now as well off as they ever should be. The following discussion will make no attempt to gloss over insufficiencies in current programs and services. Indeed, in the competition among needy groups for priority in the allocation of funds and services, and in the course of building an administrative structure to house program operations, deficiencies and peculiarities have come to light, some of which even run at variance to stated public policy. At the same time, despite these inadequacies, the central point remains that present-day programs afford a mode of accommodating the needs of the dependent individual to the demands of the community which is far superior, measured in terms of human welfare, to anything we knew in the United States prior to 1935.

Probably the most significant of all our accomplishments has been the endorsement of a policy of support to the prevailing family unit. Whether our examples are drawn from the care of children or of the aged, to cite the two groups which will receive major attention in this paper, a common thread is provided by the public policy favoring cash payments which, under most circumstances, leave undisturbed the accepted family patterns of living. That this was not always true of social welfare will be demonstrated below. The generation which has witnessed human suffering through the years of depression and holocaust may have forgotten what our pre-1935 social welfare programs were like, and the generation born following the uneasy peace of 1945 are ill-equipped to imagine a domestic economy which is not permeated by the Social Security System. The recollection of past arrangements, however, puts a useful perspective on the fundamental question of what impact welfare legislation has on families.

a brief history of welfare legislation in the united states

Until roughly one hundred years ago the predominant characteristic of social welfare in the United States was its undifferentiated approach to all needy groups in the population. Available resources, rather than any special requirements of individuals, controlled the form of help which was disbursed. Bids for community succor, which to our eyes rest on substantial documentation of human misery, were measured by the standards of a common adversity in a period when nearly every settler was engaged in an unrelenting struggle for subsistence. The memorable spokesmen for the blind, the infirm, the deaf, the orphaned, and those otherwise bereft were products of a later age when leisure, affluence, and the wondrous perils of urban living gave rise to the systematic practice of beneficence. The undifferentiated approach was also the product of ignorance about the causes of disease and social maladjustment. As a result, devices like "auctioning-off," "farming-out," and indenture of older youths or adults were grafted on the basic stock provided by a transplanted English law and grew along unique lines determined by adaptation to the special requirements of a new land. Here, just as in England, however, relief systems were intimately connected with local government. This meant that they flourished in number as political subdivisions increased and that the breadth and generosity of program varied considerably according to the attitudes of local authorities.[3] These officials presumably adopted the sentiments of voters and fashioned their poor relief schemes within the limits of parochial fiscal ability. Given this picture, it would be folly to take too seriously any generalizations about our experience in relief of the needy prior to 1935. Notwithstanding the dangers of generalizing about such a large number of political subdivisions, and the even greater danger of so doing in the absence of adequate reporting, there are bits of evidence to support a few cautious but necessary comments about pre-1935 social welfare.

In keeping with the spirit of the progenitor of American relief legislation, that famous statute of Elizabeth I, the earliest measures for support and maintenance were *ad hoc* accommodations between individual want and the community's mores and tax base. The incidence of need was seldom sufficient to justify institutionalization of appropriate remedies. Reading accounts of town meetings, for example, one gets the firm impression that local authorities were moved to act case by case and to seize on whatever appeared to be an economical plan. Thus, we may read of their renting a room in the home of the widow Smith for an indigent individual, "farming-out" an entire

[3]Edith Abbott, *Public Assistance: American Principles and Policies,* Vol. I (Chicago: University of Chicago Press, 1940), 3-17, 509-10. For an account of the parochial emphasis in English poor law administration, see Dorothy Marshall, *The English Poor in the Eighteenth Century: A Study in Social and Administrative History* (London: Routledge & Kegan Paul, Ltd., 1926).

family by stimulating the enlightened self-interest of farmer Thomas, or taking over, through lease or purchase, an entire dwelling to be manned by a hired couple who would provide care for all comers – the old and infirm, dependent children, and not infequently the mentally ill.[4]

Into the Almshouse   In burgeoning townships and counties, however, these solutions were shortly outgrown. By the beginning of the nineteenth century, coincident with early waves of immigration, the rise of cities, and the dislocations produced by America's adventure with the industrial revolution, several large cities had established almshouses, institutions large enough to accommodate hundreds of people and to afford a modest degree of segregation of men and women, young and old, purely feeble and maniacally raving.[5] From 1800 to 1900 the almshouse movement caught fire. In rural areas as well as the cities it was looked upon as offering an efficient solution to overwhelming problems of dependency, problems which increased in number and complexity as case-finding techniques improved and as increases in knowledge permitted the assertion of special competence.

Two points deserve emphasis. First of all, there seems little reason to doubt that almshouse care represented a genuine reform of preexisting weaknesses and abuses. The movement to introduce this reform was nurtured by the humanity and persistence of staunch civic leaders who presented a case for institutionalizing relief. The almshouse, as visualized by its proponents, possessed the potential for reasonably adequate care. At the same time it had the substantial advantage of permitting exercise of stringent control over grants of relief. Thus, it found avid supporters among the American counterparts of British critics of outdoor relief, that form of relief which customarily supported the family in its own home, whose experience with the Speenhamland allowance scheme confirmed opposition to non-institutional assistance in this country.[6] The almshouse possessed

---

[4]An interesting account of these *ad hoc* arrangements as applied to the mentally ill is available in Albert Deutsch, *The Mentally Ill in America: A History of Their Care and Treatment from Colonial Times,* 2nd ed. (New York: Columbia University Press, 1949), pp. 39-54.

[5]Efforts to classify and segregate the almshouse population were often dismal failures in practice. A graphic statement of the facts in one state is contained in David M. Schneider, *The History of Public Welfare in New York State 1609-1866* (Chicago: University of Chicago Press, 1938), pp. 70-75, 249-52.

[6]Interpretations of the Speenhamland system and the reaction to it which produced the Reform of 1834 in England are available in Karl de Schweinitz, *England's Road to Social Security* (Philadelphia: University of Pennsylvania Press, 1943), pp. 69-78, 114-27; and Karl Polanyi, "Speenhamland: 1795," *The Great Transformation* (New York: Holt, Rinehart & Winston, Inc., 1944). The familiarity of American observers with English developments is attested to by references to these developments in notable reform reports of Quincy and Yates, extracts of which are reprinted in Sophonisba P. Breckinridge, *Public Welfare Administration in the United States: Selected Documents,* 2nd ed. (Chicago: University of Chicago Press, 1938), pp. 30-54.

the great merit of seeming theoretically sound both to those who were promoting better care of the needy and those wishing to discourage dependency.

In the second place, it should be recognized that in many areas the popularity of the almshouse resulted in displacing other, earlier forms of relief and service. In community after community this particular institution became the exclusive technique for handling privation and sickness. Of course, there were some exceptions. We know that the almshouse proved to be an inadequate vehicle for coping with mass unemployment and that in urban localities it failed to displace time-worn remedies of soup lines, outdoor relief, and the like.[7] In the country, however, the almshouse became and remained for decades a residence for all who fulfilled the conditions of eligibility for care — settlement and destitution. Not until the latter part of the nineteenth century did specialized public institutions develop in sufficient numbers to afford any appreciable lessening of the burden carried by the almshouse. Here and there a public mental hospital or a maritime hospital for seamen or a children's home had previously arisen,[8] but these were few and far between and tended to grow up in or near the city, thus preserving undisturbed the exclusive role of rural almshouses. Broadly speaking, the establishment of these specialized institutions lagged a half century behind the erection of almshouses. In some parts of the country, in fact, the vogue for specialized institutions never took hold for reasons of economy or lack of civic and professional leadership, and in these areas, consequently, the almshouses performed recognized specialist functions — for the deaf, blind, and children, to cite examples — and continued to discharge the role of caretaker for all those many persons ineligible for the care offered elsewhere in specialized settings. A census of institutions taken in 1922 tells us that during that year 4,715 children were admitted to almshouses.[9] Thus, in certain sections of the country during the twentieth century, even children, a group quite universally regarded as "deserving" and as requiring special care, were still being denied that kind of institutional treatment which the prevailing theories of child development supported.[10]

[7]Frank R. Breul, "A History of Aid to the Unemployed in the United States," *Aid to the Unemployed,* Joseph M. Becker, ed., S. J. (publication pending). See also Leah Feder, *Unemployment Relief in Periods of Depression: A Study of Measures Adopted in Certain American Cities, 1857 Through 1922* (New York: Russell Sage Foundation, 1936).

[8]Jails had long since been established to relieve custodians of the dependent of the troublesome responsibilities of confining dangerous offenders or vagrants and misdemeanants. See Paul W. Tappan, *Crime, Justice and Corrections* (New York: McGraw-Hill Book Company, 1960), pp. 601-14; Schneider, *The History of Public Welfare Administration in New York State 1609-1866, op. cit.,* pp. 148-55.

[9]Quoted in Henry W. Thurston, *The Dependent Child: A Story of Changing Aims and Methods in the Care of Dependent Children* (New York: Columbia University Press, 1930), p. 204.

[10]*Ibid.,* pp. 202-42.

Reviewing our history, then, we may say that the almshouse of the nineteenth century was the dominant, if not exclusive, landmark of the township or county welfare scene and that its modern-day equivalent, the county farm or infirmary, in some parts of the country still discharges responsibility for a residual population, primarily older people. In contrast to the English workhouse the American almshouse was not intended primarily as a punitive device, but in operation it undeniably took on a deterrent spirit.

The almshouse in this country owes its original "therapeutic" perspective to the molding influences of Quincy and Yates, those two outstanding early-nineteenth century reformers who, through reports which bear their names, convinced the Massachusetts and New York legislatures respectively to adopt a new approach to meeting need. Both gentlemen saw in the almshouse unparalleled opportunities for better educational, restorative and maintenance services. Although the economic arguments favoring this move were not minimized in either report, we may fairly say that the dominant cause of Quincy and Yates' own enthusiasm was the potential of the almshouse for human betterment. What it could offer the young by way of education, for example, appealed to those who had seen children denied proper training because of the improvidence, ignorance, or calumny of their parents. Moral and academic training, of the kind appropriate to the child's station in life, could be assured by the almshouse's insistence on attendance at school and church or alternatively by the importation of teacher and preacher, a method apparently favored in most almshouses. The elderly too would benefit from an end to loneliness and neglect, and from superior custodial and medical care.[11]

How far short of these ideals the almshouses fell in practice is a matter of record. The squalor of these institutions indicates how important the factors of economy and deterrence of relief were as determinants of their standards of operation. Legislative reports and other documents pointed to an appallingly faulty scheme of education, poor sanitation and a low level of personal hygiene, evidence of corruption, and, most telling fact of all, death rates higher than contemporary medical knowledge could justify.[12]

What is the significance of these evils in almshouse administration for the subsequent development of remedial measures for the elderly and infirm? First, we must remember that almshouse admission ex-

[11]Breckinridge, *Public Welfare Administration, op. cit.,* p. 52.
[12]These miserable circumstances are described in Thurston, *The Dependent Child, op. cit.,* pp. 27-38; and Amos G. Warner, *American Charities,* rev. by Mary Roberts Coolidge (New York: Thomas Y. Crowell Company, 1908), pp. 195-225. According to Schneider, local dissatisfaction with what Yates and his New York State contemporaries regarded as "the perfect poor-relief system" was evident as early as 1838, only fourteen years after the county poorhouse reform had been adopted, and complaints mounted later in the century. Schneider, *The History of Public Welfare in New York State 1609-1866, op. cit.*

acted a heavy price from each inmate. This institutional relief, extended to paupers only, resulted in forfeiture of valued rights — retention of property, the right to hold public office, and, above all, the right to vote.[13] We can assume that many needy persons chose to bear great suffering in order to avoid the stigma of pauperization.[14]

And what was the view of the rest of the family toward this form of care? Affectional ties might lead them to a decision they could ill afford, if due weight were given to other factors. The irrevocability of entry into the almshouse, with its political consequences and implications of near-total isolation from relatives, made the last step through its door an event of consequence for the whole family. There is some reason to think that sentiment was not the only social force at work in the minds of the relief recipient's kinfolk. We can assume that some regard for public opinion would influence the final choice. The stigma undeniably attached to residence in the county's "catchall" rubbed off on relatives who were instrumental in committing the family members as well as on paupers themselves. As an institution which was feared by the needy whom it was supposed to aid, and abhorred by those civic leaders who appreciated the individual sensibilities of the poor, the almshouse may have exercised considerable influence on family living arrangements. While we can only conjecture at this distance from the facts, it seems reasonable to assume that many an aged person who needed additional care was assisted within the boundaries of his own family network. Hence, the three-generational family to which contemporary commentators often point with nostalgia, in some cases, may have been forced on poor families for lack of any palatable substitute. This is not to deny the importance of other factors. Certainly an agricultural economy affords the aging a different role from that available in today's economy and thus profoundly affects family arrangements. But it would be erroneous for us to assume that all past family arrangements were matters of choice over which relatives were able to exercise significant control. Indeed, in the specific cases of the aging and infirm and of children, the nineteenth-century pattern of welfare service was one which exacted separation as the price for relief of need. This was undoubtedly a price too high for some families to pay. In denying themselves the "school solution" of the 1800's, the almshouse, these families were forced to make sacrifices they could ill afford — in terms of food and clothing, and doubtless often in terms of the intangible strain of coping unaided with problems which called for specialized treatment.

[13]On disenfranchisement see Abbott, *Public Assistance, op. cit.,* p. 127.

[14]Fear of the workhouse or poorhouse is a commonly encountered theme in Dickens (see *Our Mutual Friend,* for example) and other nineteenth-century writers. The American writer Sarah Orne Jewett gives a touching account of an old woman's flight from the poorhouse to visit the city before she sees out her days in residence with other paupers. "The Flight of Betsey Lane," *The Country of the Pointed Firs And Other Stories,* Anchor A 26 (New York: Doubleday & Company, Inc., 1956), pp. 172-93.

Out of the Almshouse   The process of moving the "worthy" poor out of the almshouse began shortly after widescale introduction of that catchall repository. Indeed, the very earliest of the special schools or asylums which were designed for the deaf, the blind, orphans, and the mentally ill, to name a few groups for whom special categorical treatment was devised, antedate the main period of almshouse development. We can find an example of institutions for each of these handicapped or forlorn groups before 1825. As a broad movement to replace undifferentiated custodial care, however, the drive to establish specialized institutions took on momentum after 1850 when the rising concentration of population in cities or within the borders of a single state reached levels which would justify segregating one category of dependent from the other. The Civil War furnished added incentive for the creation of institutional facilities, particularly for the children and the widows of soldiers. Children's institutions for orphans and homes for the elderly widows left in the wake of the War (and for some of the veterans themselves) grew rapidly after 1865.

As we examine social welfare history, we can see that the movement toward categorization produced indelible results. In its earliest guise, that of segregating particular categories for custodial care, it reflects preferential treatment for certain groups to the detriment of others (who, typically, remained in the almshouse) as well as the prevailing belief that this special care required isolation of the recipients from family and community. The effect of institutional care in this sense was similar to the impact of the almshouse; in each case uprooting was prerequisite to a grant of help. To be sure, in many instances there was not much in the way of a home from which to be uprooted, but it is likely that the extent of orphanage or total loss of relatives among children and the aged has been exaggerated. If this is so, then the preference for institutional care lies in convenience of administration, a belief that institutional care was superior (generally viewed as misguided today), and a belief that costs of institutional care were lower (clearly untrue today). The marked isolation of inmates from their past environment was a natural consequence of the alleged irreversibility of the conditions which precipitated confinement. This fact is perhaps best illustrated by the attitudes which were expressed toward mental hospitalization, but to some extent the care of children in an institutional setting was predicated upon a like assumption. Here the controlling fact was the "permanent" absence or inability of parents to assume responsibility. Indeed, even in the early days of foster family care, as the founders of the Roman Catholic Prefectory in New York City vigorously complained,[15] use of that new technique was

---

[15]Supporters of this institution vigorously opposed the unnecessary separation of children from parents, which was claimed to be the result of Charles Loring Brace's innovative foster-family placement work in the New York Children's Aid Society. Thurston, *The Dependent Child, op. cit.*, pp. 125-26. We may note parenthetically that Brace's ties with Protestant ministers resulted apparently in place-

predicated on a presumed irrevocable loss of conscientious adult care-takers.

Until recent times the institutional form of care has dominated the spectrum of social welfare programs. By the opening of the twentieth century, however, there were signs of departure from this preoccupation which were destined to influence formulation of social security policies at the state level and ultimately at the federal level. Just as children and the insane had earlier been recognized as deserving domiciliary care in segregated institutions, so too other groups of able-bodied poor were gradually differentiated according to "worthiness" and accorded relief outside the confines of the almshouse. Public opinion came to support a distinction between the loafer, drunk, and vagrant types who have disquieted the taxpayer from time imme-morial, and the man whose unemployment arose in a depression pe-riod or as a result of industrial accident. For these more worthy able-bodied poor, as well as for the categories hitherto institutionalized in special settings (like children), social insurance and public assistance were created. Of the latter it may be argued that it was but a stream-lined version of outdoor relief, that type of aid which entailed support in kind (food, coal, and the like) for the family in its home. To concede that outdoor relief was practiced in the cities during the nineteenth century by private as well as public agencies does not vitiate the substance of the claim that public assistance is a twentieth century product in the United States, for such outdoor relief as agencies granted was often given grudgingly, sporadically (often in response to an unemployment crisis), and as quietly as possible. Institutional care was the preferred technique of assistance, particularly for public agencies whose standards of efficiency and honesty were widely ques-tioned in the late nineteenth century.[16]

The area first selected for the social insurance approach was that of injury to workmen. Workmen's compensation laws were inau-gurated in eleven states by 1911. These laws were designed to cope with the unfortunate by-products of industrialization, disabling inju-ries or death sustained "in the course of employment," by provision of medical care costs and support for the workman and his dependents. This completely nonfederal program evolved as an instrument of state, rather than local, policy and to this day remains subject to the force of state law and administration in the states and territories of the United States.

Insurance for unemployment came considerably later despite the

---

ment of most children in Protestant homes and that founders of the Prefectory were disturbed to see that "thousands of Catholic children were lost to the faith through a system [of placing-out] which ignored such a thing as religious rights in the helpless objects of its charity." Homer Folks, *The Care of Destitute, Neglected, and Delinquent Children* (New York: The Macmillan Company, 1907), p. 121.

[16]See discussion of changing attitudes toward noninstitutional relief of the able-bod-ied in Breul, "History of Aid to the Unemployed," *op. cit.*

active promotion of this measure by labor groups from 1916 on. Prior
to 1935 this program was in effect in only one state, Wisconsin (1932).
The tax offset provisions of the Social Security Act quickly spurred
states to passage of unemployment insurance acts. By 1939 these laws
were fully operative throughout the nation. For purposes of this discussion the enactment of both workmen's compensation and unemployment insurance laws is significant as evidence of a social and
political revolution which prepared the way for the Social Security
Act. The introduction of these programs marked a major shift in the
popular appraisal of destitution. At least when confronted by industrial injury and unemployment, the public was willing to acknowledge that these risks occurred with sufficient frequency and so little
evidence of personal culpability as to discredit a social policy of
collective inaction in the face of obvious suffering. From this position,
which postulated the inevitability of unforeseeable and unmanagea-
ble threats to earning capacity in an industrialized society, it was but a
short step to recommend state action in the form of cash benefits.
Spreading the risks meant finding a broader base of taxation and conscience than the local community possessed. And, if the incidence of
risk was seen to be unrelated to personal fault, there was then no
deterrent purpose to be served in making relief unattractive through
the almshouse or grocery-basket approach. Thus it followed that
either payment in kind (food, clothing, and the like) or application of
the means test was inappropriate. Social insurance replaced these
techniques with the innovations of cash benefits and generalized conditions of eligibility.[17]

At the same time that workmen's compensation was gaining a
toehold in the states, public assistance came into being in 1911 with
the introduction of money payments for relief of widows and dependent children. The experience in major cities with institutional placement of children had taught social reformers to question the practice
of separating young children from a parent solely for purposes of securing the child's maintenance. This practice was frequently resorted to
because of the father's death and the inability of the widow to be both
self-supporting and a caretaker for small children. In some cities,
there is evidence that the numbers of dependent children constantly
threatened to swamp all custodial facilities. A demand for home relief
of nonpunitive character arose out of compassion and a desire for more
practical management of the problem. The response was mother's
pension laws designed especially for these worthy widows and chil-

---

[17]The rise of these two social insurance programs (workmen's compensation and
unemployment insurance) is summarized in Edwin E. Witte, "Development
of Unemployment Compensation" and Walter F. Doff, "The Movement Toward
Workmen's Compensation," *Readings in Social Security,* William Haber and Wilbur J. Cohen, eds. (Englewood Cliffs, N.J.: Prentice-Hall, Inc., 1948), pp. 160-72
and 449-66, respectively.

dren. The establishment and administration of this category of law undoubtedly was aided by the built-in lobby for children which the juvenile courts offered. The courts, which commonly bore responsibility for making institutional commitments, were among the first to recognize the evils of institutionalizing the young for economic dependency only, and for many years they were among the administrators of mothers' pension laws.[18] Not until the states moved to avail themselves of the Social Security Act provisions for Aid to Dependent Children (the name which the Act originally gave mothers' pension laws) were many of our juvenile courts moved to abandon administration of this program. Such moves often occurred in conjunction with state reorganizations which were undertaken to comply with the federal plan requirement of administration of the Social Security Act provisions "by a single state agency." But the inclusion of Title IV, ADC (Aid to Dependent Children), was no open sesame for dependent children. Many states were slow to come into the program, preferring to improvise with a situation in which mothers' pensions were available in a few counties or major cities but not throughout the states as Title IV demanded. Not until 1955, when Nevada entered the ranks, were all jurisdictions participating in this grant-in-aid-program.

For the aged, the introduction of old age assistance (or pensions as they were often called) marked the first major departure from the dominant pattern of institutional care and offered this group of needy persons the choice of working out such living arrangements as suited them and their families. The growth of old age assistance, however, lagged well behind mothers' pensions. Arizona was the first state to pass such legislation, in 1915; Alaska followed in the same year, and 3 more states joined in 1923. Perhaps the obvious explanation for this lag is also the best; there simply were more needy children than needy aged, at least in urban areas where dependency is somewhat more visible and disturbing than in the country. Clearly, as already suggested, spokesmen for children were well organized and had access to a weighty and respected voice in civic affairs, that of the juvenile court judge. Perhaps in the absence of widespread urbanization the aged and their own children could not imagine the end of the extended family in its traditional form, all generations under a single roof, and therefore could not seriously consider taking steps to support independent households as acceptable, even preferable, modes of family living. In any event, income

---

[18]A fascinating account of one juvenile court judge's efforts to cope with these burdens is contained in Frank T. Flynn, "Judge Merritt W. Pinkney: The Early Days of the Juvenile Court in Chicago," *Social Service Review*, XXVIII (March, 1954), 26-30. The administrative responsibilities assumed by juvenile courts in their early days have undoubtedly influenced their present role in relation to other community child-welfare resources. For comment see Alfred J. Kahn, "Court and Community," *Justice for the Child: The Juvenile Court in Transition*, Margaret Keeney Rosenheim, ed. (New York: Free Press of Glencoe, Inc., 1962), pp. 217-34.

maintenance of the aged has been an undeniable force favoring the continuation of independent households among persons of 65 and older.[19]

In summary, then, we may say that prior to 1935 the two largest groups of dependents in the United States, children and old people, were relieved of need by techniques which were generally institutional in character and permitted little differentiation, within these broad categories, according to the special interests or requirements of the individual. Furthermore, until 1935 income maintenance was typically the business of local government, save for a few examples of social insurance and public assistance organized on a statewide basis.

income maintenance at the mid-century

Federal participation in the cost of relief on a large scale was marked by emergency depression measures which culminated in passage of the Social Security Act in 1935. Through the grant-in-aid categories and federally-administered old age insurance provisions of the Act, the United States entered an era of substantial expenditures of federal funds for income maintenance. Not only did the federal share of such expenditures rapidly assume impressive dimension, but the conditions attached to federal grants (state plan requirements) also greatly accelerated the process of centralization of relief-giving within the states. Today, although many political subdivisions are still directly responsible for *general assistance*, in terms of persons aided and moneys spent, the burden of relief falls principally on state and national governments. The undeniable gains incorporated in the Social Security Act and largely fulfilled in program administration derived in no considerable measure from removing the function of relief a step or two away from the locality which was home to the recipient.

It may seem paradoxical that income maintenance measures became more liberal and flexible as they became part of a federal system or a federal-state system and thus more remote from the human beings whose needs were to be met. Yet, in the instance of discharging the relief function, the parochial bias, as we have seen, has certain built-in features which produce a deterrent poor law and which still influence the language and operation of general assistance statutes. The narrowness of the tax base is one limiting factor of great importance. But

[19]See Lenore A. Epstein, "Living Arrangements and Income of the Aged," *Social Security Bulletin*, XXVI (September, 1963), 3-8. The Committee on Economic Security, in laying the groundwork for its recommendations of social security measures, prepared reports tracing the growth of public assistance for the aged and children and estimating current need for these groups. Social Security Board, *Social Security in America: The Factual Background of the Social Security Act as Summarized from Staff Reports to the Committee on Economic Security*, Social Security Board Publication No. 20 (Washington, D.C.: Government Printing Office, 1937), pp. 155-80, 233-49.

there are other factors which operate here. If familiarity breeds contempt, it is never more surely than with an intimate acquaintance with the poor. At close hand the ineluctable workings of a disjointed economy frequently are obscured by knowledge of the personal quirks of the needy applicant. Hence it could be, and in at least one state still is, a condition of eligibility that the person or his family be unable to maintain a decent standard of living "for *unavoidable* causes"[20] (italics supplied).

Thus, in tone, in scope, in tax base, and in administration, the titles of the Social Security Act brought about revolutionary changes in social welfare. Most significant of all, perhaps, the new programs established the principle of direct money payments to those eligible for income maintenance. Under this approach, benefits and assistance payments looked like "rights" rather than charity. In Old Age, Survivors, and Disability Insurance (OASDI)[21] this concept was reinforced by the program's contributory aspect whereby employers and their employees put sums into the system as cushions against future events in somewhat the same way that individuals purchase annuities.[22] In public assistance, "rights" did not entitle one to a fixed sum of money, nor could one dispense with showing need, notwithstanding

---

[20]Ill. Rev. Stat. ch.23, §401 (1963). General assistance plays a residual role in the social welfare system, picking up cases of emergency need, medical care for persons otherwise able to meet ordinary demands, and supplementation of wages which are below subsistence requirements because of unusual family size or needs. The general assistance caseload is subject to drastic shifts by virtue of the program's residual nature. In periods of high, long-term unemployment general assistance bears a heavy load. Addition of the unemployed parent to those covered by AFDC was designed to meet this problem (see n. 38 and 39, *infra*, and accompanying text) in part, and there have been repeated proposals for adding general assistance to the list of federally aided categories. For such information as is conveniently available on general assistance (for which reporting to the federal government, of course, is not required, as in the case of the Social Security Act categories), the reader is referred to results of a special survey: U.S. Department of Health, Education, and Welfare, *Characteristics of General Assistance in the United States,* Public Assistance Report No. 39 (Washington, D.C.: Government Printing Office, 1959).

[21]"OASDI" will be used to refer to the total range of insurance provisions contained in Title II, Old Age, Survivors, and Disability Insurance. When disability is not under consideration in the text, the abbreviation used will be "OASI"; likewise "OAI" will be used to refer to benefits to the primary beneficiaries exclusive of their survivors or dependents.

[22]The weakness of the analogy to private insurance has been exposed many times (see, for example, Frank R. Breul, "Social Insurance," *Social Work Yearbook 1960,* Russell H. Kurtz, ed. [New York: National Association of Social Workers, 1960], p. 549), but clearly the political objective of setting up OAI financing on a contributory basis was to counteract negative reactions to the means test and to emphasize the individual claim to funds as a matter of right. Cf. Franklin D. Roosevelt's remark that "'those taxes [employee contributions] were never a problem of economics. They are politics all the way through. We put those payroll contributions there so as to give the contributors a legal, moral, and political right to collect their pensions and their unemployment benefits. With those taxes in there, no damn politician can ever scrap my social security program.'" Arthur M. Schlesinger, Jr., *The Coming of the New Deal,* Vol. II, *The Age of Roosevelt* (Boston: Houghton Mifflin Company, 1958), 308-309.

the attempts of some state administrations to sidestep the needs test requirement,[23] but the detailed specification of state plan requirements and the enumeration of fair hearing procedures lent credence to a popular crusade to convince recipients that assistance was theirs by *right* with none of the stigma of the old poor relief.[24] In fact, this campaign has failed to convince many recipients, although it has convinced a few administrators and thus advanced the cause of liberal interpretation of assistance qualifications.

The money-payment principle symbolizes an effort to create for each individual a claim to a decent standard of living. Social security is a primary source of spending power for many groups in the economy and opens the door to a multitude of choices which, as we have seen, were once foreclosed by local insistence on using institutional techniques or on meeting needs by payments in kind—grocery orders, rent vouchers, and the like.[25] From the standpoint of the family, and particularly the three- and four-generational unit, the availability of cash income to a considerable degree enables relatives to work out living arrangements and patterns of spending which seem to them most fruitful. *Theirs* are the tastes and needs to be satisfied. Income data for the aged illustrate this point.

Public income maintenance is less important in terms of the total amount which it contributes to all the income available to the aged, for instance, than as a *regular* source of income for large numbers of people.[26] These latter aged persons, the ones who have been unable to continue in employment, who have been felled by heavy medical costs, who have never possessed the margin of disposable income for savings or have never been covered by retirement benefits in employment, are rescued from the bleak prospects of the old poor relief days by a system which relies primarily on cash disbursements.

Income Maintenance Through Social Insurance   In attempting to review present-day programs one is immediately confronted with the

[23]For discussion of attempts to convert old age assistance into a pension program, see generally Jack R. Parsons, "The Origins of the Income-and-Resources Amendment to the Social Security Act," *Social Service Review*, XXXVI (March, 1962), 51ff.

[24]Consider the analysis of differences in "rights" accorded claimants under public assistance and social insurance in Robert M. Ball, "Social Insurance and the Right to Assistance," *Social Service Review*, XXI (September, 1947), 331ff.

[25]General assistance is still characterized by heavy reliance on payments in kind. See U.S. Department of Health, Education, and Welfare, *Characteristics of General Assistance in the United States*, Public Assistance Report No. 39 (Washington, D.C.: Government Printing Office, 1959), p. 13 *et seq.* As of the date of collection of data for the report (January-August, 1959), the states were classified into three groups with respect to method of payment for maintenance: those which generally relied on vendor payments (10); those which used both vendor and money payments (19); and those which generally used money payments (24). In the last group of 24, some of these states used vendor payments in emergency cases or for transients.

[26]White House Conference on Aging, *Background Paper on Income Maintenance*, prepared under direction of Planning Committee on Income Maintenance, Charles I. Schottland, Chairman (1960), p. 8.

problem of selection, for in contrast to our earlier history when public programs were limited and private resources few and far between, one of the distinguishing features of the modern scene is the proliferation of programs and services. As outgrowths of individual or collective attempts to forestall dependency, these programs are so numerous as to mislead observers into believing they are also comprehensive. Furthermore, confusion is engendered by the diversity of approach which underlies program construction. Current patterns bear the imprint of special interest groups. Thus we find income-maintenance programs which are constructed on lines of age, membership in a particular group, or type of employment, to cite common examples.

For present purposes the discussion will be limited to three major income-maintenance programs — Old Age, Survivors, and Disability Insurance, Old Age Assistance, and Aid to Families with Dependent Children. This limitation will enable us to examine selected public policies regarding poverty in some detail and to make note of the consequences of these policies for family support and living arrangements.

In terms of payments and number of beneficiaries there is nothing in the United States to compare with Old Age, Survivors, and Disability Insurance. As of August, 1963, 18,790,472 beneficiaries were receiving payments under this program, of whom only about 1.4 million were receiving benefits because of their own disability or because of their dependency on a disabled person. Some 17.4 million beneficiaries were recipients of various classes of old age and survivors' benefits. Of these, roughly 10 million received primary old age benefits, and the remaining number were receiving benefits as dependents of the worker. The most common relationship among these dependents was spouse (2.6 million), but almost as many benefit payments were made to children (2.2 million). The remaining beneficiaries were aged widows or widowers of insured workers (nearly 2 million), mothers' benefits (nearly 500,000), and parents (37,000).[27] The numbers of beneficiaries under this program have risen sharply and steadily in recent years. Beneficiaries increased by more than 1 million in the year from August, 1962 to August, 1963. In 1960 beneficiaries totalled less than 15 million. Looking over the history of the Social Security Act, we can isolate several factors which account for this growth. Among them are the expanding coverage of the Act over various types of employment, a general increase in population which enlarges the potential beneficiary class, and additions to beneficiary categories. There has also been an increase in expenditures under OASDI. In 1962-63 $15.3 billion was paid out as retirement and disability benefits and survivors' benefits under the program.

[27]Information drawn from Table 5, *Social Security Bulletin*, XXVI (December, 1963), 27.

By contrast, in 1954-55 the total was $4.4 billion.[28] This increase reflects both changes under this program which produce a larger number of participants, and hence of benefits paid, and the liberalization of benefit amount and of the computation method.

Data on income *sources* would be helpful in telling us for how many families social insurance payments provide the exclusive source of cash. Unfortunately, at this time, we have little information on this point. With respect to OAI beneficiaries, we can identify some of those whose payments are insufficient for subsistence,[29] as well as the persons who have earnings from employment sufficient to disqualify them from benefits under the retirement test.[30] The former group which has increased steadily, includes those beneficiaries requiring supplementation from Old Age Assistance (OAA). The growth of this group has stimulated considerable pressure for an increase in benefit

[28]Figures are available in the most recent report in the series on social welfare expenditures. See Ida C. Merriam, "Social Welfare Expenditures, 1962-63," *Social Security Bulletin*, XXVI (November, 1963), Table 1, p. 5. Further confirmation of the relative importance of OASDI can be obtained by comparing it with expenditures in other major income-maintenance programs. The second in size is the veteran's pension and compensation program, with annual expenditures of $3.9 billion in 1962-63. Next in line are public employment retirement ($3.6 billion), unemployment insurance ($3.3 billion), and railroad retirement ($1.1 billion). Expenditures under OASDI also loom large when compared to those under organized private plans. Data for 1962-63 reveal payment under private plans of cash benefits for retirement, group life insurance, sickness, and supplementary unemployment benefits in the total amount of $4.8 billion, of which $2.3 billion represents pensions for retired workers. While it can thus be said that payments under private plans are but a relatively small fraction of expenditures for income-maintenance purposes, we should, nonetheless, note that employee-benefit plans have mushroomed in recent years. From expenditures of $678 million in 1949-50, for example, they have grown to the present $4.8 billion. *Ibid.*, Table 10, p. 14.

[29]We have no techniques whereby all persons eligible for assistance may be identified. Presumably, most persons with insufficient income for subsistence become aware of the existence of the assistance programs as a resource, supplementary or otherwise. Whether they apply, however, depends on their willingness to submit to the means test. Probably ignorance of the public assistance resource, the degrading features of eligibility investigations, at least as conducted in some states, and the application of relatives' responsibility laws deter some presumptively eligible persons from applying. Cf. observations regarding eligibility for national assistance of a group of old people studied in London: it was estimated that 20-25 per cent were entitled to supplementary assistance but had not applied. Peter Townsend, *The Family Life of Old People: An Inquiry in East London* (London: Routledge & Kegan Paul, Ltd., 1957), pp. 159-65.

[30]The retirement test reflects a compromise in policy between a requirement of complete retirement of the aged in line with OASI's basic income-maintenance objective and a policy of "equity" which permits contributors to receive value on the investment to the system which they have made through years of contributions. Under the test, beneficiaries below age 72 who earn more than $1200 per year will experience reduction in benefits for any month in which they received over $100 in earnings. Social Security Act, §203 (b), (f) (1962). The test, however, is inapplicable to persons 72 and older, which may be said to reflect the concept of "equity" with respect to the older retired worker as well as the fact that abandonment of the retirement test is far less costly when a cut-off point of age 72 is used than would be the case with a lower age. See the excellent discussion of history and modifications of the retirement test in Wilbur J. Cohen, *Retirement Policies under Social Security* (Berkeley and Los Angeles: University of California Press, 1957).

level.[31] In part, growth in the number of joint-beneficiary—Old-Age-Assistance recipients can be explained by the fact that expanding coverage of OASDI has brought into the program workers whose primary and secondary benefits are inadequate for subsistence support. One clear tendency of the extension of coverage has been to bring in more workers with marginal incomes and/or tenuous holds on employment. As a result, some contributors have a low base of earnings on which benefits are calculated, and thus require supplementation from another source. In part, however, a rise in joint OAA-OAI cases is the result of the level of OASDI benefits. Even the maximum benefit amount permitted under OASDI is clearly insufficient to provide a "decent living" for a number of families. Indeed, the extent to which this social insurance system should attempt to provide for such objectives is a seriously debated policy issue. Some critics contend OASDI is only a basic system which must inevitably be supplemented by private efforts—through savings, purchase of insurance, participation in employee benefit plans, and the like. Other critics, however, retort that there are inevitably some persons who for one reason or another do not have private sources of income and who, therefore, must look to OASDI as the principal means of support. This being so, they contend, the primary benefit level should be raised not only to reflect changes in the cost of living but to reach a more adequate level than has theretofore been achieved. That Congress has listened to the latter argument seems to be borne out by its effort, not publicly advertised, to keep average OAI benefits higher than average Old Age Assistance payments.[32] Thus, the Congressional policy appears to promote provision of subsistence support in as many cases as possible through the use of social insurance, rather than public assistance.[33]

With respect to family structure one further comment on OASDI

[31]Recent analyses of the concurrent recipient-beneficiary groups are contained in Notes and Brief Reports, "Age and Sex of Persons Receiving Both OASI Benefits and OAA Payments," *Social Security Bulletin*, XXVI (October, 1963), 15-19; Robert H. Mugge, "Concurrent Receipt of Public Assistance and Old-Age, Survivors, and Disability Insurance, *ibid.*, XXIII (December, 1960), 12-25; David H. Clark, "Old-Age, Survivors, and Disability Insurance Beneficiaries Newly Approved for Old-Age Assistance," *ibid.*, XXVI (December, 1963), 13-17.

[32]See the remark of Wilbur J. Cohen in his article, "Economic Functioning of Older People: Social Welfare Policy Issues in Providing Income Maintenance," *Toward Better Understanding of the Aging*, Seminar on the Aging, Aspen, Colorado, September 8-13, 1958 (New York: Council on Social Work Education, 1959), p. 76.

[33]The *Report* of the Special Committee on Aging, United States Senate, on "Developments in Aging: 1959 to 1963," in considering ways to increase incomes of the aged, rejects the alternative of public assistance stating that it believes "providing additional income on the basis of a needs test" to be unacceptable. Report No. 8, 88th Cong., 1st Sess., 1963 (Washington, D.C.: Government Printing Office, 1963), p. 62. A related point worthy of note is the fact that widow's benefits as a percentage of benefit amount have been increased (in 1961 from 65 per cent to 82½ per cent), and there is pressure further to increase them to 100 per cent of primary benefit amount. Again, it can be argued, Congressional policy is to provide more adequate income for old people through social insurance.

may be in order. Its nearly complete coverage of the labor force (91 per cent) means that basic provision for retirement for the overwhelming majority of American workers is lodged in a national system in which interests are readily transferable as between type of employment, employers, and geographical regions. Thus, workers need not be inhibited by the consequences for income maintenance from moving or from changing jobs as personal and family interests may dictate. By contrast, private employee benefit plans may fail to provide "vesting." Hence, the question asked by some observers regarding the impact of private schemes on the worker's mobility has been whether the growth of "fringe benefits," those important additions to base pay which are so often nontransferable and not convertible into cash, are not in effect promoting a kind of modern feudalism.[34]

In summary, Old Age, Survivors, and Disability Insurance appears as the country's chief income maintenance technique and predominant form of social insurance and is, as we shall see, an income measure which affects more than *three* times as many individuals as the various public assistances combined.[35] The program's present importance is attributable in part to changes introduced since the passage of old age insurance in 1935—the addition of survivors' and dependents' benefits, the creation of disability insurance, and the general liberalization of coverage and benefit amount. Considerable disagreement on the desirable future course of OASDI exists, not the least of it concerned with pending proposals to incorporate payment for medical care for the aged as one of the functions of this social insurance program. Other current issues relate to financing the program, the adequacy of benefits, and, most basically, the role of OASDI as a source of retirement income.[36]

For our present purposes, however, the significance of OASDI lies in its providing for cash payments without a needs test. The important features of the program's history is the extension of this cash benefit approach beyond just one risk—the original risk of retirement—to other hazards, such as dependency, survivorship, and disability. The prospects for future extension of a nonmeans-test cash benefit

[34]Cf. Titmuss, "The Welfare State," *op. cit.*, p. 9. This is not the only questionable effect of employee benefit plans, of course. For one thing it has been argued that their impact on the labor market is to increase the amount of overtime rather than the number of employees in a given firm to satisfy manpower needs because of the relative expenses of instituting employee benefit provisions for each additional employee. Consider President Johnson's proposals to stimulate industry to cut back on overtime in his State of the Union Message. *New York Times,* January 16, 1963, p. 16, col. 4. On vesting and pension "portability," see *Report* of Special Committee on Aging, *op. cit.*, pp. 85-88.

[35]Compare number of beneficiaries currently receiving social insurance benefits with the number of recipients of public assistance as of August, 1963. *Social Security Bulletin,* XXVI (December, 1963), Tables 1 and 9, pp. 23, 32.

[36]Major issues are spelled out in Cohen, "Economic Functioning of Older People," *op. cit.*, pp. 84-96. More comprehensive treatment is available in Eveline M. Burns, *Social Security and Public Policy* (New York: McGraw-Hill Book Company, Inc., 1956).

approach, whether within the framework of OASDI or within the context of a totally new structure, seem bright given the avowed preference of the public for social insurance as an income-maintenance technique.

Income Maintenance Through Public Assistance   Of the public assistances, it is Old Age Assistance and Aid to Families with Dependent Children which have been of greatest consequences. Whether measured in terms of total expenditures or numbers of recipients, these programs are impressive in both sheer magnitude and growth pattern. Some notion of current trends can be gleaned from a brief comparison of 1952 and 1962. Unlike other public assistance programs, the caseload in Old Age Assistance has decreased in this ten-year period. It hovered around the 2.2 million mark in August, 1963, in contrast to a figure of 2.6 million in 1952. The alltime peak in recipient load occurred in 1950 when 2,789,000 persons 65 years and older were aided under the program (a rate of 225 per 1000 population aged 65 and older). In the past decade, however, expenditures have risen gradually but without pause, reflecting both the upward direction of price levels and attempts by state and federal governments to improve and broaden the Old Age Assistance program, especially in the area of provision of medical care. Despite the drop in recipients, annual expenditures totalled about $2 billion in 1962-63 as compared to $1½ billion in 1952.[37] These shifts in program expense and recipient caseload, of course, reflect the substantial increase in the aged whose income needs are met through OAI, for in this same decade the number of adults in the population of 65 years and older has risen, from about 12 million in 1952 to roughly 17 million in 1962. Under these circumstances, a decline in Old Age Assistance recipients can be explained only by the availability to the aged of other income resources in 1962 as contrasted with earlier periods.

Not withstanding the picture of shrinkage in the Old Age Assistance caseload, it is widely assumed that the number of recipients will remain near the current 2 million mark. The supporting explanation rests on the prediction that there will be indefinitely a "hard core" needy aged group within our rapidly expanding 65-plus age population to whom other existing programs do not apply or for whom such programs are insufficient. Thus, even if the absolute number of recipients remains constant, as forecast, in the face of a growing number of aged persons the proportion of the aged receiving Old Age Assistance presumably will continue to decline.

[37]Expenditures rise to nearly $2 1/2 billion if we include Medical Aid to the Aged, a program established in 1961, for purposes of comparing expenditures under federally aided programs for the aged at two points in time. Current data are derived from Tables 2 and 3, *Welfare in Review,* I (November, 1963), 26, 27. The 1952 figures are available in U.S. Department of Health, Education, and Welfare, *Trends,* annual publication published in supplement to monthly Health, Education, and Welfare *Indicators.*

The prospect of a shrinking role for Old Age Assistance as an income-maintenance device for the aged, however, should not obscure the fact of the program's great importance, past and present, as an income source for those who qualify as needy. We should recall that the introduction of Old Age Assistance in 1935 provided for many the first significant alternative to almshouse or county poor farm maintenance. To the eyes of today's readers the conditions of eligibility of assistance programs may appear to be restrictive, conditioned as we are to widespread reliance on social insurance and other nonmeans-test devices. But, in 1935, Old Age Assistance represented a monumental advance over previously existing welfare strategies. It introduced statewide standards for grants of cash payment, and thereby, lent support to the belief, shared by the elderly in large numbers, that Old Age Assistance entitled them to a money grant which they were free to spend as they deemed proper. To what extent the contemporary generation of persons 65 and over looks upon Old Age Assistance as a "right" to which entitlement carries little or no stigma we cannot flatly say. Probably, however, general efforts to discredit assistance and belittle recipients have left their mark on the aged. Repeatedly, we have witnessed, as an aftermath of relief "crises," a backwash of fear and shame which innundates people, such as the aged, who are not the prime targets of contempt, investigation, or restrictive policy.[38]

Turning to Aid to Families with Dependent Children, we find it more difficult to outline the status and trends which affect this program.[39] In this program both recipients and expenditures have increased dramatically. Beginning with aid to a modest 404,000 children in 1936 (we should note that only 26 states were participating in the program by the end of that year), the numbers rose steeply following passage of legislation in 1950 authorizing the inclusion of one parent or other adult relative in the AFDC payment. Total numbers and recipient rates reflect, in their increases, changes in the child population and the general economic health of the nation and, in particular, the shifts in the labor market within individual states. Detailed analysis of state-by-state changes is indispensable to any meaningful generalizations, however. In 1961 the AFDC title was amended to permit the inclusion within the definition of "dependent child" of one whose dependency resulted from a parent's unemployment, but not until 1962 was it possible also to include this parent in the grant.[40]

[38]A long look — and a more optimistic one than the author's own — was taken recently by Elizabeth Wickenden at "The Recurrent Crises of Public Welfare — Asset or Handicap," *Public Welfare*, XXI (October, 1963), 171-74, 224.

[39]AFDC will be used in the text as an abbreviation for the Assistance Program, Aid to Families with Dependent Children.

[40]Social Security Act, Title IV, §§406 (b), 407 (1962), as amended. The Act originally provided maintenance for only the dependent child, and he was defined as "dependent" by virtue of need arising from deprivation of "parental support or care by reason of the death, continued absence from the home, or physical or mental incapacity of a parent. . . ." As noted in the text, one adult caretaker was included in the grant following amendments in 1950, and, more recently, both parents may be

As the law now stands both parents as well as their children may be included in the budget under AFDC. The states may now use federal matching funds to help support those families whose dependency results from the unemployment of the breadwinner. Not since the days of emergency relief in the early 1930's have families of unemployed parents been eligible for federal aid for reason of unemployment alone. (And one may wistfully recall that in those days, under the Federal Emergency Relief Administration, there was one national program without categories or residence requirements which disbursed funds on the basis of need!) In fact, however, states have been slow to avail themselves of the opportunity to shift families or the father himself (in cases where the rest of the family is already on AFDC) from general assistance to AFDC. The program, therefore, is not bearing the load of income maintenance for the unemployed which it could. Future developments in this program depend to some extent on the states' assessment of the relative costs of availing themselves of the AFDC-U (Aid to Families with Dependent Children — Unemployed parent) option, at a payment level generally in excess of general assistance budgets, or of depending on the old standby, General Assistance, under which local preferences and prejudices may be given fuller weight.[41] The availability of federal matching funds is not the inducement to all states it may appear to be, for these funds are conditioned on compliance with federal standards which increase the overall cost of assistance in many localities. Furthermore, the lure of extra moneys must be balanced against public attitudes toward support of the able-bodied unemployed, attitudes generally more punitive than those directed to other groups of assistance recipients. Thus, to generate public support of enabling legislation and appropriations which will permit states to take advantage of the AFDC-U amendment may be a task beyond the reach of a state's welfare officials at a particular moment.

Two additional amendments which significantly alter the potential recipient class of Aid to Families with Dependent Children must be noted. These relate to inclusion in the AFDC grant of children who are actually out of the home in placement in foster families or institu-

---

included in cases where deprivation of parental support stems from unemployment *and* the unemployed parent complies with §§407, 409 which establish availability for work and work relief conditions. These provisions of the Act are effective until June 30, 1967.

[41] As of August, 1963, only 16 states were making payments under the AFDC-U provisions to a total of 50,568 families containing 188,304 children. Table 19, *Social Security Bulletin*, XXVI (December, 1963), 39. During the same time period over 750,000 persons were receiving general assistance. Table 20, *ibid.*, p. 40. Without undertaking detailed, state-by-state analysis, however, we cannot say how many General Assistance recipients would be eligible for AFDC-U. That there would be a significant number is suggested by studies of local General Assistance units. See, for example, Frank R. Breul, *Survey of the Administration of General Assistance in Bloom Township*, Illinois, December 31, 1963 (mimeographed).

tions. The foster-family placement was permitted in 1961, while children in institutional care were added to those eligible for aid in 1962.[42] Protection against unnecessary removal of the child from the home must be part of the state plan. To achieve such protection, the Act requires a judicial determination of the need for placement, periodic review of the child's condition, services to improve conditions in the home from which he was removed, and cooperative planning in the child's behalf by the public assistance and child welfare personnel involved.

Thus, these amendments and a growing child population have affected the size of the AFDC caseload. As of August, 1963 there were 3.9 million recipients under this program, nearly 3 million of whom were children. While the program is impressive in terms of size, it would clearly be even larger were it not for the role of Old Age, Survivors, and Disability Insurance as a source of support for many otherwise needy children. Indeed, the growth of OASDI has very much altered the character of the AFDC program since the days of mothers' pension laws and the early years of the Social Security Act. Whereas the program formerly provided support for children whose dependency arose from the death or total disability of the wage earner, the expansion of the old age and survivor's coverage and the introduction of disability benefits have removed many of these children and their caretakers from reliance on AFDC. Those who remain eligible for AFDC are, to a large extent, as in Old Age Assistance, a "residual" population. In AFDC this population is composed principally of fatherless families (illegitimacy of child and desertion account for nearly 40 per cent of the children and caretakers receiving payments), families where the father is disabled (nearly 20 per cent), and families where the father is unemployed (about 5 per cent). Since these data are based on a 1961 survey, it can be presumed that the last category would now be larger, the states having had several years to take advantage of Congressional authorization of federal participation in grants to families where the father lacked a job. The most telling point, however, is that only one child in 14 was needy because of the death of the father.[43]

Disbursements under AFDC have mainly taken the form of money payments. Significant departures from this principle, however, have been introduced, beginning in 1950 with the authorization of vendor payments to suppliers of medical care. Since that time various restrictions on grants have been proposed, ranging from voucher payments to landlords and grocers to work relief requirements. As of 1963, two further restrictions have been enacted—the protective payment provision and the work relief authorization—and a third,

[42]Social Security Act, Title IV, §408. Payments in behalf of children in institutional care are permitted until September 30, 1967.
[43]Robert H. Mugge, "Aid to Families with Dependent Children," *Social Security Bulletin*, XXVI (March, 1963), 3-15.

voucher payment of rent has been proposed in Congress.[44] Strictly speaking, it may be argued, work relief as a permissible condition of receipt of assistance under Aid to Families with Dependent Children – Unemployed Parent does not violate the money payment principle, for the grant is paid in cash. Furthermore, refusal to perform work relief, unlike refusal to accept employment, may not jeopardize payment of funds to the rest of the family. The principle, however, for which the drafters of the Social Security Act labored so strenuously was that of *unrestricted* money payments, that is, cash relief to which no strings are attached beyond proof of continuing need.[45] Work relief is of a different order as a condition for receipt of funds. Its insertion in the Act can be interpreted in the light of historic attitudes toward the able-bodied unemployed, as an attempt to impose a work test, or test of worthiness and good intentions, on this most troublesome class of needy persons.

Enacted restrictions on cash grants as of this time are limited to the Aid to Families with Dependent Children program; hence, they may seem to be of remote interest so far as legislative policy toward the aged or other categories is concerned. Nonetheless, there is no reason to assume that these restrictions would not form prototypes for future exceptions to the money payment principle in other programs. This possibility will be considered below.

critique of contemporary devices for alleviating poverty

Any programs which involve expenditures of the magnitude of those in social insurance and public assistance are destined to receive critical attention from time to time. Criticism is by no means evenly distributed according to proportionate cost. Thus Old Age, Survivors, and Disability Insurance, although substantially larger than the programs of assistance plus general relief combined, has drawn comparatively little fire since the 1930's. Such attacks as have been directed toward it in recent years have been voiced largely by conscientious students of the system who debate the niceties of level premium rates, the size of the reserve, the more technical aspects of the retirement test, or the desirability of continuing the contributory principle. But criticism of the idea of social security is rarely heard, and there is every reason to believe that the program enjoys strong popular support. As already suggested, the main line of inquiry concerns the extent to which benefits to current beneficiary classes

---

[44]See protective payment, §§403 (a), 405, 406 (b)(2), and work relief and training provisions, §§407 (3), 409, Social Security Act, Title IV, as amended (1962). Voucher payment of rent was proposed in H.R. 8675, 88th Cong., 1st Sess., October, 1963, introduced by Congressman Roman Pucinski (D., Ill.). It would have affected all assistance titles, as drafted. Congress adjourned without acting on it.

[45]The money payment principle is discussed at length in Social Security Board, *Money Payments to Recipients of Old-Age Assistance, Aid to Dependent Children, and Aid to the Blind,* Public Assistance Circular #17, March, 1944.

should be enlarged and the controversial question of adding a new class of benefit, insurance for medical care, onto the system.[46] It is the public assistances, making up less than 8 per cent of all social welfare expenditures, which are the target of criticism. Since these programs are the consciously created havens of "last resort" for many of our needy and thus a crucial indicator of how our society views and treats its poor, the remaining discussion will be devoted largely to the two biggest programs of public assistance, Old Age Assistance and Aid to Families with Dependent Children.

For our purposes in this paper, the criticisms of the public assistances most deserving of mention are those which have resulted in erosion of the unrestricted money grant. If the reader accepts the position that relief of need granted in cash form has important implications for family relationships, then he may also agree that exceptions to cash payments are a potential threat not only to the dignity of individuals but to the freedom which generations of kin enjoy in establishing living patterns to their own taste. Of all the incursions, vendor payments for medical care represents the outstanding example of departure from unrestricted money grants. These vendor payments were permitted under the amendments of 1950. They were promoted on the general ground that such vendor payments would enhance the state's ability to work out the best possible quality of medical service by building in a guarantee that the suppliers of this costly service would always receive full measure for what they had rendered. Data assembled at the time persuaded Congress that some recipients had failed to pay their medical bills, to the obvious detriment of the suppliers of care. The amendment meets this complaint and, by granting the states significant control over the organization of medical resources available to recipients, it has also acted as a stimulus to those states which had previously made inadequate provision for the medical needs of clients within their boundaries. From this point-of-view, vendor payments were a compromise between governmental provision of medical care or no provision at all of such care for the economically deprived.[47] Vendor medical payments currently are a firmly established feature of public assistance. They total $94.7 mil-

---

[46]See Cohen, "Economic Functioning of Older People," *op. cit.*, pp. 84-96; Burns, *Social Security and Public Policy, passim;* and, for a ten-year-old appraisal, Arthur J. Altmeyer, "The Future of Social Security in America," *Social Service Review*, XXVII (September, 1953), 251-68. Compare the fundamental opposition to OASDI well stated in the analysis of Milton Friedman in his recent book, *Capitalism and Freedom* (Chicago: The University of Chicago Press, 1962), pp. 182-89.

[47]In addition, the 1950 amendment, by removing the money-payment restriction for medical care, allowed states to pool funds for medical services and thus average these costs and administer funds for them in a more efficient manner. For a brief description of early state practices, including operation of pooled funds, see Vivian Norman, "Federal Participation in Vendor Payments for Medical Care," *Social Security Bulletin*, XV (December, 1952), 8-10, 21. Some of the difficulties which states had previously experienced in their efforts to provide medical services are outlined in Ruth White, "Vendor Payments for Medical Assistance," *Social Security Bulletin*, XIII (June, 1950), 3-7, 10, 28.

lion a month out of an overall monthly sum of $391 million expended on all types of assistance (August, 1963).[48] Furthermore, in Medical Assistance for the Aged (MAA) and Old Age Assistance, programs which are by far the largest users of medical service, vendor payments for medical care are subject to a more liberal matching formula for federal funds than characterizes other elements in the Old Age Assistance grants.[49] Thus, in the Old Age Assistance program medical services in a sense are given preference over food, rent, clothing, and the like; in Medical Assistance for the Aged, of course, expenditures for medical services are the only ones contemplated.

Vendor medical payments opened the door to departures from the money-payment principle. In 1961 and 1962 this principle was further eroded by the introduction of protective payment and work relief and training amendments. To set the stage for discussion of these changes it may be helpful to remind the reader that for fifteen years or more a steady stream of criticism has been directed at mounting costs of assistance, rising caseloads, and particular cases of abuse and fraud on which we have documentation. While specific critics have chosen different aspects of program administration as their pet targets, they have tended to agree on the program from which they draw their examples. That program is Aid to Families With Dependent Children. There is no doubt that the two amendments, protective payments and work relief, were designed to correct abuses associated with that program, yet the author suggests that the underlying changes are pertinent to all the categories.

The protective payments amendment in effect permits the states to depart from unrestricted cash grants without jeopardizing federal matching in those cases where the state agency administering AFDC concludes that the adult relative who receives the funds is not using them for the benefit of the child. The social problem is mismanagement of funds. It is distinguishable from neglect apparently in that the relative's lack of good judgment concerns money, not corporal discipline (to choose one illustration), and presumably is not so gross as to warrant removal and placement of the child away from home. The agency may resort to a range of alternatives which run in order of severity from "counseling and guidance in the use of the payment and the management of other funds" to the invocation of state action to impose civil or criminal penalties. Fair hearing and periodic review of these cases are provided; the number of cases so treated is restricted to 5 per cent of total caseload; and the amendment is due under current law to expire in 1967.[50]

[48]*Social Security Bulletin*, XXVI (December, 1963), Tables 10 and 12, pp. 33, 35.
[49]The federal percentage for matching expenditures for medical care varies from 50 to 80 per cent, the uppermost limit being higher than the 50 to 65 per cent range which is the federal percentage for matching other types of expenditures above the first $35. See Social Security Act, Title I, §§3 (a)(1), 6(c) (1962).
[50]See statutory provisions cited in n. 44, *supra*.

Now clearly such legislation as the provisions we have sketched represents a marked departure from the concept of money payments, and equally clearly, it seems to the writer, it poses all kinds of difficulties for fair and "nonjudgmental" administration. Inevitably, the agency must identify standards on which to support a finding of money mismanagement. Is the vulnerable deed an installment contract purchase of a television set or of a mink coat? What shall we say of the mother who unwisely buys pork chops during the first half of the month and can afford only beans, and precious few at that, in the second? Are we to be guided by the home economist's idea of mismanagement or the legislator's, assuming that the ideas of these two parties differ? What we face is the fact, to use a word often employed by economists, that these expenditures involve "taste," a commodity which resists homogenization. While we may all agree that cases of abuse exist and require society's attention, as the writer certainly does, the writer would also argue that the heavy-handed solution of protective payments is an ill-chosen remedy in terms of liberty, efficiency, and ultimate economy.[51]

A related matter which requires attention is the 1961 authorization of work relief, and requirement that state plans deny assistance to unemployed parents and their families if the unemployed parent refuses "without good cause" to accept employment or undergo vocational training.[52] Here the public policy is to stimulate the search for employment and to require the performance (or training therefor) of useful work in return for the assistance payment. These provisions are limited in their application to unemployed parents, as distinct from other classes of assistance recipients, but the refusal of the unemployed parent may, in cases of refusal to accept employment or vocational training jeopardize the AFDC status of the entire family as well as of that parent himself. The intrusion onto the money-payment

[51]The author derives some support for this conclusion from the fact that the states have thus far shied away from using the protective-payment provisions. One assumes, however, that the states are seriously attempting to implement their mandate to counsel and guide recipients as to expenditures of the grants and thus it may well be the practical results are the same—a great increase in control over expenditures by officials, with concurrent restrictions on individual choice. It may also be appropriate to note here that some states have already achieved the goal of the protective-payment provision by use of vouchers with respect to certain items in the grant which exceed the maximum level of federal reimbursement. Thus, in a case where the monthly grant exceeds the maximum of federally matchable funds by, let us say, $100 and where the caretaker's mismanagement of funds is well known, a certain key item in the budget such as rent may be paid by voucher direct by the assistance agency. Such a practice has been permitted on the theory that federal funds are not involved in this portion of the grant; hence, it is argued, the money-payment principle is not violated. But the question may be asked, does the money-payment principle extend to the grant as a whole or only to such portion of it as federal funds apply? Would one argue that certain other state plan requirements may be suspended with respect to that segment of the grant which comes wholly out of state funds?

[52]See n.44, *supra.*

principle lies in the condition imposed on the grant.[53] Again, as in the protective payment amendment discussed above, the underlying problem is genuine and acute. Documented instances of malingering and laziness can be produced, and there is growing acknowledgement of low educational status as an important cause of unemployment. Work relief and compulsory vocational training thus may be said to represent the efforts of Congress to deal with an increasing burden of relief and a significant cause of unemployment.

But history tells us to beware the work relief requirement. Not only is this requirement detested by those forced to comply because of the nature and conditions of employment available, but also, in some instances, because of threats to health which are difficult to avoid in practice.[54] The work rarely is a source of satisfaction, and the difficulties of administration of these programs under conditions set forth in the amendments are immense. How can we be sure that work fills a "useful public purpose" and that payment for it is not less than the "prevailing community rate"? How can we guarantee that the work will not displace other, regular workers? Indeed, there is reason to wonder whether we have advanced far beyond the Elizabethan solutions to idleness among the able-bodied poor,[55] notwithstanding an unquestionably worthy effort to protect work relief from the kinds of abuse with which it has hitherto been riddled.

Thus far, in speaking of the recent amendments, we have spoken primarily of the Aid to Families with Dependent Children changes, but the author does not wish to imply that these changes are irrelevant to the aged. If for a worthy purpose we can carve out exceptions from the money-payment requirement in AFDC, may we not do likewise in other programs? May we not, for example, take measures to insure more effective "protection" for old age recipients? Studies of the elderly have drawn attention to their vulnerability to exploitation, though the studies do not inform us of the magnitude of the problem nationally. We may suspect that hundreds of thousands of aged persons would benefit from financial counseling and some small measure of control. Perhaps then foolish expenditures or overextensions would not be so numerous nor exploitation so profitable an opportunity for the conscienceless. But what should be the line between advice widely advertised and freely rendered (whether requested or not) and protective payments imposed through administrative, nonjudicial arrangements for the person's best interests? Certainly, in thinking

---

[53]A New York work relief statute is being tested as to constitutionality in a pending appeal from conviction under the Social Welfare Law of men who refused to work on a relief project. See Source Materials, "To Work or to Jail," *Social Service Review*, XXXVII (March, 1963), 464-71.

[54]See conscientious efforts of Congress to write in protections for the health and safety of participants in work and training programs. Social Security Act, Title IV, § 409(a) (1962).

[55]That is, punishment of the recalcitrant and provision for diligent labor on a stock of "wool, hemp, flax, iron, and other stuff" for those who would work.

about this problem, we should be clear about the necessity to define with care and precision the legal procedures to ascertain the person's need for a fiduciary and to control and supervise the one selected.[56] We should also, in the author's opinion, abide firmly by the principle that "the recipient of public aid will be subjected to no greater controls than other citizens."[57] However worthy a given objective may be, departure from that general principle carries real risk of returning the recipient to the second-class status of pauperdom.

Rent payments may come to be yet another obligation which the state will assume contrary to the money-payment principle. In a bill recently introduced in Congress the state could undertake direct payment of rent on the express finding:

> that old-age assistance is not being used effectively and consistently with the purposes of this title because of the fact that individuals receiving such aid are being compelled to pay excessively high rentals for their living accommodations or to occupy accommodations which have become unsafe, unsanitary, or otherwise substandard. . . .

The state agency as a "responsible public entity" can presumably deal effectively with landlords. The bill permits it to make direct payments and reduce the amount of money payment to which the recipient is entitled accordingly.[58] If the landlords are uncooperative about improving housing and/or lowering rents, do the old age recipients have to move? What will the state agency do to insure the cooperation of the next landlord — screen or select "approved housing"?

The simple point is that erosion of the unrestricted money grant, like the erosion of a freshly logged forest, is difficult to check. The forces behind it are often beyond our control. Having spelled out one reasonable exception, we can easily discover a rationale for others. The insidious danger of this process, in the author's opinion, is further suggested by experience with the long-sought service amendments. The year 1956 marked the introduction of *service* for more independent living as an objective in each of the four titles. The language for Old Age Assistance, for example, now speaks of "encouraging each State . . . to furnish rehabilitation and other services to help individuals . . . to attain or retain capability for self-care."[59] Title IV outlines its goals at even greater length:

> For the purpose of encouraging the care of dependent children in their own homes or in the homes of relatives by enabling each State to furnish financial assistance and rehabilitation and other services . . . to needy dependent children and the parents or relatives with whom they are living to help maintain and strengthen family life and to help such parents or

---

[56]Such procedures are described in the useful report of a project on aging, Project Director, Virginia Lehmann, *Guardianship and Protective Services for Older People*, Geneva Mathiasen, ed. (New York: National Council on the Aging, 1963).

[57]Samuel Mencher, "Perspectives on Recent Welfare Legislation, Fore and Aft," *Social Work*, VIII (July, 1963), 60.

[58]H.R. 8675. See n. 44, *supra*.

[59]Social Security Act, Title I, §1 (1962).

relatives to attain or retain capability for the maximum self-support and personal independence consistent with the maintenance of continuing parental care and protection. . . .[60]

Thus it is clear that Congress had sweeping objectives in mind when it amended the Act in 1956.

To further these goals of rehabilitation and service, urged primarily by the social work profession, Congress in 1962 adopted certain very important changes.[61] For one thing, the amendments made mandatory on the states budgetary consideration of all expenses attributable to employment, action previously optional and not permitted by some states. The purpose plainly is to provide incentive for employment by granting adequate recognition of the expenses involved in securing and attending to a job — such expenses as carfare, heavier laundry and cleaning bills, lunches, and the like. Even more important from the standpoint of incentive, however, is the authorization for the states to permit the exemption of modest earnings from the grant and, in the case of AFDC, to permit the child and his family to set aside earned or other income for future identifiable needs, such as education. These amendments indicate the degree to which Congress has accepted the behavioral science characterization of "Money as a Motivator,"[62] and is interested in offering the necessary legislative leverage to states.

But the most important feature in these amendments probably is the liberalized reimbursement formula for service. Federal matching in certain services and in the cost of staff training is increased from 50 per cent to 75 per cent, thus providing a powerful incentive to the states to improve their offerings of rehabilitative services and their investment in trained staff.[63]

As the service objectives are stated, they appear unexceptionable. One interpretation could be that, through broadened service to the needy, they merely confer explicit legislative approval on traditional social work goals which had been implicitly incorporated in these programs in the minds of supporters of public assistance since the inception of the programs. Yet, closer examination raises the question of whether "service" has a double edge, running along one side in favor of the counseling and supportive services which are badly needed by many recipients, but running along the other edge in favor

[60]Social Security Act, Title IV, §401 (1962).

[61]The amendments contained in P.L. 87-543 are described in detail, with accompanying comment on legislative history, in Wilbur J. Cohen and Robert M. Ball, "The Public Welfare, Amendments of 1962," *Public Welfare*, XX (October, 1962), 191-98, 227-33.

[62]See article by this title by Hugh A. Storrow, M.D., *Public Welfare, ibid.*, pp. 199-204, 233.

[63]See description of current efforts in Clyde W. Linville, Jr., "Staffing Problems under the New Service Amendments," *Public Welfare*, XXI (October, 1963), 201-204, 226-27. For a survey of progress in implementation, see "State Action on the Public Assistance Provisions of the 1962 Amendments," *Welfare in Review*, I (August, 1963), 1-15.

of monetary cuts or restrictions which will spur the recipient on to self-support however high the cost to self or family. One illustration, which comes to mind is the case of the AFDC mother who feels pressure to seek employment ("personal independence") despite the young age of her children and her uncertainties about her child-care arrangements.

Regardless of the spirit of the service amendments, clearly intended by professional social workers to authorize enlarged expenditures of funds and staff time on badly needed professional service, subsequent experiences with the programs surely justifies our wondering whether the identical "spirit" animates professional advocates, on the one hand, and Congressmen, state legislators, administrators, and the public, on the other. Assuming that we have long since concluded that the aged and dependent children (or families, if eligible) should be beneficiaries of a general social policy which supports them during their dependency, is it possible that we run the risk of allowing departure from this basic commitment under the guise of service? If the objective of service is, quite properly, the recipient's return to self-care or self-support, what can be the *test* of success of service but removal of recipients from the rolls? The author's concern is that heavy pressure on public assistance administrations to give evidence of service may result in premature closing of cases. Short of this hazard, pressure may also result in stereotypes of proper client responses to service which will curtail the client's freedom of choice as well as the flexibility of methods open to caseworkers within the public assistance agencies. To the reader these dangers may seem far-fetched. The author can only argue from personal experience her belief that the dangers of a frozen benevolence are real, as they have been shown to be in the field of mental health where agitation for increased staff and funds to "treat" stimulates pressures to make a record of hospital dismissals which provides evidence of treatment success. Admittedly, the dangers alluded to here are not equally great in all categories; by statutory admission, for example, our expectations of rehabilitation for the aged are limited to "self-care." Yet either formulation, self-support, or self-care permits individualized, discretionary action on cases which may run at variance with a public commitment for unrestricted money payments, a policy widely applauded when introduced in 1935.

The basic consideration which has prompted this paper has been to ascertain what peculiar effect particular forms of welfare have had on families. The author's own view has been that unrestricted money grants are a superior form precisely because they confer on families at least a modest amount of flexibility and freedom of choice. Even were this money-payment principle fully honored, however, there would remain other welfare policies whose application to individual cases produces serious repercussions within the three- or four-generational family. Most important is the application of relatives' responsibility laws since, by definition, the laws are a reflection of meaningful ties and restrict the choices open to a family member who becomes needy. By virtue of need alone, he does not become eligible for assistance. He must show that he lacks resources, one of which may be his relatives as described by law. Thus, in states which impose relatives' responsibility, he must demonstrate to the satisfaction of the assistance agency that the legally liable relatives are unable or unwilling to support him.[64] Administration of these laws raises a host of problems for the would-be recipient, the relatives, and the public assistance agency which have been documented and thoroughly discussed elsewhere.[65] Among them are the difficulties inherent in determining what amount relatives should contribute. Relatives, too, are in effect subjected to a means test, and the agency must decide whether the relatives in a specific case, to use an Old Age Assistance example, should, like the needy applicant, be reduced by the requirement of support to a minimum living standard or permitted an extra margin (and, if so, how much and for what purpose — the college education of their own children?). Furthermore, *which* relatives should be held to this obligation, those residing out of state or just those within it?[66]

In fact, the process of administering what seems as an abstraction to be a reasonable and sound objective becomes fraught with problems, and these problems are not only those associated with intrapsychic conflict but also those, far too seldom considered, which evolve in the course of attempting even-handed, objective administration of relatives' responsibility laws. Furthermore, certain inconsistencies in fundamental social policies seem to have been overlooked in connection with holding relatives to a financial duty for less fortunate kin. There is the obvious inconsistency of laying down, on the one hand, policies which favor a nonmeans-test approach to dependency (as is true of hazards covered by social insurance) and which, therefore, free the worker whose OASDI benefits and/or other re-

[64]Quite inexplicably, some few states appear to budget as paid those contributions which relatives are determined to be able to pay, even though it can be demonstrated that the relatives are not contributing to support. See Burns, *Social Security and Public Policy, op. cit.*, p. 81.

[65]*Ibid.*, pp. 80-86. An excellent discussion of current practice is contained in Alvin L. Schorr, *Filial Responsibility in the Modern American Family*, U.S. Department of Health, Education, and Welfare (Washington, D.C.: Government Printing Office, n.d.). Analysis of state laws is contained in Max Rheinstein, Chapter XI below. Ethel Shanas has illuminated public attitudes on the support duty in an analysis of responses of older people, individuals responsible for them, and a cross section of the public to questions on income sources for the aged. Her findings show that older people themselves want to be financially independent of their children. The older people and the public cross section look to government for income maintenance if personal savings prove inadequate. See Ethel Shanas, *The Health of Older People: A Social Survey* (Cambridge, Mass.: Harvard University Press, 1962), Chapter VI, "Older People and Their Families," pp. 107-41.

[66]Burns, *Social Security and Public Policy, op. cit.*, p. 84. Administrative issues are nicely identified in Floyd A. Bond, *et al., Our Needy Aged: A California Study of a National Problem* (New York: Holt, Rinehart & Winston, Inc., 1954), pp. 199-201, and *passim.*

sources cover his needs from intense scrutiny of his financial status and that of his relatives', and yet, on the other hand, supporting policies in assistance under which the less fortunate or less prudent must by their excessive or unforeseen needs subject their families to these unpopular investigations. The general popular support which the social insurances enjoy may as much reflect responsible relatives' attitudes as the personal interests of potential beneficiaries.

Compounding this inconsistency in policy is the stance which we have taken toward fluidity of family living patterns, for the application of relatives' responsibility laws in effect imposes on vulnerable families a legislative model of the extended family, with broad duties to nurture and support all its members, which does not elsewhere emerge so clearly in our welfare laws. The implicit policy is one favoring intergenerational responsibility; under OASDI, by contrast, social policy on intergenerational relationships is neutral, as indeed the author would assert it should be. Thus, the dilemma we face is that relatives' responsibility laws are more attractive in theory than in practice and produce effects upon family relationships which may be unintended and are often insufficiently recognized. That legislators hold the social policy under relatives' support laws in high esteem is undeniable, but one suspects fuller knowledge of the facts of administration would cause them some concern. At any rate, in this country the difficulties of administration of such laws are by-passed in social insurance, which may be one fundamental reason for its popularity as an income-maintenance technique.

In view of these strictures against current policy and practice in public assistance, the question remains whether prevailing programs can be so improved as to promote the kind of flexibility and freedom of choice in family living arrangements which the author has been urging, or whether more radical solutions are required. Among the ranks of social work leaders, proposals for separating income maintenance from social service, and thereby avoiding some of the problems pointed out here, have been appearing with increasing frequency.[67] One great virtue of such a division of goals and programs into a discrete approach to economic poverty, on the one hand, and to personal maladjustments, on the other, is in the heightened visibility which both these fundamental goals would acquire. As matters now stand, we can say with little fear of challenge that visibility and communicability are features conspicuously missing from present arrangements. Indeed, as the preceding discussion should have made clear, the amount of tinkering with the 1935 structure which has been undertaken in the past decade is sufficient to obscure basic policy objectives in a number of instances.

[67]See, for example, Mencher, "Perspectives on Welfare Legislation," *op. cit.;* Gordon Hamilton, "Editor's Page," *Social Work,* VII (January, 1962), 2, 128; and Eveline M. Burns, "What's Wrong with Public Welfare?" *Social Service Review,* XXVI (June, 1962), 111-22.

Thus, it has been argued that the "problem of economic assistance is linked to the economic organization of society, not the welfare system. . . . Rather than needing social work to make palatable the bitter medicine of economic deprivation [we should look for methods which] will provide dignified and realistic solutions of economic problems."[68] Flat grants, better coordinated employment services and vocational training efforts, children's allowances, and adjustment of taxation arrangements are among the suggestions which have been advanced historically for solution of the economic aspects of dependency. Parallel to these mechanisms, it has been suggested, there should exist a variety of social services, open to the self-supporting as well as the poverty-stricken, organized to deal, as best we know how, with the personal suffering and social maladjustment of which so many examples abound.[69]

By no means all of the critics of contemporary social service measures will join in advocacy of the above two-part arrangement. Some would boggle at the assignment to government of large-scale service responsibilities, as Mencher and other proponents of separation of service and income maintenance are urging. If, for the moment, however, we put the issue of service—how much and who does it—to one side, we can probably isolate a considerable area of agreement about the need for direct clear-cut treatment of the alleviation of poverty.[70]

Thus, one of the important ramifications for family life of a proposal for separation of economic from psychological or moral problems would probably be strengthening of the money-payment principle, for if the alleviation of poverty is treated as an issue requiring economic solution, it is then most likely that such a solution would find expression in cash payments. To families, availability of cash means availability of choice—choice in living as three-generation households or as independent nuclear units, choice in selecting white potatoes or sweet, choice in balancing gifts to grandchildren against requirements for medicine or recreation.

In summary, then, the thesis herein advanced has been the not surprising one that twentieth-century welfare measures have brought about improvement in the standard of living and the range of choice open to the poor. The principal means for securing these ends has

---

[68]Mencher, "Perspectives on Welfare Legislation," *op. cit.*, pp. 63-64.

[69]A variety of income-maintenance measures is considered in Burns, *Social Security and Public Policy, op. cit.*, while an imaginative approach to service planning has been outlined in Harold L. Wilensky and Charles N. Lebeaux, *Industrial Society and Social Welfare* (New York: Russell Sage Foundation, 1958) and applied to children's needs in Alfred J. Kahn, *Planning Community Services for Children in Trouble* (New York: Columbia University Press, 1963).

[70]Consider, for example, the concern expressed by Milton Friedman about the need to alleviate poverty through governmental action, notwithstanding his criticisms of OASDI, and his suggestion for a "negative income tax" approach. Friedman, *Capitalism and Freedom, op. cit.*, Chapter XII, "The Alleviation of Poverty," pp. 190-95.

been use of cash disbursements, and the most common examples are social insurance benefits and categorical assistance payments. The author has further suggested that the introduction of a heavy service component into the administration of the assistances, far from representing a "fresh" approach to the undeniable problems of the caseload, reflects "an outmoded and anachronistic view of the welfare function" and threatens regression to punitive administration of support to the destitute. Finally, the author has proposed that the test of a successful welfare system is not only the standard of living which it affords but the freedom which it confers on families to satisfy their own tastes and peculiar needs.

Insofar as the Social Security Act, through its various titles, represents a public commitment to place cash in the hands of the needy, we have by its enactment taken a large step toward establishing an economic context which does not straitjacket the family relations of the poor. Thirty years after enactment, however, we must appraise its solutions in terms of the peculiar problems of poverty and dependency in an "affluent society." The challenge of today is to maintain the progress of an earlier time while we seek to respond to ever-changing public attitudes and to write the next chapter in our history of income maintenance in a vernacular appropriate to the second half of the twentieth century.

motivation
of intergenerational behavior
by norms of law
MAX RHEINSTEIN

Having had the benefit of seeing almost all of the papers given at
this Conference in advance of our meeting, the author has gleaned a
wealth of information and of suggestive ideas from them. Once published they will be a source of stimulation not only for those people
who are professionally concerned with gerontology but also for the
members of a profession which the writers obviously had not had in
mind, the author's own profession of the law. That the writers hardly
thought of the law is made apparent by the fact that in all these papers
the law is hardly referred to at all. A conspicuous exception is
presented by the paper of Margaret Rosenheim on the history of
American public welfare.[1] After all, the author is a lawyer; she is,
indeed, a distinguished alumna of this author's own law school, the
University of Chicago. Besides, how could anyone write about public
welfare without discussing law? The very definition of welfare work
as public implies that it is carried on by governmental agencies, which
would not exist, could not act, and would have no funds, without
legislation. But even private welfare activities carried on by nongov-
ernmental organizations are, as we lawyers believe, "regulated" by

[1]See Rosenheim, "Social Welfare and its Implications for Family Living," set out
herein in Chapter X.

the law. Such is indeed the case with innumerable human activities and relationships, including those between parents and children. As lawyers, we are inclined to believe that all regulation, or even all motivation, of human activity is by the law. But if we indeed hold such a belief, we overestimate the role of the law, which is only one among the numerous regulatory forces of human life, not to speak of its motivations. If we hold such beliefs, we incur the same kind of error as those social scientists who overlook or deny the role of the law as a regulatory or motivational force of human activity.

Of adult sons contributing to the support of aged parents, only a very few appear to be motivated exclusively by the fear of legal compulsion, that is, the fear that in the case of nonsupport a court may go into action against them, may render a judgement, and that that judgment may be "enforced" by the sheriff's forcibly seizing and selling their property to raise the necessary funds, or by a court, through a prison warden, exercising pressure through imprisonment to compel the payment of support money. But quite possibly there are indeed some sons for whom the fear of such adverse governmental action, legal compulsion, is a motive. Perhaps it is not the only one; but there may be some for whom other motivations might not be strong enough without their reinforcement by the motive of fear of legal compulsion.

Here, as in other cases of conduct conforming to the law, a systematic investigation into actual motivations could yield significant insights. What indeed motivates an adult son or daughter to support, or to take care of, an aged father or mother? Is it love, pure and simple, unselfish concern about a beloved human being near to the heart? Or is it concern about what the neighbors might say or think, or is it unthinking habit or compliance with an unquestioned tradition, or obedience to a duty felt in conscience, or the fear of God, or the fear of the court, the sheriff, and the prison guards? Such research would not be easy, but it should be undertaken, if for no other practical purpose than that of determining the limits of the need and of the possibilities of legal regulation. Such research might also yield precious insights into needs of education of the young and the adult. It might also be of value to commentators on television, on the radio, and in popular magazines, insofar as they might engage in endeavors to influence patterns of behavior in the relations of members of different generations.

In his three-generation study of Minnesota families Reuben Hill mentions that none of the persons interviewed made any reference to the law.[2] This negative finding does not allow a conclusion that consideration of the law played absolutely no role at all. Motivation by fear of legal compulsion is not likely to be readily revealed to an interviewer.

[2]See Hill, "Decision Making and the Family Life Cycle," set out herein at Chapter VI.

When we consider the law as a force possibly motivating behavior in intergenerational relations, we must distinguish two different kinds of laws. There are, first, those laws which are designed directly to motivate behavior by threatening nonconforming behavior with forcible governmental action, such as imprisonment or compulsory seizure of property. In this category belong, in our context, the so-called relatives' responsibility laws, under which adult children or other close relatives can be directly compelled to pay money for the support of indigent individuals. In the same category belongs the battery of tax laws by which, under threat of direct compulsion, the funds are raised out of which the state pays old age pensions and similar grants of public welfare.

A different category is constituted by those laws which are intended to influence behavior in an indirect way or of which such motivation is but the accidental by-product of the pursuit of some other purpose. Intergenerational behavior can, for instance, be motivated by the laws on succession to property upon death. Care for parents or obedience to them may well be motivated by the expectation to inherit or the fear to be disinherited. Indirect motivation of intergenerational behavior may also be brought about by laws on income or inheritance taxes providing tax benefits in cases of gifts or legacies between parents and children or between husband and wife. If, as in the present federal estate tax law, a legacy to the surviving spouse is less heavily taxed than a legacy to children, the latter kind of legacy is discouraged.[3] If, on the other hand, the rate of the income tax can be reduced by a father's splitting his income with his children, gifts to the latter are encouraged.

In the following we shall try to survey these two types of laws with respect to their possible relevance for motivating intergenerational behavior. No exhaustive analysis can be undertaken, if for no other reason than the total lack of any previous treatment of the problem. No exhaustive inquiry can indeed be undertaken without research into actual motivations, motivations of lawmakers on the one side, and motivations of people's intergenerational behavior on the other. The desire to indicate the need for such research is, indeed, the motivation of the author to write this present article. Another motive of his has been the desire to alert social scientists to the existence of a storehouse of factual material that appears so far to have escaped their attention, viz. the material contained in such "lawyers'" publications as reports of judicial opinions, legislative hearings, and writings by legal scholars.

In all our discussions the term "intergenerational relations" shall generally be used in the restricted meaning in which it has been employed at the present Conference, that is, as referring to the relations between the generation of adult people engaged in productive

[3]See text accompanying notes 45-46 *infra*.

activity to that older generation which has retired, or is about to retire, from active participation in production. Only in special cases shall we refer to those numerous laws which are concerned with the relations between the adult generation and their still youthful offspring.

Laws of direct motivational effect in intergenerational relations are, of course, all those legal norms which directly deal with the relationship between parent and child.

In the first place we must know who it is between whom the parent-child relationship exists. To the nonlawyer the answer seems to be evident. The parent-child relationship exists between a child on the one side, and his parents on the other. But who are the parents? Apart from the rare cases of foundlings and cases of mistaken identity of babies, intentional or unintentional, it is easy to know who is a given child's mother. But who is the father? The Roman jurists had two sayings, one of fact and one of law, and both are still valid today. *"Pater semper incertus"* — Fatherhood is never certain; and *"Pater is est quem nuptiae demonstrat"* — A child's father is he who, at the critical time, was married to the mother. That rule sweeps into our compass the whole complex body of rules of the law of marriage, that is, all the detailed rules on how marriage is concluded, on capacity to marry, on nullity of marriage, and on marriage annulment. In addition to the legitimate parent-child relationship arising out of "lawful wedlock," the law also has its rules on illegitimacy, legitimation, adoption, and on persons standing to a child *in loco parentis*. But all these laws help us only to determine the relationships between parent and child. They assume practical meaning only in connection with those laws by which the incidents of the relationship are defined.

Contrary to what probably is believed by the public, these laws are by no means clear in the United States. One of the least clarified problems is indeed that very basic one of the parent's duty to support his child. Regulation of family relationships by law, that is by norms "enforceable" by sheriffs, policemen, and other governmental officers yielding power of physical compulsion, is of comparatively recent origin. In primitive society law, by definition, is absent. Social relationships are regulated by tradition, convention, ethics, and religion, including magical beliefs and taboos. When government develops, that is when a society changes from the primitive to the archaic state, government hesitates to penetrate into the circle of the kinship group. Within that group interpersonal relations continue to be determined by the command of a patriarch, by tradition and habit, and by the nonlegal norm systems of convention, ethics, and religion. Classical Rome, Confucianist China, and even Meiji Japan present neat illustrations. In all these societies the laws stopped at the threshold of the family. In the Common Law of England, which became the law in the United States, the family was not left so completely law-free, but the situation was not much different. Marriage was regulated by the commands of the Christian religion, including Christian ethics. If any judicial adjudication had to occur, it was left to the ecclesiastical courts of the Catholic Church or, after the Reformation, of the Church of England. Secular courts and secular laws were not brought into the marriage field until the former unity of faith was supplanted by modern diversity and modern religious indifference.[4] In England, the transfer from ecclesiastical to secular jurisdiction occured as late as 1857.[5] In America it had occurred earlier. In fact, in none of the colonies were any ecclesiastical courts of English pattern established at all. But the law to be applied by the secular courts remained for a long time the Canon law of the English ecclesiastical courts, insofar as such a law existed. Elaborate rules of ecclesiastical law did indeed exist with respect to marriage. But there were practically none for the parent-child relationship.

Until the eighteenth century the situation had not been much different on the continent of Europe. But the secularization of family regulation happened to occur at about the same time when rulers like Frederick the Great of Prussia,[6] Joseph II of Austria,[7] or Napoleon,[8] and their bureaucratic administrators and legal scholars felt the need for a clear and complete codification of all private law. In all the modern codes of Europe and their offspring codes of Latin America, Africa, and Asia, neat regulations are contained of all family relationships including those of parent and child. In the United States we have not had a codification; our law is based on precedent. As such it is conservative. Only occasionally has legislation stepped in to remedy glaring anachronisms; and family legislation belongs to the sphere of the states and differs widely within the nation. Much innovation has been brought about by the courts. Especially in recent years, more and

[4]On the history of Anglo-American marriage law, see 1 Holdsworth, *History of English Law* 6211 (1922); 2 *Id.* at 87; 3 *Id.* at 321; 2 Pollock & Maitland, *History of English Law before the Time of Edward I* 9, 66, 70, 364 (2nd ed. 1952); Radin, *Anglo-American Legal History* 110, 505 (1936). For modern American family law no comprehensive treatise is in existence. The voluminous work of Vernier, *American Family Laws* (5 vols. 1931-38 and Suppl. 1938) is concerned only with statute law. Madden, *Persons and Domestic Relations* (1931) is written for students and is no longer up-to-date. The best, although for the nonlawyer somewhat cumbersome way to learn about present-day American family law is that of working his way through one of the modern casebooks. The one most widely used in law schools is Jacobs & Goebel, *Cases on Domestic Relations* (4th ed., 1961). Other instructive case books are: Harper, *Problems of Family Law* (2nd ed., 1962); Ploscowe & Freed, *Cases on Family Law* (1963); and Ryan & Granfield, *Domestic Relations – Civil and Canon Law* (1963). Important monographic studies on topics of family law are collected in Ass'n of American Law Schools, *Selected Essays on Family Law* (1950). The reader's attention is finally invited to the "Symposium on Domestic Relations," 9 *Vand. L. Rev.* 593 (1956). For modern English family law, see Graveson & Crane, *A Century of Family Law* (1957). For modern Europe, see the articles by Rheinstein in *The Code Napoleon and the Common Law World* 139 (Schwartz ed., 1956), and "The Law of Family and Succession," in Louisiana Law Institute, *Contemporary Civil Law* (in press).
[5]Matrimonial Causes Act, 1857, 20 & 21 Vict. c. 85.
[6]1740-86.
[7]1765-90.
[8]1804-15.

more courts regard it as within their province to keep the law abreast with changing social conditions.[9] But a supreme court can act only for its particular state; it must wait not only until a point is raised in litigation but until such litigation is carried up to it in the hierarchy of appeals. Appeals are costly and, consequently, are rare in the family field. Development in the field of parent-child law has thus been slow, diffuse, and incomplete. Strange though it may sound, there is no general rule clearly establishing and defining a parent's duty to support his children. The only rules which are fairly clear are those dealing with the duty of a father, after separation or divorce, to support those children whose custody has been awarded to the mother. In such cases the support money is collected by the mother. But, in contrast to the European laws, no direct action for support can be brought against his father by the child,[10] and it is doubtful to what extent, if any, reimbursement can be obtained from the parents by a third person who has supplied a child with necessaries.[11]

The only third person to whom such a claim clearly pertains is the county or that other public body by which financial assistance has been granted to an indigent child. Laws entitling the parish, the county, and the like to reimbursement or to a preventive action against the parent belong to the oldest components of public assistance laws.[12] Parents are nearer in line to support an indigent child than the taxpayers. This view appears commonly to apply with respect to children below the age of majority. Should it also apply to children above that age? And what about the corollary? Are children nearer in line to support their parents than the taxpayers? On the European continent the answer is almost uniformly affirmative.

In the United States the problem was long regarded as being of little practical significance. But in recent years the mounting expense for public assistance has come to be viewed with alarm. Economy-minded legislators have been induced to believe that unpopular tax increases might be avoided by rigidly establishing the liability of all persons to support their indigent relatives and to reimburse the welfare agencies for expenses incurred.[13] There has thus been a rash of so-called Relatives' Responsibility Laws, as well as of enactments designed to prevent the evasion of these laws.[14]

---

[9]Rheinstein, "Challenge and Response in Family Law," to appear in 17 *Vand. L. Rev.* 239 (1964).

[10]See *Campbell* v. *Campbell*, 200 S.C. 67, 20 S.E. 2d 237 (1922). This case is one of the few in which a support action by a child against his father has been allowed in an American court. The cases expressing the opposite majority view are cited in the opinion.

[11]See the extensive discussion in *Greenspan* v. *Slate,* 12 N.J. 126, 97 A. 2d 390 (1953).

[12]See Rosenheim, *supra* Chapter X. The Elizabethan Poor Law of 1597-98 (39 Eliz. 1, c. 3) is the fountainhead of all this legislation.

[13]See Rosenheim, *supra* Chapter X.

[14]On the latter, see Brockelbank, *Interstate Enforcement of Family Support* (1960). The relatives' responsibility laws have been neglected in legal writing. Not a

As of 1962, laws requiring children to support a needy parent or needy parents were in effect in 35 states [Alabama, Alaska, California, Colorado, Connecticut, Delaware, Georgia (qualified), Hawaii, Idaho, Illinois, Indiana, Iowa, Louisiana, Maine, Maryland, Massachusetts, Michigan, Minnesota, Montana, Nebraska, New Hampshire, New Jersey, New York, North Dakota, Ohio, Oregon (qualified), Pennsylvania (qualified), Rhode Island, South Carolina, South Dakota, Utah, Virginia, West Virginia, Wisconsin], in the District of Columbia (qualified), in Guam, in Puerto Rico, and in the Virgin Islands.[15]

The following provisions of the Illinois Public Assistance Code[16] may be regarded as typical and are thus stated here by way of illustration:

§ 112.   Responsibility for support – Enforcement

Every person who shall be in need and unable to earn a livelihood in consequence of any unavoidable cause shall, except as herein otherwise provided, be supported by his spouse or person holding himself out to be his spouse, father, mother, a person in loco parentis to a child, children, brothers, or sisters if they or either of them be of sufficient ability.

A husband is liable for the support of his wife, and a wife for the support of her husband if he is in need of such support and is, or is likely to become, a public charge. The parents are severally liable for the support of any child or children under 18 years of age, or 18 years of age or over whenever such child is unable to maintain himself, and is, or is likely to become, a public charge. The term "child," as used in this paragraph includes a child born out of wedlock, or legally adopted child, but the liability of the father of a child born out of wedlock shall not be enforceable unless he has been adjudicated to be the child's father by a court of competent jurisdiction, or he has or shall acknowledge paternity of the child in open court or by a verified written statement.

The persons enumerated herein, for the purposes of this Section and Section 4-2, are designated as "responsible relatives" if individually or together in any combination they have sufficient income or other resources to support, in whole or in part, the needy person. In addition to the primary obligation of support imposed upon the responsible relatives,

---

single entry relating to these laws is contained in the *Index to Legal Periodicals*, which currently lists all articles published in American legal periodicals. Some information on the relatives' responsibility laws can be found in leaflets published by, and obtainable from, the Council of State Governments (1313 East 60th Street, Chicago, Illinois 60637). A brief note on the laws in question is contained in Council of State Governments, *Manual of Procedure on Reciprocal State Legislation to Enforce the Support of Dependents* (amended to 1957), reprinted in 9C *U.L.A.* at 9 (1957).

[15]9C *U.L.A.* (Supp. 1963, at 10-12). The statutes vary greatly in detail. Some, for instance, expressly establish a duty of support not only toward parents, but also toward grandparents [Alabama, Alaska, Colorado, District of Columbia (qualified), Iowa, Louisiana, Maine, Minnesota, Montana, Nebraska, New Jersey, Puerto Rico, Utah, and Virgin Islands]. The statutes of Alabama, Alaska, Colorado, Illinois, Minnesota, Montana, Nebraska, Puerto Rico, Utah, and West Virginia expressly declare a brother liable for the support of a needy brother or sister. But a sister is declared to be so responsible only in the statutes of Alaska, Colorado, Illinois, Minnesota, Montana, Nebraska, Puerto Rico, Utah, and West Virginia.

[16]S.H.A. ch. 23, §§101-903 (1958).

such responsible relatives shall be liable for any assistance or general assistance granted to a needy person for whose support they are responsible, including amounts expended from assistance or general assistance funds for the funeral and burial of such needy person. Such liability shall attach only in respect to the period of time in which assistance or general assistance was granted and during which such persons were financially able to contribute to the support of the needy person. However, in the case of an applicant for or recipient of old age assistance, the responsibility imposed by this Section shall not be enforced against the brothers and sisters of such person, and in the case of an applicant for or a recipient of blind assistance this responsibility shall not be enforced except as against the spouse or person holding himself out to be the spouse, parents and children.

Information requested of responsible relatives as herein defined under this Section shall be submitted in forms or questionnaires prepared by the Commission or the supervisor of general assistance, as the case may be, and shall be made by the relative under oath. A person who swears wilfully, corruptly and falsely in respect to any material statement or representation in the form or questionnaire bearing upon his status as such responsible relative, or upon his income, resources, or other matter concerning his ability to provide support, shall be guilty of perjury and upon conviction shall be punished accordingly.

If the needy person applying for or receiving assistance or general assistance has responsible relatives as herein defined, it shall be the duty of the Commission or the supervisor of general assistance, as the case may be, to determine whether such relatives, individually or together in any combination, are reasonably able to support the needy person in whole or in part, and, if such responsible relatives are reasonably able to give such support, to assist the needy person in obtaining said support. If such responsible relatives continue to refuse or fail to furnish such support, the Commission or the supervisor of general assistance, as the case may be, may refer the matter to the State's Attorney or to the proper legal representative of the State or governmental unit for action to obtain support, or for the recovery of assistance or general assistance granted during the period such support was not provided, or both for the obtainment of support and the recovery of the amount of assistance or general assistance granted, which action shall be prosecuted by such law enforcement officers in the manner provided in Section 4-2 or in the manner provided under such other applicable laws of this State which impose a duty of support and provide for its enforcement; provided that the Commission or the supervisor of general assistance may require the needy person to request the proper law enforcement officer to file action for non-support as a condition to the granting of assistance or general assistance during such period as his responsible relatives continue to refuse or fail to furnish such support. Actions for non-support and for the recovery of assistance and general assistance may be consolidated and the Court may assess liability proportionately against responsible relatives as provided in Section 4-2.

The provisions of this Section in relation to the recovery of assistance are subject to the conditions and limitations of Section 8-17 respecting assistance charged to the account of the recipient, or paid to or in his behalf, on account of medical, surgical, or dental services, nursing and convalescent care, or medical supplies and drugs. As amended 1959, July 8, Laws 1959, p. 560, § 1; 1961, Aug. 9, Laws 1961, p. 3014, § 1.

This lengthy statute is by no means clear in all respects. Its interpretation is rendered even more troublesome by the fact that most of its provisions are duplicated, partly verbatim, partly in slightly different form, in another section of the Public Assistance Code.[17] As so often happens in American state legislation, parallel bills are introduced in the legislature without coordination, and amendments are added to certain sections without corresponding changes in others.

Of the problems raised by the Illinois law as well as by the statutes of other states, only the following shall be mentioned here:

1. Is the heavy weapon of imprisonment for contempt of court available only for the enforcement of a judgment ordering support for the future, or also for a judgment ordering reimbursement of a governmental unit for public assistance rendered in the past?

2. What standard has the court to observe in ordering the payment of support? Is the maximum determined by the amount the needy parent would receive from the government as public assistance, or may a higher amount be awarded? If so, by what standard is it to be determined? Is the court to consider the parent's former station in life, or the station in life of the son or daughter called upon to provide support? In other words, can the rich son of a formerly rich father be ordered to pay enough to enable the father to maintain a costly household, or just the amount a pauper is to receive on public assistance?

3. To what extent can the son or daughter be compelled to cut down on his own expenses or to dig into his capital? To what extent, if any, has the court to consider the extent of the defendant's obligations of support toward other persons, especially his spouse and his children?

The statute carefully establishes an order of priority in which relatives of varying degrees may be called upon.[18] It fails, however, to establish a corresponding order of priorities among several relatives claiming support from the same individual. To what extent, if any, must a man neglect his own wife and children in order to provide

---

[17] S.H.A. ch. 23, §402 (1958).

[18] S.H.A. ch. 23, §402 (1958): "The spouse or person holding himself out as his spouse shall first be called upon for such support. The children or parents, as the case may be, ... shall next be called upon ..., and if there are no children or parents of sufficient ability, then the person in loco parentis to a child, then the brothers and sisters ... shall be called upon."

It will be noted that §112 simply declares "the responsible relatives" liable for assistance granted to a needy person and defines as "responsible relatives" all the relatives of the kind in question *"if individually or together in any combination* [our italics] they have sufficient income or other resources to support, in whole or in part, the needy person." Under this provision it seems to be possible for the public assistance agency to turn against all and any "responsible relatives" without any order of priority.

support for his father or mother or, under the laws of some states, for his grandfather or grandmother, or his brother or sister, or some or all of these?

For one interested in intergenerational relationships the last stated question is of special importance. Serious consequences could result from legislation that would compel members of the productive generation to prefer the no-longer productive over the not-yet productive.

The consequences can be serious also if a man is compelled only to reimburse a governmental unit for public assistance rendered over a longer period of the past. Just as in the disastrous case of a divorced husband, who is suddenly compelled to pay thousands of dollars of back alimony to an ex-wife who has let alimony installments accumulate, a son, his wife, and his children can be ruined by a governmental unit's claim for reimbursement of accumulated installments. The situation may even be worse than in the case of a divorced husband. As there is a judgment outstanding against him, he knows of his ex-wife's claim, even though he may have good reason to believe that she will not collect it. A son or daughter against whom no judgment has yet been rendered, has no such knowledge and may well be taken by surprise by the government's action.

Complementary to the Relatives' Responsibility Laws has been the enactment of the Uniform Reciprocal Enforcement of Support Act. Proposed by the Conference of Commissioners on Uniform Laws in 1951-52, the act was speedily enacted in 36 states as well as in the District of Columbia, Puerto Rico, the Virgin Islands, and Guam. Statutes of substantially the same kind were enacted in 14 other states. The nation is thus covered by a complete network of reciprocity laws. The case is almost unique among the uniform state laws of which only a very few have been enacted in more than a handful of states.[19] The Uniform Reciprocal Enforcement of Support Act is concerned with all types of family support claims and among them primarily with support claims of wives and ex-wives and of children, legitimate and illegitimate; but it can also be used for the interstate enforcement of support claims of, or for the benefit of, parents against their children. The Act is popularly called the Fugitive Pappy Act and is meant to put an end to that easy way of evading support claims by simply leaving the state, which was formerly available in many cases. Under the new Act proceedings initiated in the state of residence of the person by or for whom support is sought are simply transmitted to the proper court of the state of residence of the person against whom the support claim is sought to be enforced. The proceedings are meant to be simple and inexpensive.

The speedy enactment of the uniform statute is indicative of the general desire of legislators "to stem the tide of relief." Upon its

[19]9C *U.L.A.* (Supp. 1963, at 10-12).

proposal by the Conference of Commissioners on Uniform State Laws, the Act was advertised as a means to achieve possible relief savings of hundreds of millions of dollars.[20]

It would be of special interest to know how many relief dollars, if any, have actually been saved through the new statutory scheme in general and the Relatives' Responsibility Laws in particular. Perhaps they have simply shifted the relief burden from the governmental unit responsible for the support of the old man to that responsible for the support of the son and his family. If they have not thrown the latter persons on the relief rolls, how much hardship have they produced? Under the Relatives' Responsibility Laws, the enforcement of which is sought to be secured by the interstate reciprocity scheme, responsible relatives can be compelled to support the needy person not only out of income, but also out of other resources.[21] A man may thus be compelled to sell or mortgage his home. To what extent, if any, has the cost of collecting from sons and daughters stayed below the amounts recovered? How indeed do the Relatives' Responsibility Laws function? To what extent, if any, are they enforced?

To all these questions, and a good many additional ones, we ought to have answers if we are to judge whether laws of this kind are of real significance or whether they are just placebos providing psychological satisfaction to angry taxpayers. Not that such an effect would be insignificant. But we should know something more about these laws, and in order to know we need research on the actual application and functioning of these American laws.

Research would also be desirable on the foreign counterparts of our statutes. How does the United Kingdom fare, where the once-existing statutory duty of children to support their needy parents was abolished in the course of the welfare state legislation of 1948, as proposed in the Beveridge Report?[22]

---

[20]Reprinted in 9C *U.L.A.* at 3 (1957): "In June 1949 the Social Security Administration announced that the total bill for aid to dependents where the father was absent and not supporting was approximately $205,000,000 a year for the nation and the states."

[21]Illinois Public Assistance Code of 1949, S.H.A. ch. 23, §112 (1958), set out in text following note 16, *supra*.

[22]National Assistance Act, 1948, 11 & 12 Geo. 6, c. 29. In Australia, South Australia seems to be the only state where children are by statute required to support a needy parent or to reimburse the State for relief paid to a needy parent, Maintenance Act, 1926-1936,§§40, 24, 5. The Public General Acts of the Parliament of South Australia, 461-542. No such statutes appear to exist in New South Wales, Queensland, Tasmania, Victoria, or Western Australia. But in Canada relatives' responsibility laws are in force in every province:

Alberta: Maintenance Order Act, R.S.A. 1955 c. 188, §3. Children must provide "maintenance, including adequate food, clothing, medical aid and lodging."

British Columbia: Parents' Maintenance Act, R.S.B.C. 1960, c. 273, §3.

Manitoba: The Parents' Maintenance Act, R.S.M. 1951, c. 195.

New Brunswick: Parents' Maintenance Act, R.S.N.B. 1952. c. 166, §2.

Newfoundland: Maintenance Act, R.S.N. 1952, c. 35, §§2, 3. R.S.S. 1952, c. 35, §§2, 3.

   , What is the situation in the continental European countries, where the duty of children to support parents is not conceived as a means to alleviate the relief burden of taxpayers but as a duty arising out of the family relationship itself and where, therefore, the measure of support to be furnished is determined not by the amount of public assistance payments but by the circumstances of the individual parties, that is by their respective stations in life, but where also clear rules determine the order of priority among several relatives to be supported?[23]

    Nova Scotia: Parents' Maintenance Act, R.S.N.S. 1954, c. 210, §2.

    Ontario: Parents' Maintenance Act, R.S.O. 1960, c. 284, §4.

    Prince Edward Island: The Childrens' Act, R.S.P.E.I. 1951, c. 23, §73.

    Quebec: Civil Code, §166. Following the model of French law, sons-in-law and daughters-in-law are also obliged to maintain a needy father-in-law or mother-in-law. But these latter persons' obligation ceases when the mother-in-law contracts a second marriage, or when the consort, through whom the affinity existed, and all the children issue of the marriage, are dead.

    Saskatchewan: Parents' Maintenance Act, R.S.S. 1953, c. 308, §2.

    The modern statutes of the Common Law Provinces appear to be of modern origin and to be based upon the same motivation as the American relatives' responsibility laws. The provision of the Civil Code of Quebec expresses the century-old French tradition.

    All of the Common Law Provinces provide that the children's duty to provide maintenance for a parent can be enforced by the public agency responsible for providing assistance to needy persons. The relevant statutory provisions are the following:

    Alberta: Maintenance Order Act §5(6).

    British Columbia: Parents' Maintenance Act §4(2).

    Manitoba: Parents' Maintenance Act §10.

    New Brunswick: Parents' Maintenance Act §§3(2), 5(2).

    Newfoundland: Maintenance Act §§4(1) (4), 3(2).

    Nova Scotia: Parents' Maintenance Act §§3(1), 5(2).

    Ontario: Parents' Maintenance Act §3(1) (2).

    Prince Edward Island: Childrens' Act §74.

    Saskatchewan: Parents' Maintenance Act §3(1) (2).

    In New Zealand "every near relative" of a destitute person, if that relative is of sufficient ability, is liable for maintenance. The claim can be enforced by the destitute person and by certain public officers. Public assistance agencies are entitled to sue for reimbursement. Destitute Persons Act, 1910, (4 Reprint of the Statutes of New Zealand, 1908-1957, at 35-97, §§3, 4, 49, 51).

[23]The most elaborate provisions are those of the German Civil Code of 1896. They are so carefully worked out that they justify the presentation of the full text, in translation:

    Section 1601. Relatives of the descending and the ascending line are under the duty mutually to support each other.

    Section 1602. No person is entitled to support, unless he is incapable of supporting himself. A minor child is entitled to support by his parents even though he has property of his own, insofar as the income derived from such property and from his work is insufficient for the minor child's support.

    Section 1603. A person is not under a duty to support a relative if, taking account of his other obligations, he cannot provide support for another person without endangering his own adequate support. If parents are finding themselves in such a situation, they must use all means available to them to provide support for their minor unmarried children, and they must treat all such children equally. This duty does not arise if there is another relative who is legally bound to provide support. The duty also does not arise to a child whose support could be obtained by digging into the substance of such child's property.

Section 1606. Decendants are subject to the duty to provide support before other relatives. Among descendants priority to provide support is determined by the order of priority to inherit and in the proportion of the shares to which they are entitled under the rules of intestate succession. Among ascendants, the closer ones are called upon before the more remote ones. Ascendants of equal degree are obliged in equal parts. Insofar as a relative is exempted from liability by Sec. 1603, the support is to be provided by the relative immediately following him in the order of priority. The same applies where a relative cannot be sued within Germany or where such suit would meet with considerable difficulties. The claim against such a relative passes to another relative insofar as the latter has provided support. . . .

Section 1608. The spouse of a needy person is liable for support before the relatives. However, insofar as the spouse is incapable of providing support without endangering his own support, the relatives are liable before the spouse. In considering the spouse's ability to provide support, his other obligations are to be considered. The rules of Sec. 1607, Par. 2, apply analogously.

Section 1609. If there are several needy persons, and the person who is obliged to provide support is not in a position to provide such support for all, descendants have priority over ascendants, and among descendants the closer ones have priority over the more remote; the same applies among ascendants. The spouse has equal rank with the minor unmarried children. He or she has priority over other children and over all relatives. If the marriage has been dissolved or annulled, the spouse entitled to alimony has priority over children of full age and married children, as well as over all other relatives of the person who is obliged to provide the alimony.

Section 1610. The extent of the support to be provided is determined by the needy person's position in life (adequate support). Support is to cover all needs of life, and in the case of a person who is still in the process of being educated, support also includes the cost of education and of professional preparation.

Section 1611. A person who has become needy because of his own moral fault is entitled to no more than the subsistence minimum. The same limitation applies to the claim of support of a descendant, a parent or a spouse who has rendered himself guilty of a grave offense against the person by whom the support is to be provided. Analogous rules apply to the claims of support of grandparents and more remote ascendants. A needy person whose claim for support against the relative bound to support him is limited in accordance with the preceding provision, cannot turn for additional support to another relative.

Section 1612. Support is to be provided by paying money in periodical installments. The person obliged to provide the support can ask the court to be allowed to provide the support in some other way if there are special reasons to justify such an arrangement. If parents have to provide support for an unmarried child, it is up to them to determine in what way and for what periods in advance support is to be provided. In the case of special circumstances, the determination made by the parents may be changed by the orphans' court. Money payments are to be made every month in advance. The full amount for the month is due even though the person entitled to support dies during the course of the month.

Section 1613. A person may not claim support for the past or damages for nonpayment of past support, except for the period in which the obligor is in delay through his fault, or for the period following the beginning of an action for support.

Section 1614. Claims for future support cannot be waived. Payments made in advance for more than a month are effectively discharged (only for short limited periods).

Section 1615. The claim for support is terminated with the death of the person to whom the support is to be supplied, or with the death of the obligor, unless the claim is for the past or for damages for nonperformance of past support, or for demands for future support which were already due at the time

Of special interest would be an investigation into the actual functioning of the laws of Communist China,[24] of the U.S.S.R., and of other socialist countries where the family codes uniformly provide a duty of children to support their parents.[25] Why do such laws exist in countries

---

of the death. In the case of the death of the person to be supported, the obligor has to pay the cost of the funeral insofar as such payment cannot be obtained from the heirs of the deceased.

The provisions of the Swiss Civil Code of 1907 (Arts. 328-30) and of the Austrian Civil Code of 1811 (Par. 154) are much shorter, but similar in effect.

The provisions of the French Civil Code of 1804, which has served as a model for numerous other countries, are as follows:

Art. 205 (as amended by Law of August 9, 1891). Children owe support to their parents and to other needy ascendants. . . .

Art. 206 (as amended by Law of August 9, 1919). Sons-in-law and daughters-in-law owe, under the same circumstances, support to their fathers-in-law and their mothers-in-law. This obligation ceases, however, when that spouse who has brought about the affinity and all the children issue of that marriage are dead.

Art. 207. The duties resulting from the foregoing provisions are reciprocal.

Art. 208. Support is granted only insofar as it is needed with due regard to the means of the obligor.

Art. 209. If the person who receives the support no longer needs it, or no longer needs its full measure, or if the one by whom it is furnished can no longer do so, total or partial reduction may be demanded.

Art. 210. If the obligor proves that he cannot pay support in money, the court may order that he receive the obligee into his house and supply him with support in kind.

For discussion of these provisions and the extensive body of case law that has grown up in connection with them see Rouast in Planiol et Ripert, 2 *Traité pratique de droit civil français* 18.

[24]Marriage Law of May 1, 1950, Art. 13, set out in Blaustein, *Fundamental Legal Documents of Communist China* 269 (1962): "Parents have the duty to rear and to educate their children; the children have the duty to support and to assist their parents. Neither the parents nor the children shall maltreat or desert one another."

"The foregoing provision also applies to foster-parents and foster-children. Infanticide by drowning and similar criminal acts are strictly prohibited."

[25]Russian Socialist Federal Soviet Republic. Law on Marriage, Family, and Guardianship, Par. 49. Children are bound to provide support for their parents if the latter are needy and unable to work. Par. 42, sec. 3. Step-sons and step-children are bound to provide support for their step-parents if the latter are needy and unable to work, and if they, the step-children, have been supported by them for at least ten years.

Par. 55. Grandparents who are needy and unable to work are entitled to receive support from those of their grandchildren who have sufficient means and if they do not receive support from their spouses or children.

See also:

Bulgaria, Law on Persons and Family of August 9, 1949, Pars. 112, 119. The latter section reads: "The State assumes the support of those persons who have neither parents nor close relatives and who cannot support themselves out of the proceeds of their property or through work."

Czechoslovakia, Law No. 265, concerning Family Law, of December 7, 1949, Par. 70.

Hungary, Law on Marriage, Family, and Guardianship, of June 6, 1952, Par. 60, 61.

Poland, Family Code of June 27, 1950, Art. 71.

Roumania, Family Law of December 1, 1953, Art. 86.

in which the care of the aged, as of other persons unable to participate in production, is regarded as a special duty of the community?

Here we have question over question, and to answer each of these we need cooperation of law people and social scientists.

The second group of laws directly motivating intergenerational behavior are those laws under which money is forcibly taken out of the pockets of one generation and put into those of another. Of course, most of these laws are not expressly phrased in terms of generational burdens or benefits. Money raised as taxes may, theoretically, be taken out of the pockets of individual members of that very generation which is intended to be benefited as a whole. The laws here in question are of two kinds, those providing for benefits to be paid or given in kind to members of the generation of the aging and aged, and the laws meant to raise the necessary public funds. The two are not necessarily linked together. Many of the benefits, especially those of general public assistance, are paid out of funds which are raised under the general tax laws of the United States, of the states, and of the units of local government. Others, especially the funds distributed under the Social Security Act, as old age and survivor benefits, come, at least to a considerable extent, out of a tax specially earmarked for the purpose, *viz.* the federal Social Security Tax.[26] These laws of public welfare, including their history in the United States, are described in this volume in Margaret Rosenheim's paper.[27] Their impact on the distribution of the gross national product is analyzed by Juanita Kreps.[28] We can content ourselves with referring to these two papers. The general public welfare laws are supplemented, in the United States and abroad, by a host of special laws providing benefits for the aged former members of certain groups, especially occupational; such as the innumerable federal, state, and local pension laws for veterans, civil servants, teachers, firemen, policemen, armed forces personnel, and the like.

Intergenerational payments are also affected by those rules of the law of torts which provide for payment of damages to the victims of accidents resulting in invalidity or personal injury. Of course, the accident may occur while the victim is still young, but it takes him out, wholly or partially, of the producer group of society and groups him together with those who are no longer producers because of advanced age. In the United States payment of damages for personal injury is usually ordered to be made in one lump sum, on the interest and amortization of which the victim is supposed to live for the rest of his life. In Civil Law countries, payment is usually ordered to be made in periodical installments for the duration of the victim's life.[29] The inter-

---

[26]42 U.S.C. §401 (1957); Int. Rev. Code of 1954, §§3101-26.

[27]See Rosenheim, *supra* Chapter X.

[28]See Kreps, "The Economics of Intergenerational Relationships," set out herein in Chapter XII below.

[29]See, for example, Pars. 843, 844, of the German Civil Code of 1896.

generational impact of such laws is more easily recognizable than that of the American system.

The shifting of funds from members of one generation to those of another is also the effect of that vast body of laws which constitutes the legal basis of saving and investment. The laws of this category, of course, do not bring about this effect by direct motivation. The knowledge that the law guarantees the safety of our savings and investments motivates us but indirectly to save and invest for old age in the years of productivity. The basic principle of all these laws is constituted by the maxim of *"Pacta sunt servanda,"* that is, that contractual promises are to be kept. If the promise given in a valid contract is broken, a court, on the promisee's action, will render a judgment against the promisor, and in the case of noncompliance the judgment will be enforced by the sheriff or, if necessary, the armed forces of the state and the nation. Behind every judgment of a court, and be it for only one dollar or one cent, stands the entire awesome armed force of the nation.

The mark of primitive society was that there were no courts, no government, and no enforcement officers. Anyone who felt himself injured in his rights, for instance in his right to repayment of a loan, had to resort to self-help. If he would meet resistance, his kinsmen would come to his support, and, as likely as not, the adversary's kinsmen would come to the help of the latter. A blood feud would be the frequent result. It took society a long time to achieve, with many relapses, the present state in which self-help is outlawed, the legitimate use of force is monopolized by the state, the state's officers are not to go into action without being ordered to do so by the judgment of a court, the court being bound to base its decision on a rule of law democratically determined in advance and in general terms. Modern civilization, and certainly no civilization with our elaborate system of credit and investment, would never have developed without those premises. Of course, the prospect of having the contractual promise enforced by court and sheriff is not the only guarantee of saving and investment. We trust the borrower's honesty as well as his self-interest in maintaining his credit standing. But in the last resort, in relations with the dishonest debtor, or the honest but hard pressed, or the bankrupt, the heavy weapons of the law are indispensable.[30]

In economic terms, saving means that in the time of our own productivity we entrust part of our earnings to those whom we expect still to be productive when we ourselves are no longer so, and whom we expect at that time to repay us what we have entrusted to them, or to let us share, through the payment of interest or dividends in the proceeds of the enterprise in which our funds have been invested by them. The economic forms are of great variety, and so are the legal forms. They all are variants of the law of contract and its supplementa-

[30]See Llewellyn, "What Price Contract?" 40 *Yale L. J.* 704 (1931).

tion by the law of property security, of trusts, and of business associations. Of those laws more directly concerned with the safeguarding of savings and investments, we can mention only the laws on banks and banking, on savings institutions, on life insurance with its variants of annuity plans, laws on private pension funds, on investment funds, on mortgages, and on other forms of security.

The basis, however, is constituted, together with the general maxim of *pacta sunt servanda,* by the currency laws, that is in the United States, above all, the legal regulation of the Federal Reserve System. It depends on these laws and their administration whether savings retain their purchasing power or whether the savers' expectations shall be thwarted. In the German inflation of World War I and the years following, the value of the mark dwindled to one trillionth part of its pre-War value. Savings were wiped out. A vast scale system of public assistance for the aged had to be substituted for the collapsed scheme of saving. In any discussion of intergenerational relationships, consideration of the currency laws is indispensable. The best laid plans of self-reliance in old age are destroyed by inflation. It is, of course, a different question, whether inflation may not have benefits for the economy which, in overall judgment, may overbalance the destruction of savings. It may well be that a mild measure of inflation may be necessary to maintain full employment. Funds for the support of the aged might then be raised from those who benefit from the flourishing of the economy. But individual hardships cannot be avoided.

Indirectly, intergenerational behavior can be motivated by those laws which allow, stimulate, or discourage the distribution of wealth. In this category we find two large sets of laws, those on gifts and on succession to property upon death, and, intimately related thereto, the laws on income, estate, and inheritance taxation.

As generations succeed each other, the transfer of wealth, large or small, is a necessity, once mankind has passed the stage in which a primitive man's belongings were destroyed or buried along with him at his death. For this task societies have developed their systems of laws on succession upon death, supplemented by laws on gifts and by tax laws. How vital the task is of clearly determining who it is who is to be entitled to a dead man's property assets, thus to prevent a scramble in the case of death of every owner of property, and thus to preserve peace in society, is illustrated by American history. When in 1789 the vast territory Northwest of the River Ohio was opened for settlement, the Ordinance of the Continental Congress left it for future determination what rules of law, civil and criminal, were to prevail in the region. But one exception was made. In its own text, the Northwest Ordinance contained the rules on transfer of property, among the living and upon death. For the latter contingency, the Ordinance established a set of rules of intestate succession, and for wills a set of formalities was prescribed. Without such laws orderly settlement and peaceful development would have been as little possible as in a monarchy lacking clear rules on succession to the throne.

Under the system which universally prevails in modern society, but which is by no means self-evident, a man remains the owner of his property until he dies. If he becomes mentally incompetent or incapacitated to such an extent that he can no longer manage his property, it still remains his, but a conservator is to be appointed to manage the property for him.[31]

Upon the death of a property owner who is survived by issue, his property passes and descends to such issue. The members of the next generation are regarded as the natural takers.[32] But that principle may have to be qualified by the need of considering the position of the surviving spouse, who, if it is the female part, is likely to have been dependent on the deceased spouse. So strong was the idea that property ought to be kept in the blood line and ought to descend to the descendants or other relatives of the blood that the Napoleonic code refused the surviving spouse a share in the estate in any right of her (or his) own, and limited her (or him) to a life estate in a certain fraction of the estate.[33] In France and most of those countries which have taken over, or followed the pattern of, the Code Napoleon, this is still the law today. Under the system of the German Code[34] and those related to it, as well as under the statutes of practically all the jurisdictions of Anglo-American Law, the surviving spouse is entitled to a share in her or his own right, a share which, in America, in the presence of children or other issue, usually amounts to one-third of the net estate.[35] Upon the death of the survivor of the spouses, her or his share, in turn passes to her or his issue, who, however, need not necessarily also be issue of the predeceasing spouse.

In all cases of succession by issue, several children take, under American law, equal shares, and the issue of a child who died before

[31]See, for instance, Illinois Probate Act, S.H.A. ch. 3, §122 (1961).
[32]Since in the United States the law of succession on death is state law, most of those treatises which are meant to be used by legal practitioners are concerned only with the law of one state or a group of neighboring states. Of these treatises, the following may be mentioned: Bancroft, *Probate Practice* (2nd ed. 1950) (covers Arizona, California, Colorado, Idaho, Montana, Nevada, New Mexico, North Dakota, Oklahoma, Oregon, South Dakota, Utah, Washington, and Wyoming); Horner, *Probate Practice* (4th ed. 1960-61); Warren, *Heaton, Surrogate's Courts* (6th ed., Warren ed. 1949-62) (New York).

Of nationwide scope is the large treatise by Page, Wills (rev. ed. by Bowe & Parker 1960-63). A concise presentation for students, as well as for quick orientation on the general principles is Atkinson, *Wills* (1937). Rheinstein, *Decedents' Estates* (2nd ed. 1955) and Turrentine, *Wills and Administration* (1954) seek to combine the features of a students' text and a case book.

For concise surveys, see McMurray, "Succession" in 14 *Encyclopedia of the Social Sciences* at 436, and the articles on Inheritance, Intestate Succession, and Wills in the *Encyclopedia Britannica*.
[33]French Civil Code of 1804, Art. 767.
[34]German Civil Code of 1897, Pars. 1931 et s.
[35]See, for example, Illinois Probate Act §11, S.H.A. ch. 3, §11 (1961).

the property owner in question takes, again in equal parts, the share that would have come to him if he had survived (so-called succession *per stirpes*). Such equality has not always been the rule. English succession to real property followed, until 1925,[36] the rule of primogeniture. Under the old "canons of descent," males were preferred over females, and among the males the eldest son inherited all, under complete exclusion of all others. In order to prevent the uneconomic partition of farm units, the laws of several European countries provide for schemes to avoid or postpone partition, or for some special benefit for that one of several co-heirs who takes over the farm undivided and thereby assumes the burden of paying out his brothers and sisters in cash.[37]

The course of intestate succession can be changed by the making of a last will and testament. Under modern laws, a property owner has the power by himself to determine who shall obtain his property after his death. Along with freedom of contract, freedom of property transfer among the living, freedom of marriage, and those freedoms which, such as freedom of speech, make up the Bill of Rights, the principle of freedom of testation is regarded as an essential aspect of human personality in a free society. A testator may leave his property to relatives other than those indicated by the rules of intestate succession or to outsiders of the family, or to charity, shortly, to whomsoever he pleases. In the United States, a testator may completely disinherit his children, a thing he cannot do under the European continental laws, under which he must leave them at least a minimum portion of his estate.[38] Under these latter laws, complete disinheritance is possible only in the case of a child (or grandchild) who has grossly violated the commands of filial piety. In the United States the only person that cannot be freely disinherited is the surviving spouse, to whom a generous share in the estate must be left. So strong is this concern for the surviving spouse that she (or he) can, in most states, not be disinherited, even if she (or he) has given the other party a ground for divorce. Only after divorce is the tie cut, but even then not completely in favor

[36]Administration of Estates Act, 1925, 15 Geo. 5, c. 23.

[37]See French Civil Code, Art. 815, as amended by Law of January 15, 1943; see also German Civil Code, Pars. 2049, 2312, as to the right of one co-heir to take over the family farm undivided, so-called *Anerbenrecht*, which exists in several parts of Germany and Austria, or the similar Norwegian Odalsrät, and which is discussed in the article by Hallstein, in 2 *Rechtsvergleichendes Handwoerterbuch* 184 (1929) and the treatise by Enneccerus & Coing; *Erbrecht* 527 (1953).

[38]See, for example, French Civil Code, Art. 918 et s., German Civil Code, Pars. 2302 et s. Under the German Code (Par. 2333) complete disinheritance is possible in the case of a descendant who has made an attempt upon the life of the ancestor or his spouse, or has committed against the ancestor or his spouse a serious crime, or has incurred the ancestor's disapproval through a dissipate or immoral course of life. The French code, Art. 717, automatically excludes from succession a descendant who has been convicted of an attempt upon the ancestor's life, or has preferred against the ancestor an accusation of a capital crime judicially found to be false, or the descendant who has failed to report his information about another person's intention to make an attempt upon the ancestor's life.

of the innocent party. Freedom of testation also implies the freedom of tieing up the estate for some future. A testator may place his estate under a trust, limit his children or other beneficiaries, such as the surviving spouse, to the income and postpone the distribution of the capital to some future time, that, under the so-called rule against perpetuities, may be no more remote, however, than "one life in being plus twenty-one years." The possibility of postponing distribution seems to be widely used to place an estate under competent management during the period of a son's or daughter's minority or even beyond. Trust provisions postponing distribution of his share to a beneficiary until he reaches the age of 24, or 30, or even higher, appear not to be uncommon.

A testator may also subject the enjoyment of a legacy or devise to conditions. "I leave to my son Saul $100,000. This sum is to be paid to him upon his 28th birthday, provided he has by that time obtained the degree of Bachelor of Arts from a college belonging to the Ivy League, and the degree of Bachelor of Law from the Harvard Law School. If my son Saul, upon his 28th birthday, shall not have obtained these degrees, the sum of $100,000 is to be paid not to him but to the Trustees of Harvard College." Or, "I leave to my daughter Doris my piece of land called Blackacre, but she is to forfeit it if before reaching the age of 30, or before her death, whichever occurs earlier, she should ever smoke a cigar, a cigarette, a pipe, or any other instrument of tobacco smoking."

Not all such conditions are treated as valid by the courts.[39] A condition will be held invalid if it is against good morals or contrary to public policy. The courts are thus reluctant to enforce testamentary provisions tending to encroach upon freedom of religion or conditions in restraint of marriage.

However, by widely upholding testamentary conditions, the law provides an effective means for one generation for some future to control the conduct of the next generation.[40] A good measure of such control is already provided by the very existence of freedom of testation. "If you marry that man, I shall disinherit you." The possibility through such threats to maintain a measure of control over grown-up children belongs to the stock arguments adduced to justify freedom of testation.

Probably, the force of such a threat is no longer so strong today as it was in the days in which inheritance was a more important source of wealth than individual endeavor. These days are past, especially in the United States. But that attempts to control the next generation's conduct by conditions or by threats of disinheritance have not lost all

[39]See Browder, "Illegal Conditions and Limitations," in 6 *American Law of Property* pt. 27, at 591-692 (1952); Scott, "Control of Property by the Dead," 65 *U. Pa. L. Rev.* 527 (1917) reprinted in part in Rheinstein, *op. cit. supra* note 32, at 100.

[40]Consider, for instance, the provision conditioning a substantial legacy to a son upon his continuing his father's business.

significance, is shown by the occurrence of litigation finding its way into the published reports of judicial decisions or even into newspapers. The scope of conditions held by the courts to be admissible has constantly narrowed; but the line of demarcation between valid and invalid conditions is not clear. Also, beyond this, little is known about the actual use of such devices of intergenerational control of behavior beyond the grave. We need research for the benefit of scholars as well as for the guidance of the courts and of lawmakers.

Of some importance for the transfer of wealth from one generation to the other is also the legal machinery by which this transfer is effected, and, closely connected therewith, its cost. Much has been said about the high cost of dying. Most of this, at times passionate, discussion has been concerned with American funeral practices. But unnecessary shrinkage of decedents' estates is also caused by the American system of administration of estates. Following traditions which have long since been modified in their country of origin, England, in the United States, every decedent's estate or, more specifically, the personal property of such an estate, is supposed to go through the process of administration. When David Deadman dies, his assets do not directly pass to his children, his widow, or his other relatives or legatees. Title is to vest in a "personal representative," who is called executor, if he has been appointed by the decedent in his will, and administrator, if he is appointed by the court. The executor/administrator, or, as he is sometimes called, the personal representative, is to collect in his hands all the assets of the estate, to have them appraised by experts, and to list them in an inventory. He is to publish, in a newspaper, and usually three times, the fact of David Deadman's death and to call upon all claiming to have been creditors of the decedent, to file their claims with the probate court. The claims are then looked into by the court, and those which are approved are to be paid by the personal representative, along with, or, more correctly, after, the payment of estate, inheritance, and other taxes. Then the personal representative is to make up a plan of distribution of the remaining assets among the intestate takers or the beneficiaries of the will. Upon approval by the court, the estate is distributed in accordance with this plan. Thereupon the personal representative has to render his account. If it is approved, the personal representative is discharged, and the estate is closed.

The process takes, at best, nine months, but it may last longer, and it costs money. The personal representative is entitled to a fee, and so are the bondsman or the bonding company he is to present, the appraisers, the personal representative's lawyer, and all those who have rendered service to the personal representative, for example, by safekeeping the assets. Costs and complications are increased by the requirement of state statutes that express permission of the probate court be obtained by the personal representative for the sale of an asset of the estate, for example, the decedent's automobile, and for the settlement of every claim of, or against, the estate.

Administration by a middleman and carried on under the supervision of a court is an effective device to safeguard the interests of creditors, of the public treasury, of missing heirs, or of claimants in a disputed succession. But it is unnecessary where the estate is solvent, the debts are few and known, and all possible successors are in harmony. Continental laws and, to a large extent, English law, too, dispense with administration under such circumstances which, of course, are the normal ones.[41] Why do we in the United States insist in normal cases on using a device which is useful in abnormal ones, but in the great mass of transfers of property upon death is just a source of unnecessary cost and delay? How considerable a shrinkage an estate can be subjected to through this unnecessary process has been shown by the few investigations that have been undertaken so far.[42] Extensive additional research is highly desirable.

The desire to avoid the unnecessary high cost of administration or, as it is popularly, but incorrectly called, probate, has stimulated the use of transactions not designed for the purpose to bring about the effects of a property disposition for the case of death.[43] The two most popular are: the joint tenancy, especially used in the form of the joint savings account, the joint tenancy of stocks and bonds, and the joint tenancy of real estate. If a father establishes a savings account in joint tenancy with his son, the son is a co-owner with him and remains owner, or rather now the sole owner, when the father dies. The other device is the so-called tentative or Totten trust. It is frequently called the poor man's will. Father opens a savings account in his name as trustee for his son. As long as father lives, he can do with the account as he pleases, make withdrawals at any time and in any amount. When the father dies, the account automatically belongs to the son, without any necessity of its passing through administration. Such, at least, is the case law in the State of New York. To what extent, if any, the Totten trust device works in other states, is not beyond doubt.

Legal pitfalls also lurk behind the joint bank account and the other joint tenancies, as well as behind other devices which are used by estate planners to accomplish what the French say cannot be done: *Donner et retenir ne vaut*. If you wish to make a gift, you have to give it away completely; but you cannot give it away now and at the same time keep it until your death. In American law, this miracle can be performed by a skilled estate planner. But he better watch out lest he

[41]*Cf.* Rheinstein, "Judicial and Administrative Control of the Liquidation of Decedents' Estates," in 1 *Rapports généraux du 5e Congrès international de droit comparé* #229 (1960).

[42]Dunham, "The Method, Process and Frequency of Wealth Transmission at Death," 30 *U. Chi. L. Rev.* 241 (1963); Powell & Looker, "Decedents' Estates — Illumination from Probate and Tax Records," 30 *Colum. L. Rev.* 909 (1930).

[43]See Rheinstein, *op. cit. supra* note 32, at 77B; Gulliver & Tilson, "Classification of Gratuitous Transfers to Take Effect at Death," 51 *Yale L. J.* 1 (1941).

create a litigation breeder rather than a valid *inter-vivos* disposition with *post mortem* effects. Tax advantages which could once be achieved by the use of such tricky devices have long been eliminated. Congress and state legislatures have caught up with the ingenious lawyers. But the transactions are still in use, to avoid the cost of administration, or to defeat the "indefeasible share" of a surviving spouse, or for peculiar purposes of a special individual case, or just out of superstitious aversion against will-making, or as a response to advertising by trust companies.

In the present age of high taxes, the ways of intergenerational transfer of property are strongly influenced by the desire to minimize taxes. The flourishing development of the art of estate planning is motivated, although not entirely, by considerations of tax avoidance.[44]

All general tax laws have intergenerational significance insofar as they take the funds needed for public support of the aged out of the pockets of the productive. At least the major part of the tax yield comes out of that source. But some taxes, especially sales taxes and income taxes, also hit members of that very group for whose support, along with many other purposes, they are levied.

Beyond this general, directly motivational effect, certain tax laws indirectly motivate intergenerational behavior insofar as they afford tax savings for the taxpayer who engages in certain lines of intergenerational behavior. In this group belong, in the United States, the state inheritance taxes, the federal estate and gift tax, and the income taxes, especially the federal income tax.

The intergenerational influence is most obvious in the case of the state inheritance taxes. While the federal estate tax is levied upon the estate of a decedent and computed upon its totality, the state inheritance taxes are levied upon the benefits individually received by each intestate successor, legatee, or devisee, and are computed upon the amount received by each. A tax so constructed can have different rates depending upon the degree of nearness to the decedent of each beneficiary. Under the laws of most, if not all, of the states, the rate of the inheritance tax is low on estate shares coming to descendants, higher for relatives of a less close degree, and stiff for strangers to the blood.[45] For the tax-conscious property owner, this difference in rates

---

[44]The literature on estate planning is legion. Practically all of this writing is so technical that it is hardly understandable to the layman. A concise and perhaps not entirely incomprehensible survey is contained in Rheinstein, *op. cit. supra* note 32, at 831.

[45]Under the Inheritance Tax Law of Illinois, S.H.A. ch. 120, §375 (1961), which constitutes a typical example, the tax rate varies between 2% on the first taxable $50,000 in the case of an acquisition by ascendant, descendant; spouse, son-in-law, or daughter-in-law of the decedent, and 10% on the first taxable $20,000 in the case of acquisition by persons related to the decedent more remotely, such as uncle, aunt, or descendant of an uncle or an aunt. Besides, in the case of the first named class, the first $20,000 is tax free, in the case of the latter only the first $100. In the case of the first named class the tax rate on the part of the taxable acquisition which surpasses $500,000 is 14%, in the latter class the maximum rate is 30%, and it applies to that part of the taxable acquisition which surpasses $250,000.

may act as a stimulus to leave his estate to his children rather than to other persons to whom he might be tempted to leave it. Of course, the tax is no burden upon the decedent. He will be dead when it becomes payable. Nevertheless, the flourishing business of estate planners seems to indicate that, even so, property owners are influenced by the difference in tax rates. Apparently, they do not wish their estates to be depleted even after death. To what extent the motive is actually significant is unknown. Research would be desirable, although it would by no means be easy to find out about the true motives of testators. The best source would be information by estate planning attorneys as to what advice they give their clients and to what extent clients have been influenced thereby.

The motivating influence of the federal estate tax law is more subtle. Save for the exemption of legacies to charity,[46] the tax rate is independent of the relation between the decedent and the recipients. But this principle is not carried out with full consistency. Up to one-half of the taxable net estate can be left to the surviving spouse tax free.[47] Use of this so-called marital deduction seems to be widely favored in estate planning. The effect is that the surviving spouse can freely dispose of that part of the estate which is left to him or, more frequently, to her. Of course, she or he may provide for passage to the children upon her or his death, but her, or his, children may not, or not all, be also children of the decedent. But she, or he, may leave the fund to outsiders, or may give it away or use it up before death. This latter possibility may be forestalled by the estate planning device of leaving the benefit to the surviving spouse not outright, but only as a life estate coupled with a general testamentary power of appointment. In fact, under the present federal estate tax law, a fairly general pattern has developed among American testators leaving property of more than $60,000 net value in the following way:[48]

The estate remaining after payment of taxes, debts, and legacies to charity, relatives, and friends is given to a trustee, regularly a trust company, under the following trusts: To keep the estate invested profitably but safely at least for the lifetime of the surviving spouse, to whom the income is to be paid in regular installments. In case of insufficiency of the income, the capital may be invaded. Upon the death of the surviving spouse, the estate is to be distributed among the decedent's descendants, but as to one-half the surviving spouse is given the power of providing for a different distribution by her, or his, last will and testament. Where children or grandchildren are expected possibly to be under age at the time of the death of the surviving spouse, continuation of the trust management is regularly provided for their shares until the recipient reaches majority. The skilled estate

[46]Int. Rev. Code of 1954, §2055.
[47]Int. Rev. Code of 1954, §2056.
[48]See Dunham, *supra* note 42.

planner will, of course, adapt the plan to the needs or whims of the particular client, his estate, and his family. The trust provisions of the will tend to be lengthy and complex. But the general scheme is likely to be followed for the normal case, because it results in maximum tax benefits. On one-half of the estate, no estate tax is payable at the death of the predeceasing spouse, because it passes to the surviving spouse tax free under the marital deduction rule. But estate tax will, of course, be payable when, upon the death of the survivor, the fund, or what is left of it, passes, along with the surviving spouse's other assets, to her, or his, intestate or testate, beneficiaries. On the other half of the estate of the predeceasing spouse, estate tax is payable at his death, but not on the death of the survivor, because at that time no "transfer" will take place. The descendants have acquired their benefit already upon the death of the predeceasing spouse, encumbered with the life estate of the predeceasing spouse. In the technical language of the law, they have, at that time, acquired a remainder following a life estate; that remainder becomes vested on the death of the predeceasing spouse, and only possessory upon the death of the survivor.

The result of the provisions of the federal estate tax law is to favor the next generation as to one-half of the "residuary" estate, and a person who is regularly a member of the decedent's own generation, *viz.* the surviving spouse, as to the other half.

A motivation to make a disposition unfavorable to the next generation as embodied by the decedent's descendants is established by the exemption from federal estate tax, as well as from most state inheritance taxes, of legacies and devises for charitable purposes. Of course, the charity may be one that will use the fund for purposes benefiting the next generation.

Of intergenerational significance is also the possibility of saving taxes by anticipating inheritance. Gifts made by a property owner during his lifetime are subject to the federal gift tax rather than the estate tax, and the rates of the gift tax can be considerably lower than those of the estate tax.[49] Of the states, many leave *inter vivos* gifts entirely tax free; in the others, the gift tax rates are lower than those of the inheritance tax. A property owner of sufficient wealth can thus achieve sizeable savings by giving away parts of his estate during his lifetime rather than upon death. The chief beneficiaries of such gifts, of course, will regularly be the children. The stimulus to make such gifts is increased by the possibility of also saving on the federal income tax, a tax that is to be paid not by survivors after the property owner's death but by himself. The saving can be two-fold: the donor's taxable income is reduced; and the donee's income will be taxed on a lower rate, provided their total income is lower than the pre-gift income of the donor. However, as the law stands, the income

---

[49]*Compare* Int. Rev. Code of 1954, §2502 (gift tax rates) *with* Int. Rev. Code of 1954, §2001 (estate tax rates).

tax saving may not be achievable by gifts in trust for minor children. The income derived from a fund given to children for whose support the donor is responsible is, insofar as it is used for such support, regarded as part of his taxable income.[50]

All the tax-benefit provisions mentioned so far, if they have any motivational effect at all, tend to favor transfers of property from the old generation to the young. The well-known exemption provisions of the federal income tax law also tend in the same direction.[51] However, these provisions may also favor a son or a daughter who provides for an aged parent more than one-half of his total income, provided such parent's other income for the year is not higher than $600.[52]

With the exception of the last-named provision, not only social workers but also social scientists may be little interested in those rules of the succession and tax laws which have just been presented here. They do not affect the clients of welfare agencies, and generally they are of significance only for that fraction of the population which owns sizeable amounts of property; and that fraction is comparatively small even in that wealthiest of all nations, the United States. Social scientists tend to be interested in mass phenomena as reflected in statistics. But if we look at the statistics of national wealth and income, the fraction affected by the laws on succession and taxation is vast.[53] The upper-middle class and the wealthy must not be ignored by social science. After all, these persons tend to be influential in shaping the policies of the nation, and they are those who provide the major part of the expenditures for welfare, both public and private.

[50]Int. Rev. Code of 1954, §677.
[51]Int. Rev. Code of 1954, §§151-54.
[52]Int. Rev. Code of 1954, §§151(e), 152.
[53]In 1960, 50% of the total number of families and unattached persons receiving an annual income had an annual income of $5,000 or more. (1962 Statistical Abstract of the United States, table 448). According to Harrington, *The Other America—Poverty in the United States* (1963), in 1958, 45.5% of the total family income was received by families of the uppermost one-fifth group, that is, of families with an average annual income of $14,250. The table containing this figure is taken from an AFL-CIO publication, which is based upon Department of Commerce figures. It is not beyond dispute.

the economics of intergenerational relationships

JUANITA M. KREPS

Any careful consideration of the extent to which persons in the
United States are now supporting parents and grandparents, or *vice
versa,* must first take note of two developments of recent years. The
first of these developments is the growing tendency for the family
irrespective of generations to maintain its own home. This movement
toward independence in living arrangements is reflected both in the
increased proportion of aged couples and individuals who maintain
separate living quarters, and in earlier marriage and family formation
on the part of those persons who face one or more years in school
before joining the full-time labor force. A second development is the
continued decline in the proportion of both older and younger men
participating in the labor force, and thus deriving their incomes
primarily from current earnings. There appears to be a contradiction
in these two concurrent trends — the tendency for families with aged
and with young heads to maintain independent homes, while at the
same time for both groups earned income has come to be of less
significance, relative to their total incomes, than previously.

The major purpose of the present paper is to explain this apparent contradiction by focussing attention on the growing extent to which both young adults and aged persons now acquire claims against the national product of any given year without contributing to that year's output via current membership in the labor force. In a broad sense, the young and old families may be considered the children and parents of the middle-age group, who are the active participants in the production process, and who, on a current basis, are the producers of the national output. Since current consumption must come from current output, it can be argued that to an increasing degree, parents in the middle-age group are supporting both their adult offspring (and the families of these offspring), and their aged parents.

Intergenerational support thus conceived, however, is quite different from the traditional pattern in which the children and grandparents in each family were supported by the parents *of that family*. Support of one generation by another is now provided, not within families, but between one whole generation and another. Thus the employed person in the middle-age group contributes to the support of young adults via tax payments for financing education, and to the support of retired persons via the federal old age, survivors, and disability insurance tax (OASDI), whether or not he personally has children or retired parents.

One measure of the extent of intergenerational support, therefore, is to be found in the amount of income annually transferred from the generation currently in the active labor force to those adults who have not yet entered the labor force, and to those persons who have retired. These transfers, both public and private, represent dollar claims of the young adults and their families and of the aged and their families against the national output produced by the persons currently at work.

Before we examine the extent of intergenerational support evidenced by transfer payments, a brief account will be given of the recent changes in the composition of income which have accompanied the declining labor force participation of young and old men. The growing significance of income maintenance programs and the declining importance of earnings to these two age groups is thus emphasized. Intergenerational support is then considered within the context of these labor force developments, and the need for estimates of the income transfer involved between generations is indicated. Some of the economic implications of recent shifts in the pattern of intergenerational support are considered in the final section. In particular, this question is posed: will the continued rise in productivity per man-hour reduce even further the proportion of adults who are in the labor force, thereby increasing the volume of necessary income transfers? This issue involves the extent to which the evening-out of income throughout adult life seems likely to continue, and the question of the mechanisms through which the redistribution of income between age groups may be accomplished.

labor force participation and sources of income

During the twentieth century the labor force participation rates for both younger and older men in the United States have declined significantly. As a result families with either young or older heads increasingly derive their income from income-maintenance programs rather than from current earnings.

The changed education-work pattern of young men has been summarized as follows:

> At current levels, the average American male makes his first full-time entry into the labor force between his 18th and 19th year of life. At the turn of the century more than one out of every five youths 10-15 years of age were already workers.[1]

The labor force participation rate for males aged 14-19 declined from 63.6 per cent in 1900 to 44 per cent in 1962. The latter figure was much lower than had been expected; a 1959 projected rate of 46.6 per cent for 1970 indicates our failure to anticipate the rate of decline in labor force activity of young men.[2] As education and training programs for young persons receive increased emphasis, actual participation by this age group may easily fall to 40 per cent or lower by the end of the present decade.

The long-run decline in labor force participation of younger men was accelerated during the period following the Second World War; the rate fell from 54 per cent in 1947 to the 1962 rate of 44 per cent. This sharp drop, as well as the slight decline in labor force activity of men aged 20-24 during the decade 1952-1962, has been a necessary corollary of the higher educational standards that were imposed by the rapid mechanization of industry and made possible by the higher output of the economy. During the decade 1952 to 1962 the proportion of workers aged 18 and over who were college graduates rose from 7.9 per cent to 11 per cent. The proportion of workers having at least a high school education rose by 25 per cent — from 42.8 per cent to 53.8 per cent of the total.[3]

At the other end of the working life, the labor force participation of men, except for the temporary upturn in activity during World War II, has also shown a secular decline throughout this century. For men aged 65 and over, the rate fell from 68.3 per cent in 1900 to 30 per cent in 1962. As in the case of younger men, the rate of decline was faster than had been projected. In fact, projections for the year 1975 gave an expected participation rate for men, aged 65 and over, of 31 per cent.

---

[1]Fred Slavick and Seymour L. Wolfbein, "The Evolving Work-Life Pattern," *Handbook of Social Gerontology*, Clark Tibbitts, ed. (Chicago: The University of Chicago Press, 1960), p. 299.

[2]U.S. Department of Labor, *Population and Labor Force Projections for the United States, 1960 to 1975*, U.S. Department of Labor Bulletin No. 1242 (Washington, D.C.: Government Printing Office, 1959), p. 54.

[3]U.S. Department of Labor, *Manpower Report of the President* (Washington, D.C.: Government Printing Office, 1963), pp. 12-13, 156.

The decrease in work experienced by men aged 65 and over has been particularly sharp during the postwar era, labor force rates falling from 48 per cent to 30 per cent in a decade and a half. In addition, there is now a discernible downward movement in the labor force participation of men aged 60 to 64. The amendment to the Social Security Act permitting men to retire at the age of 62 may encourage some further reduction in the proportion of men in the age group 60-64 who are full-time workers.

Seymour Wolfbein has drawn dramatic attention to the combined effects of declining labor force participation and increasing life expectancy. For the first time in this century, he points out in *Changing Patterns of Working Life*, the length of working life among men in this country has declined. In summary, he cites the following data showing both the growth in numbers of years spent outside the labor force, which has occurred throughout the century, and the reversal of the trend toward increasing work life, which occurred for the first time during the 1950's.

Since these labor force trends may become progressively more pronounced for both young and old workers as the economy's manpower requirements fall short of the growing labor supply,[4] it is well to consider the effects of declining labor force participation on the incomes of the two groups, the young and the old. In particular, what sources of income are replacing earnings for the families of young men who continue in school and for the families of men who retire at age 65 or age 62? To what extent is the financial support for young and old families provided by persons in the age group 20-64 who are parents of the young or children of the aged, or both? And finally, given the

table 12-1   life and work life expectancy at birth for men in years, 1900-60

year	life expectancy	work-life expectancy	outside the labor force
1900	48.2	32.1	16.1
1940	61.2	38.3	22.9
1950	65.5	41.9	23.6
1960	66.6	41.4	25.2

Source: Seymour L. Wolfbein, *Changing Patterns of Working Life*, U. S. Department of Labor (Washington, D.C.: Government Printing Office, 1963), p. 10.

[4] F. Le Gros Clark has pointed out that a generation ago most manual workers in the "transitional phase" of 55 to 70 years of age continued to think of themselves as employable for several years. It was exceptional for such men to be retired at a given age, with little opportunity for another job. He asks whether we are not now reaching a stage at which it will be exceptional for men *not* to be finally retired at 65 or sooner. We are in danger, he concludes, of "theorizing about work and retirement in terms of an industrial milieu that is rapidly becoming obsolete." From "Changing Limits of the Employable Life," paper given at the International Social Science Research Seminar in Gerontology, Markaryd, Sweden, August 5-9, 1963, p. 6.

modern economic arrangements under which such support is extended, what are the effects of this pattern of financial support on intergenerational family relationships, and on family living arrangements in particular?

Sources of support of young families whose heads are still in school vary widely — part-time work of the young man, earnings of his wife, direct financial assistance from parents, grants by universities and foundations, and the like. Since present data do not show accurately the proportion of the young family's income accruing from these various sources, changes in sources of income which have accompanied the declining labor force activity of younger men can be described only in very general terms. It is significant, however, to note these trends: (1) the lowered age of marriage and family formation which occurred during the 1940's;[5] (2) the prolongation of the period of education of the male;[6] and (3) the recent growth in public and private expenditures for education and training.[7] The educational expenditures at colleges and universities, moreover, are expected to increase by almost two and one-half times between 1962 and 1972.[8]

Sources of income of the aged in recent years have reflected clearly the changing work-retirement pattern of older men. In brief, the proportion of the income of the aged derived from current earnings declined markedly during the decade of the 1950's while the proportion derived from social insurance benefits increased. Of the 1960 aggregate income of persons aged 65 and over, income from earnings totaled between ten and eleven billion dollars, and approximately the same amount went to recipients of old-age, survivors, and disability insurance and to retired government and railroad employees. This one-to-one ratio of earnings to benefit payments contrasts sharply with the composition of the income of the aged a decade earlier, when aggregate earnings of seven to eight billion dollars amounted to several times as much as benefit payments.[9] As total

[5]The median age of first marriage for males declined from 24.3 years in 1940 to 22.8 years in 1950; no subsequent decline has occurred. For females, the median age of first marriage dropped from 21.5 to 20.3 during the 1940's and has remained at the latter age.

[6]Improvements in educational levels, described above in terms of the proportions of workers aged 18 and over who were graduates of high schools and of colleges, during the decade 1952-62, also can be shown by the change in the number of school years completed by males 14 years of age and over. The median years of school completed rose from 9.4 in 1950 to 10.4 in 1960. U.S. Bureau of the Census, *Census of Population, 1960. U.S. Summary, Detailed Characteristics* (Washington, D.C.: Government Printing Office, 1963), pp. 1-404, 1-408.

[7]Total expenditures (public and private) on education rose from $10.9 billion in 1949-50 to $24.3 billion in 1960-61. Ida C. Merriam, "Social Welfare Expenditures, 1960-61," *Social Security Bulletin*, XXV (November, 1962), 12.

[8]Harold Wolozin, *The Outlook for Higher Education — Underlying Economic and Demographic Projections* (New York: The Fund for the Advancement of Education, March, 1963), p. 26.

[9]Lenore A. Epstein, "Money Income Sources of Aged Persons — December, 1960," *Social Security Bulletin*, XXIV (July, 1961), 6-9; and "Money Income of Aged Persons, Mid-1960," *Social Security Bulletin*, XXIV (January, 1961), 12-15.

OASDI payments continue to increase, these benefits, of course, will assume an even greater relative magnitude, unless there is a reversal of the downward trend in the labor force activity of older men. Such a reversal appears unlikely, in view of recent developments in the market forces which determine the demand for older workers' services.[10]

These same market forces also dictate the demand for the services of younger workers, and therefore to a large extent determine the composition of the income going to men aged 14-19 and their families, as well as the composition of the income of the aged. The question of income sources of both young and older families thus comes to rest primarily on the availability of jobs. Explanation of the decline in job opportunities is in one major respect the same for both age groups; technological change, paced by automation, is rapidly reducing the amount of labor necessary to produce a given volume of output. And, although the volume of goods annually produced is growing rapidly, total requirements remain too low to absorb the available labor force, which during the 1960's will be enlarged by the influx of about thirteen million new entrants. This imbalance between labor requirements and labor supply, which comes to be reflected, of course, in a mounting level of unemployment, has particularly important implications for the young and the old, since these two groups are often considered the marginal workers.

As employment opportunities for the young and the older workers shrink, income maintenance of some form (educational outlays, retirement benefits, unemployment insurance) assumes an increasingly significant role in the support pattern of these two generations. Intergenerational support in the present era can, therefore, best be approached via an analysis of income-maintenance programs, public and private, which transfer dollar claims from the generation currently engaged in production to the families of retired persons and to those who are not yet full-time members of the labor force. The need to view the pattern of income allocation in this manner rather than on a family unit basis has become clear, first, because of the rapid growth in the size of these transfers, both in absolute amount and as a proportion of the national income; and, second, because of the increased number of years of man's life in which his economic support is derived, not from current earnings and not from members of his own family, but from a social transfer of income.

claims of age groups against the national product

Dollar claims against any year's total national product are acquired through earnings from work, from capital invested, from the rental of property, and from profits. In each of these instances the in-

---

[10]Juanita M. Kreps, "Aggregate Income and Labor Force Participation of the Aged," *Law and Contemporary Problems*, XXVII (Winter, 1962), 52-66.

come is imputable to the use of a resource which, being currently in use, is contributing to the current output. But many persons who consume goods and services produced in, say, 1960, did not in fact work during that year, nor did they receive income from any other functional share. An obvious case in point is children whose claims are provided by parents.

Until fairly recently the American economy made no formal provisions for income payments other than the functionally derived shares. The unemployed worker, prior to 1935, held no regular (income) claim against the national product. His ability to consume while not employed was limited to the use of past savings, borrowed funds, gifts, private charity, or public relief. Similarly, the aged person or couple who no longer worked depended upon much the same sources of income (with the exception of borrowing, a practice rarely available to older people). Intrafamily support in such a society was obviously necessary, given the unpredictability of charitable support and relief doles. Moreover, the most economical unit through which provisions could be made for the basic necessities (housing and food, in particular) of the whole family was a single home which then housed the aged, their children, and their grandchildren.

The ability of aged persons and young adults not yet at work to maintain separate homes for their families has been greatly enhanced by the economic transition of the postwar era. During this period, society has begun to allocate a significant proportion of its national income to nonworking adults and their families. The income so allocated, being drawn from tax revenues, diverts claims against the total product from one group (the taxed) to another group (the recipients of OASDI benefits, unemployment insurance, workmen's compensation, educational outlays), which may or may not be of the same generation as the taxed. Regardless of whether these transfers of income represent intergenerational shifts—as from currently employed persons, most of whom are under 65, to OASDI recipients—or intragenerational transfers—which might characterize unemployment benefits, for example—the past two decades' growth in these transfers, both in absolute and relative terms, is of considerable import.

Present data do not permit us to derive a reliable estimate of the amount and proportion of the national product currently being transferred from one generation to another. The closest approximation to an estimate of the total socially transferred income appears in the estimates of social welfare expenditures provided by the Social Security Administration. Social welfare expenditures under public programs for all age groups (including social insurance, public aid, health and medical programs, other welfare services, veterans' programs, education and public housing, all with certain exclusions) amounted to $57.9 billion for the fiscal year 1960-61. This total expenditure represented 11.5 per cent of the Gross National Product of $505 billion. An 11 per cent increase in the expenditures for these social welfare programs occurred from 1959-60 to 1960-61, with a particularly large percentage increase (52 per cent) appearing in expenditures for unemployment insurance and employment services.[11]

The dramatic growth in total social welfare expenditures during the past two decades can be summarized as follows: from $8.7 billion in 1939-40, to $23.2 billion in 1949-50, to $57.9 in 1960-61. In dollars, the 1960-61 amount was thus about six and two-thirds times the 1939-40 figure, and two and one-half times that of 1949-50. A more relevant trend, however, is the trend in the amount spent for social welfare as a proportion of the total value of goods and services produced, the Gross National Product (GNP). As a proportion of Gross National Product, social welfare expenditures amounted to 9.1 per cent (of a $95.9 billion GNP) in 1939-40; to 8.8 per cent (of a $264.0 billion GNP in 1949-50); and to 11.5 per cent of the 1960-61 Gross National Product of $505.2 billion. Since these increases in expenditures reflect population growth and price increase, as well as an expansion in services, also useful is to note the trend in real expenditure per capita. Social welfare expenditure per capita in 1960-61 prices rose from $146 in 1939-40, to $187 in 1949-50, to $312 in 1960-61.[12]

While these data clearly indicate the upward trend in public welfare expenditures, they do not provide an adequate picture of the rate of growth in expenditure for any one age group. Only in particular instances—education, for example—is the expenditure clearly one made for one generation (in this case, generation three) from tax receipts collected primarily from generation two (the middle-age group) and to some extent from generation one (persons 65 and over). Intergenerational transfers of income via the public sector can, therefore, be described only in somewhat general terms.

With respect to the amount of income transferred to generation three, the young, a public outlay of slightly less than $20 billion was made for education in 1960-61. Another $4.5 billion of private expenditures for education brought the total to $24.3 billion, or 4.8 per cent of that year's Gross National Product. For the most part, these were expenditures made on behalf of persons not yet in the labor force. Generation three also acquired claims on the national product through other welfare programs. Aid to dependent children alone was more than one billion dollars.

For generation one, persons 65 and over, the best estimate of the dollar dimensions of the federal program of benefits and services is the one prepared for the President's Council on Aging for the fiscal year 1963. For persons aged 65 and over, the total amount involved in federal programs was $17.8 billion, this figure included income-maintenance programs—retirement income, disability payments, survivor payments, public assistance—as well as health and medical care ex-

[11]Merriam, *Social Security Bulletin*, November, 1962, *op. cit.*, pp. 3-13.
[12]*Ibid.*, pp. 7-8.

penditures and tax benefits.[13] The addition of benefits (both public and private) other than those from the federal government would swell the total dollar claims of this group considerably. Private employee-benefit programs paid about $3.8 billion in cash benefits (excluding health insurance benefits) in 1960-61, about $1.8 billion of this representing pensions to retired workers.[14]

In addition to these primarily intergenerational transfers of income, public and private expenditures for income maintenance and welfare programs serving the middle-age group (generation two) have also grown rapidly during the postwar period. Assuming that most members of the labor force are in generation two, one may view the growth of unemployment insurance as an increase in transfers to this generation, ignoring for the moment the question of the source of funds from which this transfer is made. Public expenditures for unemployment insurance and employment service rose from less than half a billion dollars in 1939-40 to $1.8 billion in 1949-50, and to $3.5 billion in 1960-61. Expenditures for private supplementary benefits made in behalf of middle-aged persons need to be added to the transfers to this group, as do expenditures for disability payments to persons under retirement age. Disability payments in total approached $6 billion in the calendar year 1960.[15] Public assistance, health and medical care programs, vocational rehabilitation, veterans' programs, and public housing give rise to further transfers of income, a large proportion of which went to generation two, the middle aged.

The Social Security Administration offers the following estimate of 1960 federal expenditures for OASDI payments, other social insurance and programs for veterans, and public assistance, by generation, as compared with 1950 expenditures.[16] Since this estimate includes only federal payments for income maintenance, it covers only a portion of the total transfers of income involved either within generation

---

[13]President's Council on Aging, *The Older American* (Washington, D.C.: U.S. Government Printing Office, 1963), pp. 54-56.

[14]Merriam, *Social Security Bulletin*, November, 1962, *op. cit.*, p. 13.

[15]A rough estimate of total disability payments to all age groups in the calendar year 1960 follows: OASDI, $586 million; railroad retirement, $146.7 million; public employee, $491.9 million; veterans' program, $2,529.2 million; workmen's compensation, $800 million; state temporary disability, $314.0 million; railroad temporary disability, $56.9 million; private temporary disability, $1,007.4 million — a total of $5,914.8 million. From the nature of these benefits, we can assume that they represent primarily an intragenerational transfer of income. See *Social Security Bulletin, Annual Statistical Supplement 1960*, p. 6; and Alfred M. Skolnik, "Employee Benefit Plans, 1954-60," *Social Security Bulletin*, XXV (April, 1962), 10.

[16]This estimate attempted to allocate benefits by age wherever possible. Payments to dependent children of retired workers, for example, are indicated as going to those under 18, rather than to the group aged 65 and over. However, no attempt was made to allocate payments under the veterans' program going to helpless children or to those 18 to 21 and in school; they are included with younger children. All payments in Aid for Dependent Children (AFDC) cases are treated as going to children under 18, since amounts for the adult caretaker are for the benefit of the child.

one, the elderly, or between generations. Nevertheless, the almost four-fold increase in total income-maintenance payments reflects the growth in significance of this source of support. Moreover, it will be noted that payments to the aged increased about five and one-half times and payments to those under 18 increased more than three times, while the payments to the group aged 18-64 doubled.

table 12-2   estimated federal payments under income maintenance programs by age group, 1950 and 1960 (in millions)

program and year	total	under 18	18-64	65 and over
Fiscal Year 1960:				
Total	$19,390	$2,090	$5,030	$12,270
OASDI	10,790	980	1,490	8,320
Other social insurance and programs for veterans	6,680	500	3,370	2,810
Public assistance: federal grants	1,920	610	170	1,140
Fiscal Year 1950:				
Total	$ 5,260	$ 630	$2,420	$ 2,210
OASDI	820	120	80	620
Other social insurance and programs for veterans	3,400	280	2,330	790
Public assistance: federal grants	1,040	230	10	800

Source: Estimate prepared by Lenore Epstein, Deputy Director, Division of Research and Statistics, Social Security Administration, U. S. Department of Health, Education, and Welfare.

In appraising the significance of these trends in terms of intergenerational support patterns, several points should be made. First, the striking growth in social welfare expenditures to all age groups during the 1950's is revealed by any one of several measures: by the growth in dollar amount (from $23.2 to $57.9 billion), by the growth in real per capita expenditure (from $187 to $312 in 1960-61 prices), or by their growth as a percentage of Gross National Product (from 8.8 to 11.5 per cent).[17] A much more dramatic picture can be drawn, of course, by tracing the figures back by two decades, showing the almost sevenfold increase in dollar expenditure since the social welfare program initiated by the Social Security Act first got under way.

Second, the figures on social transfers of income do not give a complete picture of the dollar transfers provided. Within the private sector there has been a marked increase in income transfers, particularly through the growth of private pension benefits. If these benefits continue to grow, they will provide a further important source of dollar transfers to generation one (persons 65 and over).

Third, the obvious significance of the question of intergenera-

[17]Table 12-3 shows the pattern of growth in percentage of Gross National Product of each of the major public welfare programs during the twentieth century.

table 12-3   social welfare expenditures as per cent of gross national product, selected fiscal years, 1889-90 through 1960-61

		social welfare expenditures as per cent of gross national product						
fiscal years	gross national product (in billions)	total*	insurance	public aid	health & medical services	other welfare	veterans' programs	educa- tion†
1889-90	$13.0	2.4	‡	0.3ᵃ	0.1	a	0.9	1.1
1912-13	39.9	2.5	‡	0.3ᵃ	0.4	a	0.5	1.3
1928-29	101.6	4.2	0.3	0.5ᵃ	0.4	a	0.5	2.4
1934-35	68.7	9.5	0.6	4.4	0.8	0.2	0.7	2.9
1939-40	95.9	9.1	1.3	3.8	0.7	0.1	0.6	2.6
1944-45	212.5	4.0	0.7	0.5	0.9	0.1	0.4	1.4
1949-50	264.0	8.8	1.9	0.9	0.9	0.2	2.4	2.5
1954-55	377.5	8.5	2.6	0.8	0.8	0.2	1.2	3.0
1955-56	409.5	8.5	2.6	0.8	0.8	0.2	1.1	3.0
1956-57	432.9	9.0	2.9	0.8	0.8	0.2	1.1	3.2
1957-58	440.2	10.2	3.6	0.8	0.9	0.2	1.1	3.5
1958-59	466.8	10.5	3.9	0.9	0.9	0.2	1.1	3.5
1959-60	494.4	10.6	3.9	0.8	0.9	0.2	1.0	3.7
1960-61	505.2	11.5	4.4	0.9	0.9	0.2	1.0	3.9

*Includes public housing, not shown in distribution.
†For fiscal years 1959-60 and 1960-61, includes basic research and training grants; data for earlier years not available.
‡Less than 0.05 per cent.
ᵃ"Other welfare" included with public aid.

Source: Ida C. Merriam, "Social Welfare Expenditures, 1960-61," *Social Security Bulletin*, XXV (November 1962), 7.

tional support may eventually lead to a reliable estimate of the extent to which present public and private transfers of income occur between generations and the extent to which these are shifts in dollar claims within, say, generation two, the middle-age group. Although such an estimate cannot be made at present, clearly the expenditures experiencing the greatest growth — education and retirement benefits — represent transfers to generations one and three, the young and the old.

Fourth, there is the question of who provides the income (or product) which is being shifted, either publicly or privately, to generations one and three. It might be supposed, for example, that benefits paid to retired persons and to persons not yet in the labor force are being financed by taxes on generation two, the middle-age group. To the extent that this assumption is correct, the transfer is truly an intergenerational one, and represents a shift of income claims from the middle-age group to young adults and children on one hand, and from the same middle-age group to aged persons on the other. The question of tax incidence, however, should be considered more fully.

Since children and young adults who are not yet employed pay little in taxes, most of the income transferred to generation three, the young, must come from either generation one or two or the employed members of generation three. The relatively low incomes of the youngest age group in the labor force suggests that this generation, even when employed, incurs little of the transfer liability. In general, therefore, it can be argued that taxes on generations one (persons 65 and over) and two (the middle-age group) provide the dollar claims of generation three. The source of income transferred to generation one, however, cannot be quite so clearly limited to generation two (the middle-age group), nor is it permissible to state that all the support going to generation three derives from taxes on generation two. A part of the tax liability falls on generation one.

Tax payments are for the most part not age-related, but are related instead to income, to expenditure, or to the ownership of property. In general, therefore, taxes reduce the dollar claims of persons who receive incomes, who spend money, or who own property. Taxes levied on business profits tend to reduce property owners' incomes, while excises and general sales taxes reduce the real incomes of consumers. The most important source of federal revenue, the personal income tax, is of course not age-related. Government receipts from all of these taxes would, therefore, seem to be collected from all age groups, with the result that such intergenerational transfers as are achieved occurs only when expenditures are made for the aged and the young which are disproportionately large in comparison with those made for the middle-age group.

In reality, however, taxes which are income-related fall most heavily on the middle-age group, since their incomes are much higher than either of the other two groups. Moreover, the most important single source of tax receipts involved in the transfer of income – the OASDI payroll tax on employer and employee – is a tax which reduces the incomes of the currently employed workers and provides benefits for aged persons who are not employed. At least one important tax, it might be argued, does not necessarily bear more heavily on generation two, the middle-age group, than on generation one: the property tax. To the extent that property is held by older people, this tax of course reduces the incomes of the aged. However, both the 1957 OASDI beneficiaries study and subsequent reports by the Survey Research Center of the University of Michigan have indicated that except for the ownership of a home, whose median value in 1957 was about eight thousand dollars, property owned by most aged persons was negligible.

In conclusion, then, the present tax structure seems to exact a heavier toll from the middle-age generation because this generation is employed, and has relatively high incomes and property holdings; that both the amounts expended by governments for generations one and three and the proportion of the national income transferred to the young and the aged have grown rapidly during the past two decades; and, that an equally sharp rise in intragenerational transfers has also occurred, as society has assumed some responsibility for providing income for the unemployed and the disabled, as well as continued public assistance and the maintenance of certain health and medical programs.

implications for income distribution

Growth in the volume and relative significance of transfer payments, both intergenerational and intragenerational, invites analysis of the somewhat broader issue of changing patterns of income distribution. Two questions are posed: one, what are the social forces which have brought about the trend toward greater transfers of income to nonworking groups? And, two, to what extent and in what form will these transfers continue to grow? The latter question is of considerable importance to further study of intergenerational relationships. The present concern with improving educational and training levels, for example, suggests the probability of greatly increased expenditures for young adults.

Of the many factors involved in the growth of income maintenance for persons not at work, one broad development—the rise in productivity per man-hour—is of particular significance. Increases in productivity, in fact, might be credited in large measure with both originating the need for income transfers (by requiring a more highly educated labor force, by increasing the pressure for retirement as less labor per unit of output is required, by increasing unemployment, at least in the short run, and so forth) and with providing the means of meeting this need, that is, an increased total product. Needless to say, an increased capacity to support nonworking groups does not mean that society chooses to allocate its output in such a manner. Conceivably, larger volumes of goods could continue to be distributed functionally, leaving nonworking persons and their families dependent upon private charity, savings, support by relatives, and the like. In the United States, the initial decision to allocate a portion of the nation's output to persons not currently at work was actually made at a point in the nation's history when the total output was extremely low, and when the major economic problem—unemployment—sprang not from any sudden or sharp rises in productivity, but from financial collapse and the ensuing decline in aggregate demand for goods. Thus, significant transfers of income originated in a situation in which rising productivity played no immediate role.

Since the end of World War II, increases in productivity have been a major concern throughout the world. In the United States the desire for a higher rate of economic growth (and a faster rise in productivity) has been fed by the knowledge that many other nations were enjoying growth rates considerably in excess of ours. Yet the productivity trends in this country have been substantial. Output per man-hour of workers in the private economy rose by 54 per cent, or a gain of

3 per cent per year, over the 1947-61 period. Even the productivity gain of 2.9 per cent in the later supposedly slow-growth years of this period (as compared with a 3.2 per cent for 1947-57) was above the long-run average.

The increase in the nation's output was closely related to this rise in labor productivity. Gross private product rose by 59 per cent in the years 1947-61. In the same fourteen-year period, although employment rose by 11 per cent, man-hours increased only slightly over three per cent. A decline in average annual hours of work per employee made up the difference. Thus, only a small fraction of the rise in output can be attributed to an increase in man-hours worked. For the most part, the postwar increase in gross private product resulted from the increase in output per man-hour. The productivity increase was in turn made possible by the long-run factors of technological change, improved quality of the labor force, and increasing capital investment.[18]

This increase in output per man-hour, enabling the economy to produce larger and larger volumes of goods with little or no expansion in the number of man-hours required, is precisely what gives rise to the argument that increases in productivity in fact create the need for transfers of income. Inevitably, the short-run problem of technological unemployment arises, making it necessary to provide temporary income for disemployed workers and their families. But longer-run considerations are involved in financing intergenerational shifts in income. In both the case of providing retirement income and in the providing of income maintenance during a lengthened period of education, several years' income is in question. Moreover, the particular employment problems of the very young worker in recent years have made it quite clear that the alternative to increased expenditures for education is increased expenditures for unemployment compensation.

Increased attention is being given to the problem of making young persons employable within today's technology. The need for enlarged expenditures for such a program has arisen from both the labor demand and the labor supply pattern. On the demand side, automation is now rapidly reducing the amount of labor required per unit of output in many industrial sectors, and is utilizing only workers whose skill levels enable them to cope with present-day technology. On the supply side, the number of new entrants to the labor force during the next decade will swell the total in the labor force by about thirteen million, about half of whom will be young persons seeking their first jobs. There is little doubt that the decade will bring significant increases in the volume of transfers to young persons not yet at work, and that the average age at which the young man takes his first full-time job will rise.

At the same time, the pressure of unemployment may lead to a

[18]*Manpower Report of the President, op. cit.,* pp. 67-68.

gradual lowering of retirement age, with 62 and eventually 60 possibly becoming the norm in the United States. Man's work life may thus be shortened significantly at both its beginning and its end. In addition, any increase in life expectancy will add further to the number of years spent outside the labor force. Unless this increase is offset by a decline in the number of years in which a man is involuntarily unemployed, which appears unlikely, given the postwar growth in unemployment, work will absorb a declining proportion of man's adult years.

In Wolfbein's summary of the twentieth-century changes in expectancy of life and working life at birth, cited above, he noted that a male born in 1900 had a life expectancy of 48.2 years and a work-life expectancy of 32.1 years. A man born in 1900, therefore, could expect to spend 16.1 years outside the labor force. In contrast, a male born in 1960 had a life expectancy of 66.6 years and a work-life expectancy of 41.4 years. A man born in 1960, therefore, would spend 25.2 years outside the labor force. Thus, along with the added years of life, which were divided approximately evenly between time spent in and time spent outside the labor force, the American man can see an increase of about one-half in the number of years in which he would not work. Increases in life expectancy, working life, and years spent outside the labor force were all higher for women than for men. In 1900 life expectancy at birth for the female was 50.7. Work-life expectancy was 6.3, leaving 44.4 years outside the labor force. By 1960 life expectancy had climbed to 73.1, work-life expectancy to 20.1, leaving 53.0 years outside the labor force. The latter figure is below the 1950 one of 55.8 years. Thus, for women the reversal during the 1950's of the long-term trend came in the form of a decrease in years outside the labor force, whereas for men the reversal came as a decline in work-life expectancy.[19]

Given present trends toward lengthening the period of education and reducing the work activity of older men, it is not unlikely that the number of years a man spends outside the labor force could increase significantly during the decades of the 1960's and 1970's. For example, suppose that the average age of full-time entry to the labor force rose by two years while the retirement age dropped by two years. A man would then have an additional four years in which he would be supported by nonwage income. In addition, it seems likely that most new increases in life expectancy will be added to the number of years spent outside the labor force. The former division of any extra years of life between working and not working will change, as job opportunities, particularly for older men, diminish.

If work life comes to be compressed within the years of 20 to 60, and if life expectancy increases, further modification of the distributive arrangements will need to be made. For then an increasing pro-

[19]Seymour L. Wolfbein, *Changing Patterns of Working Life*, U.S. Department of Labor (Washington, D.C.: Government Printing Office, 1963), pp. 10-13.

portion of the adult population and their families will have to be supported by income other than wages and salaries. It appears unlikely that this support will be provided primarily on a family unit basis, with generation two (the middle-age group) maintaining their children (and grandchildren) while the young complete their education, as well as maintaining their own parents who are past the age of 60. It seems equally unrealistic, despite the current growth of privately financed pension programs, to expect the middle-age group to accumulate sufficient private savings to maintain themselves through the lengthening period of retirement.

The fact that generation two, the middle-age group, does not support the younger and older members of its own family does not mean that generation two is not contributing to the support of both groups. In a financial sense, these contributions are made both by specific taxes, such as the OASDI tax, the receipts of which are used to pay benefits to currently retired persons; and by other tax payments, which provide the bulk of the services to all generations. But in a more basic sense, the age group that is currently at work provides the major support for all persons in a society, regardless of what financial arrangements are utilized. The national product in any one year results from the efforts of those people currently employed, in combination with the stock of capital goods. Insofar as the retired group owns capital goods, they, too, contribute to output In real terms—that is, in terms of producing the goods and services available for generations one (the young) and three (the old), as well as two (the middle-age group)—the age group currently at work assumes major responsibility.

The volume of goods and services produced has seen a spectacular rise in the postwar period, this rise being attributable, as was noted earlier, to steadily increasing output per man-hour. Since output is increasing without any substantial increase in man-hours worked, clearly a man can expect his lifetime output to remain at least at its present level, even if his work-life span declines, or his total man-hours of work declines through a shortened workweek.[20] In essence, the man who in the future will work from age 20 to age 60 will produce at least as much as the man who in an earlier period worked from age 18 to age 65. Very likely, the output of the man with the shorter work life will be greater, particularly if it can be supposed that his health is

[20]In the study cited earlier, Slavick and Wolfbein noted that total man-hours of work of both men and women increased during the first half of this century. This increase of about two million man-hours was caused by some small increase in the proportion of the population who worked, but more importantly by the fact that "those persons in the labor force put in many, many more years of productive life today than was possible at the turn of the century." The authors also pointed out, however, that both men and women were spending more years in retirement than formerly. See "The Evolving Work-Life Pattern," *op. cit.*, p. 300. The question of whether further increases in life expectancy will continue to increase work-life expectancy, or will bring only a further increase in years spent in retirement, seems to be clearly resolved by Wolfbein's later data on work-life patterns of the 1950's. See *Changing Patterns of Working Life, op. cit.*, pp. 1, 10.

better than that of the worker of earlier generations, and if the number of years he is forced to spend in involuntary unemployment is at least not increased.

If a man's total output is in fact rising, even though he is spending an increasing number of adult years outside the labor force, the problem of supporting him and his family through a lengthened educational period and a lengthened retirement period can be viewed in part as a problem of evening out total earnings through the life span, rather than concentrating income during the working years. A partial evening-out of the income stream need not, of course, provide the same income for each year of adult life. In fact, given the changing pattern of financial needs and expenditures through the family cycle — education, marriage, birth of first child, support of older children, the husband-and-wife family in which at least the head is still at work, and finally, the retirement period for two, and then one person — the annual income ideally would vary in accordance with changing needs. Nevertheless, it becomes increasingly important that the life earnings of husband and wife be viewed in the perspective of their lifetime needs, and that these earnings be spread somewhat more evenly through adult life, rather than being concentrated within the years of actual labor force activity.

The arrangements by which such a smoothing out of one's own life earnings are accomplished are well known. For the individual family, savings, the acquisition of a private pension claim, and the building up of equity in a home are the most frequent examples of deferred consumption during relatively high-income years in return for money or real income during retirement. The family which envisions its long-range as well as its short-run financial needs and budgets its expenditures and savings accordingly is thus evening-out its income in one direction, at least. In so doing, the family is merely extending a budgeting principle applied monthly by many families whose income is not received in twelve equal installments, but who divide their annual total income by twelve and then regulate their expenditures in accordance with this average.

The low level of savings held by those aged who have retired during the past two decades attests to the failure of these persons to postpone consumption during their working lifetimes in order to save for retirement. We should note, however, that the high level of unemployment during the 1930's, and the relatively low levels of income of these retirees even when employed (at least up until World War II) would have made the accumulation of any substantial savings for retirement extremely difficult. The more prosperous conditions and rising real incomes of the past twenty-five years, plus the current emphasis on financial preparation for retirement, may lead presently employed persons to apportion their lifetime earnings more evenly as between working and retirement years.

Growth of private pension plans, which are largely financed by employer contributions,[21] do not of course require the individual family to refrain from consumption in order to save for future expenditures. In fact, the existence of private pensions may actually discourage some families from attempting to accumulate savings simply by making these savings less essential. The traditionally high correlation between income and saving, however, suggests that the higher-income families will continue to accumulate substantial savings by the time of retirement. These same families also are more likely to have private pensions. Not only will families whose lifetime incomes are low because of deficiencies in education and training and because of recurrent unemployment throughout the work-life span find it impossible to accumulate savings; they will also usually lack private pension claims.

For an increasing proportion of the middle-income families, those with incomes in the $5,000-$7,000 range,[22] the growth of private pension plans will in the future offer important supplements to OASDI benefits. It seems unlikely, however, that an individual family in this income group will accumulate any significant savings for use in retirement, beyond the acquisition of equity in a home. For one thing, the American consumer's high time-preference for goods seems if anything to be rising, with the result that family debt, rather than net savings, is the more frequent case. Moreover, any accumulated savings are likely to be used for emergencies — illness and unemployment, for example — before retirement actually occurs. And, finally, family-held savings are increasingly necessary for the college education of the children, which occurs before retirement and is likely to be given priority over the accumulation of retirement income.

On balance, then, such evening-out of the income stream as occurs within the family unit will come predominantly from the growth of private pensions funds, which are more usually found among higher-income groups, but which will doubtless grow in significance for the middle-income worker. Except for equity in homes, savings by individual families will probably continue to be of importance only for higher-income families. The likelihood that the lowest-income group will continue to lack both savings and private pension claims, and that many of the middle-income families will have neither of these sources of retirement income suggests that public programs for evening out the earnings flow may receive increased attention.

[21]For discussion of private pension funds, their growth in recent years, financing arrangements, and the like, see Paul J. Harbrecht, *Pension Funds and Economic Power* (New York: Twentieth Century Fund, 1959). Chapter IV, "Objectives, Theory, Practice," describes employer, employee, and union rules in pension-fund growth.

[22]The 1960 median income of families and unrelated individuals was $4,791; the median for families was $5,657. Almost one-third (30.9 per cent) of the families received incomes of less than $4,000, and another third (34.0 per cent) received between $4,000 and $7,000. U.S. Bureau of the Census, *United States Census of Population: 1960. General Social and Economic Characteristics* (Washington, D.C.: Government Printing Office, 1962), pp. 1-227.

Increases in OASDI taxes (either through increases in rates or increase in the taxable base) and commensurate increases in benefits do not necessarily apportion an individual family's total earnings over the life span of that family. Instead, taxes levied on current employers and employees provide dividends to currently retired persons. The evening-out of income in this manner thus forces the present generation of workers to support the currently retired persons through a shift of dollar claims from the taxed to the retired. Intergenerational support from this major source is, therefore, no longer provided on a family unit basis in which middle-aged adults support their own aged parents, but instead on an economywide basis, in which employed workers support retirees.

The net effect of the OASDI program is nevertheless a more even distribution of income through the life span than would otherwise occur, since it reduces total disposable income available to workers and increases total disposable income going to retirees. Obviously, the higher the tax and benefit payments (assuming that they roughly balance each other), the greater the income redistribution between working families and retired families. Similarly, an extension of the Social Security Act to provide additional benefits, such as medical care for the aged, would have the effect of shifting real income from the working generation (or generations) to the aged. Since incomes of retirees are generally lower than incomes of workers, the redistribution achieved is not only a shift primarily from generation two (the middle age group) to generation one, but also a redistribution favoring a particular low-income group.

The two major public income-maintenance programs in the United States have been developed to provide income in retirement, and income during unemployment. The former is for the most part an intergenerational transfer of income. The cost of the latter, financed by a payroll tax on employers (who then shift the tax on to the consumer in the form of a higher price, or suffer some reduction in profits, or both) is borne by all generations in accordance with the extent to which they consume goods and receive profits. Since income provided goes to persons who are in the current labor force, the group aged 65 and over are not the recipients of unemployment compensation. To the extent that unemployment falls disproportionately on the very young worker, the members of generation three (the young) who are in the labor force may receive a disproportionate share of total unemployment compensation. However, the variation in state laws governing duration and size of weekly unemployment insurance payments, as well as other factors—the growing incidence of unemployment among older workers, for example—preclude any generalization on the extent of intergenerational transfer involved via unemployment compensation. The fact that eligibility for unemployment insurance requires prior employment eliminates the new labor force entrant with no work experience.

Social transfers of income to generation three, the young, have, therefore, not been involved in either of the two major income-maintenance programs. Moreover, educational outlays, which have been the primary source of income shifts to generation three, have only in recent years assumed a significant proportion of total transfers of income. Perhaps the most important question relating to intergenerational support during this decade is the question of the extent to which public educational outlays will grow. Related to the basic issue of dollar volume of expenditures are questions of the composition of these expenditures, the proportion going to higher education, the emphasis given to technical training in high school, and the like. In particular, it is important to raise the question of the extent to which public support will come to be provided for persons who are in school and for families whose head is still a student.

The pressure of unemployment, particularly among the young, has led to increased emphasis on education and training. But unless the program for extended education is accompanied by a postponement of child-bearing, some form of family support may also become necessary. Such a program would be similar in one respect to the public retirement scheme: it would provide dollar claims to the family during nonworking years, the assumption being in the case of the young family that this income would be "paid back" during the working life of one or both parents. Actually, the support in real terms is provided for both the young nonworking family and the retired family by the output of the working group.

Now being argued persuasively is that investment in human capital is a vital source of economic growth.[23] Since economists currently feel compelled to justify all activity in the name of a higher growth rate, it is not surprising that education, too, be viewed as a means to this particular end. It can be argued with equal effectiveness that society can afford greater and greater investments in education, since output is steadily increasing and since the actual production of goods requires a declining proportion of the total adult population. Not only does technological progress make it necessary to raise educational levels; it also makes it possible to do so.

In the process of meeting the educational challenge of this decade and the next, not only will public outlays for education and training grow; these expenditures will also affect markedly the intergenerational distribution of the aggregate income. On the assumption that expenditures for education will be made from general tax revenues (rather than from a special tax, such as the payroll tax which finances OASDI benefits), the cost of education will be paid less and less from

[23]See for example, *Journal of Political Economy*, LXX, No. 5, Part 2, Supplement (October, 1962); and Selma J. Mushkin, *Economics of Higher Education*, U.S. Department of Health, Education, and Welfare (Washington, D.C.: Government Printing Office, 1962), particularly Part II: "Higher Education as an Investment in People."

the individual family's savings. Increasingly, taxpayers in generation two (and to a lesser extent, generation one) will be providing for the education and family support of the students of generation three.[24] Such a support pattern for the young is somewhat analogous to the support now provided the retired group. In both instances, the transfer of income is primarily from one generation to another, rather than from the middle-aged members of one specific family to the young adult or the aged members of that family.

In the final analysis, a society's capacity to support adults for longer periods of education and in retirement depends upon that society's capacity to produce. The vast productive potential of the American economy, which is expected to make ever greater strides during the rapidly automating decade of the 1960's, is apparently capable of rendering an output sufficiently large to provide for its members both an adequate supply of goods and an increased number of years free of work. Shifts in the pattern of distribution which enable nonworking adults and their families to share in the national product, principally typified up to now by the OASDI program, may gradually be extended on a much broader scale to young nonworking adults and their families. Such shifts will further remove intergenerational support from the family unit basis, making it mandatory that persons with income from work or other sources provide support for both young adults and the aged without reference to family ties. The impersonal character of such support has obvious implications for family relationships in general and for living arrangements in particular.[25]

summary

The changing pattern of intergenerational economic support reflects the broad economic changes which have occurred during the twentieth century. In particular, increases in output per man-hour have made it possible, and seemingly necessary, for man to shorten his working life. Accordingly, man has extended both the length of time spent in education and the length of time spent in retirement. Since man's lifetime productivity is nevertheless higher than formerly, he could presumably even out his own lifetime earnings, and achieve a higher standard of living as well as the added years of leisure.

[24]Harold Wolozin, cited above, note 8, predicts that an increasing proportion of college and university enrollments will flow into the nation's public institutions. In 1950, for example, fall enrollments in colleges and universities were divided almost evenly between private and public institutions. In 1960, private institutions had 40.8 per cent of the total. It is estimated that by 1970 this percentage will drop to 33 per cent, and by 1980 only 20 per cent of the enrollments will be in private institutions. *The Outlook for Higher Education, op. cit.,* pp. 20-21.

[25]The demographic characteristics of the nuclear family in the United States is contrasted with the characteristics of the family in India, and the implications for the structure of kinship groups and households are drawn by Andrew Collver in "The Family Cycle in India and the United States," *American Sociological Review,* XXVIII (February, 1963), 86-96.

In a sense, this smoothing out of life earnings is occurring. However, it is not occurring on an individual family basis. Instead, a family during its working life contributes via taxes to the support of retirees and those young adults still not in the labor market, whether or not this working family has aged parents or children in school. In real terms, the working group, in combination with the existing stock of capital goods, produces the nation's total supply of goods and services. These goods and services are then distributed in accordance with the dollar claims held by different age groups.

In the postwar period the dollar claims available to nonworking adults have grown enormously, primarily through the growth of income-maintenance programs. One of these, the program of old age, survivors, and disability insurance (OASDI), represents primarily an intergenerational transfer of income. Current concern with improving the education and training of young persons suggests that a very substantial increase in educational outlay is likely to occur in the present decade. Such expenditures, by increasing the extent to which the working group in total provides the financial and real support for young adults not yet in the labor force, and for the families of these young adults, will shift the pattern of intergenerational support even further away from the family unit.

theoretical
perspective

extended kin relations in an industrial democratic society

EUGENE LITWAK

alternative models of kin relations

In examining the sociological literature on extended kin relations, at least four generic types have been described. First, there is the traditional extended family structure as typified by the peasant society of Poland, Italy, and China. The family is described as a complete economic and political unit composed of nuclear subfamilies all living in the same house or close by. Each nuclear subfamily is entirely dependent on the extended kin for most services in life. At the other extreme is the concept of the dissolving or weak family structure. This is sometimes implied from the work of Ogburn, Schumpeter, and Wirth.[1] The argument is made that most kin functions have been taken

[1] William F. Ogburn, "The Changing Functions of the Family," *Selected Readings in Marriage and the Family*, Robert F. Winch and Robert McGinnis, eds. (New York: Holt, Rinehart & Winston, Inc., 1953), pp. 74-76; Joseph A. Schumpeter, *Capitalism, Socialism, and Democracy*, 2nd ed., (New York: Harper & Row, Publishers, 1947), p. 157; Louis Wirth, "Urbanism as a Way of Life," *Cities and Society: The Revised Reader in Urban Sociology*, Paul K. Hatt and Albert J. Reiss, Jr., eds. (New York: Free Press of Glencoe, Inc., 1957), pp. 593-94.

over by large-scale formal organizations — leaving the family with little to do. All that is left are very tenuous husband and wife relations.

Next in line to the dissolving family type is the isolated nuclear family structure. This is the family composed of husband, wife, and small child. The assumption is made that though family functions are fewer, certain essential ones (early socialization of the child and management of tensions) have all been concentrated in the nuclear family and are sufficiently powerful to provide family stability. Between the nuclear and the extended family structure is the modified extended family structure which consists of a coalition of nuclear families in a state of partial dependence. Such partial dependence means that nuclear family members exchange significant services with each other, thus differing from the isolated nuclear family, as well as retain considerable autonomy (that is, not bound economically or geographically), therefore, differing from the classical extended family.

These four family types obviously have different implications for the solution of any given social problem. Thus, if the dissolving family was taken as a model for national policy in treating indigency among the retired population, it would suggest a large-scale organizational solution — a home for the aged or a cooperatively owned building that provided hotel services for the aged. The nuclear family unit would be devalued. If the nuclear family concept was used as a model for policy, it would suggest maintaining the husband and wife in their own residence to meet the demands of tension management and at the same time having a close relation to large organizations in order to meet the instrumental demands for living. The development of the social security program meets these conditions admirably. It permits nuclear family autonomy yet at the same time links it to the bureaucratic apparatus of the Social Security Administration for financial resources.

The modified extended family concept would suggest that the nuclear family be housed independently but remain active in situations where extended family aid as well as institutional aid can be given. In fact this is what the author feels actually does happen in our society. The nuclear family receives basic forms of economic aid from the Social Security Administration but in addition receives supplemental aid from extended family.[2] The extended family as a model for policy directives would suggest that all aid come from extended family and no forms of outside institutional aid be given or accepted unless it operated with the nepotic criteria of family before all else. Thus, legislative approaches which suggest that indigent families must first prove that there are no relatives around who are working

[2]The author feels that Marvin Sussman's and Lee Burchinal's review of the literature on parental aid might well be interpreted in this light. "Parental Aid to Married Children: Implications for Family Functioning," *Marriage and Family Living*, XXV (November, 1962), 320-32.

before they can receive public welfare, are approaches that imply that extended families are the ideal form of family structure in our society.[3] However, in a society truly dominated by the extended family concept, there may never be an older couple who are indigent since power and authority might be assigned by age. Older people in such a society might never retire but die at the peak of their social and economic power.

concept of fit

Though each of these four types of family structures—the extended family, the dissolving family, the isolated nuclear family, and the modified extended family—have their own virtues and defects, it is not clear that each type is equally consistent with the demands of an industrial democratic society. Though such a society has many demands, two general societal demands shall be discussed in this paper: (1) people should be judged on the basis of their ability; (2) large-scale bureaucratic organizations are necessary if the high standard of living engendered by technological progress is to continue.

We should understand this point if the framework of this paper is to be judged by empirical data. For what is being said is that if a democratic industrial society is to exist, then certain types of family structures will be more congenial to such a society than others. The author is not saying that these family types do in fact exist in current society. Other family structures might well exist. But insofar as the family structures compatible with an industrial democratic society do not exist, then we will have less industrial progress and greater class crystalization with persons less likely to be rewarded on the basis of their ability. Thus, Willmott and Young are able to point out the psychological benefits of extended family relations in the center of London.[4] At the same time, they also inadvertently point out the great degree of occupational and housing nepotism that occurs among these families. If such a phenomenon were to be prevalent throughout the society, then we would have a lowering of technological progress and crystalization of class lines.[5] The existence or lack of existence of certain family types will not in themselves prove or disprove the views

[3]Alvin L. Schorr, *Filial Responsibility in the Modern American Family*, U.S. Department of Health, Education, and Welfare (Washington, D.C.: Government Printing Office, 1960), pp. 19-39.

[4]Michael Young and Peter Willmott, *Family and Kinship in East London* (London: Routledge & Kegan Paul, Ltd., 1957), pp. 159ff. As Robert Blood points out in a personal conversation, where there is surplus labor or housing, the issue of restriction of geographic mobility becomes less important.

[5]Many studies which assume they are testing Parsons' hypothesis on the functional utility of nuclear family structures in the United States in fact do no such thing. What these studies in effect do is to demonstrate the existence or lack of existence of nuclear family relations. However, the test of Parsons' views would be one which demonstrated that nuclear family structure permits technical efficiency and

suggested here. It is the relation between these types and technological progress and democratic society which must be investigated.

With these thoughts in mind, kinship structure in an industrial society must fulfill several requisites if the demands for technological progress and democracy are to be maintained. These requisites are:[6]

1. *Kinship Efficiencies for Goal Achievement.* One must first point out in what sense kinship groups can aid in the accomplishment of goals. If in fact their functions can be handled more efficiently by other organizations as implicitly suggested by some writers, then there is less basis to justify strong kinship structures in industrial democratic societies.[7]

2. *Capacity to Get Along with Bureaucratic Organizations.* Since bureaucratic formal organizations are thought to be necessary for technological progress and since the former tend to be organized on a different basis than the family (objective, impersonal, segmental, transitory relations, and less face-to-face contact than the family which has emotional, diffused, and permanent relations), the ideal family structure must be able to operate side by side with bureaucratic organizations.

3. *Differential Occupational Mobility.* Since both a democratic society and technological progress demand that people be appointed to positions on the basis of their ability, kin structures must be such that differential occupation mobility is possible. The kin structure should not prevent its members from moving occupationally even when such movement results in members of the kin group being in different socio-economic classes.[8]

4. *Differential Geographical Mobility.* The demands of technological progress are such that people are presumed to be able to go where jobs are available. This means that the kin structure must not discourage people from taking jobs even when such occupational choice results in geographical distance between kin members.

---

democracy more than other family structures. The existence of an extended family structure might simply indicate a less efficient technology or a class crystalization —both consistent with Parsons' theory. To measure family relations without measuring class crystalization or technological efficiency might frequently lead the investigators to assume they have invalidated Parsons' hypothesis when in fact they have substantiated his view.

[6]There is no assumption that these requirements are exhaustive. The only claim made is that among the possibly many such criteria these will be extremely important.

[7]William F. Ogburn, "The Changing Functions of the Family," *op. cit.*, pp. 74-76. This should be coupled with Max Weber's assertion that bureaucratic organizations might be the most efficient for achieving social goals in a mass society; *From Max Weber: Essays in Sociology,* Hans H. Gerth and C. Wright Mills, trans. and eds. (New York: Oxford University Press, 1946), pp. 196-244.

[8]This assertion assumes that there are status differences attached to different jobs. If, as argued by Tumin, status does not necessarily cling to occupational differences, then this requirement need not be imposed on the family structure. Melvin Tumin, "On Inequality," *American Sociological Review,* XXVIII (February, 1963), 19-26.

The four conditions outlined above are the requisites which kin structures must satisfy if the minimal needs of an industrial bureaucratic society are to be met. In what follows, the four different types of kin structure will be examined in terms of their consistency with the above prerequisites of an industrial society. This analysis should indicate the virtues and defects of each kinship type.

kinship efficiencies for goal achievement

The four types of kinship structure each claim different functions for the kinship system in our society. The dissolving family structure, as developed by Ogburn, is one where most of the duties of kin have been taken over by the large-scale formal organization. The only function clearly remaining with the kin structure is the supplying of affection.[9] This function, however, is unlikely to substitute for lost functions of the kinship group, and, as a consequence, family bonds are likely to be very weak.

The concept of the isolated nuclear family as suggested by Burgess and Parsons is one where it is argued that extended kinship functions have disappeared. Certain of these functions have gone to formal organizations while others have become concentrated in the nuclear family. There is a division of labor between formal organizations and the nuclear family groups, with the latter handling the early socialization of the child and the management of tension while the formal organizations handle most of the other functions.[10] Because of this division of labor in which each has its own sphere of functions, both nuclear family and formal organizations are necessary for the survival of industrial democratic society.

The modified extended family approach differs from the nuclear family approach in two ways.[11] First, it argues that the family is not concentrated in a few specialized functions. Quite the contrary, the family actively intervenes in all functions — manufacturing, protection, medical care, education of the older child, old-age security, and so forth. However, in each of these areas it contributes only part to the achievement of goals. The other part is contributed by the formal organization. Second, the kinship unit is larger than the nuclear family. It consists of several nuclear families who exchange meaningful services. However, these families are semiautonomous; they are linked together in an equalitarian coalition. In contrast, the extended family concept suggests that all functional areas are completely con-

---

[9]William F. Ogburn, "The Changing Functions of the Family" *op. cit.*, pp. 74-76.

[10]Talcott Parsons, "The Social Structure of the Family," *The Family: Its Function and Destiny,* Ruth N. Anshen, ed. (New York: Harper & Row, Publishers, 1949), pp. 190ff; Talcott Parsons and Robert F. Bales, *Family, Socialization and Interaction Process* (New York: Free Press of Glencoe, Inc., 1955), pp. 3-19.

[11]Eugene Litwak, "The Use of Extended Family Groups in the Achievement of Social Goals: Some Policy Implications," *Social Problems,* VII, No. 3 (Winter, 1959-60), 178-79.

trolled by the kinship group with no help from the formal organizations. The kinship groups are tightly bound economic and geographic units with a single hierarchical authority system.

Power—The Theoretical Basis of Primary Group Efficiency   Thus, we can see that the claims of the kin group range all the way from the dissolving family where the implicit assumption is made that the formal organization can take over just about all meaningful activities of the primary group to the extended family concept where it is argued that the family can take over all meaningful functions of the formal organization. In order to determine what is the optimal role of the family and the formal organization, the author should like to engage in an analysis of the modes of social influence or power and see to what extent and under what situation the formal organizations provide the best basis and under what circumstances the primary groups provide the best basis for the exercise of such influence and, therefore, the achievement of social goals.

The analysis of social influence or power may be approached in many different ways. One which seems congenial is that which suggests that there are four bases for power in our society: (1) expertness; (2) reward and punishment; (3) legitimation; and (4) attraction or reference orientation.[12] The writers on social influence have rarely sought to examine the extent to which each of these forms of influence are encouraged or discouraged by the organizational setting in which they are located.[13] In this section, an attempt will be made to pinpoint the circumstances where the family as an organization can exercise these forms of influence better than the bureaucratic organization and those circumstances where the contrary is true.

Expertise as a Form of Influence.   If Weber's concept of bureaucracy is examined, it is clear that one of the chief bases for his highlighting of certain dimensions was because the latter provided an organizational milieu within which the knowledge, experience, and ability to accomplish the task of the organization would be maximized. Through the concept of specialization, this bureaucracy provides the maximum time to become proficient in a given task. The demands for impersonal relations and *a priori* delimited duties and privileges are ways by which the organization insures that evaluations are based on the individual's ability and avoids favoritism and nepotism. The demands of hierarchical authority and the use of rules for regulating behavior are ways for insuring proper coordination in a situation where there are

---

[12]John R. P. French and Bertram Raven, "The Bases of Social Power," *Studies in Social Power*, Dorwin Cartwright, ed. (Ann Arbor, Michigan: The University of Michigan, 1959), pp. 155-65.

[13]There are some notable exceptions to this assertion such as Elihu Katz and Paul F. Lazarsfeld, *Personal Influence* (New York: Free Press of Glencoe, Inc., 1955), pp. 48-65. This discussion of social reality can be interpreted as suggesting the organizational basis for primary group influence.

many different subgroups working on a given job. In these ways the bureaucratic organization provides an organizational base for the maximum development of the "trained" expert.[14] When Weber makes the claim that the bureaucratic organization is the most efficient organization in a mass society, in part what he is saying is that the bureaucratic organization provides the social bases for bringing the maximum amount of knowledge to bear on any given problem. Insofar as knowledge is a relevant variable in the solution of a problem, his claim would indeed be valid.

The comparison of the family with the bureaucracy along these same lines further illustrates Weber's claims for the bureaucracy. First, the members of the family are recruited biologically or on the basis of affection (not on the basis of the person best able to handle instrumental tasks). Second, family activities cover a wide range of behavior which makes it difficult to develop a specialist and *a priori* to delimit duties and obligations. Membership in the family is relatively permanent, which makes it difficult to advance or eliminate people on the basis of their capacity to perform. The family is small, which makes it difficult to develop a specialist in all necessary areas. Finally, the family encourages nepotistic considerations between family members — family bonds are an end in themselves — which makes it difficult to assess people on their instrumental task performances.

From this analysis it would seem reasonable to argue that where trained experts are needed the bureaucratic organization is in a better position to produce such experts than the family.

The question which arises is, in what circumstances do we need trained experts and in what circumstances do we not? For instance, if a child is in the path of an oncoming automobile, an adult passerby — regardless of his knowledge about rescue — is in a better position to aid the child than a trained policeman who is not at the scene. Or again, during a disaster such as a tornado, where large numbers are endangered, it is best for untrained family and neighborhood people to pull individuals out of burning or collapsing houses rather than wait the hour or two necessary for the trained fireman or policeman to arrive to do the job. Many disasters are characterized by the fact that most victims are rescued by relatives, friends, and neighbors before the professional groups are able to reach the scene.[15]

If we generalized from these illustrations, it could be argued that in some cases the trained expert is not as important as speed of reac-

---

[14]The trained expert is differentiated from other kinds of experts by virtue of the fact that there is a definite organization designed to train him or there is an explicit job-training program. By contrast many mothers become highly expert on the moods of their children without undergoing any special training but just as a by-product of their everyday interaction.

[15]For instance, William H. Form and Sigmund Nosow claim that well over 75 per cent of the people were rescued within the first three hours by friends, neighbors, and relatives — before the formal agencies could intervene. See *Community in Disaster* (New York: Harper & Row, Publishers, Inc., 1958), pp. 33-82, 112-13.

tion when dealing with highly idiosyncratic events. There are two reasons for this. First, an expert can only be reserved for those events that are relatively frequent over time and that concern large numbers of people. The more idiosyncratic the event, the more experts necessary to cover all possible contingencies—a policeman for every child crossing a street, rescue organizations on constant alerts for tornadoes that may occur once in twenty years. This requires an extravagant expenditure of funds. Second, if an event is truly idiosyncratic—happening only a few times and then never again—it would frequently mean that experts cannot be trained in time. Even more disturbing is that once trained such experts may well seek to maintain a specialty for which there is no longer any need.[16]

There is still another area where the trained expert may be of little use. These are the problem areas where the amount of knowledge known or necessary is so small that the ordinary person faced with the problem can handle it equally well as the trained expert. Thus, the amount of knowledge necessary to push a child out of the path of an oncoming car is trivial—most persons react in this situation without special training. To say that where there is no real knowledge the

---

[16]Several different meanings of idiosyncratic will be used interchangeably in this paper. Though an explicit consideration of these differences suggests further subtleties of analysis, the author is making the assumption that such an effort would not contradict the general theoretical frame being developed here. As a consequence, the possible implications of these differences are not explored. The first meaning of idiosyncratic is an event that happens infrequently. Such an event might be an earthquake or a tornado that strikes a country once in fifty years. Another more relativistic definition is an event that is relatively rare. Thus, on an absolute level, the number of children being hit by cars might be very large. Yet compared to the possible combinations of children and cars interacting, it is an infinitesimally small ratio. This is what makes it so difficult to provide successful institutional safeguards for children—other than primary groups supervising them. Another notion of the idiosyncratic deals with events that only affect a small group of people. In a small minority of families the parents might be more able and have more time to educate their children than the schools. However, this event may be so rare as to make it a socially unique event. Finally, there is a meaning of idiosyncratic which has to do with knowledge. Thus, having no knowledge of a particular event, the person has no basis for predicting its course, and as a consequence it seems idiosyncratic. This area of knowledge may involve very complex problems where there is some knowledge, but because of the complexity of interacting variables, this knowledge is not always usable to solve problems. Thus, those working on the polio vaccine had a fairly delimited problem. By contrast the psychoanalyst or persons dealing with personality interactions have a far more complex set of variables with which to deal. The issue of idiosyncracies should not be mixed in with the issue of social value which will be discussed later in the paper. Thus, an event which has high probability of occuring might still be treated as an idiosyncratic event because of the high value put on it combined with the refusal to take risks.

The clinging of outmoded experts to their jobs is manifested in many ways in our society. Thus, management invidiously refers to the union's demands for "featherbedding." On a more "respectable" basis, the service rivalries between the army, navy, and air corps frequently involve an attempt to maintain professional distinctions that technological progress has made obsolescent. The cost to the economy and the defense posture of these specialists clinging to their outmoded specialties might be very high.

trained expert has no advantage over the ordinary person is another way of talking about the nonuniform or idiosyncratic event.[17]

Obviously, too, there are times when we seek trained experts even when the event is relatively idiosyncratic. Thus, we seek to use trained scientists to deal with frontier areas in knowledge which almost by definition are idiosyncratic. We train people to deal with problems of psychosis despite the fact that our knowledge is so limited that each psychotic is treated as though his case were unique. This suggests another basis for utilizing experts. In those instances where a society places a high value on dealing with a given problem, then trained experts will be used. Where the event is unique, this means that the society is willing to bear the heavy costs involved in using trained experts for unique events and to be satisfied with their comparative inefficiency; that is, the expert does not do much better than the knowledgeable layman, or it takes the expert an extremely long time to get results. As noted before, extreme neurosis or psychosis are frequently defined by society as a "must" for treatment even though these ailments involve little understood phenomena and as such constitute unique events.

One way of looking at the concept of social values is to examine the minimal standards that society sets up in all areas of life— medicine, care for the aged, retirement, housing, education, protection against violence, care of children, and the like. Society will not tolerate people falling below these standards, and as such these standards constitute operational definitions of the level of social value in each area. By social value as the term is used here, we mean publically agreed-to standards. Private opinions might differ considerably.[18] The

[17]There are other reasons why trained experts might not be as useful as the "non-trained" expert. Thus, Lewin and his colleagues suggest that in order to have commitment, people must participate in decision making. Insofar as meaningful participation is related to commitment and insofar as commitment is the goal that is being sought for, then the trained expert is not as useful as discussion and participation among the participants (nontrained experts). See Kurt Lewin, "Group Decision and Social Change," *Readings in Social Psychology*, Theodore M. Newcomb and Eugene L. Hartley, eds. (New York: Holt, Rinehart & Winston, Inc., 1947), pp. 330-44.

[18]Quite a distinction may occur between private and public values. This may be a consequence of invidious norms. Thus, status aspirations must almost by definition be private. If such aspirations are publically expressed, they might lead to a loss of status. Then again, people may act the way they think other people want them to act rather than on their own private beliefs. Thus, people might vote for Sunday blue laws not because they believe in them but because they feel this is what others want. In addition, certain values might be considered private because they pertain to such a limited number of people no one else would be interested in them. However, it should also be understood that public values do not necessarily mean majority values. Rather, it means those values which are advocated in a public manner by individuals who occupy the power centers to implement these values. These people might indeed be a small minority of the population. It should not be assumed that private values are any less important than public values to the individuals involved. Quite the contrary—the meaning of life might be more centrally tied to the private than the public values. What is central to the concept of public values is that they encourage some kind of cooperation between people,

public nature of the value is essential in any consideration of the trained expert because such training requires cooperation among many people. At the same time this suggests that there are many areas where there will be no trained expert because the situations are not covered by public value. To insure that the levels of social values are being maintained, the society assigns the job of maintaining minimum standards to professionals and formal organizations or the trained expert. The accomplishment of goals above and beyond these socially set minimums frequently involve the family primary groups — especially where the family deals with the idiosyncratic event and the personal goals of individuals.

To summarize, there are several classes of situations where the trained expert is of little use: in situations which are not uniform and where the minimal standards set by society are not involved. By contrast, the formal organization might be more effective in uniform situations where high social values are involved.[19] The question arises as to whether the family as a primary group might not be superior to the formal organizations in these areas.

The author would argue that the family structure is able to deal more easily with the idiosyncratic event because the family has more continuous contact over many different areas of life than the professional organization. Because of its smaller size, the family has speedier channels for transmitting messages that had no prior definition of legitimacy. Further, because it is less likely to have explicit rules on what is and what is not legitimate, it is more likely to consider events which have had no definition. The bureaucratic agency in the extreme case is prevented from considering events without *a priori* definition of legitimacy by law. In most instances the bureaucratic agency is specifically prevented from acting, by explicit rules which define the area of legitimacy ahead of time.[20]

The family, because of its small size, can define much more uniquely what is to be valued. The number of people who must

---

such as the development of formal organizations. As such, public values seem to be one of the requisites of formal organization.

[19]This paper does not deal with all possible combinations of the two variables (social values and uniformity). Thus, where the situation has both social value and uniformity, then one has the greatest stress for the Weberian bureaucratic organizations. Where the opposite extreme occurs (private values and idiosyncratic events), a great stress occurs on primary groups. The mixed categories lead to variations on bureaucratic organizations and primary groups which we will not discuss here because it would not basically change the main point of this paper though it would involve some interesting elaborations of organizational types.

[20]This is pointed out in the literature on bureaucratic organizations. Several authors have pointed out that where the bureaucrat is faced with an issue which has not been clearly defined as part of the intake policy, one of several errors in operation can occur: (1) he can apply a rule which is inapplicable; (2) he can pass the information to the top and wait for a reply (bureaucratic red tape); or (3) he can apply his personal values which may not be applicable to the purposes of the organization. In none of these cases, is the bureaucracy making full use of the trained professional's expertise.

cooperate are much fewer, and because they are involved in affectional relations, they are more inclined to accept each other's personal definition of values.

From these considerations, the author would argue that where knowledge was equal—in nonuniform situations and in situations where there is little public value—then the family primary group is in a much better position to implement goals than the trained specialist in the bureaucratic organization.

Reward and Punishment as a Form of Influence.   The virtues and defects of the two types of organizations, family and bureaucracy, become even clearer when reward and punishment as a mode of influence is examined. The question is whether the primary group or the bureaucratic organization is in a better position to reward or punish the needs of the individual. The formal organization, such as the police, are in a better position to train specialists in various aspects of crime detection, such as taking and cataloguing finger prints, laboratory equipment for autopsies, and the like. These in turn permit the decision as to whether a person should be punished. In a similar manner formal organizations can develop specialists, such as entertainers and television equipment, to provide the population with leisure-time pursuits.

However, one of the chief problems in using a reward and punishment mode of influence arises over the inability to observe the situation one is trying to influence. The reward and punishment mode of influence assumes an expedient orientation on the part of the recipient, and, where he is not in a position to be observed, he might well respond to neither reward nor punishment in the way the influencer would like. In this regard it can be argued that the more idiosyncratic and private—rather than public—the behavior, the more difficult it is for the professional to use his special skills and facilities. By contrast, the primary group is in a better position to use reward and punishment. This is clearly seen in the area of morality. It is very difficult if not impossible to convict a couple of adultery where they have willingly engaged in this activity. The nature of the event is so private and so idiosyncratic that the law has no rationale for assigning people to watch each man and woman within a given age span. A similar problem arises in the area of political behavior where a government wants to avoid an incipient revolt by making sure all people really believe the existing government to be the best possible one. Attitudes are difficult to determine or observe by ordinary policemen. The police power would be faced with the prospect of keeping close tabs on all the adult population during a considerable part of their waking hours.

In such situations, the primary group has the advantage of fairly continuous contact with its members. Moreover, the positive affect between members makes it easier to penetrate most areas of privacy.

Thus, adultery may be much more quickly spotted by primary group members than the police.

The Chinese and Russian governments when faced with the possibility of incipient revolts utilized the family as an instrument for insuring proper social attitudes. Thus, they urged family members — especially children — to report deviant attitudes. The Nazi Government did much the same during the height of World War II when the problems of social control were maximal.[21]

To summarize, the argument is that when dealing with the idiosyncratic and the private area of values, the family is in a better position than the formal organization to utilize reward and punishment, while the opposite would be true where the situation is uniform and has high social value.

Legitimacy and Attraction as Modes of Influence. There are two other modes of influence called legitimation and attraction. Legitimation is the situation where people agree to obey norms because of their belief that the larger group defines these norms as valid. In order to use this method of influence, one must be in a position to identify with the norms of the group or must be in a position to create norms. The more the formal organization seeks to utilize legitimation when dealing with idiosyncratic situations, the more difficult does its task become. If, in fact, the formal organization had to develop a different norm of legitimation for each situation or each group that exists, its work would be difficult if not impossible. By contrast, the family with a much smaller base can with considerably more ease deal with the view of each of its members; that is, it can tailor the concept of legitimation to the needs of its members or develop its own norms of activity.

The same argument holds for attraction as a basis of influence. The formal organization can utilize the "man on the white horse" as a mode of influence, but only on those issues which are central to a large number of people. If one is dealing with idiosyncratic issues — a situation in which no two groups consider the same issue important — then the use of a common man to appeal to all groups becomes somewhat difficult to conceive. By contrast, the small group because of its limited base can tailor its reference individuals to the needs of each member of the group. The formal organization has the advantage of having experts and equipment at hand for promulgating their heroic figure, and this expertise is decisive when the formal organization has a common target. However, it becomes less meaningful the more diverse and idiosyncratic the target groups become.

In the analysis thus far two points have been made. First, most concepts of interpersonal influence suggest at least four basic types of such influence: expertness; reward and punishment; legitimation; and

---

[21]Seymour M. Lipset, Martin Trow, and James S. Coleman, *Union Democracy* (New York: Free Press of Glencoe, Inc., 1956), pp. 73-82.

attraction. Second, the formal bureaucratic organization is a better base for using these modes of influence where tasks are relatively uniform and have a high social value, while the primary family groups are a better base for using these modes of influence when events are idiosyncratic or in the area of personal rather than social values. This discussion is best summarized in Table 13-1.

table 13-1   organizational base for social power

forms of social influence	uniform-repetitive events or socially defined value	nonuniform events or personally defined value
Expertness	Bureaucratic	Primary group
Reward-punishment	Bureaucratic	Primary group
Legitimation	Bureaucratic	Primary group
Referent power	Bureaucratic	Primary group

The reader should be clear as to the importance of this discussion for the purposes of this paper. What has been done thus far is to establish theoretically the basis for primary group efficiency in goal achievement vis-à-vis the formal bureaucratic organization.

Importance of Uniform and Nonuniform Tasks   Having established the theoretical basis for family and bureaucratic efficiencies, the question arises: how important are uniform and nonuniform tasks?[22] Once this question is answered, the importance of kinship structures and bureaucratic organizations for achieving goals can be stated in its most general form.

One can argue that nonuniform tasks will be a part of the industrial society in the foreseeable future. First, nonuniform tasks are the consequence of having a society geared to technological progress. Technological progress leads to many unanticipated social consequences. Therefore, at any given moment of time, large masses of people will be confronted with events for which they have no prior trained experts or social norms to which they can look for guidance.[23] Second, in a large industrial society with its complex role structure, there is every reason to assume that socialization into roles will never be perfect. As a consequence, in any given interaction people invariably will be confronted with unanticipated events for which they have little guidance in standardized role definitions.[24]

---

[22]We can also ask how important are those sectors of life dominated by private and by social values. This problem will not be discussed in this paper, but it should be understood that the private sectors are as important if not more important than the public sectors. Thus, to a mother, her child's momentary unhappiness over a broken toy or a young man's infatuation with a given girl may be far more important than the efficiency of the educational system for turning out a trained labor force.

[23]For a detailed statement of this point of view, see Nelson N. Foote and Leonard S. Cottrell, Jr., *Identity and Interpersonal Competence* (Chicago: University of Chicago Press, 1955), pp. 36-60.

[24]William J. Goode points out some of the issues which arise from this situation in "Norm Commitment and Conformity to Role-Status Obligations," *American Journal of Sociology*, LXVI (November, 1960), 246-58.

But what is most central to this paper is the argument that in almost any area where we have been able to reduce the idiosyncratic to a predictable event, we have at the same time opened up entirely new areas of the unknown or the idiosyncratic. This is well understood in the natural sciences where the reduction of previously unexplainable events has coincided with the opening up of new problems which scientists could not even anticipate as problems until they had solved the old ones.[25]

This same process works in the social world as well. For instance, we have been able to rationalize production and thereby separate it from the family and locate it in a factory. Once having located the work in the bureaucratic organization, we found that an important technical problem is work motivation — above and beyond that thought of as sheer monetary gain.[26] This problem was not manifest while the work was located within the kinship structure. However, the very separation of place of work from the home seems to have produced this problem in ways it had not occurred before. There is good evidence that such work motivation plays an important role in productivity and that the family plays a central role in developing and maintaining this work motivation.

The implications of the remarks on the permanence and the likelihood of nonuniform events in all areas of life are twofold. First, in all areas of life there will be aspects of a given task for which the family will be superior to the formal organization, and there will be other aspects for which the opposite will hold. Second, in all areas of life the family and the formal organization must coordinate their behavior if the optimum achievement of goals is to take place. Only by such coordination will there occur the combination of trained experts, speed, and flexibility.

Empirical Illustrations of Shared Functions Some reanalysis of prior material can illustrate the nature of the functions shared by the family and bureaucratic organizations as well as resolve some past paradoxes. First, the argument that the family has a few areas of functional specialization, such as the management of tensions and early socialization of the child, while the formal organization has other areas of specialization can be examined.[27] The theory suggested herein would argue that areas such as the management of tension involve a rela-

---

[25]Not only will these nonuniform events continue to exist, but further these nonuniform events may be extremely important. Thus, saving lives in a situation where there is an unexpected tornado is important. Dealing with a little understood disease which takes lives is extremely important. Trying to understand the complexities of a modern industrial economy is important even if little understood. For example, it is difficult if not impossible to predict the turn of economic events except in gross forms.

[26]This is, of course, the heart of the entire development of the human relations approach in industry that has so characterized modern industrial research and management training.

[27]See Footnote 10.

tively new discipline. Only since the early 1900's have we developed any cogent theories of personality that permit the training of professionals (the psychiatrist) for dealing with tension management. As such, this aspect of life has much in the way of nonuniformity, and the family as a primary group is better suited than a formal organization for dealing with it. However, there is no reason to assume that this is inevitably so. The historical evidence suggests that just the opposite may be true. Since the 1900's there has been a rapid development of professions concerned with tension management—psychiatric social worker, clinical psychologist, psychiatrist, and psychiatric nurse. The development of these professions plus the agencies which house them is evidence for the fact that tension management can be dealt with by formal organizations. The rate of growth of these specialties suggests that eventually the family might share this functional area with the formal organization in the same ratio as it shares other areas. One area in which there seems to be great likelihood of institutional expansion is in the development of family life courses in high schools and colleges.

The second argument that the formal organizations have taken over most "instrumental" functions of the family, such as basic education of the school-age child, medical functions, productivity functions, and protective functions would also be disputed by the theory suggested herein. The theory of shared functions would suggest that in each of these areas the formal organizations have taken over those parts which have been standardized and which have been given social value, while the family groups have specialized in those aspects that are nonuniform and have private values.

In the field of education the assumption is made that the schools have taken over the educational functions once the child reaches the age of five. The family is no longer assumed to play a major role. Yet, for those who have empirically examined the problem of education, it has become increasingly clear that without proper family support throughout the educational process, the child will do poorly in school or drop out of school. This point becomes very obvious when the low income areas of our society are examined. In such areas close to 80 per cent of the pupils in some schools drop out before they finish high school, as compared to a national average of around 30 per cent. In these same areas children who stay in school might score a year to a year and one-half below the average in achievement tests.

In England, where there is free education through the university level, it is still true that the working-class families provide an extremely low percentage of students compared to their proportion of the population.[28] This difference is attributable only in part to the

[28]Brian Jackson and Dennis Marsden, *Education and Working Class: Some General Themes Raised by a Study of 88 Working-Class Children in Northern Industrial City* (New York: Monthly Review Press, 1962), *in passim.*

staffs of schools. It is also true that a considerable part of the lack of success of the working-class child in school is a consequence of the working-class families' ignorance of the kinds of information the child must have, the kinds of deferred gratification the child must learn, what forms of concepts must be developed, and when children should be encouraged and when discouraged from taking a job. The massive nature of the failure of the educational bureaucracy in the lower-income groups has highlighted the role of the family, a role which was more or less taken for granted in the middle-class groups.

When education was the sole province of the family, the teacher was not differentiated from the everyday man in point of knowledge. However, as educational levels advanced and specialists took over the standardized areas of education such as the transmission of prior knowledge, a higher standard of learning put greater pressure on the student to develop abstract concepts, educational motivation over long periods of time, and the ability to defer certain gratification. It became important to have some group deal with these problems of education, and insofar as they are (at this point in time) nonuniform, they can most efficiently be taken over by the family.

As professional educators have seen this point more clearly, there has begun a swing back from the closed-door school policy of yesterday with its insistence that the schools are the only basic institution for education of youngsters. This has led in turn to a series of changes eventuating in programs of school community agents whose job it is to bring the family closer to the schools, so that the power of the family can be better coordinated with the powers of the schools.[29]

At the same time that the family is encouraged to participate in the educational process, the development of preschool nurseries and professional specialists who deal with the very young child (such as the pediatrician, child analyst, and nursery school teachers) suggest that the formal organizations are moving into the area previously claimed as the exclusive function of the family—the socialization of the very young.

An analysis comparable to that made in the field of education can be made for the area of medical problems. Socio-economic differences are related to a variety of medical problems, such as infant mortality, types of mental retardations, acceptance of free medical innovations such as the Salk vaccine, and responsiveness to preventive medicine. In these cases, we are speaking about situations where the economic resources of the particular family are not the dominant issues. The dominant factors here are rather the attitudes and habits developed in the family dealing with such things as diet, hygiene, keeping up with

[29]The school system of Detroit has embarked on an experimental program which explicitly takes this approach. Similarly, the school systems of Flint and New York as well as those in many other cities utilize this approach in various special programs they are developing.

recent developments in medicine, and a knowledge of and respect for the doctor's role in maintaining the health of the individual.

As in education, when the medical professional took over certain medical functions from the family, the problem of motivation to use medicine became increasingly important as a factor in maintaining health. In addition, as doctors became more sophisticated and discovered new areas of ignorance, they found it useful to include family participation as a preliminary diagnostic tool. Thus, the initial symptoms of a disease such as cancer are so idiosyncratic and the rate of growth so unknown that to maintain complete medical control of this disease would involve the examination of the entire population on a weekly or monthly basis. Since this is an impossibility, through a program of preventive medicine the family has been given the function of preliminary diagnostician. In a similar manner, the importance of the family environment in health maintenance is becoming increasingly apparent. We have come to the point in some places where medical men speculate that further reduction in the mortality rate of infants will arrive through changes in the social environment rather than through the introduction of new drugs or medical procedures.[30]

As pointed out earlier, within the world of work there is an increasing understanding of the role of the family in maintaining work motivation. In addition, it can be demonstrated that the family plays a major role in shaping occupational aspirations and in providing funds and support for the initial occupational training of the young, for example, higher education. In addition, some reason exists for believing that the family plays a role in handling the difficult years around the retirement phase.[31] As mentioned earlier the taking over of certain work functions by trained specialists has opened up the new frontier areas of work motivation, occupational training, and problems of retirement. In these areas the family plays a specialist role.

Finally, the consideration of the army, which many cite as the ideal bureaucratic organization, illustrates most explicitly the role of the family. With the professionalization and bureaucratization of the armed forces it has become increasingly clear that troop morale plays a major role in the efficient running of the army. Furthermore, the maintenance of morale is very much a function of the family. Therefore, the army has very explicit and systematic ties with the family. The magnitude of this commitment can be illustrated by the attempts of the government of the United States to redress an unfavorable balance of trade with Europe. The Department of Defense sought to withdraw the wives of servicemen from Europe in order to reduce the spending

[30]Raymond Illsley in a personal conversation reports this view as being held by some doctors regarding Aberdeen, Scotland.
[31]This would seem to be the burden of the evidence which suggests fairly close ties between families and their retired parents. For a general summary article see Gordon F. Streib, "Family Patterns in Retirement," *The Journal of Social Issues,* XIV, No. 2 (1958), 46-60.

of American dollars abroad. The reaction to this policy was immediate, powerful, and negative, and the order was cancelled. The fact that the army felt it necessary in the first place to have the families housed next to the troops indicates how closely it associates its success with the family. The fact that grave economic dangers could not change this relationship is even more explicit testimony to the role of the family. The importance of the family is heightened during an actual war when it is national policy for the family to maintain the morale of the troops. The Shils and Janowitz study suggests the wisdom of such an approach.[32] It indicates that one of the few appeals which destroyed the German Army's will to fight was the appeal that their families were being hurt. This finding takes on added significance when it is suggested that the fear of death, the knowledge that the war was lost, or the sense of loyalty to the national cause did not have a similar effect.

These illustrative statements of the role of the family in several diverse areas of life is meant to make the point that the family plays an important role in all areas of life. The family does not specialize in one function, and the organization in another. This may sometimes appear to be the case because at any given moment of time the state of the arts may not have reduced events to the point where the professional expert and formal organizations can play a role. However, a close look at most major areas in our society suggests that formal organizations and primary groups both play a role. This shared functioning is the best way of achieving social goals because these two types of organization bring together different but complementary means for achieving such a goal.

In some ways this is too extreme an assertion. A more exact statement is: if society seeks to maximize its goal achievement, it must employ both formal organizations and primary groups such as the family. This point can be empirically documented by examining periods of crisis where society is obviously seeking to stay alive (disasters, wars, and revolutions). In such periods, the author would hypothesize, the complementary role of the family and the formal organization would become even more obvious.

Research Implications of Shared Functions   The theory of shared functions of family and formal organization has some very direct consequences for research design. Any question which seeks to determine the source and kind of aid a given family receives should be so worded as to permit the respondent to indicate that he receives aid from both formal organizations as well as kin. In other words he should have at least one of the four following choices: (1) receives aid from both family and institution; (2) receives aid from family alone; (3) receives

[32]Edward Shils and Morris Janowitz, "Cohesion and Disintegration in the Wehrmacht in World War II," *Public Opinion and Propaganda*, Daniel Katz, Dorwin Cartwright, Samuel Eldersveld, and Alfred McClung Lee, eds. (New York: Dryden Press, 1954), pp. 553-82.

aid from institutions alone; (4) receives aid from neither. Furthermore, the question should be so worded to differentiate the different types of aid in the same area—that which is uniform and that which is idiosyncratic. Thus, in the field of old age the regular provision of income to meet the minimal standards set by the society is one kind of income aid. Such income aid is generally provided by a bureaucratic organization such as the Social Security Administration. Another kind of income aid deals with the fringe area, that is, buying durable goods items, such as television sets, providing funds for a vacation, extra clothing, and so forth. This aid may well be supplied by the family. A question which simply asks who supplies your source of income forces the respondent to choose between family and social security, when in fact both are used. The exact wording of such a question would depend in part on the socio-economic level of the respondent. When dealing with a wealthy retired family, the nature of kinship aid might differ from that which might occur among poorer families.

From this point of view the following question which has been used in some surveys of old people would be considered ambiguous: Who do you think should provide for the older person who has stopped working if he needs help? If this question were structured to indicate the differences between supplemental aid and standardized aid, the author would hypothesize radical differences in the proportion of people who suggest the kin groups.[33] The author feels the point of view suggested herein is reflected in the responses to another item: "If a parent needs financial assistance, how much should children be expected to help? A great deal (8 per cent), help some (50 per cent), help little (33 per cent), and not expected to help (9 per cent)."[34] The response category "help a great deal" suggests that the family takes over the major function of help, and according to the theory of shared functions this would be inefficient. The middle categories ("help some" and "help little") suggest the sharing concept, and close to 88 per cent of the population accept this position. The Sussman and Burchinal exhaustive reviews of the literature on the nature of kinship help suggests very much the same kind of phenomenon.[35]

[33]Gordon F. Streib and Wayne E. Thompson "The Older Person in A Family Context," *Handbook of Social Gerontology,* Clark Tibbitts, ed. (Chicago; University of Chicago Press, 1960), p. 480 present findings to this question. Thirty-three per cent of the people said the family should provide help when problems arose, while 42 per cent said they should help out with medical expenses. The respondents were permitted to make more than one choice, and 53 per cent said the government should help with problems, 45 per cent said the company or his employer, and 34 per cent said his state government. With regard to medical expenses only the government outranked the family (49 per cent). However, if one is dichotomizing into primary groups and formal organizations, clearly formal organizations are the majority sources of help in both cases. If this question had differentiated between types of aid, we would predict percentages of closer to 80 per cent for the family and the formal organizations.
[34]*Ibid.*
[35]Marvin B. Sussman and Lee Burchinal, "Parental Aid to Married Children: Implications for Family Functioning," *op. cit.*

ideal kin structure and shared functions

The discussion thus far has pointed out in what sense kin structures have a unique role in Western society, and why such kin structures will always have a place in a society seeking to maximize technological progress and a democracy. However, little has been said as to which of our four types of kin structures would most efficiently perform this role: the dissolving family; the nuclear family; the modified extended family; or the extended family. On logical grounds, the two extreme types (dissolving and extended) can be ruled out; the former because it provides such a weak family structure that the family cannot perform its part of the shared function, and the latter because by definition it seeks to service all functional areas by itself, rejecting the aid of the formal organizations. This leaves two types of family structure which permit both family and institutional aid to exist side by side, the modified extended and the nuclear. In terms of the problem of maximizing available resources, the author would hypothesize that the modified family would be a more efficient unit than the nuclear — all other things being equal. This results because the modified extended family, confronted with a problem, has a greater pool of resources to draw on than the nuclear family.

In order to illustrate this point, the function of tension management (one area in which the nuclear family is thought to be supreme) can be examined. If the problems of anxiety and tensions are examined and the question, what is one major source of tension for family members, is asked, most practitioners will answer: the problem of husband and wife disputes. If this is indeed the case, it should be quite clear that here is one major area of tension management for which the nuclear family is unsuitable. By contrast, the modified extended family is more suitable to manage these tensions because in such situations the disputants can go to their kin for succor. More generally, any time the nuclear family as a unit is hit by some such event, the nuclear family will be less suited than the modified extended family to provide tension management. When the family moves to a new location because of the husband's job transfer, the husband is concerned with his new job, the wife with a new house, new shopping, and making new friends, and the children with a new school, and so forth. Again if a major illness strikes any one member of the family, all members are equally hit by tension. In all such instances, the modified extended family has the additional virtue of having kin members who are able to provide succor and support. Basically, the same logic would apply in all problem areas. The modified extended family has a greater pool of financial resources, service resources for baby sitting, nursing, and the like. The only problem with the modified extended family is that aid once given might lead to undue dependence of one nuclear family on the other, which in turn would lead to the development of extended family structure and the negating of other demands of industrial society — differential occupational and geographic mobility, as well as the avoidance of nepotism and favoritism in the operation of formal organizations. Before we take up these issues, the discussion of kin structure and maximal use of shared functions is summarized in Table 13-2.

table 13-2   capacity of kinship structure to use family and institutional sources of aid

kinship structure	capacity to use formal organizations	capacity to use family aid	capacity to use both
Dissolving family	High	None	Low
Nuclear family	High	Some	Moderate
Modified extended family	High	High	High
Extended family	None	High	Low

This table shows that the modified extended family has the highest ranking in its ability to use both family and institutional aid, the nuclear family the next highest ranking, while the other two family types, each for a different reason, have lower rankings.

nature of kinship exchange

The concept of the modified extended family presented here highlights a very important theoretical and empirical problem for research: under what conditions will kinship exchange permit the semiautonomous development of the nuclear family and under what conditions does such exchange cause the modified extended family to degenerate into the classical extended family structure. Some suggested conditions under which exchange will not lead to the dependence of the classical extended family are outlined below.

Partial Aid or Competitive Aid   In this analysis we have pointed out that the modified extended family receives only part of its services from the extended kin while the rest comes from the formal organizations. Where the giver is never in a position to provide the entire service, then he is not in a position to ask for complete subservience. The explicit norm of partial services would go a long way towards insuring that modified extended relations never degenerate into the classical extended relations. Sussman reports a good illustration of the norm of partial services in describing a situation where a new grandfather seeks to pay the total hospital bill for his daughter's confinement and is immediately rebuked by his son-in-law for having gone beyond the legitimate boundaries. By contrast the son-in-law will accept the present of a layette.[36] To understand the nature of

[36]Marvin B. Sussman, "The Help Pattern in the Middle Class Family," *American Sociological Review*, XVIII (February, 1953), 22-28.

kinship aid, the empirical questions which must be resolved are the extent to which the norm of partial aid is accepted by giver and recipient and, also, whether the aid is truly partial or complete.

Furthermore, Blau has pointed out that when there is partial aid—two or more donors and one recipient—then the problem of competition between the donors becomes crucial.[37] Where the donors are in severe competition with each other, the recipient of such aid might not only achieve independence but a certain modicum of control over the donors. This is quite clear in international relations where "neutrals" such as Yugoslavia and Egypt have maintained their autonomy by playing off the aid of Russia against that of the United States. In kinship relations, it is difficult to visualize such competition between the formal organization and the kin structure. Such competition would seem most likely to occur between two different sets of in-laws providing aid to a given nuclear family. Still, the competition between various donors of aid is an empirical question which should be investigated when studies of kinship aid are made.

Reciprocity of Aid   Where the exchange of aid between kin is reciprocal, such aid is less likely to lead to undue dependence of one family on the other. Reciprocity may or may not be in kind. Thus, two married siblings may exchange baby sitting services, an exchange in kind. By contrast, parents of a young family that is just starting out, might supply economic support through loans, substantial gifts, or a monthly supplement to income in those cases where the young couple is going to college. The parental family in exchange might receive the following kinds of psychic satisfactions: (1) satisfaction derived in helping someone with whom they are psychologically closely identified; (2) a sense of status achievement which may no longer be derived from their own occupation because of an early career plateau; (3) an opportunity to keep close to grandchildren, who provide them with a sense of continuing life as their own lives approach an end. These psychological kinds of exchanges should be remembered, because if one concentrates only on more obvious forms of service or money exchanges, it will often seem that no reciprocal exchange has taken place when in fact it has. The strength of this kind of exchange can be illustrated by the case of the young married couple who use threat of withdrawal as a weapon to keep the parental families in line. Finally, exchanges may occur over a period of time. Some parents might help their children financially with the understanding that when the parents retire, the children will reciprocate. Another important area for empirical investigation, therefore, is to determine the degree and nature of reciprocity in kinship exchanges.[38]

[37]Peter Blau reported this in a private conversation. This was an oral report on an untitled manuscript dealing with the problem of exchange.

[38]In this regard the work of Edwin J. Thomas would seem to be especially useful, "Effects of Facilitative Role Interdependence on Group Functioning," *Human Relations*, X, No. 4 (1957), 347-66.

Normative Occasion for Exchange   Where exchange of aid takes place within an institutionally approved situation, it is less likely to be experienced as a gift by the respondent. Where a social norm makes gift giving by the grandparents mandatory at the birth of a grandchild, the father is in a position to accept such a gift without having a sense of personal obligation to the gift giver. Moreover, the donor, robbed of some of his discretion by the mandatory nature of the norms may feel less able to trade off gift giving for subservience. Blau points out that such normative gift giving also has the property of providing an indirect exchange.[39] In such instances the gift giver might derive status from his peers by giving a gift to his child. Thus, a parent giving a lavish wedding for a child and providing an extravagant gift might be seeking status from his peers rather than any power over his child. Knowing this, the child may feel no sense of obligation to the parent even though the parent's gift might be extremely useful, because the child has been an indirect vehicle for reciprocity. To understand kinship exchanges fully they should be examined in terms of their normative implications, that is, are services exchanged on holidays, birthdays, births, and so forth.

Exchange of Aid over Social and Geographical Distance   The modified extended family as defined herein consists of nuclear families that exchange aid over geographical and occupational distances. The function of such distances is to make the immediate, everyday supervision of nuclear subgroups very difficult. The donor finds it difficult to control the recipient's everyday decisions in such circumstances. Another topic for investigation is the determination of how much kinship aid takes place over such distances.

Initiative for Exchanging Aid Comes from the Donor   As has been pointed out by some investigators, within the kin group, the person in need of aid may never directly ask for it.[40] Rather, a sibling may be informed of the need, and the sibling in turn speaks to the parents. The parents as potential donors, if they give aid, must then initiate the aid sequence, and by so doing rob themselves of the discretion customarily assigned to the donor. Studies of aid, therefore, should also investigate the extent to which the recipient of aid has requested such aid, and the extent to which the initiative for aid has come from the donor.

Aid Given Only in Areas Reserved for Kinship Structures   If the modified extended family is to be preserved, then it must restrict its aid to that area reserved to the kinship structure, and it must not impinge on the institutional structure. Thus, in the occupational world the family can deal with the problem of work motivation and training.

[39]As reported by Peter Blau in a private conversation. This was an oral report on an untitled manuscript dealing with the problem of exchange.
[40]Morris Zelditch, Lecture given at Graduate Sociology Department Seminar, Columbia University, January, 1958.

Furthermore, through supplemental sources of income it can affect the standard of living of the young family by supplying noncollateral loans, giving help in buying durable goods, and the like. However, it would be inappropriate for the family to seek to place people in jobs or to seek to advance them or promote them.

In a similar fashion the family can provide first aid in emergencies, or they might provide some housekeeping services for a person who is sick, but the family should not seek to provide medical diagnosis and treatment for basic problems. Again, the family might provide supplementary forms of protection for its members by seeing that a male member walks women members home late at night or by walking young children across the street. However, it would be inappropriate if the family sought to provide the basic services for apprehending criminals and punishing them.

The empirical question which arises in this instance is the extent to which families exchange services within a strictly delimited area of family responsibilities, and the extent to which they see the entire spectrum of services in a society as open for family intrusion.

Future Studies of Family Exchange   Some of the procedures by which family exchanges of services can be prevented from moving in the direction of the classical extended family dependency are outlined above. These procedures indicate ways in which the introduction of nepotism and the exclusion of the bureaucratic organization as a source of aid can be avoided. No claim is made that the present analysis is anything but a preliminary discussion of an important issue. However, for empirical purposes, it is suggested that any future studies of family exchange should seek to determine which if any of the above conditions bind the exchange. Whether the exchange is useful for optimal achievement of social goals or not cannot be understood apart from these conditions.

kinship and bureaucracy—conflicting atmospheres

The analysis to this stage has pointed out that the family and the formal organization have much in common—they are both necessary for goal achievement. This in no way negates an opposing point, the structures of these two organizations are antithetical. The structural contradictions between these organizations may be summarized:

1. The family has relatively permanent members. The members of the family are defined by biological consideration or relatively inflexible laws. The expectations are very strong that people once entering the group will stay. By contrast in the work group, a formal organization, people are judged by their performance and frequently expected to move.

2. The family is based on emotional relations with love being central.

Even the most human-relations oriented bureaucracy does not encourage the intensity of affect that is developed in the family.

3. Relations in industry are instrumental with each individual expected to act in a fashion that will promote company goals and his individual success. In contrast, a family member is expected to view his family relations as ends in themselves and value these relationships for their own sake.

4. The work relation is relatively specialized over a small range of phenomena. Family relations, on the contrary, are diffused. They can range through the entire spectrum of life activities — work, leisure, love, religion, politics, and the like.

5. Family relations are governed by face-to-face contacts. Work relations, relatively speaking, make much more use of written rules.

To summarize, even the most human-relations oriented bureaucratic organization would differ considerably from the family, and these differences must be taken into account in deciding which type of family structure ideally will meet the needs of an industrial bureaucratic society. The dissolving family structure adjusts to the industrial society by losing its family character and adopting the milieu of the bureaucracy.[41] The extended family structure meets this same dilemma by introducing nepotistic norms within the bureaucracy and thereby destroying the industrial bureaucracy.[42]

Parsons, by contrast, suggests that the two types of systems, family and industrial bureaucracy, can live side by side with antithetical atmospheres if they are kept isolated from each other. One way of keeping them isolated is to have only one member of the family in both systems. It is partly on this basis that he argues for a sex-linked division of labor with only one person from the family in the occupational force. The insistence on the nuclear family rather than the extended family has the same consequence. There will be only one person from the family in the labor market. The view that these two systems, family and bureaucratic organization, can be isolated, in part rests on the theory that the two systems operate in completely different spheres of life.

By contrast, the theory of shared functions states that the family and the bureaucratic organizations share functions in all areas of life. Keeping the two systems isolated in the manner suggested by Parsons might lead to a breakdown in coordination between them and a loss of goal attainment. Yet, moving the two systems too closely together might well lead to the disruption of either system because of their

[41]Joseph A. Schumpeter, *Capitalism, Socialism, and Democracy*, 2nd ed., *op. cit.*, pp. 157ff.

[42]Talcott Parsons, *The Structure of Social Action* (New York: Free Press of Glencoe, Inc., 1949), pp. 542-52. Max Weber, *The Theory of Social and Economic Organization*, A. M. Henderson and Talcott Parsons, trans. (New York: Oxford University Press, 1947), pp. 354-58.

antithetical atmospheres. Insofar as both of these propositions hold true, there must be some balance theory of linkage to account for kinship structures existing side by side with bureaucratic organizations.[43] The mid-point of social distance would seem to be the ideal balance point. Extreme distance and extreme closeness both tend to disrupt goal achievement.

The contradictions in group structure between family and formal organizations raises an important empirical issue for it suggests that aid accepted from formal organizations must come in certain forms if it is to be consistent with ideal kin structures. The nature of contact between the two should be such as to maintain a balance in social distance. Thus, where the family is very distant to start with, the organization might use a process of communication which builds up intimacy, such as sending people out to the family to make friends. However, when the family is very close to the agency, it must utilize forms of communication which are relatively formal, such as the mass media. A glance at the relations between on-going agencies and families indicates that there are indeed such linkage mechanisms, and, in principal, there is no reason why the antithetical atmospheres of the bureaucratic organizations and family group cannot be maintained at a mid-point of social distance by these mechanisms.[44]

Several other considerations might be added to this general point to indicate why in current society families can come much closer to formal organizations than was true in the past. The professionalization of occupations provide more public ways for assessing favoritism and merit, eliminating the necessity of using crude rules of nepotism. Thus, to be a doctor or an engineer one needs a certain specialty education and, in the case of medicine and sometimes engineering, a license to practice. These formal requirements provide a firm basis for merit, so that if nepotism occurs within these occupations, it is not as likely to be harmful to goal achieving. With professionalization has come bureaucratization of the job organization, which means that individuals are no longer in a position to hire or fire or promote people at will. There may be a group of specialists who do this. The jobs are no longer there to be given by the father to the son. Finally, an overall

[43]For a detailed statement of one such theory of linkages, see Eugene Litwak and Henry Meyer, "A Balance Theory of Coordination Between Bureaucratic Organizations and External Primary Groups," unpublished manuscript, 1963.

[44]The following are illustrative of types of linkages that formal organizations use to reach outside groups: mass media; detached experts, such as workers with delinquent gangs; voluntary organizations, such as school P.T.A.'s; formal authority, such as school truant officers; settlement house-like arrangements, such as the opening of the school building for after-hours community participation; and opinion leaders, illustrated in the Shaw-McKay concept of treating delinquents through the use of indigenous leadership. If these various procedures for reaching out are analyzed in terms of contemporary theories of communication, one can easily see in what sense they are differentially suited for closing and opening social distance between formal organizations and primary groups. Litwak and Meyer, *ibid.*, present the detailed analysis for this approach.

change in norms has occurred since the early stages of the development of bureaucracy. In the past, a considerable proportion of the population were engaged in small family-owned farms or businesses. Rules of nepotism were the norm, if not legally required. The owner passed on his land or business to his son or relatives, not to the person who was most able. A bureaucratic organization emerging in a society dominated by such norms would have to take extreme actions to screen out nepotism and to stress the isolation of family from the work situation. By contrast, in current society where the norms of merit might be prevalent because the bulk of the jobs are either professionalized or bureaucratized, there is not as great a need for the formal organization to maintain social distance.

From this analysis it would seem pertinent for researchers to investigate specifically the extent to which norms of merit actually prevail in our society, the extent to which relatives can control jobs, and the extent to which there are public, objective criteria of success.[45]

In summary, the question might yet be asked how does each of the family types deal with the problem of antithetical atmospheres. As has already been pointed out, the extended family and the dissolving family cannot deal with this problem. The nuclear family deals with it by the mechanisms of isolation. The modified extended family deals with it by mechanisms of linkages which keep the family at a mid-point of social distance. The research investigator, if he seeks to understand which of these kin structures is indeed ideal for goal achievement, must carefully examine the way in which the formal organization communicates with the kin group. When the investigator finds that the most efficient organizations vary their modes of communication from intimate to formal, dependent on the distance of the family they are seeking to reach, the investigator can assume that the theory of shared functions and linkage mechanisms is in operation. If these formal organizations maintain great social distance in all circumstances, then they have assumed the nuclear family concept of kin structure.[46]

kinship structure and occupational mobility

As mentioned in the introduction, one of the demands of an industrial society is that people be assigned occupationally on the basis of their merit. Unless it is assumed that all people in the family are equally talented and have an interest in interrelated occupations, this

---

[45]For instance, Herbert H. Hyman reports on a national survey where people were asked what it takes to get ahead. At most 18 per cent gave a response which could be interpreted as nepotistic—that is, getting along with the boss or friend or relative of the boss. See: "The Value Systems of Different Classes: A Social Psychological Contribution to the Analysis of Stratification," *Class, Status, and Power*, Reinhard Bendix and Seymour Martin Lipset, eds. (New York: Free Press of Glencoe, Inc., 1953), p. 437.

[46]Maintaining great social distance is usually associated with specific kinds of linking mechanisms, such as the mechanisms of isolation suggested by Parsons (only one person in the labor force), or the use of formalistic procedures, such as the mass media which do not encourage intimate contact.

demand raises the question as to which kin system is best able to tolerate differential occupational mobility. Since the author has dealt with this problem extensively elsewhere, we shall only summarize the discussion at this stage.[47] The prior work pointed out that there were at least three reasons why people felt that differential occupational mobility would be inconsistent with extended kin structures. These were: (1) invidious status comparisons would lead to estrangement;[48] (2) class socialization process would develop different values, different styles of life, and different communication patterns which would lead to estrangement;[49] and (3) differential mobility is not consistent with the relatively constant authority patterns of the extended kin structure.

These arguments may be met by counter-arguments. Invidious status distinctions are based on the concept that status is derived by association with those on the same socio-economic level or higher. However, there is another form of status gratification. In this instance, status is gained by deference. Such status involves associating with people who are at lower status positions. If both forms of status – that derived by association with presumed equals and that derived by association with presumed inferiors – are considered simultaneously, there is no reason why kin on different levels would not both derive gratification if they use different criteria of status; that is, the higher kin member gains status by deference, and the lower one, status by association. However, the same person generally cannot derive both forms of status in the same relationship.[50] Family and friendship groups, however, can be separated so that any given individual can achieve both types of status provided he uses different reference groups; that is, the family provides status by deference, and friends provide status by association. In addition, the analysis previously referred to stated that kin through their resources can provide services and funds that can assist the mobility of any given nuclear sub-unity. To determine which point of view about status is valid, it is important to gather empirical data about the forms of status orientation which members of the family have towards each other and the extent to which family and friends are kept separate.

The position that there are class differences in values and styles of

[47]Eugene Litwak, "Occupational Mobility and Extended Family Cohesion," *American Sociological Review*, XXV (February, 1960), 9-21.

[48]*Ibid.*, p. 9.

[49]Herbert H. Hyman, "The Value Systems of Different Classes . . .," *op. cit.*, pp 426-42.

[50]Robert Blood pointed out in a personal conversation that where two forms of status gratification – deference and status by association – operate between family members who are on different class levels, there is a real threat to the concept of the modified extended family as an equalitarian confederation. This would be true to the extent to which both partners of this exchange did not feel mutually dependent on each other for their gratification and to the extent to which status is not also derived independently from family as suggested in the modified extended family concept.

living is not to be denied. However, what is crucial for maintenance of kin structure is the magnitude and the direction of these differences. Are such differences growing or shrinking, or are they staying the same. With regard to the magnitude and direction of class differences, in a previous report, the argument was made that there has been an absolute rise in the standard of education with the great bulk of the population (over 70 per cent) now completing a high school education. This absolute rise may mean that the communication problems between the social classes are becoming less difficult. The differences in styles of living between the classes may reflect differences in the division of spoils rather than *major* differences in class values or aspirations.[51] To make this point is not to deny that there are differences. But it is to deny that these differences are of sufficient magnitude to prevent family identification across class lines. The argument is not that families in the same class will not have greater identification, each with the other. It is argued, however, that such high degrees of identification are not necessary to maintain a sense of obligation and significant exchange of services across class lines. In short, class identification is not always a dichotomous variable with high identification leading to the extended family and low identification leading to a nuclear or dissolving family. The middle ranges of identification are extremely crucial and permit the semiautonomous state suggested in the modified extended family concept. An important empirical question is the measurement of the degree of family identification over and within class lines. Such measurement should indicate at least three points on a given scale—high, medium, and low —so that the hypothesis advanced here can be tested.

The argument that differential mobility upsets the authority structure of the kin system rests on the assumption that such systems demand a single authority. The modified extended family concept, by contrast, suggests a confederation as ideal, and the prior discussion on the nature of exchange suggests ways in which services can be exchanged while maintaining such a confederation. As an empirical issue, it would be important to distinguish between a single authority system, the complete independence of the nuclear family, and the concept of the confederation. Too often, we have assumed a dichotomy in this area. After showing that the traditional extended family authority system does not hold in our society, we have assumed that complete nuclear autonomy was the only alternative.

The question arises as to which form of family structure can best deal with the problem of mobility. The hypothesis on this issue is summarized in Table 13-3.

In the first column of the table is the amount of status one can gain by differential mobility, taking into account both types of status, that

[51]Eugene Litwak, "Occupational Mobility and Extended Family Cohesion," *op. cit.*, pp. 12-13.

table 13-3   kinship structure and differential occupational mobility

	supports for mobility			
kinship structure	status gained by differential mobility—through association and through deference	resources available for differential mobility	consistency between authority structure and differential mobility	overall evaluation
Dissolving family	Moderate	Low	High	Moderate
Nuclear family	Moderate	Low	High	Moderate
Modified extended family	High	High	High	High
Extended family	Low	Moderate	Low	Low

gained through association and that gained through deference. The extended family kin structure is lowest on this scale because it discourages all differential mobility. The nuclear and dissolving family are classified as moderate, because not having kin they are more likely to have a choice of one form of status or the other. The modified extended family is thought to be highest on this scale because it has a greater possibility of using both forms of status since it can separate the family and the friendship populations. In the second column the four types of kinship structure are classified by the resources available for differential mobility. It may be argued here that the extended family and the modified extended have the greatest resources. However, the extended family is unlikely to agree (except in emergencies) to use these resources for differential mobility. In the third column a rating is made of the consistency between differential mobility and the authority structure of the various kin systems. It is argued that all systems except the extended family are consistent. From this analysis it would be argued that the modified extended family is the most able to deal with differential mobility, the extended family the least able, while the other two types of kin structures have a middle rating.

An important question for consideration is the extent to which this model of kinship structure and occupational mobility can be applied in research. Parenthetically, it can be reported that the Jewish groups, who have a modified extended family structure, are one of the most upwardly mobile groups in American society.

kinship structure and geographical mobility

The point has been made that any kinship structure in a modern society must permit both occupational mobility and differential geographical mobility. Since this premise has been discussed in some detail in a prior article, only a brief summary and elaboration of certain points will be undertaken here.[52]

The prior discussion stated that there were basic arguments

[52]Eugene Litwak, "Geographical Mobility and Extended Family Cohesion," *American Sociological Review*, XXV (June, 1960), 385-94.

against the co-existence of differential geographical mobility and extended kinship structure. These arguments were: (1) high extended family identification would make differential moves unlikely; (2) it is difficult to move a large extended kin and still find jobs; (3) it is difficult to maintain kinship identification over geographical distance, so that where differential mobility has occurred, there will be no extended kin identification.

Against these arguments, a number of counter-points were raised to indicate that there is no reason why extended kin cannot legitimate differential mobility. Kinship groups have done so in the past, when survival was at issue. Insofar as it can be demonstrated that economic well-being of the unit members is related to geographical mobility, the kinship group might very well legitimate such moves in current society.[53] Further, once they legitimate such moves, the extended family has greater resources, economically and in terms of communication channels, to encourage such movements.[54]

The second point raised against geographic mobility is partially irrelevant since the needs of an industrial society call for differential geographic mobility not large extended kin mobility. It was hypothesized in the prior study, however, that there are instances when the extended family can coalesce geographically without going counter to the demands of rational distribution of labor. Where two or more members of the family have reached a career plateau then there is no reason these members cannot move to the same area. This would be especially true where one member is retired. It would also be true for the nonretired person if the place where he moved were large enough so he could find an equivalent job in the geographical area near his close relative. The possibility of future coalescence further enhances the legitimation of differential geographical moves at an earlier state. Further research is needed about the extent to which people legitimate differential geographical mobility and their expectations of future kin coalescence.

The answer to the third point—the inability of kin to maintain identification over large geographical distance—is that the modern techniques of communication have decreased the social significance of geographical distance. Further, we live in a monetary economy, which means that the family can arrange for most services simply by wiring money.[55] The fact that geographical distance no longer has the same social significance it had in the past supports the family legitimation of differential mobility.

No claim can be made that two families living forty miles apart can match the intensity of identification of families living in the same

[53]This is especially true if, as noted below, family members have a sense that such moves do not involve a loss of contact with their kin.
[54]Litwak, "Geographical Mobility and Extended Family Cohesion," *op. cit.*, pp. 386-87.
[55]*Ibid.*

household. However, it can be argued that families today living forty miles away are, in terms of contact and identification, no different than families of the past living in the same small community. As such it is postulated that a sufficient amount of family identification can be maintained despite geographical distance to continue family exchange of services. There is no need to argue that this identification is the same as that which distinguished the traditional extended family.

With these thoughts in mind, the four kin structures can be examined in terms of their implication for differential geographical mobility. The results of this examination are given in Table 13-4. The argument would be that the dissolving family, nuclear family, and the modified extended family would all legitimate differential occupational mobility. For the first two types, differential occupational mobility is not really an issue since they have no kin to leave behind. The one family type that is unlikely to legitimize such moves except under dire emergencies is the classical extended family. The other consideration on the issue of geographical mobility is the resources families have for supporting a move – granted such a move is legitimate. All other things being equal, the modified extended family and the extended family have the greatest amount of pooled resources. The nuclear family and the dissolving family have the least. Summing up, it is argued that the modified extended family is most able to promote differential geographic mobility. It would be of some importance to see whether empirical research actually verifies these assertions.

table 13-4   Kinship structure and differential geographic mobility

kinship structure	dimension encouraging differential mobility		
	legitimation of differential geographic mobility	availability of financial resources for differential geographic mobility	overall evaluation
Dissolving family	Very high	Low	Moderate
Nuclear family	Very high	Low	Moderate
Modified extended family	High	High	High
Extended family	Low	Moderate	Low

pluralistic family types in an industrial society

Having devoted most of this paper to the establishment of the idea that there might be an ideal type of family structure which most clearly meets the needs of an industrial society, the author would now like to indicate those points where we think this approach is limited. In the presentation thus far the assumption has generally been made that one family type is ideal for most of the demands of an industrial democracy. Empirical research and further theory might well lead to a more complicated assertion, which is: one family type is most desirable in satisfying one of these criteria of industrial democracy, and another family type is more desirable in satisfying another. This means that the investigator might not be able to suggest a single type of family structure as most important in industrial society, but instead must confront society with the legitimacy of different types.

Further, a need for a pluralistic concept of family structures might result from the fact that at any given point of time the standards set for each of the conditions of an industrial democracy (differential mobility, unique function, and agreeability with bureaucratic organizations) might vary considerably. This is especially a problem in a large industrial society geared to great change. At any single point in time, such a society might resemble a complex social mosaic rather than a single continuous substance.

Let us examine the problem of congeniality between formal organizations and primary groups. As pointed out in a previous discussion, there might have been great utility in advocating a nuclear family structure in the early stages of industrialization when the society adhered to nepotistic norms. In such a culture it might have been necessary to advocate an extreme position in order to produce any change at all. Similarly, in contemporary American society, white migrants from the mountain areas of the South come into urban areas with a strong extended family structure. It might be best to split nuclear subunits off rather than to try to change this entire structure. Such change would be necessary to shift it to a modified extended family stage.

If the problem of differential economic mobility is examined historically, it is easy enough to point out that some of our major industries started out as family concerns. As such, they seemed to flourish despite the lack of differential occupational mobility. Thus, where an area of endeavor requires little technical knowledge, there is no reason why a family might not compete by drawing people with sufficient ability from within its own boundaries. However, in an area in which scientific research plays a great role, the organization which restricted itself to family members would probably lose out to the organization which used the entire world as its manpower source. This historical analysis of the growth of different industries has equal relevance to the situation. There are constant innovations in modern industry, and in the early stages of these innovations little technical knowledge may be required. In such cases there is no reason why family enterprises cannot be successful. Further, no real demand for differential occupational mobility need be made on these families.

Similarly, with regard to differential geographical mobility, this may not be as great a problem in the future when man better learns to control his environment. In addition, we might point out that for many occupations sufficient job opportunities arise within a large city or metropolitan area to negate large-scale geographic moves. Finally, as has been indicated, differential geographic moves might vary within the life cycle. The individual who reaches his career plateau is able to move near a kin member in a similar situation without disturbing the rational allocation of labor.

With these qualifications in mind a more precise statement of kinship structure in a highly industrialized society would be one which says: For the large bulk of the population there is one ideal form of kinship structure (modified extended family), but room must be left for a variety of types that involve substantial minorities. Thus, with regard to the issue of retirement of the aged, one might want to utilize independent home life with aid from social security as an ideal form, but at the same time one should not rule out the need for homes for the aged or their more luxurious modern counterparts.

conclusion

This paper attempts to provide a theoretical base for the effectiveness of primary groups and bureaucratic organizations, coexisting in an industrial society. To do this it was first necessary to show the relationship between theories of social power and theories of organizational structure. From this analysis emerged a theory of shared functions between formal organizations and primary groups. Secondly, this paper attempted to point out some key essentials of an industrial bureaucracy — the need for bureaucratic organizations and primary groups to live side by side and the need of each to deal with differential occupational and geographical mobility. Then, an attempt was made to assess four types of family structure in terms of these criteria. Each of these family types presented certain problems in meeting the demands of industrial society. Some of these problems, such as the problem of exchange in a modified extended family, were explored in great detail. From this arose an initial assessment that the family type here called the modified extended family might be most effective in the maintenance of a democratic industrial society.

Given this analysis, the author would draw two conclusions. For the policy-maker pressed for a decision, before all the possible facts are in, this paper might provide a guide line for which family type he would seek to perpetuate. For the social scientist seeking to better understand social life, or for the policy-maker seeking information for long-term planning, this paper should be treated as a series of reasonable hypotheses pointing out several avenues of fruitful inquiry.

commentary
and criticism

a social psychologist
looks at
kinship structure

KURT W. BACK

the problem as discussed in the papers

This discussion will concentrate on the papers by Sussman, "Relationships of Adult Children with their Parents in the United States"; Stehouwer, "Relations between Generations and the Three-Generation Household in Denmark"; Townsend, "The Effects of Family Structure on the Likelihood of Admission to an Institution in Old Age: The Application of a General Theory"; LeVine, "Intergenerational Tensions and Extended Family Structures in Africa"; and Goldfarb, "Psychodynamics and the Three Generation Family." This group of papers shows clearly the continued presence of the extended family in urban and industrial society. References to empirical data gathered in a host of situations, to clinical observations, and to theoretical considerations all agree in this respect. The importance of kinship grouping in industrial society has been underestimated in some current theory. We recognize now that an organizational principle, such as kinship, is adaptable to many kinds of cultures.

The failure of theory based on observation of the contemporary must give us pause. We recognize, of course, that sociological theory cannot be an exact representation of actual conditions. Theoretical work in any science requires a certain amount of abstraction from the empirical givens. The early theorists who discovered the growing importance of the nuclear family and especially the later theorists, such as Ogburn and Parsons, therefore, abstracted the decay of kinship structure as the relevant inference. They acted on what we recognize today as insufficient evidence. Parsons' article, which is cited most frequently as the prototype of the nuclear family position, rests on two very disparate foundations.[1] One is an analysis of kinship nomenclature similar to that used by anthropologists studying tribal cultures, and the remainder is an impressionistic description of family life as it would exist if his hypothesis were true. If the assumption that kinship structure is decaying seems plausible enough, this latter description apparently has struck sufficient readers as familiar to their own experience. Evidence presented in the papers under discussion, especially Sussman's and Stehouwer's, does demonstrate the continuing importance of the extended family. Existing kinship structures were not errors for the social theorists to disregard in deriving principles of family organization, but were the important social facts. New theory and research is called for which considers the continuity of family structure under conditions of social change from rural and agrarian to urban and industrialized society, and which does not exaggerate the differences.

Sussman feels that the methodology of typology and the statistical tool of the Chi-square test are to blame for this extreme emphasis on the shift in family structure. He seems to put the blame on the wrong point, however. In statistics, the treatment of continuous variables has progressed at about the same rate or even faster than that of qualitative variables, and sophisticated typologists recognize that pure types are theoretical constructs, while gradations between them are the empirical facts. Both the statistician and the typologist use dichotomies if there are no means to capture the underlying complex of variables. In order to investigate gradations of kinship structure, we must be able to distinguish and to handle fine structural and dynamic gradations. If it is possible to do that, we can then address ourselves to the varying social and psychological problems of varying kinship structure, the implications dealt with in these papers for the three-generation family.

Seen in this light, the papers deal with the different social and psychological consequences of different degrees of extended family structure. Discussion of these papers will be helped by starting with the somewhat abstract treatment of gradations of structure and dynamic connections which make possible gradations in family struc-

---

[1]Talcott Parsons, "The Social Structure of the Family," *The Family: Its Function and Destiny*, rev. ed., Ruth N. Anshen, ed. (New York: Harper & Row, Publishers, Inc., 1959), pp. 241-74.

ture. We shall then be able to deal not with social units but with a network of social interrelationships in the manner of a social psychologist. We shall sketch first the mathematical and logical tools which enable us to deal with degrees of kinship networks and the degrees of meaning which such networks can have for individuals.

formal methods

Graph Theory The tools for the study of structure have been developed in matrix and graph theory.[2] Both these theories are studies of the properties of linkages and of figures drawn on the basis of these linkages. Harrison White has recently used this method in a limited analysis of kinship structure.[3] Both his method and his limitations are instructive for our purposes here. He starts with eight elementary role relationships based on sex, generation, and type of relationship. These relationships are: father and mother, brother and sister, son and daughter, and husband and wife. From these elementary linkages we can build up all possible kin relationships, such as mother's brother, mother's father, sister's husband, brother's daughter. For each person, each ego, this method can build up a relation of all his possible and actual relatives, which of course very quickly ramifies to an excessively high number. The specific cultural conditions or societal conditions now enter into simplifications of this network. Some relationships are almost universally identical: thus brother's brother is a brother, brother's sister is a sister, father's wife is usually the mother, although, of course, it could be a stepmother. These are relatively trivial simplifications. The more interesting modifications enter in with the classificatory kinship systems. Thus, if we call father's brother "father" and treat all his linkages as if they were linkages of the father, a great amount of simplification is achieved. White finds it possible to construct models and to analyze various patterns of marriage roles found in various societies by introducing suitable kinds of equivalence relationships. When we look at American and Western European society, we can see immediately that these societies do not recognize the nuclear family exclusively. In these societies not only the primary one-step relationships are recognized. It is not even true that only one-step relationships are recognized when all other relationships are put into an equivalence condition. Some two- and three-step relationships, even collateral ones, are distinguished by special names which may imply a special kind of role relationship. What is crucial, however, for our argument is that even beyond those special

[2] For the most comprehensive account of graph theory and its relevance in this context, see Claude Flament, *Applications of Graph Theory to Group Structure* (Englewood Cliffs, New Jersey: Prentice-Hall, Inc., 1963).
[3] Harrison C. White, *An Anatomy of Knowledge* (Englewood Cliffs, New Jersey: Prentice-Hall, Inc., 1962).

relationships there exist generic terms for relatives which include quite a number of steps. Those relatives may be counted as cousins, uncles, kin, or relations, but they are distinguished from people who could not be reached by any steps along this tree.

Thus, the first underlying dimension which can bring us over the dichotomy of extended and nuclear family is the description of a specific graph which can represent the kinship nomenclature of a society and the number of steps distinguished in such nomenclature, and, at best, after how many steps no more relationship is recognized. An understanding of the dynamics of kinship based on this structure is more difficult. In cross-cultural studies the main use of the description of the kinship system has been an all-or-none determination of definite relationships. Prominent among them are marital requirements and taboos, and this is White's primary interest. Other features which are closely related to the structure are residence requirements, inheritance, and status rights and duties. All these relationships have made kinship an important part of the discussion of social structure.

The value of graph theory in this discussion is the possibility which such theory offers in distinguishing degrees of network connections. We can distinguish more and more differentiated networks, and other networks which have a great amount of equivalence between positions. On the one hand, we find now that the argument deriving from nomenclature simply means that there is a great amount of equivalent position, not that there is no more kinship structure; and on the other hand, it is possible to distinguish the importance of kinship extended family from the existence of corporate extended family structures with definite unity. It is possible to have overlapping networks of kinship structure which can still be analyzed as meaningful structures. We can thus define even quite simplified kinship structures without saying that only the nuclear family exists. We can define quite complicated systems without having to depend on the corporate entity of one extended family. This technique gives us, therefore, the possibility of distinguishing family structure beyond the dichotomy of nuclear versus extended family. The other dichotomy to be evaded is the content of this relationship, saying that because kinship does not have the same activity as the nuclear family, that kin are dealt with as we deal with strangers. We, therefore, need a way of dealing with the degree of relationship.

Modal Logic The traditional logical framework which influences scientific thought is bivalued. It admits of a proposition that it be either true or false, or of a relationship either that it exist or not exist. To obtain a degree of relationship or a degree of likelihood of activity or to order sentiment and obligation, we are usually constrained to use a combination or ratio of these yes-no answers, as in the calculus of probability. Many applications of this calculus, however, do violence to the topics with which we are dealing. First of all, they promise too much, implying the acceptance of all mathematical rules comparing different sentiments. On the other hand, the necessary assumption of random events is not what we mean by likely or probable, for example, in the sentence: A person would rather help a cousin than a nonrelated person. This sentence does not mean a probability, but a definite link between cousins, although the link may be weaker, for instance, than the link to one's spouse. Put another way, we cannot measure the strength of the link between kin by the relative frequency with which one follows a certain obligation. The link is just as definite, but weaker or different. What is needed, therefore, is a kind of logic which will admit of these qualitative differences without putting them into a framework of dichotomized or arithmetical relationships.

We need a logic which is analogous to the kind of geometry which graph theory provides. Graph theory still preserves the concept of distance in structure, but not in the metric sense, and thus the corresponding logic should preserve the notion of degree, not in the sense of arithmetic, but making it qualitatively different. Such a kind of logic is the logic of modalities, which can admit of qualitatively different relationships such as true-false, possible, and necessary or obligatory and permitted.[4] Thus we have a variety of types of relationship possible with each kin link, and this gives us the possibility of describing different kinds of relationships and prevents us from too easily inferring one type of relationship from a change in another one. For instance, if a society no longer requires responsibility for a certain kinsman, that does not necessarily mean that help for this kinsman will never be given, but it also means that the pure frequency of this kind of relationship is not an adequate measure. In general, if we find that the extended family does not live together, does not work together or even work in the same occupation, and has no ironclad responsibilities for each other's support, then we can be led easily into overgeneralization about the nuclear or even the vanishing family. What we do not see is that even though structural links cover some definite pattern, they also carry some less definite patterns of different degrees of possibility of choice which may be directed more into one channel than into another. That is, certain activities, certain interaction, and certain feelings may be channeled into possibilities of action toward certain people. There is a choice of the individual toward whom action may be directed, but there is also a preferred choice. What the papers demonstrate is less a change in kinship patterns in industrial society, but rather that the structural methods which have been used to study

---

[4]For some of the basic systems of modal logic, see: Clarence I. Lewis and Cooper H. Langford, *Symbolic Logic*, 2nd ed. (New York: Dover Publications, Inc., 1959); Arthur N. Prior, *Time and Modality* (Oxford: Clarendon Press, 1957); Georg Henrik von Wright, *An Essay in Modal Logic* (Amsterdam: New Holland Publishers, 1951); and A. R. Anderson, "The Logic of Norms," *Logique et Analyse*, I (1958), 91-94.

kinship have become inappropriate in such an industrial society. Let us expand a bit on this statement.

In looking at social structures, we can distinguish certain events which are either necessary or impossible because of the cognitive state of the society: that is, its technical knowledge and scientific sophistication.[5] Beyond this we can see certain actions which are either obligatory or prohibited: those are the normative actions within the society. Beyond both these fields of discourse, the cognitive and the normative, there is an intermediate range of events which are determined neither cognitively nor normatively and which allow individual freedom of action. As far as societies know, events can be technically possible but still be prohibited. Other combinations of those two dimensions are possible. We can call the domain of all acts which are either limited by norms or by technical knowledge the structural necessities of the society. However, even in the most regulated society, there are some acts which fall outside either cognitive or normative specifications. These acts do not occur at random; they too are partially influenced by societal and by individual predilections, but they need to be dealt with in different terms. It can be argued that this is the subject matter of social psychology. In different societies, different and more or fewer actions are left over in this field.

application of the formal models

We propose, then, to look at the dynamic characteristics of kinship relationships in this framework. As in discussing the structural relations, we cannot say, therefore, that the change is from kinship to no kinship, but rather that the relation between kin becomes continuously different, as they are pushed from a purely normative framework to a framework of individual decisions. Industralization and urbanization have less destroyed the fabric of family relationships than increased the choice of behavior and the number of relationships which are possible. Short of developing an absolute measure of strength of tie based on some emotional involvement, number of interactions, or amount of time spent, the importance of each relationship network can only be stated comparatively. That is, in answer to the question, "What are the different kinds of relationships which compete with kinship: local, occupational, fraternal, voluntary association, or political?" we even find that some approximation of the kinship relationship is carried through society through transfer of funds in the public sector. Further, what are the distinguishing characteristics of the kinship relationship in comparison with all these other structures? Fi-

[5]A more statistical exposition is given in Kurt W. Back, "The Proper Scope of Social Psychology," *Social Forces*, XLI (May, 1963), 368-76; an application in Kurt W. Back, Reuben Hill, and J. Mayone Stycos, "Population Control in Puerto Rico: The Formal and Informal Framework," *Law and Contemporary Problems*, XXV (Summer, 1960), 558-76.

nally, does the evidence suggest that one characteristic of modern Western society is the greater domain of what we have called the social-psychological act, as compared with the normative act?

The papers in this symposium would seem to be a recognition of this fact. The earlier theoretical speculations dichotomized between normative and nonnormative. As normative kinship relations declined, the conclusion drawn was that all kinship relations declined. The reaction against this simplification is shown in the papers which demonstrate where kinship relations are still important and which introduce the social-psychological variables. In reviewing these papers now, let us keep in mind the framework we have developed for such a review and for the evaluation of the data which the papers give on this new social-psychological domain of kinship relationships. The conceptual tools developed in the last two sections are helpful in addressing ourselves to the classification of the papers under discussion.

None of the papers accept the easy dichotomization of nuclear and extended family, of kinship and no kinship, of break or link between generations. However, having accepted a more complicated formulation, they are forced to address themselves to a somewhat more difficult problem. They raise such problems as the connections of kinship structure with other structures within the society, qualitative changes in the kinship networks, the effects of the changes on the problem of individual choice, and the cost which this individual choice entails. The different papers address themselves principally to different problems within this list. The papers of Sussman and Stehouwer discuss mainly the evidence for the change in kinship networks, Sussman within the United States and Stehouwer on a cross-cultural basis. Townsend and LeVine discuss the question of psychic cost, Townsend the cost of complete rupture between generations, especially in situations where this rupture is relatively rare, and LeVine the psychic cost of extended family relations in a situation where this rupture is not possible at all and where the norm of obligatory kinship structure is still very strong. Finally, Goldfarb discusses the qualitative nature of different links between people in families and generations from the point of view of the individual. He then can define his different links in an individual, clinical fashion similar to the different types of links we have developed logically from a social point of view. Let us now discuss some of the major points brought out through the different points of view represented in the papers.

Sussman   Sussman presents a massive amount of evidence for the survival and even for the strengthening of the extended family in American urban culture. In the face of this evidence, it is hard to see why a contrary opinion has been entertained by many leading sociologists. Several comments are, therefore, in order here. In addition to the empirical evidence, there is not even a particular theoretical reason (even accepting the views of the social disruption of urban life) why kinship structure should weaken with urbanism. It could be argued just as well that the breaking of the community links involved in moving from the village to the city would throw the person almost exclusively on his own family. In fact, studies in France have shown that consanguinal marriage is indeed greater in cities than in the surrounding countryside, and it has been suggested that consanguinal marriage occurs in the same situation where marriage through newspaper ads also occurs.[6] As long as city life is impersonal, these are practically the only sources for finding a mate. Thus purely logically, urban disorganization by itself could lead just as well to strengthening of kinship structure as to its weakening, and some of the data cited by Sussman point in this direction. Although the same people who have proposed the nuclear family hypotheses also seem to have a distorted view of the city, these two points of view thus do not necessarily go together. We must, therefore, look elsewhere for explanation of the strength of the theory which Sussman so successfully attacks.

To do so, we can turn now to the possibility that the kinship structure has changed qualitatively, although the quantitative measures, especially of behavior such as age and social contact, have not changed, or have even increased. There is a difference between the social reality of a kin group or the existence of an extended family as such, and behavior and relations with kin.

Mathematically speaking, the graphs may have changed from distinct wholes to more indistinct structures with a great number of equivalent strengths: that is, people may recognize kinship relationships while the kinship unit as a unit has lost its distinctiveness. Secondly, the kind of dynamic relationship exemplified in the kinship link may have changed, such as a change from necessity to voluntary choice and permission. These changes, if they occur over a short time, may not encompass the expectations of the older generation, and they may be exaggerated by them and may have gradually contributed to the myth of the nuclear family. Shanas has shown evidence that the myth of children's neglect may have been propagated by the parents who frequently, in an almost paranoiac reaction, have complained to those people dealing with the old about imagined or real slights.[7] In this way, a myth was fixed in the minds of gerontologists and other professionals dealing with older people, who hardly ever had the means of correcting this one-sided impression. Thus, slight changes in norms and in some behavior may have led to a social myth of much larger changes and much different kinds of behavior. This distinction between norms and behavior, and thus consideration of the quality of

[6]J. Sutter and L. Tabah, "Frequence et Repartition des Mariages Consanguines en France," *Population*, III (1948), 607-630.
[7]Ethel Shanas, "The Unmarried Old Person in the United States: Living Arrangements and Care in Illness, Myth and Fact," paper presented at the International Social Science Research Seminar in Gerontology, Markaryd, Sweden, 1963.

links appears in Sussman's own data, although somewhat neglected. The indication in a few studies that aid, especially from parents to children, has to be hidden and given in ways not officially recognized as aid shows an important social fact. Although economically the aid is just as great in whatever form it is given, hidden aid leads to a different interpretation of the kinship link. In the extreme, as is demonstrated in Juanita Kreps' paper, it does make a difference whether income is transferred from one generation to another through the social sector in the form of taxes and public support or whether it is given as direct aid to one's own relatives. It thus seems that a change has occurred in norms and behavior which is not apparent. However, the difference in the mode of social relationships was not actually reflected in amount of kinship aid or amount of contact, yet, for different reasons the people affected and the scientists studying them were led to believe that the change in the quality or texture of behavior was a change in quantity.

Stehouwer   Stehouwer's data on kinship relationships, especially of adult children with their parents, extends the idea of kinship structure over different societies. These studies show the lack of obvious relationship between physical conditions and social behavior. Lack of contact does not necessarily mean any diminished relationships, and the smaller forms of mutual aid in Denmark do not say anything about the quality of kin relationships in this country. Both the common elements and the differences between the three countries found by Stehouwer are striking. There has been a change in all countries in the amount of common residence and in the direct financial responsibility of parents and children toward each other. However, different historical and geographic conditions seem to be related to the manner and degree in which this change has been effected. The smaller distances in Denmark, especially as compared to the United States, have made it more likely that parents live relatively close to their children. In the same manner it has made it less likely that parents will stay overnight in the children's homes or vice versa. Thus, we can see similarly how the early development of comprehensive social security in Denmark has played down the importance of actual cash transactions between parents and children or grandparents and grandchildren in the latter country. In Great Britain, by contrast, in spite of the development of social security, parents are most likely to live with their children, while in matters of financial aid the conditions in that country lie between Denmark and the United States. These behavioral indicators lead to interesting speculations about the quality of emotional relationships between adult children and their parents. However, the special conditions which explain some of the differences at the time of changes also make it difficult to use these behavioral indicators as indicators of some quality of relationships. From these data, we cannot see whether of not the quality of relationship between generations is different in the three countries. The data collected in the three-nation study provide a valuable compendium of facts about the relations between generations in the three countries, and they show us clearly the limitations of factual knowledge. The interpretation of the meaning of facts is always difficult, especially in such an emotion-laden subject as this.

Townsend The importance of kinship links and their particular quality can also be evaluated negatively; that is, by investigating what is missing if those links are lacking. This seems to be the particular value of Townsend's paper. Concentrating on that part of the older generation which lives in institutions, the paper can describe the meaning of the kinship ties which are lacking in many of these cases. From this point of view it is particularly fortunate that Townsend was working in England, the country in which, by comparison with Denmark and the United States, the older generation is most likely to live with their children. Thus, the alternative of living alone is less common, and a greater proportion of the people do feel abandoned if they enter an institution or home for the old. We see here clearly the different degrees in meaning of different kinship relationships. The point made in many of the interviews that, let us say, a sister's child is not the same as one's own child; or the author's difficulty in deciding what can be called an available relative, would seem to point more to qualitative than to quantitative differences. Townsend is not dealing with a differing strength of relationship, but a different kind of relationship where different behavior is appropriate. One could go farther in looking through the "wrong end of the looking-glass" at the kinship structure. What the subjects in the study have in common is that they do not live with their relatives or even accept aid from them. One could look for the reasons why they do not live with different kinds of relatives. This is done in part in the paper, and it is clear from different parts of it that the reasons for not living with children are of a different kind than those for not living with other relatives, and also that there are different reasons for rejection within the latter group. These different reasons for separating from the kin group can give us inferences of the different kinds of links existing in these different kinship relations.

LeVine The last two papers, those by LeVine and Goldfarb, treat more with the psychological stress which can occur in these kinship linkages. LeVine's paper is a very clear reminder that even in the well-defined kinship groupings of African societies, tensions can and do occur. Two kinds of these structural stresses seem to be particularly relevant to our discussion. One is that the definition of the kinship group, the extended family, as a corporate social group, submerges the individual and the varying demands of his life cycle in the organization of the group itself. The assumption of certain responsibilities, rights, and property does not depend on the age or maturity of the

individual himself, but on his place in the kinship group and especially on the survival of members of the older generation. It is this
stress between the needs of the individual's personal life cycle and
the needs of the group which fosters most of the bases of aggression
shown in the paper. The other stress factor is the multiplicity of functions which the extended family provides. The additional economic
and social functions which in Western society are taken up by other
institutions also make any stresses within the family system or any
other kind of stresses more strongly felt. The description of the cause
of putting all relationships into one kind of system again exemplifies
the quality of the relationship and the different meanings this relationship has in a system where the different kin relations are so definitely
defined. This comparison with the more perfect kinship structure,
such as presumably existed earlier in Western culture, shows that
even in the traditional kinship system we cannot have a simple,
undifferentiated network of linkages. Relationships between humans
are not simply connections between points, and there are always ways
in which a required connection conflicts with individual desires and
there are also ways of either expressing this tension or making adjustments in required relationships. The possibility of migration to new
land is one example. Further, the African kinship systems show a great
variety of obligations and gratifications which can be put on the same
link, which is not customary in modern Western society. Thus, in
analyzing the latter, instead of trying to assess the absolute importance
of kinship links, we have to compare the kinship network with those
networks which carry the alternative economic and social functions.

Goldfarb   From this perspective of the stresses encountered in a
well-defined extended family system, we can evaluate Goldfarb's typology of the different psychodynamic factors involved in linkages in
our society. In the early part of the paper he shows that not only
generational relationships but also age differences as such have always been thought to produce certain types of linkages. Psychody-
namically, that is, in its meaning for the person himself, Goldfarb then
distinguishes two major types of relationship which can act as a cohesive force within the kinship grouping and in the society as a whole,
a dependent or independent kind of relationship, both with various
subclasses to define more subtle kinds of behavior. Both types can
provide a cohesive base for interpersonal relationships; that is, each
type is equally strong, but they are qualitatively different. Fitting with
our earlier logical classification, we can characterize the dependent
type as putting more stress on necessity or obligation, especially from
the other person, while the independent type stresses more possibility and permissiveness. Dealing mainly with clinical material, Goldfarb can show how far the type of linkage depends on the individual
and stays consistent throughout the individual's life. It would be instructive to know now how these kinds of relationships fit into a social

context, whether the same type of relationship exists in the same kinship group or in different socially defined groups, and even how invariant it is in different contexts for the same person. The two theoretically oriented papers discussed, Sussman's and Goldfarb's, treat the two extremes of the problem of kinship structure, Sussman's the extent of linkages within society and Goldfarb's the type of linkages of which the individual is capable. As we have seen, the three other papers, which were mainly empirically oriented, have presented data commenting on one of the other aspects of the joint problem.

The combination of these theoretical approaches and the empirical studies, all of which are done independently of each other, throws light on our present theoretical position on kinship structure and the lines of future fruitful research. It seems best to conclude this discussion by considering the methodological problems and insights resulting from this convergence of views.

methodological problems

The first methodological pitfall in intergenerational studies is that of taking one social network, such as kinship structure, by itself. People are bound together by several networks. One is familial, one is local, one is territorial, one is occupational; others are religious or dependent on voluntary association. Speaking about strength of kinship makes more sense if we are able to compare all of these. If kinship is the main bond which holds people together, then we can speak about the importance of the extended family, as in West Africa. However, in our society clearly other bonds are important too. Then the question does not become, "Are kinship bonds important?" Just as in comparison with previous times of different cultures, such bonds can become more or less important. The question is, "Under any condition, is kinship more important, or are other bonds?"

This brings us to the second question, namely the time dimension. If we measure at any time, it may well be that occupational bonds, local bonds, or others are more important than family and kinship structure; that is, people may have more contacts with their occupational peers, may use them more as reference groups, may get help from within the locality, may give help within it, and so on. At any time, this may be more important than a kinship structure, and this is in fact what is meant by the lessening importance of kinship. However, if measured over the years, we also find that the structure of locality and occupation involves different people. People change, there is turnover, there is mobility, and the same intensive relationship may occur with different people. Meanwhile, the background relationship with kin and the extended family remains stable. It is always the same person who is one's father, one's cousin, and whatever the different extended family relations are. Thus, if asked for a specific person to whom he might turn, a respondent might give a relative who is a constant person, instead of a person in a certain relationship (for example, neighbor) who may be a different person from time to time.

The third problem is what can be called the *need orientation*. In order to study the crucial problems in the relations of different members of the kinship structure, the researcher necessarily concentrates on the most visible points; that is, help, illness, financial help, and behavioral crises. Now, even in old persons, those are not the most common occurrences. Here, we probably get into the difference between what has been called interaction orientation and the discussion of people living together, and the discussion of what kinship structure really means when people do not live together. Again, the extent of time may play a crucial role. A certain relationship may be important in the event that a hurricane strikes or something like that, but people may get along for a long time, even sometimes a lifetime, without something like that happening. Part of this crisis orientation, of course, we get from the helping professions, social workers, physicians, public health nurses, who see the person when the crisis strikes.

Application to the Papers   These cautions may guard us against suddenly switching from exclusive attention to the nuclear family to exclusive attention to kinship structure. Except for people who succeed in blinding themselves completely because of theoretical presupposition, people have rarely accepted as a fact the position that the extended family does not matter at all. Hence, the main question is, "What kind of an extended family do we have?" and by this the author does not mean types, but more specifically, "What does the nuclear family do, who are the people who live together, which people do live together, and what is the meaning of relatives who do not live with you as compared with other people who do not live with you?" This again may be meant positively or negatively. LeVine did us a service in pointing out the stresses which may occur from the kinship structure. Now let us relate this discussion to aging and to the relationship of the adult child to the aged parents. Here we have evidence, especially from the three-nation study, that not living together does not diminish emotional ties and mutual reliance. Besides this negative statement, however, there are many problems which arise. It may be hard to understand the difference between the three nations by just concentrating on the family. It is, for instance, harder for the author to understand offhand why parents living with children are most frequently found in England, then in the United States, and least in Denmark. We may have the explanation for Denmark in its social services, but certainly England has better services than the United States. The larger prospects of comparing these relationships with different ones may give us some explanations.

Looking at the relation to age, we have to extend our vision a little further yet. Old people are not only different because they are old, but because they belong to a different generation. The supposed transition toward the nuclear family has been said to be generated just in that period in which the older generation of today was growing up. Therefore, the reaction of today's oldsters may not be predictive of today's generation two, the middle-aged, or generation three, the young. In fact, the adult child of today whose parents resist institutionalization may be quite willing to accept institutionalization when he is old. As the active member of the economy and the bearer of political power today, the middle-aged adult may even succeed in having acceptable institutions built before he needs them. Again, this is not thrown out as a definite fact, but as a possibility which should be taken into account before we get too far away from the concept of the nuclear family.

final suggestions

The papers on the three-generation family and on the question of kinship structure in the industrialized, urbanized Western world of today have given several suggestions:

1. The necessity of studying the family not by itself but as part of the society and of treating it in conjunction with the other social links within the whole society. It may be that too facile theorizing about this relationship is equally dangerous; such as industrialization and urbanization must lead necessarily to the nuclear family. But, in our studies, we should be able to compare these linkage systems and then see what strains they cause and what consequences they have.

2. This point follows from the one before. We need more facts and probably more methods for measuring these facts. The combination of the survey and the economic methods may be important, but still, what is the relative importance of the social intergenerational help and the direct individual help, or would people be willing to pay higher taxes and how much, if they were then completely relieved of any responsibility for other generations? The whole controversy about medical care for the aged may have something to do with this question. Similarly, methods can be found to evaluate the relative importance of the different linkage systems and especially the day-by-day importance of those systems. Is disengagement important, and if the disengagement theory is correct, then will the importance of all linkage systems decrease, or is disengagement theory just a rationalization of the middle generation?

3. Can our methods really predict a trend, or do we talk about the world situation at one point, and especially so in intergenerational studies? It becomes important to see each generation not only as part of an abstract social relationship to the other generations but also as a

representative of the progress of time. This is to say that this young generation when it becomes old may be really different from the old generation of today.

4. A special question is the relation of the professional, especially the social scientist, to the topics under study. How much of the theorizing and the direction of research is caused by the social situation, and even the personal situation, of the theorist, and how can that be overcome? That is, there are certain reasons which we can identify within a society which push social science once toward the nuclear, then to the extended family; and conversely, how far does this social scientist affect exactly the processes which he wants to study? How much has the influence of Freud, and even Parsons, affected not only social workers but their clients directly, and how can we know whether our studies use the influence of social science as part of the study of the social process?

intergenerational relationships: problems and proposals

IRVING ROSOW

Seldom has social science had the opportunity to settle disputes through a concise body of definitive research on which a discipline can clearly agree. Only rarely can such consensus be symbolized by a particular conference which represents the settlement of an issue. To some extent, the Duke Symposium is such a bench mark of the final respects paid to the isolated nuclear family before its interment. It culminated an intensive series of studies which destroyed the stereotype of this family as the modal, functionally optimal type in industrial bureaucratic society. As Marvin Sussman stated at one Symposium session: "The isolated nuclear family is a myth. This has already been conclusively demonstrated. It does not merit any further attention of the field, and I, for one, refuse to waste any more time even discussing it."

Indeed, in the past few years, work in America and abroad, including Symposium papers, leaves the issue in little doubt. Essentially, people in the modern world are embedded in extensive kinship networks, if not the classical extended family, rather than isolated in the family of procreation. The Duke Symposium may epitomize the final packaging of this finding, complete with the handle of accumulated documentation and the shiny ribbon of semiofficial consensus. Because of this informal settlement of the issue, any dissent after this Symposium may be raised only cautiously *sotto voce* with impregnable evidence. To this extent, the conference was significant.

But as in all scientific growth, the resolution of this problem opened up a new series of questions for study. The Symposium was rich in these. Consequently, the present paper will discuss several of these issues which were explicit or implicit in the proceedings. Although the author will range freely over the contributions, the discussion is drawn primarily from the following papers:

1. Margaret Blenkner, "Social Work and Family Relationships in Later Life with Some Thoughts on Filial Maturity."

2. Reuben Hill, "Decision Making and the Family Life Cycle."

3. Alan C. Kerckhoff, "Nuclear and Extended Family Relationships: A Normative and Behavioral Analysis."

4. Juanita M. Kreps, "The Economics of Intergenerational Relationships."

5. Eugene Litwak, "Extended Kin Relations in Industrial Democratic Societies."

6. Max Rheinstein, "Motivation of Intergenerational Behavior by Norms of Law."

7. Margaret Keeney Rosenheim, "Social Welfare and its Implications for Family Living."

Obviously, this discussion cannot be exhaustive. It will integrate several papers around some common problem and will handle other disparate points separately. The selected issues are not of comparable importance or complexity, and they do not demand equal time and attention. But all of them warrant some consideration.

conceptualizing family types

The conceptualization of families by Professors Litwak and Kerckhoff poses a basic problem: whether we shall work with descriptive or analytic types. We can operate either with global qualitative descriptions or with systematic typological constructs. In the absence of sharp criteria of judgment, the looser approach depends on impressionistic classification of families with the attendant problems of validity and reliability. The more rigorous approach specifies objective criteria and makes the typological schema exhaustive and mutually exclusive. These criteria also clarify the nature of the concept.

The descriptive types are liable to various difficulties. For example, consider one of Kerckhoff's unexpected findings which should not have been unexpected at all. On the basis of a review of the literature, he initially defined three family types: extended, modified extended, and nuclear. He then operationalized their differences by two variables: propinquity and aid. This presumably resulted in the following types:

family types	propinquity	aid
Extended	+	+
Modified extended	−	+
Nuclear	−	−

He investigated his problem in this framework and then encountered a troublesome latent fourth category in his behavioral typology which he called individuated. On analysis, this simply turns out to be the logically missing fourth combinations of + − on the propinquity-aid variables. Though starting with three descriptive types, he commendably indicated the criteria to distinguish them. But he did not apply them systematically to generate the exhaustive schema which they intrinsically encompassed. Obviously, the permutations of two independent variables necessarily yield *four*, not three, types. This is true under all conditions, even when one combination may be a logical, but not an empirical possibility.

Thus, his preliminary thought led to two variables which should then have been the new starting point for a disciplined construction of family types. Had he approached the problem in this way, he would have uncovered the four basic patterns and disclosed a gap in his original thinking about family types. For the missing + − pattern implies a distinctively different orientation than his other three types defined *a priori*.

This is only a simple illustrative case, for Kerckhoff's approach might not have differed materially even if he had constructed his types more systematically. But we cannot prejudge this by any means. For in considering the full set of combinations, he might have arrived at new factors which he had not previously considered or even at different hypotheses (and the failure of his second hypothesis indicates that some explanatory principle is still missing). In any case, a more disciplined approach would have avoided the intrusion of an unexpected type — one implicit in his logical schema and certainly not deviant (even statistically, for it contained more cases than either the nuclear or the modified extended families).

Litwak's case is similar in principle, but more complex, for his description is richer and more diffuse. In the Symposium paper and elsewhere, he invoked a larger range of descriptive factors which presumably distinguish family types: propinquity, hierarchical authority, nepotism or occupational involvement, pooled resources, continuing aid, reciprocal services, association, affection, socialization, tension management, and others. Litwak also limited his types *a priori* and proposed the following four: extended, modified extended, isolated nuclear, and dissolving.

Insofar as Kerckhoff and Litwak were both abstracting to the same problem of classification, it is significant that Litwak reached four types and Kerckhoff three, especially since Litwak's fourth (dissolving) is not Kerckhoff's latent fourth (individuated). Yet this is precisely the kind of difficulty with which typological construction can help. The specification of analytic variables can clarify such discrepancies and give some purchase on differences in analytic richness.

Yet Litwak did not sift his descriptive factors for their value as analytic elements or criteria for the distinction of his types. Had he done this, even as Kerckhoff started to do, he might have gone further toward clarifying his concepts.

One can, of course, suggest some factors which seem central to his analysis. For purposes of illustration, with no assumption that these factors are definitive or that Litwak would pick the same ones, let us arbitrarily abstract the following: propinquity, pooled resources, socialization, and affective bonds. Litwak's four types might then be distinguished as follows:

family types	propinquity	pooled resources	socialization	affective bonds
Extended	+	+	+	?
Modified extended		+	+	+
Isolated nuclear			+	+
Dissolving				+

Significantly, Litwak does not suggest an extended family rating on affective bonds, an omission which indicates the lacunae to which descriptive types are subject. But let us assume that it is + and that all other ratings are correct. In that case, the types resemble a Guttman scale: the more + attributes, the closer a type approximates the classical extended family; the fewer, the closer it is to dissolving.

More generally stated, these four family patterns represent *perfect* scale types on an implicit scale. The four dichotomous variables encompass sixteen combinations, of which Litwak's patterns are the first four pure scale types (the fifth being minus on all variables).

This has two major implications. If Litwak's classifications are pure scale types, then they vary according to these specific variables. The relative importance of the variables is ordered and in turn orders the pure family types. Analytic elements which do this are conceptually central to a problem. Therefore, the specification of criterion variables clarifies the nature of the family typology and what the concept subsumes. Variables which distinguish among family patterns and have high predictive power to critical dependent variables obviously may cast the basic concept in a new perspective.

However, an implicit scale of sixteen types means that Litwak's four types are certainly not exhaustive, and one wonders about their adequacy. How would an empirical distribution of families be divided among his four pure types and the other eleven or twelve patterns? If his types are truly adequate, a distribution should yield a .90 criterion of reproducibility for the full scale. And, types could then be collapsed according to normal scaling practice. In any case, it would certainly be important to test the adequacy of Litwak's proposal empirically. For if his types can be specified in analytic terms and absorb 90 per cent of American families, this in itself would have major value. But, if his types absorb only 60 per cent, then some further rethinking is necessary.

But this should not distract us from the central point. Typologies can be systematically and rigorously constructed. They may equal descriptive types in qualitative richness, imagination, and insight, and exceed them in clarity and sophistication. The specification of analytic elements not only sharpens definitions and reduces operational measures to their essentials, but also obliges us to assume critical responsibility for our ideas by testing, deepening, and strengthening our concepts.

functional integration of family and bureaucracy

Litwak has presented an important theoretical paper which is a logical extension of his previous work. Earlier, he questioned dubious assumptions about the nuclear family which had been uncritically taken for granted. His skepticism was instrumental in exploding the stereotype of the isolated nuclear family, though this may result in a new orthodoxy which we would find embarrassing. But this is a risk of originality.

In his Symposium paper, Litwak goes beyond nuclear family isolation to the general issue of family-bureaucratic integration in advanced societies. Although his analysis becomes fine-grained at various points, the overall problem formulation is too loose and does not tie together the basic parts of the problem clearly enough. Too much is left implicit and unfocussed. Therefore, we will first clarify our view of his problem as the basis of this discussion.

Litwak is concerned with two sets of variables: familial and bureaucratic. He proposes four ideal family types according to the implicit variables which we discussed in the preceding section. He then describes industrial democracy in terms of: (1) rational bureaucracy, (2) norms of ability, and (3) technological growth. These attributes are not only means, but become ends as well. The initial problem is the relationship between family types and these industrial democratic goals: which family type is most functional for the attainment of the industrial democratic ends?

Clearly, the industrial democratic goals are taken as givens. Then the problem requires criteria of family functionality. Litwak draws these from four *functional prerequisites* of industrial democracy: (1) geographic mobility, (2) occupational mobility, (3) the compatibility of other institutions with bureaucracies, and (4) "kinship efficiencies for goal achievement." Family types which maximize these prerequisites presumably are the most functional for bureaucratic society. Thus, the functional prerequisites are intervening variables between family operation and the goals of industrial democracy: their realization is necessary to sustain bureaucracy and technological progress.

Thus, the basic problem can be reformulated: *which of the family types maximizes the four functional prerequisites of industrial democracy?*

The balance of Litwak's paper considers the relation between family types and the functional prerequisites, notably that of "goal achievement." His analysis is summarized in four tables which show the modified extended family as the optimal type for a mature industrial democracy. It presumably maximizes geographic and occupational mobility (and a rational allocation of labor), use of both familial and bureaucratic resources, and shared functions between the institutional spheres, and it effectively resolves the conflict of bureaucratic and kinship norms.

Incidentally, some of the family ratings in these four tables seem arbitrary. For example, Table 13-2 ranks the kinship types' ability to utilize bureaucratic and family assistance. Here the rating criteria are unclear, although they could be easily clarified. What is the referent of the ratings: the *capacity* to use either form of aid, the sheer *need* of aid, the *available volume* of resources, or the *orientation* to different sources? In the absence of explicit criteria of judgment, this table and its underlying analysis run the risk of being tautological. However, such weaknesses are secondary and can be corrected, but possibly only at the expense of a basic revision of the four functional prerequisites themselves.

Nonetheless, Litwak is not dealing with trivial issues; he has raised a series of significant theoretical questions which can engage sociologists for years. This is an imaginative, searching "think piece" in middle-range theory. It is a measure of the complexity of the problem that Litwak has not achieved full analytic closure and pristine clarity in a single definitive paper, but further development is necessary. Therefore, this discussion will indicate some of the problematic areas which future theory and research may profitably address in an effort to refine the conceptualization. The following discussion cannot be exhaustive, but is limited to the more important issues.

The most problematic feature of Litwak's formulation is the ambiguity of goals and their referents. Whose goals are involved? Are family and bureaucracy to be analyzed in relation to the goals of industrial democracy (bureaucracy, competence, technological growth)?

Or, as we have inferred here, in terms of the functional prerequisites of industrial democracy (geographic and occupational mobility, institutional compatibility, and "kinship efficiencies")? Or, indeed, in terms of family objectives or functions? This is quite unclear.

The problem logically seems to require the functional prerequisites as the implicit ends or dependent variables (and the basis of criteria for family evaluation). But this creates some difficulties. For example, the prerequisite of compatibility of family and bureaucracy is virtually tautological, for this is the central problem under study. It demands explicit, *independent* criteria of compatibility rather than treating compatibility as its own undefined criterion. In other words, the problem cannot be properly solved by assertion, but requires independent objective standards to test effects.

This prerequisite leads to Litwak's analysis of uniform and non-uniform tasks and his theory of shared functions. Presumably all tasks contain both standard and idiosyncratic elements, which are optimally the respective provinces of bureaucracy and family. Bureaucracy can most effectively handle standard problems and the family idiosyncratic ones. This distinction between uniform and non-uniform elements is conceptually necessary, but the basis of their empirical classification becomes difficult, even in Litwak's illustrations. For example, fairly standard processes of socialization, tension management, motivating members, maintaining morale, and so on occur in both family and bureaucracy so that the institutions have overlapping rather than exclusive functions. Further, when nonuniform tasks are performed within the family, it is unclear how these tasks can distinguish among the family types. All the families are primary groups and presumably have such idiosyncratic tasks. Hence, how can the dissolving, isolated nuclear, and modified extended families be analytically differentiated by these functions? It would be difficult to maintain that even the dissolving family does not perform all these "nonuniform" functions or serves them less effectively vis-a-vis the functional prerequisites than the modified extended structure.

One might argue cogently that the family types differ in their intensity of conflict with bureaucracy over roles, ends, or loyalties. But this involves other variables outside Litwak's schema (although akin to his normative conflict). Such factors might be more fruitful and easier to operationalize than his variable of uniform and nonuniform tasks.

The articulation of functions between family and bureaucracy is, of course, a crucial matter. While his detailed analysis of their functional links is basically sound, Litwak has not conceptualized this linkage in the clearest, most powerful terms. Its place in his theory is still fuzzy and requires sharper delineation.

The ambiguous relationship between different segments of the problem is emphasized by his section on kinship exchange and dependency-autonomy of nuclear units vis-à-vis the larger kinship network. Here Litwak analyzes how family types meet internal needs. Do they achieve self-sufficiency and maximize dependency of constituent units on the total network or leave a residue of unmet needs which generates linkages with external bureaucratic structures? The analysis focuses strictly on internal kinship patterns without reference to their external consequences, particularly on the functional prerequisites of industrial democracy. Different mutual-aid patterns are obviously significant for internal functioning of the family network. But what is their general impact on family-bureaucratic relations and their specific effect on the attainment of the functional prerequisites? Litwak virtually ignores this and leaves it dangling in open-ended implication. These consequences cannot simply be assumed as self-evident, for they are at the heart of his problem and must at least be indicated explicitly. The internal patterns of differential aid, reciprocity, initiative, and conformity to normative occasions or kinship spheres are not equally relevant to family-bureaucratic interaction, nor do they necessarily have different implications for the functional prerequisites. For example, aid within the network may be competitive or not. But from this fact, we cannot simply extrapolate to relations between donor, donee, or the larger network and the functional prerequisites. This is the problem to be analyzed.

This shift in focus arises mainly from the ambiguity about goals and their referents. The dependent variable of the larger problem is vague and unclearly specified. We are floating around among several sets of possible referents, with no clear principle of relevance to discriminate among them. Therefore, the discussion tends to shift adventitiously from one to another rather than according to the demands of a clear-cut problem. Whose goals are, after all, at stake in the problem? Various social objectives represented by the functional prerequisites or those of industrial democracy or those internal to kinship units? Or indeed those of individual actors? How does the problem specify the proper goals? Until the dependent variable is clearly defined, the analysis of localized issues has no clear-cut frame of reference. And the relations between family and bureaucracy cannot be meaningfully articulated.

Thus, the major difficulty is theoretical: the problem definition, the specification of the dependent variable, the goals in focus, the relationship between parts of the problem, and the relevant criteria of judgment to be employed. Once this basic framework is worked out, the subsidiary issues can be clarified and can fall into perspective. But the sheer untanglement of the secondary issues has little effect on the formulation of the central problem. The consequential difficulty is essentially conceptual.

This must be borne in mind in the remaining discussion which considers some of these subsidiary issues. The definition of the central problem is crucial and takes precedence over the localized points below.

Litwak discusses the bases of power in American society. He postulates four: (1) technical competence, (2) reward and punishment (implicitly, the control of resources), (3) legitimation (or the consensus on norms of authority), and (4) group attraction (or reference orientations). He then analyzes the conditions under which the family or bureaucracy can exercise each type of power more effectively for "goal attainment." Presumably, this can clarify the optimal division of power and social labor.

Power may be an unfortunate concept here, and the analysis might be better served by another. Power is more relevant to total societies and large social units, including bureaucracies, than to primary groups and families where it may mean something else. Because of this ambiguity, the analysis tends to treat social and purely interpersonal influence as if they were synonymous and mixes them indiscriminately. Yet the two forms of influence cannot be casually equated. Not the least objection to this treatment is the different significance of personality in each context.

Further, Litwak's power bases are not exhaustive, nor are the variables on the same analytic level. For example, he does not mention role responsibility as a possible base, and it is only implicit in technical competence among those bases he lists. Although his discussion mentions the "man on the white horse" as a basis of bureaucratic "influence," he ignores charisma, as well as legal and traditional authority—even though some of the power bases inhere in the Weberian schema. And is legitimation on the same level of abstraction as technical competence or reward and punishment? Thus, there are difficulties about the exhaustiveness of power bases, the confounding of personal and social power, and possibly the concept of power itself.

But let us examine the discrete power bases more intensively. In his analysis of technical competence, Litwak distinguishes between uniform and idiosyncratic problems. He concludes: "Where knowledge was equal—in nonuniform situations where there is little public value—then the family primary group is in a much better position to implement goals than the trained specialist in the bureaucratic organization." He illustrates this with pushing a child from the path of an automobile, and finds the nonspecialist as competent as the professional. However, where knowledge of the trained and untrained is equal, then it is irrelevant. It begs the basic assumption of *relevant* competence by excluding expertise as a factor at all, thereby ignoring those situations where specialized training is germane to the exercise of power. The issue is not whether the family is more effective than bureaucracy in any rare idiosyncratic event, but only in that which involves specialized knowledge. For example, children and adults are

occasionally accidentally poisoned through carelessness, faulty prescriptions, defective food, leaving toxic substances accessible to children, and the like. Clearly, this is a rare, unpredictable event. But the
family cannot cope with this precisely because it involves technical
problems of biochemistry, physiology, and pharmacology. And expert
knowledge is required to select effective antidotes, a need which is
commonly met by emergency poison centers in many large cities. This
is quite a different problem from pushing a child out of the way of a
car. To be sure, many unpredictable, idiosyncratic events do not require special knowledge. But the critical variable in comparing family
and bureaucracy in the exercise of technical competence is not the
frequency of a problem, but the technical knowledge that it invokes.
The next question would concern the proportion of idiosyncratic
events that do require specialized knowledge.

In terms of reward and punishment as a basis of power, Litwak
again argues that the family can exercise this effectively in idiosyncratic, private situations while bureaucracy can use it in dealing with
uniform, consensual public situations. His gross analysis may be correct as a first approximation, but it requires further refinement to deal
with systematic variation. Litwak writes:

> ... the more idiosyncratic and private – rather than public – the behavior,
> the more difficult it is for the professional to use his special skills and
> facilities. By contrast, the primary group is in a better position . . . In
> such [private] situation, the primary group has the advantage of fairly
> continuous contact with its members. Moreover, the positive affect be-
> tween members makes it easier to penetrate most areas of privacy. Thus,
> adultery may be much more quickly spotted by primary group members
> than the police.

Of course, families do tend to have more access than other primary
groups to private information about members. But this is not invariably true, especially in areas of *segmental roles* and *normative devi-
ance*. Litwak's example of adultery is a fine case in point. To be sure,
"primary group members" may spot it more quickly than the police.
But the family may be the very last to learn about such violation of
norms precisely because it is the major target of concealment. At least,
that is the first administrative problem of the game. Indeed, the
French farce as an art form has subsisted for fully three centuries on
the stock character of the cuckold. Everybody in the world except the
poor devil himself seems intimately conversant with his spouse's lia-
sons. And he typically learns of them from some friend (or "friend"), a
primary group member outside the family. Adultery is only one sort of
deviant behavior which is effectively concealed from the family (children and adolescents know many more), but which typically comes to
the attention of other primary group members.

Furthermore, some private behavior, including normative viola-
tions that become known, may be more effectively controlled by reward and punishment of large groups, including bureaucracies, than

of the family. For example, gossip and censure informally regulate behavior in small towns and in community circles in large cities. Within formal organizations, control may be imposed by manipulation of opportunity, perquisites, reward, promotion, transfer, discharge, and other variables of career fate. The informal system, of course, has its own mechanisms. Thus, the critical factors in reward and punishment include the effective reference group and its control of an actor's success in terms of his motives and goals.

Segmental role behavior also involves differential ignorance because of differential exposure. Primary group members outside the family have knowledge about an actor in their role set (including those in bureaucracies) which the family shares much less.

Hence, several points are clear. First, families and other primary groups are *not* synonymous. Their power based on reward and punishment and that of bureaucracy will vary with the situation and other factors. Second, sheer amount of contact between actors is not always related to *visibility* of all behavior, especially in segmental roles and private normative violation. Third, control of public and private behavior through reward and punishment sometimes may be as effectively exercised by large groups, bureaucracies, and other primary groups as by the family. Fourth, a crucial condition of this power base is the relation between an actor's goals and reference groups, and their command of significant rewards and punishments. Fifth, *which* public and private behaviors can be effectively influenced through reward and punishment by family, other primary groups, and bureaucracy?

Finally, Litwak extends his uniform-idiosyncratic, public-personal distinctions to power based on legitimation and on group attraction. Again this may be adequate on a gross level, but it leaves several implicit problems. First, there is an underlying difficulty with the standard-idiosyncratic dichotomy. Of course, bureaucracy is the sphere of many standard, socially valued functions. But this does not reduce family functions to a residual category of the unpatterned, idiosyncratic, and privately valued. Indeed, the major family functions are institutionalized. They deal with standard, patterned cultural imperatives which are socially valued and widely shared. Socialization, the maintenance of class and ethnic norms, child care, mate-selection, occupational choice, career aspirations, and consumption patterns are clear instances of standard family problems. All are functionally significant in the society and are typically centered in the family rather than in formal organizations. The distinctive factor, then, is not sheer uniformity-idiosyncracy; uniform functions are not the simple touchstone of the optimal division of social labor between family and bureaucracy. This variable is an inadequate explanatory principle.

Other variables are necessary, and they apply equally to legitimation and group attraction. The uniform-idiosyncratic distinction may be supplemented, for example, by two of Parsons' pattern variables which discriminate the relevant role relationships. Standard tasks may be divided between family and bureaucracy according to the primacy of affective involvement-neutrality and expressive-instrumental goals. Clearly, the family can specialize in those standard functions requiring affective involvement (for example, socialization) and major expressive relations. This may be some help, but it is not the final answer. Many legitimate family functions remain instrumental. And although bureaucratic power cannot be legitimized by affective attachments, bureaucratic group attraction may be (for example, congenial faculty colleagues).

Quite apart from its sheer brevity, Litwak's treatment of legitimation and group attractiveness as power bases is incomplete. The normative basis of legitimacy requires closer analysis. The uniform-idiosyncratic and public-personal variables do not systematically discriminate legitimate familial and bureaucratic functions. Similarly, group attractiveness requires some rethinking. It might even be completely reconsidered as a significant power base. Possibly this factor is reducible to several more fundamental variables, such as dependency on the group and others.

In any case, a general need exists to sharpen the concept of power (if it is to be retained) and to delineate more closely its relation to the central theoretical problem.

Litwak concludes his analysis of uniform and nonuniform tasks by inquiring into their relative importance in industrial society. His reasoning centers on social change as endemic in such a social order. Change inevitably creates unpredictable new problems for which there is little advance socialization or training. Adaptation to these problems may routinize their handling, but it in turn tends to produce other novel, unexpected problems. Therefore, the idiosyncratic remains with us and maintains a sphere of efficient family operation. Thus, Litwak concludes, the family is the most effective institution for coping with unanticipated consequences of social change.

Change may indeed be endemic, and new situations continuously arise, sometimes from the institutionalized solution of earlier novel problems. This does not mean that all novel situations are equally significant or that rationality is steadily undermined by the diminishing returns of a Malthusian model of change in which solutions increase arithmetically while problems are generated geometrically.

But Litwak's analysis contains a major nonsequitor and a seriously misplaced emphasis. For he invokes the family as the distinctive compensator for bureaucratic inflexibility in the face of nonstandard problems. This is surely unwarranted. It ignores the most fundamental modern contribution to bureaucratic theory: the function of the *informal* system. If there is anything that we have learned about bureaucratic organization, it is that the informal system compensates for inadequacies of the formal system in dealing with atypical problems. It improvises and holds the fort until uniform formal procedures are developed. This is absolutely basic bureaucratic theory.

Invoking the family, an external structure, as the compensatory mechanism for new internal problems is literally an unwarranted *deus ex machina* solution. It begs the basic question of bureaucratic adaptation and inappropriately shifts the theoretical ground. Litwak arrogates to the family central bureaucratic processes with which the organization must cope. Nor are these functions significantly shared by the two institutions. To render appropriate functions unto the family is legitimate; but to expand these by indiscriminate definition is an unwarranted form of theoretical imperialism.

It would be theoretically significant to refine the division of family and bureaucratic labor in deeper terms of "kinship efficiencies." What functions — socialization, the development of aspirations, maintenance of motives, reinforcement of norms, and others — can the family perform more effectively than bureaucracy? In what terms can a complementarity between the institutional spheres be more fruitfully conceptualized and systematically analyzed? What are the most significant variables that distinguish optimal function? Possibly some theory of complementary specialization might improve on the theory of shared functions.

Several problems arise in Litwak's analysis of the family types' accommodation to the conflicting norms that govern family and bureaucratic role relationships. These norms adapt Parsons' pattern variables: the family is regulated by ascription, affectivity, expressiveness, diffuseness, and particularism, and the bureaucracy by performance, affective neutrality, instrumentalism, specificity, and universalism. Litwak contends that families accommodate to these "conflicting atmospheres" differently and that the modified extended family is the most successful type. It establishes "linkages" which keep it at an optimal "mid-point of social distance" from bureaucracy, enabling it to share functions, use bureaucratic resources, maintain internal kinship autonomy, and minimize role conflict.

But the contrasts of the other family types may be questioned. Litwak argues that the dissolving family cannot reconcile the different norms and effectively succumbs to the bureaucracy ". . . by losing its family character and adopting the milieu of the bureaucracy." Surely this is empirically untenable. There is no evidence that the dissolving family is more universalistic, instrumental, affectively neutral, and so on than the reverse; nor that it has adopted these norms significantly more than the isolated nuclear or modified extended families. Whatever the virtues of a symmetrical analysis, they do not warrant this conclusion.

Further, the classical extended family would resolve the normative dilemma ". . . by introducing nepotistic norms within the bureaucracy and thereby destroying the industrial bureaucracy." Presumably nepotism violates the cardinal bureaucratic requirements of affective neutrality, universalism, and performance. The general proposition is so basic that we seldom bother to question it.

But recent evidence raises the paradox that under some conditions nepotism and universalism might co-exist: universalism might function within a *nepotistic, particularistic field of eligibles.* Social change in India shows the persistence of caste as a principle of industrial recruitment and allocation. Key departmental supervisors or company executives systematically tend to recruit new labor from their own caste, often from their own village, so that the caste dominates the composition of the unit under supervision. Although this may not be the most rational principle of labor allocation, apparently it has not prejudiced performance and efficiency. Similarly, in Japan, the familiar paternalism of bureaucratic enterprises virtually assures a young person lifelong tenure with an employer once he is hired. Regardless of the company's economic vicissitudes (short of bankruptcy), the employee remains with the firm and makes his entire career there. Of course, this gives tremendous job security at the expense of labor mobility. While this may not seem optimally rational, Japanese industry and production are generally efficient.

The value of this evidence is not completely clear. The caste nepotism of India may be effective only because of a vast labor surplus that assures adequate competence in almost any ascriptive status group in the labor market. But we cannot judge the relative effects of universalism and particularism under conditions of severe labor shortage or balanced demand and supply. Similarly, in Japan, we cannot gauge the effect on industrial performance of labor mobility and immobility. Particularism might be relatively efficient under special conditions such as surplus labor or early industrialization, although large Japanese firms cannot be construed as primitive bureaucracies. On the other hand, Japanese technical development might have advanced more rapidly with universalistic labor allocation.

But, we may profitably reexamine some basic assumptions about the functional prerequisites of bureaucracy and principles of bureaucratic organization. We may seriously consider possible alternatives under various conditions. For other principles may be equally functional, especially in the framework of the total system. Universalism and geographic mobility might produce higher average performance on the job than nepotism and labor immobility. But lower cohesion, greater worker turnover, and lower commitment might reduce total output, raise overhead, and increase unit costs. So the advantages of the universalistic pattern might be more localized than general, more apparent than real under some conditions. Hence, alternative possibilities should be considered, and the functional prerequisites not taken as valid for all conditions. Possibly the nepotism and particularism of extended families might be compatible with bureaucracy at various times rather than invariably destroy it.

Finally, Litwak indicates that the nuclear family deals with the conflict of family-bureaucratic norms by the sharp isolation of the institutional systems. His analysis rests on Parsons, but his interpretation is overdrawn, and some perspective may be restored. Presumably, according to Parsons, normative conflict is reduced by separation of the two systems, mainly through a sex-linked division of labor that places only one family member in both systems. Litwak argues that this analysis assumes that family and bureaucracy operate in completely separate spheres, an assumption explicitly denied by his theory of shared functions. He asserts that excessive isolation would lead to a breakdown in linkages while being too close would lead to disruptive normative conflict. Consequently, he urges a "mid-point of social distance" as an ideal solution.

This reading of Parsons damns him unduly. Logically, reducing the number of participants in both spheres should minimize role conflict. But, more important, Parsons might argue that the crucial factor is the isolation of *roles* so that appropriate norms are clear and do not spill over between systems. Parsons' theory has always been based on a differentiated, integrated social system, and he would probably agree with Litwak's basic theory of shared functions (aside from details). While Parsons may have been incorrect about the predominance of the isolated nuclear family, we must recall that his main point of reference was the traditional extended family. And he saw this as inimical to bureaucratic organization, just as Litwak does. He did not consider the modified extended family explicitly, although there is nothing in his schema to exclude it. This is a refinement or subcategory that he did not reach. So much of the apparent disagreement is a matter of emphasis and timing, partly because Litwak is concerned with refinements beyond those of Parsons. When Litwak urges a "mid-point of social distance" (some separation) to minimize conflicting norms, is this essentially different from Parsons' urging of separation as a means of precluding normative conflict? The basic reasoning is the same—although Litwak does go on to examine linkages that Parsons gave little systematic attention. While there are genuine disagreements, those that reflect different concerns or emphasis are reconcilable. Hence, we should distinguish between specious and real issues. Some windmills are more equal for tilting than others.

The remainder of Litwak's analysis focuses on the last two functional prerequisites of industrial democracy—occupational and geographic mobility. He considers the main arguments that they are inimical to kinship solidarity and in each instance postulates counter-arguments. We will examine the case for occupational or social mobility and then for geographic mobility.

First, let us examine the view that invidious status distinctions lead to estrangement within the family. Litwak retorts that, in social contacts, status differentials create a symbiosis in which the higher-status member receives deference and the lower-status member gains prestigious association. Yet this ignores important evidence of very genuine strain and alienation that do develop with differential social mobility. For example, Peter Townsend reports that in London, nonmobile children showed intimacy, close contact, and affection for aged parents while mobile children had infrequent, ritualistic contact and were essentially estranged. Hence, the possible symbiotic gratification was not compelling enough to sustain close, solidary relationships.

Second, let us look at the view that differential socialization and life styles lead to alienation. Litwak denies "... that these differences are of sufficient magnitude to prevent family identification across class lines." Obviously, this is strictly an empirical matter to be settled in research. However, the issue is not whether mobility eliminates identification, but whether it significantly weakens it, and to what extent. Litwak asserts that the differences in basic values and aspirations are not really very great, and that the successful achievers (the mobile) personify the stable group's aspirations and thereby reinforce the latter's identification. Research shows that the values of mobile groups are between those of their class of origin and their class of achievement, although generally closer to the latter than to the former. This does not vitiate genuine value differences between mobile and stable kin. Nor does it follow that aspiring failures continue to identify with successful aspirants—particularly when their relationship may be complicated by sibling rivalry and so on. Invidious distinctions between people with similar aspirations, but different success contain massive forces of alienation. Although this may not apply to noncompetitors with different aspirations, Townsend's evidence is not encouraging on this score. In any case, this is a problem of reference group theory. The conditions under which identification persists between stable and mobile kin must be studied.

Third is the view that differential mobility is inconsistent with a stable power structure. Litwak replies that disrupted authority is balanced by a confederation of autonomous modified extended family units. This again is an empirical issue whose resolution largely depends on the concept of balance. That one pattern changes into another is apparent. But that they are functional equivalents is another matter which cannot simply be taken for granted. In any case, the idea of balance or adequate compensation must be defined, not only for clear criteria of judgment, but simply for the problem to be examined in a stable frame of reference.

Generally, Litwak's counter-arguments about kinship solidarity seem tenuous. Even if they were correct, they only indicate redeeming features, conditions which *moderate* the disruptive effects of differential occupational mobility. Voluntary association tends to be selective among peers, confined to those of similar status; conversely, status differentials discourage informal contact. This is an elementary fact of social stratification. Furthermore, Homans has shown the direct relationship, even in primary groups, between interaction and sentiment. So the overall hypothesis may be drawn that status differentials discourage interaction and undermine sentiment. Consequently, with differential mobility, change should definitely develop toward *weaker* kinship bonds and greater estrangement—even though normative obligations and affective ties may persist. Indeed, Litwak later concedes in another context: "There is no need to argue that [the strength of] identification is the same as that which distinguished the traditional extended family." Hence, the direction of change is not problematic. But in view of some inevitable decline in closeness and solidarity, the *strength* of the residual bonds remains in question.

Litwak also raises objections to several familiar arguments that geographic mobility is inimical to kinship solidarity. First, let us consider the view that high family identification significantly prevents residential mobility. He denies this and argues that extended kin can and do legitimize such mobility. He may well be right. There is no hard evidence to our knowledge that extended kin systematically discourage occupational and residential mobility. Indeed, even in classic folk tales, the young boy who goes into the world to seek his fortune leaves behind him heavy hearts, but carries his family's blessings (legitimacy and encouragement) and a full knapsack (assistance). But the next two points are more problematic.

Secondly, let us consider the view that it is hard for extended kin to preserve a close-knit group by migrating together or to the same locality because of job scarcity. Litwak retorts that diverse local opportunities are congenial to such group migration. He also adds: "...the extended family can coalesce geographically without going counter to the demands of a rational division of labor." Thus, presumably maintaining the integrity of the extended kinship group does not prejudice an optimal allocation of labor.

But we must be careful about this. Litwak's analysis is most applicable to kin who are occupationally *homogeneous* and enter the same segment of the labor market. Then, aside from special problems, such as the discrimination against older workers, kin may be able to settle together in a locality where there are jobs. The real problem arises, however, with occupationally *heterogeneous* kin who are in different labor force categories. In this case, propinquity becomes a function of opportunity, or relative labor *demand*, not supply. One cannot assume with Litwak that local opportunities cover the diverse range of employment required by the family. Local labor-market demand is not necessarily uniform for all skills. It may be high for scarce labor categories and nonexistent for others. The forces which govern rational labor distribution are sensitive to the needs of the entire labor

market, especially in labor scarcities, and insensitive to the preferences of occupationally heterogeneous families. Therefore, the
effective opportunity for collective *geographic* mobility may be limited by differential *occupational* mobility within the family, except
under conditions of pervasive labor shortages. Mobile workers with
different skill levels must be willing to pursue shifting market opportunities as *nuclear* family units, for extended kin are no viable unit
of labor supply.

Third, let us examine the view that it is hard for the geographically
mobile to maintain identification with extended kin over distance.
Litwak counters that modern communication does enable identification to be preserved, at least to the extent of sustaining mutual aid in
the family network. His earlier research and Marvin Sussman's recent
studies certainly bear this out. Reciprocal obligations and assistance
in crisis are maintained by the modified extended family.

But these functional supports cannot be casually equated with
strong emotional ties or with the close identification resulting from stable workaday association. As the earlier discussion showed, reduced
contacts from occupational or residential mobility necessarily weaken
the intensity of sentiment and the closeness of affective bonds. In other
words, there may well be a flow of help in emergency, but with the
reduction of intimate contact, there must also be an inevitable waning
of feeling. Insofar as mobility has increased in recent decades, we may
even be in a transitional period in which the modified extended family
is a *temporary* form in a historical shift from the traditional extended
to the isolated nuclear families. Such a shift may have weakened emotional ties without yet destroying the normative obligations which
support mutual aid. But another generation or two might see the decay
of sentiment below the threshold necessary to sustain normative obligations. (In that case, Parsons may have been off chiefly in his timing,
and contemporary isolated nuclear families may actually be advanced
cohorts of a general family change.) Of course, this is pure speculation,
but it touches on a definite theoretical possibility. Nonetheless, it is
important to investigate two problems: the extent to which mutual aid
and emotional closeness may vary independently in the kinship network; and the degree to which normative obligations are maintained
with increasing emotional distance.

Several problems also appear in Litwak's Table 13-4 which summarizes the analysis of geographic mobility. On the legitimation of
geographic mobility, he rates the dissolving and nuclear families as
very high, but the modified extended family only *high*—a purely arbitrary distinction without any discernible basis. And, on available
financial resources, he rates the modified extended family *high*, but
the traditional extended family only *moderate*. This is surely untrue or
at least unwarranted as a strict function of the family types per se
(independent of such correlates as living standards or productivity of

the total economy). In this rating, is the key factor "availability" of existing resources or their amount? Is the traditional extended family less sympathetic to migration of its members, and does it withhold resources as a means of discipline, control, and disapproval? If this should be the case, then "availability" would be a function of legitimation rather than a true independent variable. Thereby, available resources would be contaminated and not independently measured. Furthermore, it is dubious that the total evaluation would accurately predict the relative frequency of migration resulting from the family variables (aside from other migration determinates). Do family factors really enable modified extended families to migrate more than the isolated nuclear or dissolving kinship unit? Or have members of traditional extended families migrated significantly less, whether in contemporary life (for example, the Southern Negro and Puerto Rican migration to Northern cities) or historically (for example, the American immigration of 1870-1910)? Certainly legitimation and available resources seem central to family influences on geographic mobility. But other variables may also be important in distinguishing those conditions—antagonistic, necessary, and sufficient—which account for the kinship structure's effect on migration.

Finally, at the conclusion of his paper Litwak enters a curious disclaimer that calls into question much of his analysis. In pointing out some possible limitations of his approach, he states:

> In the presentation thus far the assumption has generally been made that one family type is ideal for most of the demands of an industrial democracy. Empirical research and further theory might well lead to a more complicated assertion which is: one family type is most desirable in satisfying one of these criteria of industrial democracy, and another family type is more desirable in satisfying another. This means that the investigator might not be able to suggest a single type of family structure as most important in industrial society, but instead must confront society with the legitimacy of different types.

Obviously his awareness of alternative prospects is excellent. But why so late? At this point, he introduces for the first time the possibility that optimal family types may vary according to the functions under consideration. But this qualification never figured in his initial premises and may be responsible for some of the ambiguities that developed in his treatment. Indeed, if the problem had allowed for variably optimal structures, then the ambiguity of goals might not have arisen so sharply. The goals (or functions) might have been more systematically specified. But Litwak's implicit hypothesis was not quite so flexible. His assumption was not simply that "one family type is ideal" for industrial democracy, but specifically that the modified extended family was that ideal type. Hence, his analysis concentrated on the functional linkages between it and bureaucracy. This was fine as far as it went, but it did not go far enough. As we have seen, the analysis encountered many conceptual and substantive difficulties. And there was no corresponding attention to possible disfunctional linkages (without prejudging what these might be). In other words, the analysis did not cover the full range of possibilities.

What seems to be lacking is the consideration of possible alternatives. The linkages between bureaucracy and other family types seem prematurely written off. The dissolving and isolated nuclear families implicitly seem more closely linked to bureaucracy than the modified extended family, closer than his "mid-point of social distance." But this does not seem disfunctional for *bureaucracy* and the *functional prerequisites*. (If the lack of kinship linkages is disfunctional for the *family unit*, this too must be set into perspective by the focus of the problem.) Closer attention to the problem definition and the criterion variables, the functional prerequisites, might have kept strategic alternatives in perspective.

And other alternatives are also theoretically germane. For example, could other societies (for example, Japan, India, the USSR) attain efficient industrial bureaucracies with different family types? If so, how? And how could this prospect be accommodated by Litwak's theory of institutional integration? Would such alternative types rest on different variables? Do the functional prerequisites exhaust the goals crucial for institutional integration? Can those chosen simply be taken as definitive? Are there conflicting cultural goals which are relevant to the central problem and which may ultimately account for some of the tenuous points of analysis?

None of this discussion of Litwak's paper is intended as pejorative criticism. The very subtlety and complexity of his problem virtually precludes an exhaustive, definitive analysis on the first attempt. Indeed, the central concepts and variables may have to be developed in several stages and refined in a series of successive approximations. Therefore, this discussion is intended solely as a guide to those issues which require clarification. For all its problematic aspects, the paper is a major, significant attack on a profound theoretical problem. Litwak has raised strategic issues and any shortcoming in their analysis can definitely be redeemed.

intergenerational transfer payments

Professor Kreps' paper provides a vital perspective on intergenerational relationships in the context of the total society. Her simple, trenchant arguments focus on factors which public officials and social scientists may ignore only at the expense of the older generation whose welfare presumably is at stake. She considers the basic developments of the economy, those changes which determine or limit the life chances and social position of older people – their employment, earnings, social roles, dependence and independence, general life conditions and relationships in the later years. In other words, as Professor Kreps indicates, the economic facts of life govern the range of effective policy alternatives.

This economic picture is clear-cut. The American economy has attained enormous productive potential which, despite complaints about its sluggishness, continues to grow significantly. Technology and automation have had tremendous impact on this growth, and their expansion promises to accelerate in the future. The technical and scientific basis of this increasing productivity, of course, will make the economy more complex and demand greater skills and sophistication of its workers. These trends will have several immediate effects: (1) sheer productivity will steadily reduce the size of the necessary labor force, (2) higher technical qualifications required for new entrants to the labor force will prolong the period of young adults' education, (3) scientific advance and technological refinement will accelerate the obsolescence of mature workers and generate pressures for their early retirement, (4) the length of work life, consequently, will be significantly shortened (and the United Auto Workers is already making formal proposals to this end), and (5) there will be a growth of nonproductive young and old generations outside the labor force. The young will be in training and the old obsolete; productive work life will be concentrated in a diminishing period of middle age. Hence, the dependency ratio of nonworkers to workers will increase. *Earned* income, therefore, will be largely confined to the working middle generation, while the old and young (dependent generations one and three) will essentially live on *nonearned* income.

With earlier retirement and gradually lengthening life expectancy, the older generation faces a long period without earnings — one which eventually may become as long as the dependent period in youth before entering the labor force. Hence, the vital problem in the later years is basically that of *income* and income maintenance.

As we have seen, this cannot be solved through dependence on wages and salaries. Neither does the solution essentially lie in transfers of *wealth* to the older generation, for Max Rheinstein has shown that such transfers normally flow from the old to the young. Nor do income-bearing *investments* offer much hope for income maintenance, for only a small, perhaps insignificant, minority of the aged have such investments. In youth and middle age, the consumption and expenditure pressures of raising a family and educating children effectively drain the income of most wage earners. These workers cannot sustain a large enough investment portfolio for an adequate retirement income. While private investments may conceivably yield minor increments as frosting on the retirement income cookie, this cannot meet the basic needs of the older generation as such. Hence, successful income maintenance strategies cannot be based on transfers of wealth or private investments.

We will presently consider some alternative approaches to income maintenance. It will become apparent that many of the relevant issues involve not only specific economic beliefs, but broader social philosophy as well. While economic problems may be objectively analyzed (often on the basis of premises which are neither self-evident nor universally accepted), social values are less amenable to rational demonstration. Nonetheless, the basic issues must be explicated.

The first general problem is Professor Kreps' point about the proper locus of fiscal responsibility for the older generation. Specifically, to what extent is income maintenance to be the province of the family or of the economy and nation as a whole? Professor Kreps appropriately insists that the kinship structure cannot assume the responsibility for stable financial support because of limited resources and legitimate competing claims on these resources. Many families are simply too insolvent to support aging parents and relatives directly. Furthermore, as Reuben Hill demonstrates, the balance between resources and needs is not always sensitively adjusted throughout the family life cycle, so that surplus and deficit vary irregularly from one period to another. Typically, aged parents in generation one require help when generation two may be under severe financial pressure in educating generation three and helping generation three through the early stages of marriage and family formation. With these cross-pressures, generation two must establish priorities of need, and this may commonly come at the expense of generation one. The justice of this is at the moment irrelevant. But balancing equitable benefits (between generations one and three) and equitable sacrifices (among members of generation two) may generate severe internal family strains.

The critical factor, however, is that even the pooled resources of modified extended families may be inadequate for the diverse needs within the kinship structure. They cannot cover short-term emergencies (as, for example, medical or business) *and* heavy expenses for moderate periods (for example, college education) *and* moderately heavy expenses for long periods (that is, retirement income). Therefore, however effective the larger family unit may be in meeting limited financial emergencies, it cannot be equally effective in maintaining retirement income, except at the expense of other more valued or pressing claims. Thus, financial responsibility can only be stablized outside the family.

In summary, earnings, wealth, investments, and the family offer no firm prospect of adequate income maintenance. The fundamental strategy must center on *transfer payments in the larger economy,* whereby current earnings are redistributed from the productive to the dependent generations in the form of social insurance. There are no viable alternatives to this basic approach.

Actually, there are only two possible bases for retirement income:

(1) private pension plans, and (2) social insurance or a public system of social security. The choice between them can seldom be resolved on the purely rational basis of sound economics, for it often involves arbitrary assumptions about objective issues or value premises which can only be asserted, but not demonstrated. Let us briefly consider these alternatives.

Despite their proliferation, private pensions are still quite limited in the number of people they cover and will remain so at least for another decade. Indeed, many groups of workers probably never will be covered by private plans. But even for those who are covered, private pensions have certain disadvantages. The first, of course, is that inflation reduces real retirement income, which is not compensated by increased benefits. Secondly, coverage tends to be inequitable, favoring the higher-income ranks of professional and managerial employees and discriminating against the least secure manual workers. Third, equity in private plans is not transferable and discourages labor mobility. If workers are mobile, they move through a series of jobs with and without pension systems. At best, they patch together a retirement income quilt based on diverse programs in different companies, a complicated and inconvenient arrangement. Fourth, the beneficiary of private pension plans does not have the consumer's freedom of choice in the market, but is subject to the decisions of administrators who select the group plan and the insuring company. In the choice of program, cost advantages to management may take precedence over retirement benefits to the individual. Fifth, no private pension plan can cover as many persons as a vast public program, which can by its size minimize rates through high volume. By this principle, veterans' insurance premiums are only fractions of the lowest charged by private firms for comparable coverage. Finally, one may question the very propriety of public services such as retirement income being commercial enterprises.

As a public program, social security obviates most of these disadvantages. Previously uninsured persons, whether or not they are profitable risks, can be covered by legislative action. The effects of inflation can be counteracted by legislation to raise benefit levels and preserve real income. A centralized program, administered by a single agency, can assure continuity of standard coverage despite job changes. Governmental programs are subject to public scrutiny, and their deficiencies are amenable to legislative correction through organized political action. A federal program eliminates conflicts of interest in selecting an insuring agency. Major savings are possible when insuring a vast public, especially if corporate profits are not required. These savings can be reflected in higher benefits for any given level of contributory premium.

Clearly, the choice between private and public insurance may be governed by ideological as well as purely economic considerations.

This may be quite appropriate insofar as basic social philosophies are involved. Yet interminable arguments under the guise of economic controversy may only obscure the underlying value conflict when this should be exposed and engaged.

To make the author's own bias clear: the author is unequivocally in favor of social insurance. There are general and specific reasons for this. In the area of social problems, the author is convinced that common goals are not only worthwhile, but necessary, and that policies about them must be clear and explicit, bolstered by strong programs and strong commitment. The author does not believe that they can be entrusted to private enterprise, if only because of the conflict of interest that they engender. Such social objectives have strong economic and social consequences which are too important to yield up to practices of the market place. Social insurance in particular must rest solely on principles of public obligation and the common good without regard to private profit. Responsibility for economic security should neither depend on the dubious ability of individuals to provide adequately for their own old age in a society based on maximum personal consumption throughout life nor on competition for the limited resources of extended families. Insofar as conflicting interests of public and private groups are involved, this problem will eventually have to be fought out in the political arena where the essential issues that go beyond the few raised here may see the light of day.

The affluence and productivity of the total economy can compensate for the major weaknesses of both private pension schemes and individual family resources if the government is free to exercise public policy in this area on behalf of the larger society. Retirement income can be adequately assured if the problem of intergenerational support can be completely divorced from the individual family and dealt with in a framework of *total generations,* as Professor Kreps has proposed. Then national resources can be allocated among generations on the basis of productivity and need through the mechanism of transfer payments. In other words, social programs of adequate retirement income can be stabilized without either making the older generation a hostage to fortune dependent on family patronage or subjecting it to the humiliation and strain of chronic competition for scarcities within the family.

The transfer payments principle entails several problems. The first involves a set of policy decisions regarding allocation: (1) How much of the Gross National Product will be required for transfer to generations one and three, the old and the young, and (2) how will this amount be divided between the dependent generations, that is, the ratio of old/young transfers? These questions raise pure value choices in the selection or redefinition of those national goals to which we are willing to be committed—notably the balance between private consumption expenditures and social welfare expenditures. Further, by what principle will priorities be assigned to the general range of competing public claims (for example, education, conservation of resources, urban renewal, regional planning, public recreation, highways, and the like) and to the relative welfare of young and old in particular (for example, education and the prevention of delinquency as opposed to retirement income and medical care)?

The second set of problems concerns the mode of financing transfer payments. As Juanita Kreps clearly indicated, any principle of social security is a means of prorating earnings over a lifetime. Social security taxes are always collected on the earnings of generation two (the middle generation) during its productive years. Theoretically, these taxes may be handled in one of two ways. They may be transferred promptly to retired contemporaries in generation one, the old. Or, they may be reserved in a fund until generation two gets old and retires to claim the benefits that it paid in. In either case, income is prorated over the lifetime since it is spread out over a longer period than the work life itself. But the alternative modes of financing differ significantly. Private pension plans provide funding, whereas the social security scheme does not.

The funded reserve resembles the equity of personal savings, except in that funds are accumulated in one account from which people withdraw pensions roughly proportional to their deposited contributions. Thus, the fund is strictly cumulative and grows very large. It may become huge during the decades after its establishment because the premiums paid into the fund greatly exceed the benefits paid to retirees. And it remains huge.

At first, the funds collected through the social security tax also accumulated in this fashion, since the benefits were minimal during the early years. In recent years, however, this program has shifted to a pay-as-you-go plan, with benefits being roughly offset by tax receipts for any year. Thus, current claims are essentially financed by current contributions. A much smaller reserve is held as a contingency fund to stabilize payroll tax levels against the effects of short-run fluctuations of the economy and labor force while social security claims hold steady or increase. And the social security tax levels can be geared directly to present, not future benefit levels. This eliminates the need for huge reserves whose accumulation may adversely affect fiscal policy. Also, it is possible to reduce the effects of inflation by providing retired persons with current income measured in real terms. Thus, the benefit levels under the social security program can be sensitively adjusted not only to changing prices but also to increasing productivity. Thereby, benefits and taxes reflect the same set of economic forces instead of one lagging a generation behind the other.

Although funded private pension plans enable workers of generation two (those in the middle years) to provide for a guaranteed fixed income in retirement, the financing of such plans has significant shortcomings. Payment of annuities from these funds is a transfer payment for which no service is currently being rendered. Consequently, the pension paid the retired worker is based on "obsolete" dollars, so that the fund provides absolutely no protection against inflation which systematically erodes the real value of the annuity. At any given time, payments into the fund are predicated upon future premium levels, but after three or four decades of inflation, the pension the fund may provide may prove completely inadequate for satisfactory income during retirement. Thus, the major problem presented by the funded reserve is the declining value of retirement pensions owing to inflation, and long-run inflationary trends are well established. This inflationary effect only exacerbates the inequities of differential annuities which are governed by length of service in a company and the amount of income earned in this period by workers who are covered by these plans.

The rapidly rising productivity of recent decades underscores the importance of conceiving retirement income in terms of the economy as a whole, divorced from individual family responsibility. For productivity gains can be diverted to those social objectives that we choose, simply as a matter of social policy, without reference to the resources or decisions of individual family networks.

adequate retirement income

Discussion of transfer payments almost invariably leads to the problem of adequate social security benefits. Because of our productivity and affluence, this is not a genuine economic issue, but purely one of values: how much of our Gross National Product are we willing to expend on retirement income?

This value judgment underlies Professor Rosenheim's basic question: how much is an adequate retirement income? The problem invokes contrasting perspectives on social security. At one extreme of a continuum is the rugged individualism of some citizens which denies both the virtue and the necessity of any social security system at all. Indeed, crude proponents of this view often regard social security as a fundamental affront to human integrity and self-reliance.

In the middle of the continuum is the basic philosophy of our own Social Security system, namely, to provide some token retirement income as a minimum shield against sheer destitution. Social Security benefits have been abysmally low from the outset and remain so now. Revisions in benefit levels were first made in 1950 and on three subsequent occasions during the fifties, all coincidentally during election years, and again in 1961. These increases in benefit level managed to keep pace with rising prices. The original benefits were so low, however, that the level of payments still remains inadequate. A retiree in 1940 received an average monthly benefit of $22.60 (or $47.10 in 1959 dollars). By 1959, this payment had increased to $55.10. A worker who retired in 1954 started with an average benefit of $66.10 (or $73.15 in

1959 dollars). Subsequent adjustment raised this to $71.00 in 1959 (a drop in real income over these five years). Social Security is important because it is by far the major source of retirement income,[1] both in dollars and in number of recipients. Yet, despite the increases in benefits, their average levels do not approach the Bureau of Labor Statistics standards for a modest but adequate budget.[2] Many beneficiaries draw the present minimum monthly payment of $40. Even doubling this for a single person or quadrupling it for a married couple would not suffice for the bare essentials of a decent, dignified life.

Furthermore, retirees have by no means shared in the general prosperity of the United States. Between 1940 and 1960, average Social Security payments (in adjusted 1959 dollars) have increased by only 17 per cent as compared to an increase of over 50 per cent in average real income (after taxes) of the population as a whole.[3] Thus, despite adjusted benefit levels, retirees on Social Security have fallen behind in relation to younger generations and to our gross output of goods and services. Certainly retirees have enjoyed less than one-third of a *pro rata* share of our increased productivity in the past generation.

The proliferation of private pension plans since the war simply documents the gross inadequacy of present Social Security benefits. If Social Security payments did support decent living standards, the pressures for supplementary private pensions would be weak. But private pension plans reflect a genuine market and an actual need. To this extent, they indicate the completely inadequate levels which Social Security affords. Indeed, it is the exceptional case, in which even home-owning recipients of maximum benefits can manage comfortably solely on these benefits alone.

The reasons for adopting such inadequate standards for Social Security payments are another matter. In part, these reflect the pressures of large employers to limit the earnings which are subject to Social Security taxes (a major sum for large employers). Furthermore, workers themselves probably are loath to pay increased Social Security taxes and reduce current earnings. Although this attitude may seem shortsighted, its consequences are independent of its causes.

The low levels of taxable earnings and benefits under Social Security reflect our national values. We place a premium on children and youth (the future) and on current consumption of consumer goods

---

[1] Lenore A. Epstein, "Sources and Size of Money Income of the Aged," *Social Security Bulletin*, XXV (January, 1962), 12-17; and "The Aged in the Population in 1960 and Their Income Sources," *Social Security Bulletin*, XXIV (July, 1961), 3-10, *et. seq.*

[2] Margaret S. Stotz, "The BLS Interim Budget for a Retired Couple," *Monthly Labor Review*, LXXXIII (November, 1960), 1141-57.

[3] White House Conference on Aging, *Background Paper on Impact of Inflation on Retired Persons* (Washington, D.C.: Government Printing Office, July, 1960), pp. 18-23.

(the present) rather than on retirement (the past). To this extent, the Protestant ethic may be declining in our pragmatic society. But, our low Social Security benefits indicate that the aged have a low status, that we place a low value on nonproductivity, and that claims on income are legitimized by *current* rather than former productive roles. Thus, as a nation, we have little use for people who retire, despite our pious disclaimers and protestations. For in our Social Security decisions, we are restricting possible income and thereby withholding from the retired the foremost material symbol of status that we can confer—money. Indeed, low retirement income itself may be one of the greatest barriers to a new valuation of retirement leisure in our society.

The other end of the ideological continuum assumes that social insurance should be more than a minimum barrier against destitution; it should be adequate to support people in comfort and security according to some norm, such as the Bureau of Labor Statistics standard budgets. Elsewhere we have proposed Social Security revisions which essentially call for genuinely adequate income in retirement, assured by automatic revision of benefits according to fluctuations in the price index, and extension of coverage to *all* nonworking household heads or survivors who reach retirement age.[4] These revisions are based on the premise that older people should have a decent living standard and an equitable share of our economic growth. Put another way, benefit levels should not simply trail haltingly along with prices, but retirees should be entitled to greater benefits in accordance with increased productivity and workers' rise in *real* income.

The issues discussed here represent genuine value choices in any social security problem. The Social Security program adopted reflects the actual decisions made about these values. The purpose of setting forth the three alternative positions is to clarify their ideological assumptions. One can argue cogently enough in favor of any of the alternatives, but the determinate factors in a choice ultimately are value commitments.

The author's conviction is that we can afford many social programs without impoverishment or even serious sacrifices of our personal comfort. To be sure, we may gain some of the benefits of adequate retirement income (or superior education or urban renewal, and the like) at the expense of other things. But the choice is clearly our own and is, regretably, being made quite consciously. We are choosing between alternatives in which adequate retirement income and other social programs compatible with our productivity and purchasing power literally are being opted *against*. Our preference for military investments, private consumer goods, and personal luxuries leaves too

[4]Irving Rosow, "Old Age: One Moral Dilemma of an Affluent Society," *Gerontologist,* II (December, 1962), 182-91.

little for social investments such as an adequate retirement income.

We are indebted to Professor Rosenheim for raising the question of adequate retirement income because this query exposes the value problems at the very heart of all the discussion of the economic issues in old age.

composite institutional studies

The papers of Professors Kreps and Hill open the prospect of a complementary study of support between generations. Kreps focuses on intergenerational transfer payments in the larger economy, independent of the family. Conversely, Hill could examine support between generations within the family, independent of the economy. Taken together, the two perspectives encompass Litwak's general problem of the sharing of economic functions by families and bureaucracies. Admittedly, both sets of data have limitations: public figures are crude, incomplete, and unrefined, and they combine categories that should be separate in intergenerational analysis; Hill's sample is localized and selective, and he has no intensive data on income sources. But both these weaknesses could be corrected, so that the combined approaches could give a composite picture of intergenerational support.

The two perspectives could be integrated in highly refined, sophisticated research on income sources and expenditures. This would be based on a coordinated study of *public transfer payments* and a *sample survey of families.* The advantage of combining them lies in relating public transfers to other income *at the family level.* If both levels were studied in the same terms, this would clarify the effectiveness of public economic programs and their articulation with familial and other institutional resources. Without such a composite design, one cannot now relate the disparate data from current studies on each level.

On this basis, one would first classify public transfer payments (certainly federal and as much of state and local data as possible) in terms of sources and beneficiaries by *age groups*. This would be supplemented by the sample survey of income sources and support payments within family units in the same set of categories. The two sets of data would complement one another so that gaps at one level might be filled by tentative extrapolation from the other. Thereby, one could approximate the role of various public funds (for example Social Security, unemployment compensation, civil service retirement, aid to dependent children, old age assistance, federal scholarship) in conjunction with extra-familial private income (for example, earnings, private pensions) and supports within the family (for example, regular contributions, payment of rent or medical bills, gifts).

One possible model for such a study is Wassily Leontief's input-output analysis of production.[5] Leontief divides the total economy into different sectors and distributes among these sectors investment or capital sources and production of goods and services. Thereby, capital production (output) of one sector is distributed as investments (inputs) in other sectors as a basis of their production (output). In this manner, not only can the productivity of each sector and its significance in the total economy be assessed, but the functional connections of each sector can be specified.

Despite its complexity, this model is conceptually related to sociometric methods in sociology. The categories in this model are variations of a basic "from-to" or "who-whom" schema. In Leontief's work, the categories are units of economic structure (sectors), while in sociometry they are units of group structure (members). But their objectives are similar: the synthesis of more complex structural aggregates and the analysis of their relationships. The conceptual framework is flexible and can accommodate different categories and substantive problems.

A simple sociometric table basically organizes group members' reciprocities in the manner shown in Figure 15-1.

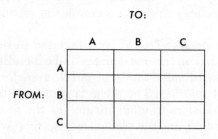

fig. 15-1   members' choices

This allows a complete distribution of all members' choices in terms of the person choosing and the chosen person. From these base data, cliques, reciprocal preferences, stars, and isolates can be abstracted as components of group structure. Thus, the connections between parts of the system can be specified.

Similarly, Leontief's input-output analysis can be adapted to the problem of intergenerational supports, for such supports are conceptually similar to sociometric choices. Payments (outputs) are like choices given, while income sources (inputs) are like choices received. This might be schematized in the oversimplified illustration shown in Figure 15-2.

Here the basic approach is slightly elaborated, but the complexity centers on details rather than the overall framework. The problems

[5]Wassily Leontief, *et. al., The Structure of the American Economy, 1919-39* (New York: Oxford University Press, 1951); and *Studies in the Structure of the American Economy* (New York: Oxford University Press, 1953).

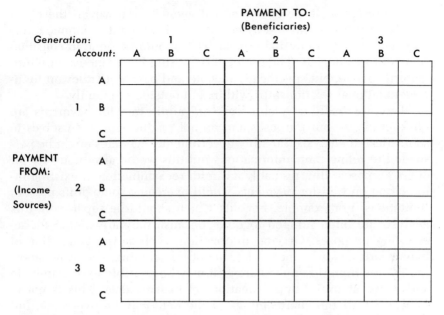

fig. 15-2 intergenerational payments and benefits

cluster in the "Accounts" categories which are *the same* on both axes. Accounts are the discrete classes of income sources (From) and beneficiaries (To). The Accounts should exhaust the range of refined categories of transfer payments, extrafamilial and intrafamilial funds, for both sources and recipients. They are cast in generational terms to clarify the volume and channels of intergenerational transactions. Regardless of inevitable crudities of some internal estimates, *all* income sources and receipts within one framework would support a comprehensive analysis of the effective claims for support secured by generations one and three, the old and the young, from generation two — within the family and outside.

Several problems arise in formulating the Account categories. The first of these is the development of mutually exclusive categories suitable for the analysis of propositions such as those advanced by Litwak. They must clearly distinguish various institutional spheres, minimally public or governmental at different jurisdictional levels, semipublic or private organizations, and family subsystems. This would clarify the extent to which specific functions, such as intergenerational support, are shared by different institutions.

The second problem is the use of *identical* Accounts in the transfer payments study and family sample survey. To insure comparability of both sets of data, they should be classified in the same categories according to the same criteria. This would have the incidental advantage of using information from the family survey to make estimates for data gaps on the larger economy, as, for example, in funds from private bureaucracies or local governmental agencies. However, these Accounts must be formulated by economists in straight economic terms most appropriate to available data. This should be done in consultation with sociologists. The problem is not simply income-expenditure patterns per se, but specifically income and payments relevant to intergenerational relationships within and outside the family.

Parenthetically, available data on public transfer payments are quite crude for our purposes and do not readily lend themselves to sophisticated analysis. Possibly governmental agencies might be persuaded to refine their information, and this would also be useful for other purposes. But, probably a careful reexamination of existing information on transfer payments would overcome some of its present limitations. For example, benefits which should be separate in this analysis are often lumped together because they are similar for accounting purposes. Or vital information, such as the generation of beneficiaries, may be incomplete or entirely missing. Yet, by juxtaposing figures from different sources, it may be possible to discriminate and arrive at useful approximations of missing data. This is not to imply that all the shortcomings of the data may be overcome, but simply that the present value of the data might be extended by bringing information from one agency to bear on information gathered by another.

But even if public data collection were drastically redesigned, this would not solve all the accounting problems posed by this schema, especially those related to the generation of beneficiaries. We may illustrate the general problem through educational subsidies. Most direct federal scholarships may be allocated to generation three, the young. But what about institutional grants which are ultimately divided between generations two and three—for example, research funds to generation two, the middle-aged, which are partially used for fellowships or research assistanceships in generation three? Such information is normally not available and cannot be reliably estimated or collected except at prohibitive cost. Nor is the age of the ultimate consumer always the critical factor. For example, capital investments in dormitory or classroom construction cannot be easily allocated, for the immediate "consumers" may be generation three, but the investment is strictly institutional. Here the very concept of "beneficiary" becomes fuzzy and requires sharper definition. One might arbitrarily regard all benefits which pass to institutions as "nongenerational." How would one classify Old Age, Survivors' and Disability payments or Old Age Assistance payments to the institutionalized aged which pass directly to the institution itself? Obviously, the issues involved in determining the generation of beneficiaries are fairly complex and require clear principles for the allocation of income sources and receipts to different generations.

The sample survey suggested above demands not only a full range of family types, but also that the *complete* kinship unit should enter into the analysis. This problem may be solved by a special two-stage format of primary and secondary samples.

The primary sample would consist of a national random sample of households, large enough to include a substantial segment of older (generation one) members with a broad range of support patterns. This would provide full coverage of family types, with members in all age groups. The secondary sample would branch out from the primary to all the consanguinal and affinal kin of the primary sample members (within a given cut-off point of kinship distance). Thus, primary sample households would be entree points to the larger kinship unit, and the secondary sample would consist of all the collaterals of the primary. Thereby, taken together, the primary and secondary samples would cover total kinship networks. The basic idea adapts and systematically extends the technique of Ethel Shanas' study of the health of old people in which selected kin of aged respondents were used as informants.[6]

In this fashion, the primary sample would yield respondents from all three generations within households, and these in turn would be supplemented by their near kin of all generations outside the household. Thus, a household of a middle-aged couple (generation two) with children would ultimately lead to both sets of older parents (generation one), the middle-aged siblings of the primary couple (generation two) and the nephews and nieces of the couple (generation three). These units would reflect different living arrangements and degrees of extension, but they would all constitute bounded systems of ostensible kinship obligations.

Complete data on income sources and payments would be secured from family units in both samples. Ultimately, a complete picture could be built up of intergenerational transfer payments within total family networks. This would not only delineate the patterns of financial reciprocity of such networks but also would clarify the relation of internal family supports to various external payments and transactions.

A study along these lines would permit several assessments beyond the sheer description of who supports whom. First, the effects of public policy could be evaluated. Purposive programs could be appraised according to their operation at the family level. While such programs have given objectives, their effectiveness must be related to different family contexts. Clearly, retirement income schemes or other transfer payments may have different impact as kinship units vary. Thus, the meaning of these programs must be related to the family systems on which they impinge.

[6]Ethel Shanas, *The Health of Older People: A Social Survey* (Cambridge, Mass.: Harvard University Press, 1962).

Secondly, such a comprehensive study, repeated at intervals, would measure trends in support patterns in the national economy and within families. Not only could innovations in support patterns be evaluated, but also the internal dynamics of various combined programs could be clarified. For example, retirement income has been increased in recent years by several forces, including the extension of Social Security coverage, raising of benefits, growth of private pensions, and the like. After each increase, some older people have left their children's homes and established independent households. But we know little beyond this. We know almost nothing about the characteristics of these people, their family circumstances, whether the marginal increase in income alone enabled them to move or whether supplemental contributions from other family members were also required, and the like. Thus, periodic studies of the type proposed would clarify changes in the division of economic functions between family and other institutions.

Of course, there are difficulties with such research even beyond the many problems of income studies. There are major problems of sample design, and of supervision and coordination of field work in the location of the secondary sample. With little prior experience as a guide, there is almost no basis for an accurate estimate of the probable size and location of the secondary sample or of field costs. But one thing is certain. This would be quite expensive research. However, the total expense would be proportionately reduced if the sample survey were carried out at eight- or ten-year intervals and the cost prorated over this period. Then the annual budget for the survey might be consistent with that of many short-term studies.

miscellaneous issues

Several other Symposium problems warrant brief discussion.

Relational Meanings Shanas, Sussman, Hill, Litwak, Townsend, and others have effectively refuted the predominance of the isolated nuclear family in the United States and Great Britain. These investigators have shown that most people are actually embedded in kinship networks: (1) most older people live fairly close to some adult child, (2) intergenerational contact and interaction tend to be regular and frequent within the network, and (3) even when it is dispersed, the network is a viable unit of mutual aid, especially in meeting crises. Marriage may modify, but does not cancel these relationships or dissolve reciprocal obligations.[7]

However, the sheer fact that such affiliations persist may be a strong invitation to misinterpret them and to extrapolate too casually

---

[7]For a detailed list of studies of family and kinship, see the bibliography in the paper by Marvin B. Sussman, Chapter IV above.

to other conclusions without proper evidence. Just as Parsons' original deductions about the isolated nuclear family were uncritically taken for granted without study or even skeptical reflection, so their refutation raises the prospect of a similar fallacy: the confusion of interaction with its quality. Homans may have to be qualified: while sentiment wanes with low contact, high interaction may not sustain affective bonds. High interaction is a necessary, but not sufficient condition for emotional closeness.

Because there is considerable intergenerational contact, we tend to conclude that this necessarily signifies emotional warmth and closeness between the actors. But the evidence for such emotional warmth is inconclusive. This is an empirical problem yet to be studied, and we should be careful about confusing the fact of association with its meaning to the participants.

Several distinctions should be borne in mind. First, assistance, especially in emergencies, is not synonymous with stable, continual contact. This is especially relevant to the dispersed kinship units in Litwak's earlier work. His clear evidence of pooled resources – financial aid for medical emergencies or help in sending a child to college – acknowledges reciprocal obligations. But his examples are not synonymous with regular, workaday, face-to-face relationships. Though they may be highly correlated, the emotional meaning of help may differ significantly from the meaning of stable primary-group association. Thus, irregular or critical assistance is not tantamount to steady interaction.

Secondly, we must distinguish between possible elements in association, principally emotional warmth and ritualistic contact. Sheer contact may indicate obligation (structural integration) rather than emotional closeness (affective integration), so that the fact of association may conceal an ideal-real discrepancy. Fairly strong forces of social change may limit the experience shared by different generations and may even serve to alienate them from one another. Under these conditions, the strains of emotional distance may develop which ritual observance could serve to ease or control. Thus, symbolic behavior – ritualistic visitation (the Sunday visit to grandma) or ceremonial observance (attendance at births, graduations, anniversaries, illness) – can adumbrate the forces which separate people. Thereby, it becomes possible to meet obligations and maintain appearances with or without strong emotional attachments, so that different emotional meanings may inhere in similar participation patterns. Hence, the sheer fact of interaction, notably its frequency, does not indicate its quality nor specify its emotional meaning to the actors. The next order of research business in these areas, as many of the Symposium participants have indicated in their writing and comments, is to move from the quantitative to the qualitative to document the character of these relationships.

Generational Differences The data on consumption patterns presented by Professor Hill are drawn from a broad spectrum of possible generational differences in belief and behavior (for example, religion, politics, sex roles, manners, morals and taste, and so forth). The underlying problem which confronts us is the meaning of such differences. Do these reflect different *life stages* or general *social change?*

Two contrasting theories may account for generational differences: (1) the *developmental*, and (2) the *historical*. The developmental would assume generic processes of growth and change fairly common to all people as they traverse the life span. Therefore, there should be few differences between generations if they were compared at similar points in the life cycle. Consequently, apparent differences between age groups are not genuine generational differences, but simply a function of their different stages in the life cycle. On the other hand, the historical theory emphasizes differential socialization of successive generations in the culture. Presumably, the ethos and experience of a period stamp each generation in youth with distinctive patterns which remain fairly stable throughout life, but distinguish successive generations from one another because of social change. Hence, the meaning of generational differences shifts according to these theories. The developmental theory explains such changes by the occupation of different points in the life cycle at the same time. The historical explains them by differential socialization or by persons coming to maturity at different times under different influences because of social change.

The contrasting frameworks imply conflicting views of any given generational difference. For example, consider the stereotype of political conservatism in old age, documented by voting patterns of various age groups. The developmental approach would attribute this conservatism to emergent forces in old age, the historical approach to progressive liberalization of political beliefs through time. The former implies a generic, irreversible process, while the latter implies flexibility and reversibility according to the currents of political change. Presumably, in forty years, the generation reaching adulthood under Roosevelt would be more liberal than its offspring growing up under Eisenhower. Thus, the two theories are mutually exclusive.

However, their differences are significant for family theory, problem formulation, and the direction taken by future research. To this extent, it is important to resolve the conflict between these theories and choose between them in order to guide future thought more effectively. But the generational differences which appear in our data cannot do this because they are consistent with both theories. The fact of difference is only documentary and cannot discriminate between the conflicting interpretations. Hence, studies which would untangle the web of meaning in favor of one approach or the other would be of strategic importance.

Low-Frequency Problems   Old age is a social problem with many inherent pressures toward social action. Because of this, our perspectives tend to become distorted in the direction of practical (rather than theoretical) problems, action programs (rather than understanding problems, even with no ready solution), material (rather than relational) concerns, and highly visible (rather than subtle) difficulties. Consequently, our vision gets cloudy, and we focus on problems salient to the professional worker, magnifying their apparent importance and overestimating their incidence.

For example, in the array of older people's problems, a disproportionate emphasis is placed on housing. This is a practical, tangible, simple area which can be readily grasped and an action program readily outlined. While housing problems may be acute when they occur, seldom do even 5 per cent of any older sample have serious housing difficulty. Yet, professional concern about this gives the impression that perhaps 60 per cent of the aged are so afflicted. Thus, there tends to be a confusion between quality and quantity and an uncritical substitution of one for another. Our bias causes the proportion of affected people to loom considerably larger than their actual numbers. This also smacks of a confusion between the part and the whole, as if some conspicuous problems of minorities were typical of the older generation in general.

On the whole, the Symposium papers are not particularly guilty of this error. But there are moments when our resistance may be weak and we require a bit of lashing to the mast in the manner of Ulysses and the Sirens. Problems that demand caution in maintaining our perspective include Rheinstein's concern with inheritance and transfers of wealth which may provoke strain within a small proportion of families. He indicates that estate administration is an unnecessary burden under *normal* circumstance — when there are no financial complications and "all possible successors are in harmony." Further, "rules of succession and tax laws ... are of significance only for that fraction of the population which owns sizable amounts of property; and that fraction is comparatively small even in the wealthiest of all nations." Even though the amount of testamentary wealth is disproportionate to the number of families involved, this tends to be redistributed within the privileged class owning "sizable amounts of property." Hence, its significance for the family is mainly confined to the wealthy elite, and only part of this group experiences profound strain over inheritance. So the consequences impinge on relatively few families, and the problem must not be overgeneralized. Another problem is that of quite marginal family structures, as in Stehouwer's small percentage of three-generation Danish *households* (as opposed to three-generation family networks). Finally, there are those abnormalities of behavior drawn from special minority groups, such as the institutionalized aged (3 per cent of the older population) or social-work clients. These may include the related problems of filial immaturity raised by Blenkner and the neurotic relationships in three-generation families.

Clearly, such special problems and groups have their place in the range of phenomena of multi-generational family systems. But they are instrinsically low-frequency problems which we must keep in perspective without inflation or overgeneralization.

This emphatically does not mean that minority problems should be given short shrift or ignored, nor that they are necessarily unimportant either practically or theoretically. After all, Freud's neurotic patients spawned one of the two major intellectual revolutions of this century.

But an uncritical confusion of the nature and frequency of various problems may be embarrassing and self-defeating, diverting limited resources from major to minor action programs and from theoretically crucial to fruitless concerns. Hence, a strong *caveat* is in order so that we do not mistake practical for theoretical importance, pathological conditions for the norm, and low-frequency problems for modalities.

indexes

name index

Stutter, J., 333n
Stycos, J. Mayone, 331n
Sussman, Marvin B., 5, 47, 48, 49, 62-92,
    94n, 95n, 149n, 291n, 308, 310-311,
    326, 327, 332-334, 341, 358, 374
Sweetser, Dorrian Apple, 81-82

T

Tabah, L., 333n
Tappan, Paul W., 211n
Thomas, Edwin J., 311n
Thompson, Wayne, 48, 70n, 308n
Thurston, Henry W., 211n, 212n, 214n
Tilson, 262n
Timmons, John F., 78n
Titmuss, Richard M., 169n, 207n, 224n
Tonnies, F., 64, 66
Townsend, Peter, 5, 6, 48, 70n, 143n,
    146n, 163-187, 222n, 326, 332, 335,
    356, 374
Townsend, Ruth, 163n
Townshend, Rev. Chancey Hare, 12
Trow, Martin, 301n
Tumin, Melvin, 293n
Turrentine, 258n

U

Utting, John, 179n

V

Vandiver, Joseph S., 75n
Vernier, 245n
von Wright, Georg Henrik, 330n

W

Walker, Jan, 163n
Warner, Amos G., 212n
Warren, J., 76n, 258n
Wasser, Edna, 51n, 53n
Weber, Max, 64, 66, 293n, 295, 296, 314n,
    349
Wedderburn, Dorothy Cole, 179n
Weiss, Viola W., 46n
White, Harrison, 328, 329
White, R. Clyde, 69n, 70n
White, Ruth, 230n
Wickenden, Elizabeth, 226n
Williams, Richard, 123n
Williams, Robin, 97
Willmott, Peter, 70n, 149, 292
Wilson, James Q., 87-88
Wirth, Louis, 66, 290
Witte, Edwin E., 216n
Wolfbein, Seymour, 269n, 270, 281, 282n
Wolfe, Donald, 119, 126n, 127
Wolozin, Harold, 271n, 287n
Woodroffe, Caroline, 163n, 165n

Y

Yates, F., 64, 210n, 212
Young, Michael, 70n, 149, 292

Z

Zelditch, Morris, 312n

subject index

Urbanization: (*Cont.*)
  kinship structure, 88, 327, 333, 339
  social insurance and public assistance, 215
  three-generation households, 150

V

Values, social, 298-300, 304, 317-318, 351, 366, 367-369
Vendor payments, 220, 228, 230-231
Vesting of retirement insurance, 224
Vienna, three-generation households in, 151, 154
Vital force concept, 12-13
Voucher payments, 220, 228-229, 232n

W

Wealth, transfer of, 243, 257-266, 277-278, 284-285, 377
Welfare programs:
  analysis, 206-240
  criterion, 6-7, 52, 292
  criticism, 53-54

Welfare programs: (*Cont.*)
  Denmark, 143, 155-157, 158, 159, 162
  income transfer, 364-365
  input-output analysis, 369-374
  insurance (*see* Insurance, social)
  legal analysis, 241, 255-266
  public assistance (*see* Public assistance programs)
  source of help, 58, 124, 125
  support patterns, 268, 270, 271-272, 273-279, 282, 284-288
  three-generation households, 150
Western Europe:
  estate administration, 262
  graph theory, 328
  housing arrangements, 150-151, 160
  legal family regulation, 245, 246, 252
Witchcraft accusations, 194, 195, 197-198
Work, motivating, 303, 306, 312 (*see also* Labor force)
Work-life expectancy, 281-283, 287-288, 312
Workmen's compensation laws, 215, 216
Work relief test, 229, 231, 232-233
World Health Organization, 49

DATE DUE